LET'S ROCK!

LET'S ROCK!

HOW 1950S AMERICA CREATED ELVIS AND THE ROCK & ROLL CRAZE

Richard Aquila

ROWMAN & LITTLEFIELD
Lanham • Boulder • New York • London

Published by Rowman & Littlefield
A wholly owned subsidiary of The Rowman & Littlefield Publishing Group,
Inc.
4501 Forbes Boulevard, Suite 200, Lanham, Maryland 20706
www.rowman.com

Unit A, Whitacre Mews, 26-34 Stannary Street, London SE11 4AB

British Library Cataloguing in Publication Information Available

Library of Congress Cataloging-in-Publication Data

Names: Aquila, Richard, 1946–
Title: Let's rock! : how 1950s America created Elvis and the rock & roll craze / Richard Aquila.
Description: Lanham : Rowman & Littlefield, 2016. | Includes bibliographical references and
index.
Identifiers: LCCN 2016011928 (print) | LCCN 2016015726 (ebook) | ISBN 9781442269361 (hard-
cover : alk. paper) | ISBN 9781442269378 (electronic)
Subjects: LCSH: Rock music—United States—1951–1960—History and criticism. | Presley, Elvis,
1935-1977.
Classification: LCC ML3534.3 .A75 2016 (print) | LCC ML3534.3 (ebook) | DDC 781.660973/
09045—dc23
LC record available at https://lccn.loc.gov/2016011928

Printed in the United States of America

For Marie

CONTENTS

ACKNOWLEDGMENTS

I would like to thank everyone who helped this book become a reality. Both Penn State University and my previous institution, Ball State University, encouraged and funded my research. Rowman & Littlefield Publishers, especially editor Natalie Mandziuk, offered valuable advice and excellent support. And Robert Pruter, Bill Schurk, Steve Cichon, and Michael Randolph, executor to the estate of photographer William "PoPsie" Randolph, graciously provided illustrations.

Countless others contributed in less obvious but still important ways. First, there were the singers, songwriters, disc jockeys, and all the other rock & roll pioneers, whose impact on American life proved to be far more significant than most people could have imagined back in the 1950s. My older brother, Phil, and I discovered the joys of the new sound in 1955 when we were just little kids. Every night we tuned in to hear George "Hound Dog" Lorenz playing rock & roll on WKBW radio in Buffalo, New York. A few years later, Phil even taught me how to dance fast like Bob and Justine on *American Bandstand*. (I still haven't forgiven him for teaching me the girl's part!)

My thoughts about rock & roll were shaped by others along the way. My parents encouraged my interest in music and bought me my first record player and 45s. The girls and guys I met in school made me aware—sometimes painfully so—of the music's power and importance. What young baby boomer couldn't relate to Dion and the Belmonts singing "Teenager in Love?" In high school and beyond, Dan Sawers has been a rock & roll kindred spirit. Our many arguments about which songs and singers were best undoubtedly improved both our musical tastes. My college roommate and friend Jim Meighan broadened my rock & roll vision by introducing me to Dylan, Eric Andersen, and other folkies. Later friends and colleagues like Pete Tallman, Drew Cayton, Mark Fissel, Dan Goffman, and Ken and Trudy Feltges helped me clarify my ideas about rock & roll and history.

Both the music and I changed as the years went by, but rock & roll's spirit lived on. Even after I "grew up," got married, and had children, the music remained a constant in my life. I continued to seek out the latest performers and songs. I sang rock & roll lullabies to my kids, Stephen and Valerie, and got them off to a good start in life by introducing them to rock & roll classics. As a professional historian, I explained rock & roll to a wider audience. With the help of Ball State University radio station manager Stewart Vanderwilt and producer/engineer Stan Sollars, I even got the chance to write and host *Rock & Roll America*, a radio show that ran on Indiana Public Radio for two years and then on NPR and NPR Worldwide for another two seasons. That weekly program gave me ample opportunities to think seriously about rock & roll as history and to interview numerous rock & roll artists. Many of the insights gleaned from those interviews are included in this book.

Over the decades, my wife, Marie, always encouraged my interests in rock & roll. She listened patiently to my innumerable comments and mini-lectures about the music as history. And she smiled knowingly whenever I said, "Let me play just one more song for you." That's why "this is dedicated to the one I love."

INTRODUCTION

History You Can Dance To!

When most people think about early rock & roll, images of switch-blades and leather jackets come to mind. They recall wild rock & rollers like Elvis Presley wiggling his hips on stage, Jerry Lee Lewis pounding his piano while singing suggestive songs, or Little Richard screaming and shouting out lyrics with abandon. Those images certainly made headlines, but they don't tell the whole story.

Let's Rock! shows that the rock & roll reality was actually far more complex and interesting. This book is a history of the music's birth, but it is also a history of the times. The tale begins in the late 1940s and early 1950s when a handful of artists pioneered the new sound by blending various musical styles. But then everything changed when an uninhibited young singer with long hair, sideburns, and flashy clothes grabbed the national spotlight in 1956. The arrival of Elvis transformed rock & roll into an unstoppable cultural phenomenon. Neither popular music nor the country would ever be the same (see figure I.1).

ROCK, ROLL, AND 1950S AMERICA

Rock & roll was born in the shadow of World War II. After 1945, the United States was the top military and economic power in the world. The nation boasted a booming economy, new technologies, new media,

Figure I.1. Brooklyn Paramount marquee showcasing Alan Freed's live rock & roll show in 1955. (Photo by "PoPsie" Randolph L.L.C.; provided by Michael Randolph, executor to the estate of William "PoPsie" Randolph)

and liberty and justice for all. The "American Century" had arrived but not without potential problems. The nation had to adjust to rapid social and cultural change unleashed by the Second World War. And it had to contain the growing threat of communism.[1] The historical forces swirling around in 1950s America set the stage for the coming of Elvis and the rock & roll craze.

"No future history concerned with the life and times of the twentieth century can leave out rock 'n' roll," wrote Herb Abramson of Atlantic Records back in 1956. "It's that important."[2] Abramson was right on the mark. From the very beginning, the new music was closely intertwined with the times. Rock & roll became one of the most significant cultural developments in post–World War II America, reflecting and shaping everyday life and thought, yet its origins are shrouded in myth and legend.

Let's Rock! reclaims the lost history of rock & roll. Like other books, it covers all the well-known performers. But *Let's Rock!* goes beyond the well-traveled roads of rock & roll history. It explores areas not typically found in history or music books, including obscure artists, minor hits, disc jockeys, record executives, producers, rock & roll movies, TV shows, and magazines. It shows that teenagers were active participants rather than just passive audiences in the story of rock & roll's birth. Set against the backdrop of 1950s America, this dramatic tale offers a revisionist history of the music as well as a nontraditional history of the times.

Based on years of research and interviews with Dion, Bo Diddley, Pat Boone, Dave Bartholomew, and other rock & roll pioneers, *Let's Rock!* offers new information and fresh perspectives about early rock & roll and 1950s America. It explains how and why the music appeared when it did, and it analyzes the significant roles that radio, TV, movies, and print media played in the expansion of the music.

Like a vast oral history project, rock & roll documented the thoughts and actions of its producers and consumers. Rock & roll artists generally were the same age and had the same socioeconomic backgrounds as their listeners, so they could relate to audiences' needs and wants. Dion, who found success in the 1950s and '60s as both a solo artist and lead singer of Dion and the Belmonts, explains: "When we had our first hits, we were just high school kids ourselves. We knew exactly the kinds of music our friends liked." Mike Stoller, who partnered with Jerry Leiber to write and produce hit records for Elvis Presley, the Coasters, and numerous others, has a similar story. "We wrote to amuse ourselves . . . we were our audience, and we were, on some level or another, typical of the people who bought our records. Not necessarily that we were the same as they, but we were not that far removed. There was something universal about the humor, or the emotional content, that caught the teens."[3]

Rock & roll's close ties to its audience make it a valuable source of history. The music offers evidence about ordinary people and everyday life that historians might otherwise miss. These sonic snapshots from the 1950s provide new perspectives on political, social, cultural, and economic trends of the day, including demographic changes, technological advances, the growth of consumer culture, the expansion of mass media, and the rise of a cold war culture that endorsed traditional values to guard against communism.

Rock & roll's unique view of the 1950s yields new details about the rise of a post–World War II youth culture and other aspects of American life.[4] The evidence suggests that early rock & roll was not nearly as rebellious as myth has it. More often than not, the new music reinforced the values, dreams, and fears of the era's dominant cold war culture. Rock & roll singers and songs supported centrist politics, as well as traditional values and mainstream attitudes toward race, gender, class, and ethnicity. The birth and growth of rock & roll suggests that America's cold war culture was much more broadly based than previously thought. The new sound reveals that most teenagers of the 1950s were not that different from their parents and grandparents. It suggests that both the young and old were preoccupied by the same concerns, tensions, and insecurities. Rock & roll contained some elements of rebellion, but it also reflected the era's consensus behavior, conservatism, and conformity. This dichotomy suggests that 1950s youth culture and rock & roll were never as monolithic or rebellious as myth has it. The notorious generation gap would not open for another decade.

Rock & roll served as a cultural binding force for a new generation. It enabled young people to deal with the pressures of growing up in an age marked by rapid political, social, and cultural change. The new music spoke to listeners' hopes and dreams, fears and anxieties. And it helped clarify their attitudes toward major issues involving youth culture, race, ethnicity, and gender. Rock & roll became a mirror and matrix for the era's youth culture, as well as a public forum for ongoing discussions about issues, events, beliefs, and actions. Perhaps rock superstar Bruce Springsteen summed up the music's importance best: "Rock 'n' roll, man, it changed my life. It was like *The Voice of America*, the real America, coming to your home."[5]

LET'S ROCK!

Despite rock & roll's historical and cultural importance, the story of the music's birth and growth has been given short shrift in most history books and even music books. For most people, the rise of rock & roll is like the dark side of the moon. They know it exists but don't really see it. *Let's Rock!* throws light on that distinct period and explores what the coming of rock & roll reveals about the times.

Rock & roll's early years deserve detailed coverage. All too often, books either omit or just mention in passing the birth of rock & roll before concentrating on the late 1950s when Elvis Presley, Chuck Berry, Fats Domino, Ricky Nelson, and other big-name rock & roll stars dominated the charts. No book has given the initial wave of rock & roll artists—the true pioneers of rock & roll—their proper due. Focusing on the period between the end of World War II and 1956 allows us to take a detailed look at all the early artists and all their hits, as well as the entire rock & roll scene. In keeping with the time period, this book uses *rock & roll* as a generic term to describe the popular music of young people in the early 1950s. Such an approach allows us to explore the historical significance of all the songs that made the rock & roll charts—regardless of style or performer.

The story of the coming of rock & roll ends in 1956. By that time, the new sound was firmly established in all its various shapes and forms. Rock & roll would enter a new phase in 1957. The arrival of Dick Clark's *American Bandstand* introduced new artists, new dances, new sounds, and new ways of promoting rock & roll. And, by the late '50s, most of the first wave of rock & roll singers were gone, replaced by newer stars. Even the rock & roll audience changed as millions of baby boomers reached puberty, providing reinforcements for the initial post–World War II youth culture.

Part I of this book traces the origins of the music and explains how the new sound was linked to some of the most important social and cultural changes of the day. Part II analyzes the coming of Elvis Presley and his relationship to the times. Part III demonstrates how the media and various musical forms—including rhythm & blues, country & western, and traditional pop—all rode the Presley wave throughout 1956. The conclusion places rock & roll in the context of American history by focusing on the connection between the new music and the era's cold war culture.

Approximately sixty years have passed since the pioneers of rock & roll first appeared on the scene. Black-and-white images of a young Elvis wiggling his hips on the Milton Berle show or Chuck Berry doing his duck walk across the stage are etched into a nation's collective memory. And classic rock & roll hits such as Presley's "Hound Dog," Carl

Perkins's "Blue Suede Shoes," and Fats Domino's "Blueberry Hill" have become part of the American songbook. But the legacy of these rock & roll pioneers is more than just a catalog of gold records. It's history you can dance to!

I

Before Elvis: The Rise of Rock & Roll (1946–1955)

1

MYSTERY TRAIN

The African American Roots of Rock & Roll

One of the first songs Elvis Presley ever recorded was "Mystery Train." Presley's 1955 release on Sun Records was a remake of a rhythm & blues song done two years earlier by Little Junior Parker and the Blue Flames. Parker wrote the song and recorded it in the same Memphis studio later used by Elvis. The original was a regional hit but never made the national R&B record charts. Elvis's version did somewhat better, making it to number 11 on the national country & western charts (see figure 1.1).

The two records were very different in style and approach. Junior Parker's version was slow paced and pure rhythm & blues. Parker's blues-influenced vocal tells a sad tale of loss and despair. The Blue Flames' music adds to the dark mood of the record. Instrumental riffs mimic a train chugging slowly down the tracks, while a wailing sax captures the woeful sound of a "mystery train sixteen coaches long." The somber record ends on a downbeat note, with Parker imitating a train hissing to a stop. The song's protagonist is left with little hope for the future. Just as easily, the brooding song could reflect the plight of African Americans in early 1950s America. Its anguished vocal, pessimistic message and mournful repetition suggest hopelessness and the realization that the future will be no better than the past.

Elvis Presley's "Mystery Train" sends a very different message. Presley's rendition is faster and combines elements from both R&B and

Figure 1.1.   Elvis Presley and Junior Parker both recorded "Mystery Train" for
Sam Phillip's Sun label. (Richard Aquila Collection)

country & western music. If Parker's version emphasizes the *blues* in
rhythm & blues, Presley's spotlights the *rhythm* through a fast-paced

vocal powered by energetic country-style guitar pickin'. Where Parker's down-bound train plods along toward its sad end, Elvis's more upbeat musical express seems hard put to stay on the tracks, always threatening to soar upward. Unlike Parker's plain lament, Presley's defiant vocal is drenched in echo and careens up and down the dark landscape. Elvis's backup band adds a sense of urgency to the song's mysterious mood, with Scotty Moore's lead guitar and Bill Black's slap bass providing musical momentum like a runaway train. Elvis ends on a high note, imitating the whistle of a train rushing through the night. The result is far more ambiguous than Parker's original. Despite the song's ominous mood and cryptic lyrics, Elvis makes it clear that he is not going to be defeated by the mysterious forces at work. Presley's young audience could relate to his optimistic, maybe even defiant, stance just as much as Junior Parker's primarily black audience could relate to his darker, more pessimistic message.

In retrospect, "Mystery Train" is an excellent metaphor for early rock & roll. Elvis's version—which combines R&B and country music—clearly demonstrates that the new sound was a musical hybrid. Rock & roll was no mere imitation. It often had a different feel, sound, and message than rhythm & blues—one that was more in tune with white teenage interests and dreams. Equally important, the song's enigmatic title suggests the ambiguity, if not confusion, that cloaks the arrival of rock & roll. The speeding train offers revealing glimpses of Eisenhower's America. Racial boundaries begin to blur and youth culture comes into view as the rock & roll mystery train thunders across the rapidly changing American landscape.

ORIGINS OF ROCK & ROLL

Although rock & roll exploded onto the American scene in the 1950s, its roots run deep in the past. Some experts trace its origins to backcountry ring shouts of African American slaves. Others locate the roots of rock & roll in sanctified gospel music and spirituals heard in black churches during the 1920s and '30s.[1] Still others find rock prototypes in various musical styles of the mid-twentieth century. Pop music hits of the 1930s such as Duke Ellington's "Rockin' in Rhythm" (1931) and the Boswell

Sisters' "Rock and Roll" (1934) used the words *rock* and *roll* to describe dancing.[2]

Rhythm & blues music (R&B) frequently employed both words as euphemisms for sex and wild partying. In 1922, Trixie Smith recorded "My Man Rocks Me (with One Steady Roll)." Arthur "Big Boy" Crudup—who later became a big musical influence on a young Elvis Presley—enjoyed success in 1945 with "Rock Me, Mama." Even more important was "Good Rockin' Tonight," which became a major R&B hit in 1948 for both Roy Brown (who wrote it) and Wynonie Harris. The song's tremendous popularity set the stage for similar R&B hits, including Wild Bill Moore's "We're Gonna Rock, We're Gonna Roll" (1948), Jimmy Preston's "Rock the Joint" (1949), and Amos Milburn's "Let's Rock a While" (1951).[3]

Rock & roll prototypes can also be found in country & western music. The bluesy sound of country artists like Jimmie Rodgers and Hank Williams are often cited as influences on Elvis Presley, Buddy Holly, and early rockabilly singers. Authors Jim Dawson and Steve Propes even include country hits such as Hank Snow's "I'm Movin' On" (1950) and Hank Williams's "Kaw-Liga" (1953) as possible choices in their book, *What Was the First Rock 'n' Roll Record?*[4]

No doubt all these songs and styles provide prototypes for later rock & roll. But rock & roll was always more than just one type of music. Jerry Wexler, who helped pioneer the new sound as a producer for Atlantic Records in the 1950s and '60s, offers what may be the best approach for understanding the origins of the music: "One of the psychological and sociological reasons for the development of rock and roll was the exposure of white people to black music," explains Wexler. "They began by listening to it. The next thing they did was attempt to play it, quite poorly, but the ones who persisted managed to learn their instruments and soon became as proficient as their black role models—but maybe not with the same gravamen of authenticity. So it became something else."[5]

The music that Wexler is describing became "something else" sometime in the early to mid-1950s when both black and white artists began combining elements from rhythm & blues, country & western, and mainstream pop. The result was a musical hybrid that was neither white nor black. A product of the dominant culture with important links to the era's rising civil rights movement and emerging youth culture, the music was multicultural and multiracial before those terms were invented. Rock & roll was at once an electrified folk music that sprang up from young people and a commodified pop music sold to the young. By 1953, rock & roll had arrived. Although few people suspected at the time, the music would eventually establish itself as one of the most significant musical forms in American history. The story of rock & roll begins with black rhythm & blues in post–World War II America.

The Rise of Rhythm & Blues

Prior to World War II, record companies generally used the term *race music* to describe songs done by black performers for black audiences. As the civil rights movement picked up momentum by the late 1940s, the term became increasingly more embarrassing, so the record industry tried a variety of euphemisms, including *ebony, sepia,* and *tan tones.* In 1949, Jerry Wexler, then a staff writer at *Billboard,* suggested that the trade magazine should try *rhythm & blues* as an alternative. The new name soon caught on as the description for pop music aimed at black audiences.[6]

Rhythm & blues music was the product of several important demographic, economic, and technological forces that were unleashed during the first half of the twentieth century. Perhaps the most important demographic change was the mass migration of blacks out of the South during and after the two world wars. Searching for better employment opportunities and hoping to escape southern racism, millions of African Americans headed for industrial cities in the North and West. The promise of industrial jobs in Chicago during World War II, for example, attracted over 50,000 blacks from Mississippi alone. These African Americans comprised a small percentage of a much larger group. Chicago's black population jumped from 40,000 in 1910 to approximately 500,000 by 1950. Most of these migrants settled in poor neighborhoods on the South Side or West Side, finding employment in the stockyards, meat-processing plants, steel mills, and other industries.[7]

Among the cultural baggage brought along by black migrants were two musical styles—*gospel* and *blues.* The former sprang from African American churches, while the latter was rooted in the cotton fields of the rural South, particularly the Mississippi Delta. Some experts maintain that blues was simply gospel music with secular themes. Blues singer Dwight "Gatemouth" Moore notes that when somebody asks him to explain the difference between blues and gospel, "I say one word and smile. 'Lyrics.' No other difference."[8]

Pioneer blues singers such as Big Bill Broonzy, Blind Lemon Jefferson, and Sonny Boy Williamson worked in Chicago's factories by day and played in bars at night, specializing in the country blues that Delta migrants had grown up on. Homesick black migrants packed into smoke-filled joints on the South Side to hear the familiar blues and wailing sounds of bottleneck slide guitars and mouth harps.

The new urban environment soon transformed both the music and performers. One of the most important technical innovations was the introduction of the electric guitar. It is hard to pin down who the inventor was because, as is often the case in history, once a new technology is available a number of people start tinkering with it. By the late 1920s or early '30s, several people were trying to amplify acoustic guitars. Most historians cite George Beauchamp as the first to actually accomplish this somewhere between 1928 and 1930. But he did not get a patent until 1937, by which time numerous other people were also producing versions of electric guitars. By the late 1930s and early '40s, T-Bone Walker had introduced the instrument to blues music, Oscar Moore and Charlie Christian were using it in jazz, Merle Travis used it in country music, and Les Paul and Mary Ford were using electric guitars on pop hits.

The two electric guitar pioneers who were undoubtedly the most important to the roots of rock & roll were Les Paul and Leo Fender. By the late 1940s and early '50s, both had developed solid body electric guitars. Les Paul's love affair with music began in 1927 when the eight-year-old got his first guitar. Over the ensuing decades, his eclectic musical tastes spanned country & western, jazz, blues, and pop. Between 1950 and 1955, he and his wife, Mary Ford, were a fixture on the pop charts, earning twenty-two Top 20 hits, including two number 1 records, "How High the Moon"(1951) and "Vaya con Dios" (1953). Audiences were intrigued by the duo's harmonies and unique guitar-driven sound. Most of the pop audience, however, was not aware that behind the scenes Les Paul was a technical genius. He built his own recording studio and experimented with multitrack recording, echo effects, and sound-on-sound recording. He also designed a solid-body electric guitar with twin pickups, which the Gibson company began marketing in the early 1950s. The Les Paul Gibson model was soon adopted by Carl Perkins, Roy Orbison, James Burton, and other early rock & rollers, as well as later rockers like Paul McCartney, John Lennon, Eric Clapton, Neil Young, and Keith Richards. The Les Paul Gibson became one of the most popular electric guitars of all time. In recognition of Les Paul's contributions, he was inducted into the Rock & Roll Hall of Fame in 1988 and awarded a Grammy for technical achievements in 2001.[9] (figure 1.2).

Unlike Les Paul, Leo Fender was not a musician. He was an inventor and manufacturer. In 1950, he began marketing an electric guitar called the Esquire. Over the next few years, Fender introduced other models, including the Telecaster and his most famous model, the Stratocaster, which was offered in a variety of colors including gold,

Figure 1.2.   Les Paul, an innovator with the electric guitar and in the recording studio, with singing partner and wife, Mary Ford. (Photo by "PoPsie" Randolph L.L.C.; courtesy of Michael Randolph, executor to the estate of William "PoPsie" Randolph)

black, and red. Fender's mass-produced guitars were the musical equivalent of Henry Ford's Model T. They made the new technology inexpensive and available to thousands of aspiring rock & rollers, including
Buddy Holly who became famous with his Stratocaster. One rock & roll
group even named themselves after the inventor. The Fendermen
found success in 1960 with an electrified version of Jimmie Rodgers's
country classic, "Muleskinner Blues." Later rock guitarists such as
George Harrison, Jimi Hendrix, and Mark Knopfler also gained fame
with Stratocasters. Leo Fender's important contribution to rock & roll
history was officially recognized in 1992 when he was inducted into the
Rock & Roll Hall of Fame.[10]

The electric guitar paved the way for changes in blues music. T-
Bone Walker first started using the instrument in the 1930s, and Muddy Waters and Howlin' Wolf adopted it in the 1940s. The amplified
guitar not only improved their bottleneck slide sound, but it also allowed them to be heard in loud urban bars. "When I went into clubs,"
explains blues great Muddy Waters, "the first thing I wanted was an
amplifier. Couldn't nobody hear you with an acoustic." Blues changed
in other ways. According to musicologist Arnold Shaw, the music took
on "a resounding backbeat" and "back boogie and shuffle—the rolling
eight-note figuration in the bass and the wailing blue notes in the melody—a sound absent from white pop since the 1930s." Shaw notes one
other change: "Instead of maintaining the twelve-bar form and the simple three-chord progression . . . it adopted a gospel or pop structures of
eight and sixteen bars. Progressions varied greatly but a patterned bass
held the recording together. It was a carry-over of the riff in swing, save
that the repetition of a group of notes assumed the form of a bass
rhythm figure."[11] (figure 1.3).

Electric guitars, organs, and basses joined with tenor saxes and
drums to give the new music driving rhythms and danceable beats. By
the late 1940s, electrified urban blues was an eclectic mix of blues,
gospel, swing, jazz, boogie-woogie, pop, and country & western. Billy
Ward and the Dominoes fused a gospel feel with a blues sound. The
Orioles mixed white pop harmonies with jazz bebop. Fats Domino
blended a New Orleans Dixie style of piano playing with country &
western–influenced vocals. Joe Turner stirred together large doses of
blues with a frenetic gospel delivery. The "rhythm & blues" style soon
became the music of choice for black urban America. The fresh sound

Figure 1.3.   T-Bone Walker pioneered the use of the electric guitar in R&B music. (Robert Pruter Collection)

reflected both the hopes and fears of urban blacks in post–World War II America. Unlike traditional country blues, which dealt mainly in despair and resignation, R&B captured the optimism of working-class blacks. The new music allowed listeners a temporary escape from the stockyards, factories, or other types of hard labor through promises of material goods, sensual pleasures, and above all else, a solid dance beat.

But if R&B reflected a postwar mentality of optimism and hedonism, it also triggered fears in an era known for conservatism. With moderates such as Harry Truman and Dwight Eisenhower in the White House and conservative politicians, ministers, and cultural critics standing guard against communist infiltration or threats to American culture and morals, any music not in tune with mainstream values was suspect. "R&B music was felt to be degrading," noted Don Robey of Peacock Records, "and not to be heard by respectable people." Many middle-class blacks, as well as middle-class whites, condemned rhythm & blues as the devil's music and insisted that lewd lyrics should be censored. Upper- and middle-class African Americans were also offended by R&B stereotypes (many of which came from white composers) that depicted blacks as lazy ne'er-do-wells interested only in alcohol, gambling, and sex.[12]

Their concerns were not totally unfounded. Jackie Brenston's number 1 R&B hit from 1951, "Rocket 88," equated a car and its powerful engine with sex and carousing. Just to make sure nobody missed the imagery, Brenston's label, Chess Records, issued an advertisement that featured a shapely girl in a skimpy bathing suit straddling a huge phallic rocket with "Rocket 88" written on the side. The Dominoes' "Sixty Minute Man," also a hit in 1951, featured bass singer Bill Brown boasting about his sexual prowess. He insisted he could satisfy all his girls with fifteen minutes of kissing, fifteen minutes of teasing, fifteen minutes of squeezing, and a climactic fifteen minutes of "blowin'" his "top." Other risqué R&B songs included Dinah Washington's "Big Long Slidin' Thing," the Swallows' "It Ain't the Meat (It's the Motion)," and the Toppers' "Baby, Let Me Bang Your Box."[13]

Despite objections by both black and white middle-class listeners, rhythm & blues would not go away. R&B's soaring popularity was aided by the rise of "indies" (i.e., small, independent record companies). The way had been cleared during the hard economic times of the 1930s and '40s when major record companies such as Capitol, Mercury, Columbia, Decca, and RCA all but abandoned blues music, believing the audiences were too small to warrant the expense and effort.[14] Further opportunities for independent labels popped up when major record companies slowed or shut down operations in 1942–1943 due to a strike by the American Federation of Musicians. Indies filled the void by making separate peace with the union and recording new songs with new musicians and writers.[15]

A feud between two music publishing rivals likewise spurred the growth of independent record companies. The American Society of Composers, Authors, and Publishers (ASCAP) was formed in 1914 to ensure its members would be paid royalties whenever their songs were performed. The coming of radio in the 1920s complicated matters. "The ASCAP members historically had made their money from the sale of sheet music. . . . When people stopped playing the piano and started playing the radio, sheet music sales dropped," explains telecommunications professor Patrick R. Parsons. "ASCAP's long-standing remedy was to charge the radio stations for the use of the music, but as royalty fees went up, so did the friction between ASCAP and the radio industry." In 1939, radio stations set up their own licensing organization, Broadcast Music Incorporated (BMI), and began making plans to boycott all ASCAP music. "Since ASCAP had a virtual monopoly on most of the popular music of the time," notes Parsons, "BMI was forced to go to the musical fringes for material. BMI 'rediscovered' country and western (hillbilly music), various forms of folk music, and rhythm & blues." The rise of BMI offered indies numerous opportunities for music publishing and radio airplay throughout the 1940s and early '50s.[16]

The lack of competition from the majors combined with the rising demand for rhythm & blues led to the creation of hundreds of independent record companies in the late 1940s and early '50s. Among the most successful were Atlantic Records in New York, Chess in Chicago, King/Federal in Cincinnati, Ace in New Orleans, Savoy in Newark, Peacock in Houston, and Imperial and Specialty in Los Angeles. A few of the owners were motivated by love of rhythm & blues. "Some of this music moved me so much it brought tears to my eyes," recalls Art Rupe, the founder of Specialty Records. "I decided that this was what I wanted to do." Most, however, were attracted by the money to be made in the new industry. Sid Nathan, for example, founded King Records because he thought he could profit by targeting the "music of the little people," that is, race music, country & western, and other markets neglected by major companies.[17]

Though the majors scoffed at records that sold only a few hundred or a thousand copies, those numbers were sufficiently large to turn big profits for small, local companies with lower overheads. Not only was there a growing and increasingly more prosperous African American market for R&B records, but there were a variety of ways to squeeze even more money out of unsuspecting artists. Unlike major labels, which paid royalties to singers and composers, indies often paid just small lump sums to poor artists. Other times, indies would get eager performers to sign away songwriting credits and publishing rights for almost nothing. "We used to bring 'em in, give 'em a bottle of booze and say, 'Sing me a song about your girl,'" recalls Saul Bihari of Modern Records. "They'd pluck around a little on their guitars, then say 'O.K.' and make up a song as they went along."[18]

New recording techniques helped indies get established after World War II. Prior to the war, the record industry had been limited to large companies that could afford to use the expensive, elaborate recording studios located in large urban areas such as New York City, Los Angeles, or Chicago. But the magnetic tape recorders developed by Hitler's Germany during the war years soon brought sweeping changes to America's recording industry. Along with offering easier editing capabilities and better sound quality, the new, inexpensive magnetic tape recorders made it possible for small companies to record artists anywhere in the United States. For less than a $1,000 investment, independent record companies could record local acts and sell enough records locally to turn a profit.[19]

Technological change aided R&B in another way. The coming of television after World War II staggered the radio industry, which responded by searching for new formats. One of the most successful was "narrowcasting." Chris Spindel, program director at Memphis's WDIA in the late 1940s and early '50s, first learned about the concept from a speaker at a broadcasters' convention. "Whether it's teenagers, fourteen to sixteen, or older folks thirty-nine to ninety-five," explained Spindel, "the man was saying that you need to gear your program for one group."[20] Not surprisingly, radio stations in cities with large black populations soon found a perfect narrowcast format in rhythm & blues. In the process, they inadvertently helped spread the sound to a new group of listeners—white teenagers.

Black Music—White Audiences

Although black R&B artists had a difficult time trying to crack the predominately white popular music market of the late 1940s and early '50s, their rhythm & blues soon found the way onto the radios of dial-twisting white teenagers who eagerly listened to the strange new sound. A young man named Robert Smith—who later gained fame as disc jockey Wolfman Jack—is a perfect example. From his home in Brooklyn, New York, Smith could pick up Gene Nobles's R&B show that originated a thousand miles away at WLAC–Nashville. On a clear night, WLAC's powerful signal beamed as far north as Canada and southward to the Caribbean. "The Nashville station had a signal strong enough to reach Brooklyn because they appealed to the FCC with the idea that black people in some rural areas around the South didn't have any stations in their own area with the kind of programming that they wanted to hear," explains Wolfman Jack. "So WLAC got permission to have one of the most powerful signals in the country, so long as they carried rhythm and blues."[21]

Millions of white teenagers across the country discovered black rhythm & blues the same way the young Wolfman Jack did. Lying in bed late at night, they would twist the radio dial until they filtered out enough static to pull in those hypnotic rhythms. The heavy beats and gritty lyrics of rhythm & blues were unlike anything they had ever heard. Memphis disc jockey George Klein could have been speaking for an entire generation of white teenagers when he said, "We were so tired of playing Doris Day, Eddie Fisher, and Perry Como."[22]

Gene Nobles of Nashville's WLAC was only one of many disc jockeys playing rhythm & blues in the 1940s and early '50s. In some ways, this type of programming was not that new. Since the early days of radio, programmers had occasionally tried to reach black audiences.[23] But programming aimed at blacks was the exception rather than the rule prior to World War II. The move toward narrowcasting in the mid- to late 1940s ushered in a new era. *Sponsor* magazine reported in 1949 that African Americans constituted a huge but neglected market that could potentially yield $12 billion a year in sales. Little wonder that by the late 1940s and early '50s, radio stations across the United States were flocking to rhythm & blues programming as a way to reach the "forgotten 15 million" black consumers in America. *Variety* magazine reported in early 1953 that 260 radio stations were programming rhythm & blues due to "the music's widespread and almost unique acceptance by Negro audiences."[24] What the writers at the show business tabloid failed to grasp was that blacks were not the only ones listening to R&B broadcasts.

While most of the hosts of these new R&B shows were white, there were a few black disc jockeys. In the late 1940s and early '50s, Memphis's all-black station, WDIA, boasted numerous African American talents such as Nat D. Williams, "Hot Rod" Hulbert, and Dwight "Gatemouth" Moore. R&B recording artists B. B. King and Rufus Thomas actually began their careers as WDIA disc jockeys. B. B. King's initials came from his radio moniker, "the Beale Street Blues Boy." Black deejays could also be found elsewhere in the early 1950s, including Jack L. Cooper and Al Benson in Chicago, Tommy "Dr. Jive" Smalls in New York City, and Douglas "Jocko" Henderson in Philadelphia.

Most of the initial jobs for R&B jocks, however, went to whites—not surprising given the era's discrimination and racism. All the contradictory claims make it impossible to determine who the first R&B deejay was, but it is safe to say that the pioneers arrived on the R&B scene shortly after World War II. As early as 1946, Bill Gordon was on the air playing R&B in Memphis, while halfway across the state, "Daddy" Gene Nobles was spinning R&B records in Nashville. A short time later, John Richbourg (known on radio as "John R.") joined Nobles on the same Nashville station. Hunter Hancock became Los Angeles's first R&B jock in 1948. Around the same time, "Jumpin'" George Oxford began spinning R&B platters farther to the north in San Francisco. Dewey Phillips got his start in Memphis in 1949. The story of how Hunter Hancock got involved with rhythm & blues is fairly typical. The white deejay began playing jazz music on Los Angeles's KFVD radio in 1943. He recalls that in 1948 a promo man from Modern Records "told me that if I wanted to reach average Negroes, jazz wouldn't do it. Thank God that I had the good sense to listen to him and switched my shows to an exclusive diet of r&b disks." That's an understatement. For the next twenty years, Hunter Hancock remained one of the most popular jocks in the LA market.[25]

The number of white deejays playing black R&B grew rapidly in the early 1950s with the addition of colorful jocks like George "Hound Dog" Lorenz in Buffalo, Alan "Moondog" Freed in Cleveland, Dick

"Huggie Boy" Hugg in LA, Clarence "Poppa Stoppa" Hamman Jr. in New Orleans, and William "Hoss" Allen in Nashville. Many of these white R&B disc jockeys, either consciously or unconsciously, adopted the vocal mannerisms of African Americans. Historian Louis Cantor, who is white but worked as an engineer and part-time disc jockey at an all-black radio station in Memphis back in the 1950s, does not believe this was just a coincidence. After all, this was a time when white stations were trying to reach black audiences, but they were still reluctant to hire black disc jockeys. "The trick," says Cantor, "was to get a white announcer who would appeal to blacks, either by attempting to mimic what they considered a black dialect or by playing almost exclusively the new so-called race music." Not everyone agrees with Cantor. William "Hoss" Allen of Nashville's WLAC insists that he and other white jocks were not just copying African Americans. Many of them naturally talked, acted, and dressed like blacks. "John R. [Richbourg] was from Charleston, and I grew up in a small [southern] town," says Allen, "so we could revert back to our childhoods, when we played a lot with black children, remember the colloquialisms, the street talk. That was the thing we used on the air." Allen even socialized more with blacks than with whites: "When I'd get off the air, I'd go down to the New Era, which was a big black club in Nashville, and hang out."[26]

Frequently, listeners couldn't tell if a deejay was white or black. That's what made the famous scene from *American Graffiti* ring so true—the one where Richard Dreyfuss's white teenage character is shocked to learn that the jive-talking disc jockey played by Wolfman Jack is white not black! That scene was probably played out in real life by hundreds if not thousands of teenagers who assumed, wrongly as it often turned out, that they were listening to black R&B jocks.

Dewey Phillips is a perfect example. The white deejay with flaming red hair and a pale, freckled face was the host of *Red Hot 'n' Blue*, a wild R&B program that aired nightly on WHBQ–Memphis. His program chatter consisted of a nonstop barrage of words and syllables, spoken so rapidly that he often sounded more like an auctioneer than a radio announcer. He hawked a variety of products from Old Amigo Flour to hair-straighteners for blacks, all the while frantically setting the stage for gritty Delta-style blues music. Because of his vocal mannerisms and extensive use of black slang, many listeners assumed he was African American. But Dewey Phillips was no mere imitator. His speech patterns and love of blues music reflected the multicultural influences of the rural South in which he was born and raised.[27]

While some fans might have wondered about his race, none ever questioned his authenticity. Ratings consistently showed that *Red Hot 'n' Blue* was one of the most popular and influential R&B programs in the country, capturing the hearts and minds of both black and white audiences. Phillips took Memphis by storm. A local paper reported in July 1951 that Dewey's signature line—"Tell 'em Phillips sent 'ya"—had listeners doing just that all over town, "so much so that merchants who don't even advertise on the show are demanding to know who-the-heck is Phillips?" Further testimony to Phillips's crossover appeal among blacks and whites was a tribute song appropriately titled "Phillips Sent Me," done by a black R&B group, Joe Liggins and His Honeydrippers. Perhaps blues singer Rufus Thomas summed up Phillips's crossover appeal best: "Dewey was not white. Dewey had no color."[28]

Not all African Americans were as receptive to white R&B disc jockeys. A few claimed the white jockeys' imitative style mocked African Americans. Others suggested that white disc jockeys were taking jobs away from blacks. Some of the most pointed attacks came from the black press. The *New York Age Defender* reported in the summer of 1954 that hundreds of blacks in the New York area were opposed to the rumored hiring of Alan Freed by WINS radio because the white deejay's "manner of broadcasting is in bad taste and shows a degree of contempt for the intelligence of the Negro public." The newspaper quoted one critic who said, "Freed is worse than *Amos and Andy* ever dared to be and if WINS brings him into New York it will be a disgrace to the entire Negro race."[29]

Most African Americans, however, were willing to accept white disc jockeys playing rhythm & blues as long as their love of R&B was real. "If measured only by the numbers—the audience ratings of their shows and the turnouts at personal appearances," explains journalist Ben Fong-Torres, "blacks seemed to accept the white disc jockeys as friendly purveyors of the music they loved."[30]

R&B disc jockeys provided the first large public showcase for rhythm & blues. This type of exposure in hundreds of cities across the country helped spread the black sound to new white audiences, leading to increased record sales and greater attendance at R&B concerts. White teenagers no longer had to sneak into juke joints or listen to R&B

records surreptitiously. Black rhythm & blues—also called "cat" music—was now readily available on the airwaves. The fact that white deejays were spinning the platters probably made the music less objectionable for some whites. Ironically, the appearance of R&B on white-oriented radio stations helped make the music more acceptable to many blacks, as well. Music expert James Miller explains, "The fact that this music was aired on a predominantly white station gave it a new kind of cultural cachet among blacks, even as it permitted white listeners to tune in without guilt."[31]

In a very real sense, white R&B disc jockeys were straddling a cultural crossroads. It was contested terrain: capitalists versus consumers, black culture versus white culture, old ways against the new, the Establishment versus the common people. And to the victor went the right of cultural control. R&B disc jockeys had to please a number of constituents, including station owners, program directors, record companies, advertisers, listeners, and fans. Their performance ultimately depended upon the close ties they developed with audiences.

Radio allowed direct contact between broadcasters and listeners. President Franklin Roosevelt used that to his advantage with "fireside chats" during the 1930s and '40s. So did R&B "personality jocks" in the late 1940s and '50s. Because they beamed right into teenagers' bedrooms, an intimate relationship developed between deejays and fans. Disc jockeys became more than mere announcers; they became teenagers' close friends and advisors. Like minstrels in blackface, R&B jocks sporting cat clothes and jive-talk introduced millions of white teenagers to black culture and music. If white deejays were white teenagers' trusted guides into the strange new world of black rhythm & blues, then black deejays were often the first African Americans white teenagers ever "met." In either case, R&B jocks emerged as influential cultural brokers between white America and black America of the 1940s and early '50s.

R&B disc jockeys introduced white listeners to an exotic African American world filled with swinging sounds, new slang, flashy clothes, and "cool cats." Like Pied Pipers leading white teenagers down a new road toward the promised land of black rhythm & blues, these white hipsters personified Norman Mailer's 1950s abstraction of "white negroes"—nonconformist existentialists who knew how to live dangerously. Not only were R&B deejays cool, but they also held the key that could unlock the mysteries of "cool" for white teenagers. The deejays knew the way to a hip underground musical world where excitement, sexual freedom, and liberation were accepted ways of life. What more could white teenagers ask for in an era that stressed conformity and controlled behavior?

R&B disc jockeys paved the way for the civil rights movement.[32] Significantly, the spread of rhythm & blues music to white audiences was contributing to cultural integration long before *Brown vs. Board of Education*. At a time when blacks had to sit in the back of the bus, disc jockeys brought black singers right into the living rooms and bedrooms of white America. Granted, racist attitudes toward blacks changed slowly, but the spread of rhythm & blues to white audiences was at least a beginning.

The growing presence of black rhythm & blues on white-oriented radio stations cracked the walls of segregation. Not only were many whites becoming increasingly more interested in and tolerant of black musicians and culture, but African Americans were also beginning to develop a newfound pride in their heritage. Some young African Americans applauded black R&B disc jockey Al Benson because he never tried to act white. "[Benson] sounded black," remarked a fellow black deejay, "and most of us were proud of the fact." African Americans were even more proud when Al Benson hired two white men in 1956 (shortly after an anti-desegregation court ruling) to distribute 5,000 copies of the U.S. Constitution in Jackson, Mississippi. Obviously, the coming of rhythm & blues did not mean the end of segregation, but it was an early step toward cultural integration.[33]

Along with radio, jukeboxes enabled white teenagers to listen to rhythm & blues. In the 1890s, the Rudolph Wurlitzer Company introduced coin-operated player pianos. While this "nickel-in-the-slot" machine was a forerunner, the modern jukebox did not appear until 1927 when AMI (the Automatic Musical Instrument Company) introduced the Selective Phonograph. Wurlitzer, Seberg, and other companies soon launched similar models. During the 1930s, these early jukeboxes enabled audiences to at least listen to the records they could no longer afford to buy during the Great Depression.

By the late 1940s and early '50s, jukeboxes could be found in almost any public place: bars, diners, skating rinks, ice cream parlors, theaters, bowling alleys, department stores, hotels, grocery stores. A 1951 advertisement for the Rock-ola Rocket 51-50 reveals why storeowners and patrons were attracted to the jukes. A sketch depicts a futuristic-looking machine with large speakers, chrome trim, and lots of modern push-buttons. The copy boasts "America's Finest Phonograph" that would bring operators reliability and "beautiful tone quality." The Rock-Ola Rocket 51-50 allowed operators to use [the newer] 45-rpm or [the older] 78-rpm records and the flexibility to adjust "any combination coin play" right on location, "whether you prefer 1 play 10c, 3 plays 25c, 2 plays 10c, 5 or 6 plays 25c, or even 1 play 25c, or whatever coin play combination you desire."[34] The machine's sleek appearance was designed to appeal to the modernism of the post–World War II generation, while its practical features enabled operators not only to keep pace with rapid changes in the record industry but to also make necessary adjustments to increase profits. Even the name, Rock-Ola Rocket 51-50, evoked the new rhythm & blues music, as well as sexy images of potent, powerful rockets or Oldsmobile rocket engines.

By the time the streamlined Rock-Ola hit the stores, jukeboxes were generally showcasing all types of music, from traditional pop to country & western to rhythm & blues.[35] The potential profits from jukeboxes were enormous. Records that cost operators thirty-five cents to buy scored hundreds, even thousands, of hits at a nickel or dime a play. When interest in the song waned, used records would then be sold to record buyers eager for good deals. Given such potential, it is not surprising that by 1940 approximately 44 percent of all records were being sold to jukebox operators.[36]

Jukeboxes were delivering big profits in part because they offered white teenagers easy access to the new R&B sound. Advertisements made store owners and operators aware of rhythm & blues' drawing power. A 1951 record ad advised operators: "Grab the Nickels with Imperial's New Hit! 'Sometimes I Wonder' [by] Fats Domino." That same year RCA Victor Record Company attempted to pump up its R&B department by sending out free samples of rhythm & blues records to 600 leading jukebox operators across the country.[37]

White teenagers jumped at the chance to hear rhythm & blues. Historian C. Warren Vander Hill can recall when R&B songs first began appearing on jukeboxes when he was a teenager in Queens, New York, during the mid-1950s: "I vividly remember the change in the jukebox. Goodbye, Rosemary Clooney and Frankie Laine. Hello on the candy store jukebox to new R&B groups." The young Vander Hill was witnessing an important transition that was playing out across the country—African Americans were becoming more visible not only on jukeboxes but throughout American society and culture. In 1954, *Ebony* magazine suggested to its readers that anybody interested in learning about the changes occurring in race relations need only take a look at the nearest jukebox. There, "on an R&B record purchased for forty-five cents at the dime store," scholars would find "the real inside story."[38]

Live performances provided another venue for white teenagers to hear rhythm & blues. By the late 1940s, almost every major city in the Northeast had at least one theater or club that showcased black talent. Among the more famous were Harlem's Apollo Theater and Washington, D.C.'s Howard Theater. A loose network of bars, night clubs, juke joints, and ballrooms—sometimes called "the Chitlin' Circuit"—existed throughout the country. An entertainment trade paper reported in 1951 that R&B clubs on the West Coast were doing phenomenal business, explaining that the success of night spots such as Hollywood's Waldorf Cellar and the Dixie Club "results from multiraced enjoyment of blues artistry, with most audiences 30–60 percent white."[39]

White R&B disc jockeys jumped at the chance to make big bucks by staging R&B concerts. Hunter Hancock of KFVD–Los Angeles hosted his first rhythm & blues variety show on August 5, 1951. Alan "Moondog" Freed of Cleveland's WJW earned notoriety on the night of March 21, 1952, when he staged his initial R&B concert—"The Moondog Coronation Ball." The event turned into a near riot when thousands of ticketless young people tried to crash the gates of the Cleveland Arena, already filled to its 10,000 capacity. Bill Randle, Cleveland's top disc jockey at the time, noted, "[The Moondog Coronation Ball] was the beginning of the acceptance of black popular music as a force in radio. It was the first big show of its kind where the industry saw it as big business."[40]

Not surprisingly, other R&B shows soon followed. Freed followed up the Coronation Ball fiasco with a series of successful R&B dances and concerts throughout eastern Ohio; Bill Randle promoted a Cleveland R&B dance in June 1953; and earlier that year *The Biggest Show of '53* launched a six-week tour of one-nighters throughout the South. Not to be outdone, Alan Freed ended the year by putting together the biggest package tour in R&B history—aptly called *The Biggest Rhythm and Blues Show*—featuring Wynonie Harris, Ruth Brown, the Clovers, and other R&B greats. It is important to note that the audiences at these live R&B shows were overwhelmingly African American. One of Freed's friends recalls seeing Freed walking out onto the stage "amidst a sea of black faces."[41]

Audiences at R&B concerts became increasingly more integrated, though, as the 1950s progressed. Freed's "Moondog Birthday Ball," held on June 25, 1954, at an armory in Akron, Ohio, attracted an audience that was reputedly one-third white. Seven months later, in January 1955, a Freed concert in New York City drew a huge audience, 70 percent of which was white.[42]

All of these live R&B performances represented—literally and figuratively—the barriers of segregation coming down. *Ebony* magazine reported one such incident in 1949 at a rhythm & blues concert held in Knoxville, Tennessee. Wanting to see rhythm & blues performers in person, white teenagers "jammed the upper balcony" of a local "Negro dance hall." But they didn't stop there. Defying local laws of segregation, the white kids demanded "the right to go onto the floor, mingle with the Negroes and get a better look at R&B singer Bull Moose Jackson."[43]

The growing popularity of rhythm & blues resulted in more whites buying R&B records. Ahmet Ertegun and Jerry Wexler of Atlantic Records noticed the trend in the early 1950s. Record store owners observed the same thing. Cleveland record store owner Leo Mintz reported in early 1952 that white teenagers were eagerly buying up all the black R&B records they could find in his store. That same year Dolphin's Hollywood Record Shop, a black retail store in Los Angeles, noted that their business was 40 percent white. Within a short time, white teenagers didn't even have to leave their neighborhoods to purchase rhythm & blues. At least one R&B label, Okeh Records, was shipping records to white pop outlets by 1952.[44]

Records sales, attendance figures from concerts, jukebox plays, and the proliferation of R&B on white-oriented radio stations all indicate that by the early 1950s black rhythm & blues was spreading rapidly to white audiences. Jerry Wexler, who joined Atlantic Records in 1953 as a record producer, believes the trend began in the South: "In those years, a top R&B record could go to four hundred thousand. Sales were localized in ghetto markets. There was no white sale, and no white radio play. . . . At some point we became aware that southern whites were buying our records, white kids in high school and college. This happened long before the kids in the North began to dig R&B. A kid like Presley was picking up on R&B long before the other kids around him." Wexler surmises the reason had a lot to do with southern family culture that was neither black nor white. "It was southern proletarian, southern agrarian, and these people—truck drivers, farm hands—worked together. Their churches were very much alike. A white Baptist church had the same screaming and carrying on as a black Baptist church—the euphoria, speaking in tongues, the falling down, rigidity, tambourines, responses, and the minister blues talking." Wexler added with irony, "People can hate each other's guts even though they come from a common culture—and that's the way it was in the South."[45]

Actually, R&B's growing popularity among young white listeners may not have been as regional as Wexler suggests. After all, white deejays such as Hunter Hancock in Los Angeles, Alan Freed in Cleveland, and George "Hound Dog" Lorenz in the Buffalo/Niagara Falls area were playing R&B music by the late 1940s and early '50s. Since it is impossible to segregate airwaves, their audiences had to include blacks and whites. Regardless of where the trend began, though, the result is clear: by 1953, black R&B music had spread to white audiences nationwide. Like many converts, these young people often became zealots. They couldn't get enough of the new sound. They listened to R&B music on the radio. They played it on jukeboxes. They attended R&B clubs and concerts. And they purchased the latest records by their favorite artists.

No one knows for sure why white teenagers were so attracted to black rhythm & blues, but there are a lot of possibilities. For one thing, the music sounded fresh. The traditional white pop that was commonly heard on the radio in the late 1940s and early '50s was bland and formulaic. Even worse, to many young ears the music of Perry Como, Eddie Fisher, Vic Damone, and other crooners was terminally boring. No way could young people work up a sweat dancing to the music of the Four Lads or Patti Page. Many white teenagers wanted something different, something that was theirs alone, something real that they could relate to, something befitting the new post–World War II era. R&B fit the bill on all counts. It had an authentic sound that was fresh and exotic, as well as a lively beat that was made for dancing. Sam Phillips, the founder of Memphis's Sun Records and the man who would discover Elvis Presley, first learned about the growing R&B phenomenon in the early 1950s from jukebox operators, record distributors, and deejays who "tipped [him] to the fact that [white] teenagers were falling in love with Negro music. They wanted to hear that rocking, pounding, down-to-earth stuff."[46]

Simply put, white teenagers thought the music was cool. Warren Vander Hill, born and raised in Queens, New York, recalls what attracted him most to R&B: "It's the rhythm. It was dance music." Vander Hill still remembers driving around Queens with other members of his high school basketball team listening to Fats Domino songs that were being played on a radio station in faraway Memphis. After graduation he attended Hope College in Michigan, a church-related school that "frowned on dances." They did have "footfunctions," but "we never heard R&B played there." Vander Hill and his friends, like numerous other white teenagers across the nation, thought "cat" music was cool.[47]

R&B had an added benefit. Since most adults hated the new music, it set teenagers apart from the older generation. Ironically, the era's segregationist attitudes also may have contributed to the spread of black music to young white audiences. R&B's status as "forbidden fruit" made it that much more tempting to rebellious white teenagers.

Black performers and their music might have been attractive for other reasons, too. Throughout American history, white observers have viewed the black minority as outsiders living on the margins of mainstream culture and society. Paradoxically, these "other" Americans came to represent personal freedom, since they did not always have to conform to middle-class norms. In colonial America, some whites equated blacks with sexual power. In the nineteenth century, says historian Eric Lott, white minstrels performed in blackface in part "to become black, to inherit the cool, virility, humility, abandon, or *gaite de couer* that were the prime components of white ideologies of black manhood." Historian Michael Bertrand suggests that these "appropriators were attempting to forsake not their whiteness but rather a bourgeois or middle-class ethic that they considered repressive. That they chose African Americans to embody their model of liberation . . . is significant." He adds, "No one can deny that society had traditionally denied African Americans full membership into the American mainstream and economic marketplace; societal prejudice and economic barriers had compelled many to retain traits antithetical to the middle-class ethic. Those traits had great appeal to those opposed to the dominant culture."[48]

White mimicry of African Americans continued into the twentieth century. Al Jolson's character in the 1927 film *The Jazz Singer* sang in blackface to symbolize his abandonment of traditional responsibilities. Writers in post–World War II America likewise equated African Americans with social freedom. Norman Mailer's "White Negroes" were cultural rebels opposed to the conformity of 1950s America. Jack Kerouac's hipster characters in *On the Road* viewed blacks as the antithesis of, if not the antidote for, America's boring middle-class culture. The white teenagers who turned to black rhythm & blues in the late 1940s and early '50s were not that different from Mailer and Kerouac. Like the two authors, they also were seeking more freedom and fun through African American culture. Black R&B singer Rufus Thomas has a succinct explanation. "I always tell white folks: 'If you could be black for one Saturday night, you never would want to be white anymore.'"[49]

Whatever the motive, the changing musical tastes of white teenagers had important implications for race relations. Seeds of integration were being planted as white teenagers began buying R&B records, cheering black performers, attending R&B concerts, and trying to be like blacks. "Rhythm and blues music no longer is limited to what used to be considered a rhythm and blues audience," concluded *Cashbox* magazine in 1955. "The meaning of all this is that people are just recognizing that the tastes of other people in other regions are as valid as their own. And with an open mind, they are learning to appreciate qualities which they never could see before."[50]

R&B music of the late 1940s and early '50s had much in common with early rock & roll. Not only did R&B songs like Wynonie Harris's "Good Rockin' Tonight" (1948) or Jimmy Preston's "Rock the Joint" (1949) use the terms, but they and other R&B hits such as Lloyd Price's "Lawdy Miss Clawdy" (1952) and Clyde McPhatter and the Drifters' "Money Honey" (1953) sounded almost identical to early rock & roll. In fact, those four songs were later recorded by numerous rock artists and are now considered rock & roll classics. R&B's power came from its electric guitars, prominent rhythms, insistent backbeats, expressive lyrics, and emotional, shouting vocal styles. "Listening to many of these

[R&B] stars, one can hear elements of 1950s rock & roll," concludes music historian Joe Stuessy.[51]

R&B's growing popularity allowed several rhythm & blues songs to cross over onto the pop charts in the late 1940s and early '50s. The Orioles' ballad "It's Too Soon to Know" made it to number 13 in 1948. In 1951, the Dominoes' "Sixty Minute Man" climbed to the number 17 spot, while Joe Turner's "Chains of Love" made it to number 30. The following year, Fats Domino's "Goin' Home" also came in at number 30 on the pop charts. Not coincidentally, these black singers were integrating the pop charts just as African Americans were gaining a higher national profile. Following World War II, the black population of northern and western cities continued to grow, transforming civil rights from a regional to national issue. Headlines spotlighted black achievements. Jackie Robinson broke the color barrier in baseball when he joined the Brooklyn Dodgers in 1947. President Truman desegregated the military in 1948. And *Amos and Andy* became the first TV show with an all-black cast in 1951.

Despite R&B's growing popularity, it was still rhythm & blues, not rock & roll. It was being sung by black artists primarily for black audiences. All that was about to change, though. Within a short time, white artists like Elvis Presley and their predominately white audiences were about to answer the question posed in Wynonie Harris's 1948 rhythm & blues hit "Good Rockin' Tonight": "Have you heard the news? There's good rockin' tonight!"[52]

2

GOOD ROCKIN' TONIGHT

From R&B to Rock & Roll

In September 1954, a teenager named Elvis Presley entered a tiny studio at Sun Records, 706 Union Avenue, Memphis, Tennessee, to record a new version of Wynonie Harris's 1948 R&B hit, "Good Rockin' Tonight." Only a handful of people in Memphis were even aware of the session that ultimately would rock America forevermore.

Presley's rendition of "Good Rockin' Tonight" was strikingly different from Wynonie Harris's original. Wynonie's mature vocal was controlled, and the song chugged ahead with a slow-paced, steady rhythm. Elvis's youthful-sounding voice, on the other hand, shot up and down and around and around like a high-speed rollercoaster, giving the vocal a dramatic sense of urgency. Harris was backed by a 1940s-sounding R&B combo that featured a swinging saxophone and a beat driven by handclaps and bass. Presley was supported by just two country pickers—Scotty Moore on electric guitar and Bill Black on slapping bass. But the three created an original, high-energy sound that was pure excitement. Even the lyrics on the two records were different. Harris sang about R&B jubilees and made constant references to earlier R&B songs. Presley dropped those rhythm & blues allusions and created a new one as he kept shouting the phrases "We're gonna rock! Let's rock! C'mon rock!"[1]

Significantly, the two singers were aiming their performances at two totally different audiences. Wynonie Harris was singing for black listeners. Elvis Presley was alerting white teenagers to the news—"There's good rockin' tonight!" By 1954, the song Presley was singing was no longer just rhythm & blues. It had morphed into something new. Part black, part white, it was now rock & roll in everything but name. And that, too, was about to change (figure 2.1).

BLACK INFLUENCES ON WHITE SINGERS

Elvis certainly was not the first white singer influenced by African American music. Mainstream pop music of the nineteenth and twentieth centuries frequently borrowed from black spirituals, blues, ragtime, and jazz. Early country & western singers such as Jimmie Rodgers and Hank Williams incorporated black musical styles. White pop artists of the 1950s were also inspired by black music. Frankie Laine was influenced by Cab Calloway and other black artists to such an extent that many listeners initially assumed that he was a black vocalist. The same is true for Johnny Ray. "Billie Holiday influenced me a great deal," he says. "When my first record hit, a lot of people thought that I was black."[2]

While Johnny Ray and Frankie Laine were being influenced by black music, another white musician, Bill Haley, was copying rhythm & blues note for note. Haley was not the first white to try his hand at R&B. Others had been involved with the music for years, including record company owners Ahmet Ertegun and Sid Nathan, producer Jerry Wexler, band leader Johnny Otis, and songwriters Jerry Leiber and Mike Stoller. What made Haley different was that he aimed his R&B efforts at white, not black, listeners. In the process, Bill Haley blazed a trail for the coming of rock & roll.

Haley was born in 1925 in Highland Park, Michigan, near Detroit. A few years later, his family moved to Chester, just outside of Philadelphia. It was there that Bill became interested in country & western music. "My mother was a piano teacher. My dad, who was from Kentucky, played mandolin," explains Haley. "And I suppose that was where the country influence came from. I started to play guitar at the age of seven and I was a country-and-western fan. I used to go around entering amateur contests."[3]

Figure 2.1. R&B singer Wynonie Harris had a number 1 R&B hit in 1948 with "Good Rockin' Tonight." (Courtesy of Music Library and Sound Recordings Archives, Bowling Green State University)

By the time Haley was in his late teens, he was singing with country & western bands that toured the Midwest and South. He even cut three or four records, all of which flopped. Haley tried everything—from billing himself as either "Silver Yodeling Bill" or "The Rambling Yodeler" to fronting a band called the Four Aces of Western Swing—but nothing clicked. In 1947, Haley returned to Chester, broke and doubtful that he would ever have a career in music. He landed a job as a disc jockey and bandleader at a local radio station, and for the next few years, he hosted a daily program that allowed him to perform with his latest country & western group, Bill Haley and the Saddlemen.

In June 1951, Haley's career took an unexpected turn. The white country & western artist decided to record black rhythm & blues. There are two different versions of how that came about. Dave Miller, who owned and operated a local record label called Essex Records, insists that it was his idea, not Haley's. Miller claims that he made a business trip down South, where he heard and bought a copy of Jackie Brenston's R&B hit "Rocket 88." He brought the record back to Philadelphia, gave it to Haley, and asked the singer, who was fairly popular throughout the Philadelphia area, to record a new version of the song. Miller recalls that he really had to twist Haley's arm to convince him to record the "race" record.

Haley remembers the story differently: "On [my] station there was a show called 'Judge Rhythm's Court'. . . an hour of rhythm & blues, [which] ended just before I came on live for an hour with my band. All of this led me to think: 'Why shouldn't a country-and-western act sing rhythm & blues music?' It was unheard of in those days. . . . I didn't see anything wrong in mixing things up. I liked to sing rhythm & blues and I sang them." Haley recalls that he often used to go on the air still humming Jimmy Preston's R&B song "Rock the Joint," which the previous show used as an ending theme song. "About this time," continues Haley, "Dave Miller . . . came to see me. He and his sister and mother had been listening to my radio programs and he thought I had something different: singing rhythm and blues with a country-and-western background. So I agreed to make some records. And the first side we cut, 'Rocket 88,' an R&B hit, did quite well for us."[4]

Regardless of whose idea it was, this was the first time a white artist had consciously attempted to duplicate the sound of a black rhythm & blues record. Cover records (i.e., new versions of songs already recorded) were not new to the 1950s. Throughout the first half of the twentieth century, most of the profits in the music industry came from song publishing, so it made good economic sense to have as many artists as possible record a song. That explains why Bing Crosby, Charlie Spivak, Gordon Jenkins, and Freddy Martin all had hits with "White Christmas" in 1942. Or why in 1948, "A Slow Boat to China" was recorded by Kay Kyser, Eddy Howard, and Snooky Lanson. By the early 1950s, some white pop artists were even covering black R&B songs. In

1951, for instance, Patti Page had a number 1 hit with a pop rendition of Erskine Hawkins's R&B record, "The Tennessee Waltz" (which in turn was a version of the original by country artists Pee Wee King and Redd Stewart).

But even if cover records were not that new, white cover records that attempted to imitate a black rhythm & blues original were. When Haley and his band covered Brenston's "Rocket 88" on June 14, 1951, they nudged the music industry a little closer to rock & roll. Equally important, Haley's record established a pattern that would be used by later cover records. In order to make the R&B song more acceptable to white audiences and radio stations, Haley toned down the lyrics, deleting all references to sex, drinking, and carousing. Although Haley's "Rocket 88" was a bad imitation of the original, it still managed to sell 10,000 copies locally. That was good enough to justify Haley's subsequent covers of other R&B hits. Bill Haley & the Saddlemen followed up with an equally tepid version of Jimmy Preston's "Rock the Joint," which did somewhat better, selling 75,000 copies.

Haley and his group were convinced they were on to something. Band member Johnny Grande recalls that for about a year nobody knew what to do with them. They were no longer country & western, but they weren't rhythm & blues either. "What I still think of as our 'desperation huddle' brought the turning point," says Grande. The group discussed the situation and decided to perform for free at local high schools as a way to reach the teenage audience. "That's how it happened that we played 183 high-school assemblies. It was tough to do at the time, but it proved the smartest thing we ever tried," insists Grande. "The kids taught us. We tried our experiments on them. When their shoulders started moving, their feet tapping, and their hands clapping, we knew that particular tune or style was worth keeping in the act."[5]

Even though the group's popularity was on the rise, Bill Haley realized that his group's name and image were confusing disc jockeys and audiences. The Saddlemen appeared to be a country & western act, but they sounded like rhythm & blues performers. So Haley came up with a plan. He renamed the group "Haley's Comets with Bill Haley" and gave them a new look. "Soon we got rid of our cowboy boots and we shaved off the sideburns," explains Haley. "We bought tuxedos and became a pop act."[6] Though no one suspected it at the time, Haley's Comets were about to light up the rock & roll universe.

THE BIRTH OF ROCK & ROLL

Change was in the wind in 1953. When Eisenhower was sworn in as president, he became the first Republican to occupy the White House in twenty-four years. A few months later, the presidential retreat in Maryland was renamed Camp David, in honor of Ike's grandson. Other firsts included the American Stock Exchange, which came into existence; Harvard Law School awarded its first degree to a woman; American Airlines began nonstop transcontinental flights between New York and Los Angeles; Chevrolet introduced the Corvette; scientists announced the discovery of DNA molecules in all living cells; and new TV programs included *The Danny Thomas Show*, Walter Cronkite's *You Are There*, and a novel quiz show called *Name That Tune*.

Rock & roll offered its own innovations. In 1953, Haley's Comets with Bill Haley earned their first national hit with "Crazy Man, Crazy." Written by Haley and released on the Essex label, the song combined the musical stylings of country & western and rhythm & blues with lyrics aimed at white teenagers. "The musical world was starved for something new," recalls Haley. "I felt then that if I could take, say, a Dixieland tune and drop the first and third beats, and accentuate the second and fourth, and add a beat the listeners could clap to as well as dance this would be what they were after." He added, "From that the rest was easy . . . take everyday sayings like 'Crazy Man Crazy' . . . and apply to what I have just said." The Comets' keyboard player, Johnny Grande, remembers how Haley came up with the title: "Bill noticed that the kids' favorite expression was 'Crazy.' A crazy sweater, a crazy tie, a crazy beat. Bill took their word—and their football chant 'Go! Go! Go!'—and gave it back to them in a song."[7]

"Crazy Man, Crazy" became a million-seller in 1953, peaking at number 12 on the national pop charts. The song was so popular it was covered in the United States by the Ralph Marterie Orchestra and in England by both Ted Heath and Oscar Rabin. A very strong case can be made that "Crazy Man, Crazy" is the *first* rock & roll record. Prior to this, R&B songs performed by black R&B artists had crossed over onto the pop charts. But, this time things were different. This was a white group singing an original song they had written for a white teenage audience. Although their record was influenced by rhythm & blues, it was more than just rhythm and blues. "Crazy Man, Crazy" was a musical hybrid that blended R&B beats, country & western vocals, and white pop lyrics. In effect, R&B had been transformed into something new, something different.

Ironically, the new sound's message was being delivered by an anachronistic messenger. Bill Haley and His Comets looked more like the old swing-style type of band that would be hired to play at a wedding reception than they did musical revolutionaries. Haley seemed shy and self-conscious on stage. His portly appearance and thinning hair made him look older than he was (he was only twenty-eight when "Crazy Man, Crazy" was released). The rest of the group also seemed middle-aged. They tried to look "cool" by wearing matching tuxedos and slicking down their hair, but it didn't even come close to working. The tuxes (complete with bowties) simply made them look like lounge singers. The hairdos were even worse. Haley looked the strangest with greased-down hair and a weird spit curl in the middle of his forehead. But what they lacked in appearance, they made up for with effort. Haley's Comets were determined to give young audiences a wild show, patterning their act after raucous R&B performers. They played solos while lying on their backs, jumped in the air, and played their instruments over their heads just like spirited jazz and R&B musicians (figure 2.2).

Audiences loved the sound and style, convincing Haley that his band had crossed a threshold. Bill later said that rock & roll was born when Cleveland disc jockey Alan Freed began playing his group's songs on the air, adding, "Of course, we didn't realize what we had until 'Crazy Man, Crazy'. . . went over a million." The song's success likewise impressed the Comets' Johnny Grande: "['Crazy Man, Crazy'] was the first nonclassifiable tune to break over into pop record sales. Riffs we had invented in our band were [soon] copied by others. Our rrroom-pah was picked up everywhere. The big back beat was rocking the country." Years later, Haley recalled, "We were something new. We didn't call it that at that time, but we were playing rock & roll." Eventually, critics would acknowledge Bill Haley's contribution by labeling him "the father of rock & roll."[8]

Haley's Comets managed two additional hits in 1953, "Fractured" and "Live It Up." Both seem contrived next to "Crazy Man, Crazy" but still managed to make it onto the Top 30 record charts. Equally impor-

Figure 2.2.   Bill Haley and His Comets perform. (Photo by "PoPsie" Randolph L.L.C.; courtesy of Michael Randolph, executor to the estate of William "PoPsie" Randolph)

tant, Bill Haley's success opened the door a little wider so black R&B performers could also make it onto the predominately white pop charts.

Prior to Haley's "Crazy Man, Crazy," only four R&B records had ever made the Top 30 pop charts: the Orioles' "It's Too Soon to Know" (1948), the Dominoes' "Sixty Minute Man" (1951), Joe Turner's "Chains of Love" (1951), and Fats Domino's "Goin' Home" (1952). In the few months after Haley's hit, four additional R&B songs charted: Fats Domino's "Goin' to the River," the Orioles' "Crying in the Chapel" (which was an R&B cover of Darrell Glenn's country & western hit), Faye Adams's "Shake a Hand," and Joe Turner's "Honey Hush."

The gates of the pop music charts were thrown wide open in 1954 as ten R&B or R&B-influenced records became Top 30 hits. Fittingly, these African American sounds provided background music for the nation as the most famous civil rights case of the day—*Brown vs. Board of*

Education—made its way through the courts. A story in *Billboard* magazine noted the new musical craze: "Once limited in sales appeal to the relatively small Negro market, rhythm and blues has now blossomed, with disk sales last year reaching an all-time record of $15,000,000. And indications are that 1954 sales will surpass even this mark." The trade magazine explained that white teenagers who craved "music with a beat" were responsible for R&B's sudden surge in popularity. Jukebox operators were among the first to notice the trend. California operators reported that "popular records take a secondary position to R&B" on the jukeboxes at almost every teenage hangout.[9]

Many white teenagers were particularly intrigued by the R&B harmony sound that later became known as "doo-wop." Nowadays, the term is commonly used to describe a musical style popularized by rock & roll groups of the 1950s and early '60s. Based on the harmony sound of rhythm & blues groups, it used human voices to duplicate the sounds of instruments. More often than not, the doo-wop sound was characterized by a prominent bass singer, a soaring falsetto, and three or more additional voices providing complementary harmonies. Here's a sample of two early doo-wop songs:

- "Doot doo-doo doot, doo-doo doot, doo-doo doo-doo-doot / Doot doo-doo doot, doo-doo doot, doo-doo doo-doo-doot / Love that girl" (The Crows' "Gee," 1954)
- "Shoo doo in dooby doo / Shoo doo in dooby doo / Shoo doo in dooby doo / Shoo doo in dooby doo" (The Five Satins' "In the Still of the Nite," 1956)

Even just a quick glance at those nonsensical syllables demonstrates why this R&B harmony sound became known as doo-wop. Actually, the term was not used until the early 1970s when New York disc jockey Gus Gossert popularized it. Back in the 1950s and early '60s, the sound was viewed simply as a vocal group variation of either rhythm & blues or rock & roll. The harmony sound originated in the 1940s when R&B groups began experimenting with blends of pop music, gospel, blues, and jazz. Of course, using voices to imitate instruments was around long before rhythm & blues arrived on the scene. "Vocal group harmonizing, whether religious or secular, black or white, male or female, sophisticated or innocent, a cappella or accompanied, has produced some of the most astonishing sounds ever created," explains music expert Bob Hyde, "and for the generation or two for whom the popular mode of musical expression was rock 'n' roll, doo wop was the primary vocal group contribution."[10]

Prior to the rise of doo-wop, harmony groups on the pop charts were either white pop groups or African American singers like the Mills Brothers and Ink Spots who mimicked white pop harmonies. R&B groups such as the Ravens, the Crows, and the Five Keys changed all of that. By the late 1940s and early '50s, they were singing black vocal music aimed at blacks, not whites. While doo-wop came out of African American urban communities after World War II, its roots can be traced back to earlier African American musical traditions. Doo-wop "comes from the desire of four or five black youths to get together to create a sound with harmonized voices," explains doo-wop expert Robert Pruter. "They could get together anywhere—on the street . . . in the hallway . . . [even] the boy's washroom. But what they wanted . . . was to create a sound with vocal harmony. And so doo wop is taking a very old tradition in black music that goes back to the 19th century and is attaching this tradition to the new sense of rhythm & blues and rock & roll in the '50s."[11]

The melodies, lyrics, and harmonies of this urban folk sound were usually uncomplicated and straightforward, as evidenced by the simple lyrics and basic instrumentation on early doo-wop records such as the Spaniels' "Goodnight, Sweetheart, Goodnight" (1954), the Jewels' "Hearts of Stone" (1954), or the Moonglows' "Sincerely" (1954). "Some of the best doo wop is as primitive and unschooled as it can get," notes musician Billy Vera. The Orioles, who are often credited as the first doo-wop group, are a perfect example. They went from practicing their amateurish harmonies on the street corners of Baltimore to having hits on the national charts such as "It's Too Soon to Know" (1948) and "Crying in the Chapel" (1953). But Vera is quick to point out that "amateurism is not necessarily the essential component of the genre." There were numerous examples such as the Moonglows and the Flamingos that were "hard-core professionals who rehearsed in real rehearsal halls with real musicians (or, in some cases, were musicians themselves)."[12]

While doo-wop may have begun in the rhythm & blues field, it soon became an integral part of rock & roll. By 1954, doo-wop records by R&

B groups were attracting white listeners, as well as blacks. One of the earliest national hits was the Crows' "Gee," which appeared on George Goldner's Rama label, a small, independent record company in New York City. Goldner was a major figure in the history of early rock & roll. As the owner of an independent record company, a talent scout, and record producer, Goldner had a tremendous impact on the direction the music took in the mid-1950s. He began his career in 1948 when he established Tico Records, which specialized in Latin American music. He soon noticed that many young Latinos in his New York City neighborhood were buying R&B records. So, in early 1953, he started up Rama Records, a subsidiary label that would specialize in rhythm & blues. He would go on to record some of the greatest groups in doo-wop history, including Frankie Lymon and the Teenagers, the Chantels, and the Flamingos.[13]

Goldner's first big success came with the Crows' "Gee," an up-beat harmony song that the group had written in ten minutes. The record became a national hit in 1954 when a West Coast disc jockey, Dick "Huggy Boy" Hugg, began playing it repeatedly because his girlfriend really liked the song. Whether the stunt impressed the girl is unknown, but the exposure on one of the most popular radio stations in Los Angeles did wonders for the record. When the Crows' song started selling on the West Coast, Goldner began promoting "Gee" nationally. Eventually, the R&B song climbed all the way up to number 17 on the national pop charts.[14]

The success of "Gee" led to the white discovery of other R&B doo-wop songs, including the Clovers' "Lovey Dovey," the Moonglows' "Sincerely," the Spaniels' "Goodnight, Sweetheart, Goodnight," the Penguins' "Earth Angel," and the Chords' "Sh-Boom." Eventually, it sparked a cover-record craze that would dominate the national pop charts until early 1956.

The growing popularity of rhythm & blues did not go unnoticed by either major record companies or white recording artists. In 1954, Haley's band (now officially known as Bill Haley and His Comets) earned their first hit on a major record label. Haley's success the previous year with "Crazy Man, Crazy" had landed him a recording contract with Decca Records. His new producer was Milt Gabler, the same guy who had co-written and produced several hits for R&B great Louis Jordan in the 1940s. Haley's first release on Decca, "Rock Around the Clock" (which used the black slang word for dancing and sex), did reasonably well, peaking at number 23 on the pop charts. The record would do even better the following year. It became a number 1 hit in 1955 when it was rereleased after it appeared in the soundtrack of the film *Blackboard Jungle*. Even the record's modest success in 1954 was important, though, because it demonstrated to the record industry that songs by white artists that alluded to black R&B could sell in the pop market.

Shortly thereafter, major record companies jumped on the R&B cover-record bandwagon. The McGuire Sisters, who had already gained fame on Arthur Godfrey's television show, were the first to hit it big by covering (i.e., copying) a rhythm & blues hit. They made it all the way to number 7 on the pop charts in 1954 with a polished, pop-style version of the Spaniels' R&B doo-wop ballad "Goodnight, Sweetheart, Goodnight."

The Crew-Cuts found even greater success with their 1954 cover of an up-tempo doo-wop song called "Sh-Boom." The song had been written and released earlier in the year by the Chords, a black rhythm & blues quintet from New York City. Years later, one of the Chords recalled how the song came about. He was sitting around one day watching television when all of a sudden news came on about an atomic bomb test at Bikini. "Wouldn't that awesome sound of a big bomb exploding make a wonderful song title?" he thought. He and his group, the Chords, got right to work, and the result was their 1954 record, "Sh-Boom," which went to the top of the R&B charts and sold fairly well on the pop charts. The song serves as an excellent metaphor for how early rock & roll dealt with America's cold war culture in the 1950s. Though the record might have been inspired by a thermonuclear blast, its lyrics dealt with romance, not bombs or the cold war. Like "Sh-Boom," most hits from rock & roll's early years did not mention political, social, or cultural concerns directly. Nevertheless, America's cold war culture often lurked just beneath the surface of these seemingly innocent songs.[15] (figure 2.3).

The Chords' R&B song attracted lots of attention. Arnold Shaw, who helped Hill and Range Publishers acquire rights to "Sh-Boom" in 1954, vividly recalls the first time he heard the Chords' record: "The disk opened with two unaccompanied 'Life could be a dream . . . life could be a dream,' hoarse and strident, and bounced into a bright, unabating shuffle. Explosive 'Sh-Booms' punctuated both the vocal and R&B ten-

Figure 2.3.   The Chords wrote and recorded the original version of "Sh-Boom."
(Richard Aquila Collection)

or-sax solo," explains Shaw. "The phrase, 'Hello, hello again' came out of nowhere several times to keep the rhythm going, as did other nonsense syllables. The bass voice solo, traditional on R&B records, had a nostalgic feeling of longing. Lyrically, the song was a compound of cliché phrases. . . . But it kept repeating the inviting promise of 'Life could be a dream.' I found it irresistible."[16]

Audiences were likewise captivated. The Chords' R&B song—released on the indie label Cat Records (a subsidiary of Atlantic)—shot up to the top of the pop charts in Los Angeles, causing a major record company, Mercury, to rush one of their pop groups, the Crew-Cuts, into the studio to record a cover version. The Crew-Cuts looked and sounded like the perfect All-American boys (even though they hailed from Toronto, Canada). Always well groomed, they even wore coats and ties in the recording studio. The group's name, which referred to the popular hairstyle sported by clean-cut white teenage boys during the Eisenhower era, underscored their positive image. The Crew-Cuts sounded as white as the Chords did black as they substituted pristine, 1940s pop-style harmonies for the Chords' grittier, jazz-based scat singing. Even the big band musical arrangements on the cover record blared "WHITE POP!"

The Crew-Cut's rendition exploded onto the pop charts, climbing all the way to number 1. But the Chords' version wasn't exactly blown out of the water. The R&B original did almost as well. It became the first doo-wop record to make pop music's Top 10 charts, peaking at number 5. Significantly, the Chords' version won out in the long run. Nowadays, it is the Chords' version that is still remembered and played on oldies stations, not the Crew-Cuts'.

Many experts insist that "Sh-Boom" was the first rock & roll record,[17] but that claim is dubious at best. "Sh-Boom" was not the first R&B song to make the national pop charts. In 1948, the Orioles' "It's Too Soon to Know" became the first R&B ballad to make the pop charts, while the Dominoes had the first up-tempo R&B crossover in 1951 with "Sixty Minute Man." "Sh-Boom" was not the first white cover of an R&B record, either. That honor goes to Bill Haley, who remade "Rocket 88" back in 1951. Even if the field is limited to white covers that became Top 10 hits, the McGuire Sisters' "Goodnight, Sweetheart, Goodnight" still predated the Crew-Cuts' record. "Sh-Boom" was not even the first R&B-influenced hit to be recorded by white artists. That honor also goes to Bill Haley and His Comets for "Crazy Man, Crazy."

But even if "Sh-Boom" was not the first rock & roll record, it still is extraordinarily important. "Sh-Boom" was the first R&B-influenced song to make it all the way to number 1 on the pop charts. The song threw the doors of the white pop charts wide open to black rhythm & blues. It also became a prototype for later doo-wop songs that used nonsense syllables as lyrics. The record's tremendous success guaranteed that numerous other cover records would follow.

Bill Haley, who pioneered the cover-record phenomenon three years before the Crew-Cuts made it to number 1 on the pop charts, was not about to be left behind. When Joe Turner's R&B song "Shake, Rattle, and Roll" began climbing the pop charts in the summer of 1954, Bill Haley and His Comets rushed into Decca's studio and cranked out a cover version. Haley's record soon outpaced Turner's, making it all the way to number 7 on the national pop charts while Turner's better-sounding original stalled at number 22. Just as Haley had "cleaned" up the lyrics on his earlier renditions of "Rocket 88" and "Rock the Joint," he rewrote the words to Turner's suggestive jump blues song. The original record begins with the lead singer ordering his woman to "get out of that bed" and into the kitchen to "make some noise with the pots and pans." Haley avoids the bedroom scene completely, telling his girl "Get out in that kitchen, and rattle those pots and pans / Roll my breakfast 'cause I'm a hungry man." Where Turner sings, "Well, you wear low dresses, the sun comes shinin' through / I can't believe my eyes that all this belongs to you," Haley changes it to "You wear those dresses, your hair done up so nice / You look so warm, but your heart is cold as ice." Haley simply omits what might be Turner's most suggestive verse: "I said over the hill, and way down underneath / You make me roll my eyes, and then you make me grit my teeth."[18] Bill Haley later explained why he rewrote lyrics: "We steer completely clear of anything suggestive! We take a lot of care with lyrics because we don't want to offend anybody. The music is the main thing, and it's just as easy to write acceptable words."[19]

Whether Haley's tinkering with R&B lyrics was justifiable is debatable, but there is no doubt that Haley's success, along with the Crew-Cuts', ignited a cover-record craze that swept through the music industry in 1955 and early 1956. These white covers—which frequently followed Haley's approach for dealing with suggestive lyrics—would steal the commercial thunder away from the R&B originals. By the end of 1954, white groups like Bill Haley and His Comets and the Crew-Cuts had changed the equation for rhythm & blues. It was no longer a marginal sound aimed at a minority group. R&B was mainstreamed. In the process, the music was transformed into something else, something new—a musical hybrid that blended black R&B, white pop, white country & western, and other musical styles. All that was needed was a new name. By the end of 1954, that, too, would come to pass.

THE NAMING OF ROCK & ROLL

Rock & roll fans, critics, and historians have long credited disc jockey Alan "Moondog" Freed as the man who coined the name *rock and roll*. Right up until his death in 1965, Freed insisted that he was the one who invented rock & roll. That claim eventually made it into cyberspace when the "Official Alan Freed Website" opened its virtual doors on the web, billing itself as "covering the life and work of the man who coined the phrase 'rock n roll' and helped shape the future of popular music." Indeed, one of the most important reasons for locating the Rock & Roll Hall of Fame and Museum in Cleveland, Ohio, was because Freed allegedly came up with the idea for rock & roll while he was a deejay on WJW–Cleveland.[20] (figure 2.4).

Despite the claims made by Freed and his supporters, he certainly did not coin, create, or invent the phrase "rock and roll." It is debatable whether Moondog even applied the term to rhythm & blues music prior to 1954. The words "rock" and "roll," as well as the entire expression—"rock and roll"—had been used in black music since at least the 1920s as code words for sexual intercourse, dancing, revelry, or any combination thereof. Just prior to Freed landing his show on WJW–Cleveland, there were well-known R&B hits such as Wynonie Harris's "Good Rockin' Tonight" (1948), Bill Moore's "We're Gonna Rock, We're Gonna Roll" (1948), and John Lee Hooker's "Rock 'n' Roll" (1950). Yet, even if Alan Freed did not invent the expression "rock and roll," he certainly did much to popularize it (at least after 1954). Moondog became, in the words of musicologist Arnold Shaw, "rock 'n' roll's superpromoter."[21]

Figure 2.4.   Alan Freed launched his "Moondog" rock & roll show on Cleveland's WJW and later became a successful disc jockey in New York City. (Robert Pruter Collection)

Freed's rise to fame was intertwined with the birth and growth of the music that eventually became known as rock & roll. As Freed tells it, he was approached in early 1951 by Leo Mintz , the owner of the Record Rendezvous store in Cleveland, who told him that white teenagers were eagerly buying up all the black R&B records they could get their hands on. Freed went to Mintz's store to see for himself, and later described the scene: "I heard the tenor saxophones of Red Prysock and Big Al Sears. I heard the blues-singing, piano-playing Ivory Joe Hunter. I wondered. I wondered for about a week. Then I went to the [WJW] station manager and talked him into permitting me to follow my classical program with a rock 'n' roll party."[22]

Leo Mintz remembers it differently. He insists that Freed initially refused to play R&B, because he did not want to get involved with "race" music. But Mintz persisted, and Freed eventually relented. Freed's most reliable biographer, John A. Jackson, believes that Mintz's version is closer to the truth. Jackson notes that the story about white teenagers buying R&B records is probably exaggerated if not entirely made up, since Freed's initial audiences for both his radio show and concerts were almost entirely black. Mintz, who already advertised on WJW, simply wanted an all–rhythm & blues program on the air so he could sell more records. One of Freed's close associates reinforces Jackson's argument, explaining that Mintz bought the time on WJW, hired Alan for the program, and told Alan what records to play. But although Freed was "pushed" into doing the show by Mintz, "he got to like the music very much."[23]

Freed's rhythm & blues program debuted on WJW on July 11, 1951. Significantly, Freed was not the first white disc jockey to play R&B music. Deejays such as Hunter Hancock in Los Angeles, Dewey Phillips in Memphis, and Gene Nobles in Nashville were all spinning R&B records on their radio programs by the late 1940s. But if Alan "Moondog" Freed was not the first, he certainly became the best known. He was perfect for the new, unconventional sound. "Freed possessed the personality, the command of jive talk and even the voice to become [rock & roll's] supersalesman," remembers Arnold Shaw, who was in the music business at the time. "An operation on his vocal chords to remove a polyp left him with a gritty hoarseness that made him sound like a blues shouter." More traditional disc jockeys probably winced every time Moondog howled at the records, screamed along with the music, rattled a cow bell, and banged out a beat on a telephone book with his fists. Sometimes, even young listeners were confused by the histrionics. Freed's tour manager noted that a kid "would buy the record, bring it back to the store and say, 'Hey, this ain't the record. I want the one with the guy screaming.' And there'd be arguments in the record shops, fights, every damn thing."[24]

Freed eventually began calling his program "The Moondog Rock 'n' Roll House Party." The deejay later claimed that in order to sneak black rhythm & blues music past white radio station managers and white parents, he had to call it something else—so he invented the phrase "rock 'n' roll."[25] While the story sounds possible, maybe even reasonable given race relations in the early 1950s, the facts do not support Freed's contention.

Some experts question whether Freed's original program was even called "The Moondog Rock 'n' Roll House Party." Arnold Shaw remembers its initial title as "Record Rendezvous" (named after sponsor Leo Mintz's store). Only later was the name changed. John A. Jackson's detailed research supports Shaw's recollection. The biographer suggests that Freed's program might have been on the air for several days, maybe even weeks, before the disc jockey inadvertently stumbled across the Moondog idea. Evidently, one evening Freed was playing an obscure song by Louis Hardin called "Moondog Symphony," which featured a hound baying at the moon. The deejay interrupted the song, saying, "Come on now, Moondog, please stop howling or you'll wake up the neighbors." The switchboard lit up immediately. Listeners wanted to know what the heck was going on. The next night, says Jackson, Freed's "Moondog" persona "took to the airwaves, baying like a moonstruck hound." Freed even began referring to his theme song, Todd Rhodes's "Blues for the Red Boy" as "Blues for the Moondog."[26]

Even if Freed's claim that he originally titled his program "The Moondog Rock 'n' Roll House Party" is allowed, it is likely that the disc jockey was using the phrase "rock 'n' roll" to describe the show, not the music. An audio clip of the deejay's introduction to one of his shows in 1953 provides evidence. He begins by saying, "Hello everybody, how're y'all tonight? This is Alan Freed, the 'ole King of the Moondoggers. And it's time again for another of your favorite rock 'n' roll sessions—blues and rhythm records for all the gang in the Moondog Kingdom from the Midwest to the East Coast. . . . Enjoy Erin Brew [the beer company sponsor] as you enjoy the Moondog Show."[27] Notice that Freed refers to the show as a "rock 'n' roll session" (i.e., a dance session) of "blues and rhythm records." That suggests that when Freed called his radio program a "Rock 'n' Roll Party," he was using the expression as an adjective to describe the program rather than as a noun for the type of music being played.

Not until late 1954 does Freed actually apply the phrase to the music he played. "Freed eventually claimed he gave rock & roll its name," explains John A. Jackson, "and, by 1960 the deejay incorrectly maintained he had named the music rock & roll in 1951."[28]

Before 1954, Alan Freed seemed far more interested in emphasizing his Moondog identity than the notion of "rock 'n' roll." A 1953 audio clip ends with Freed telling his audience to "enjoy the Moondog Show." He doesn't mention rock & roll. An early photograph of a promotional event for the program depicts a banner that reads "Record Rendezvous Sponsors the Alan Freed's Moon Dog Show [on] WJW 850 on Your Dial." The posters for Freed's first major R&B concert in March 1952 likewise refer to Freed's program as "The Moon Dog Show." In neither case is "rock 'n' roll" even mentioned.[29]

While all sorts of questions surround the title of Freed's program and his initial use of the phrase "rock 'n' roll," there is no doubt that the program had an immediate impact. Cleveland listeners had never before heard anything so outrageous on the radio. At first, audiences were primarily black, but within months, Freed also began attracting young white listeners who tuned in nightly to hear this crazy guy rant and rave about wild new rhythm & blues sounds.

The show's success prompted Alan Freed, Lew Platt (his manager and booking agent), and Leo Mintz to branch out into live concerts. On March 21, 1952, they staged the Moondog Coronation Ball at the Cleveland Arena. The dance concert, which featured the Dominoes and other black R&B artists, turned into a fiasco when a mostly black crowd numbering somewhere between 16,000 and 25,000 tried to crash through the gates of the 10,000-seat arena. Police immediately turned the house lights on and cancelled the concert.[30]

At first glance, the event seemed like an unmitigated disaster for Freed and his partners. They didn't make any money. Local newspapers condemned them for the near riot. And city officials threatened to arrest the promoters for selling too many tickets (charges that were never proved). But, in the long run, the Moondog Coronation Ball catapulted Freed into the rhythm & blues spotlight. The Moondog's appeal did not go unnoticed by either the record industry or the national media.

Throughout the rest of 1952 and into 1953, Alan Freed's star continued to rise as his nightly radio show took Cleveland by storm and subsequent R&B concerts proved to be both highly popular and profitable. Freed's career was given another boost in late 1953 when WNJR, a small radio station in Newark, New Jersey, agreed to air tapes of his program. They didn't pay him much, but Freed wasn't worried. "The hell with the money," said the Moondog, "I'm being heard in the New York area!"[31] Freed had every reason to be optimistic. The momentum continued to build: the WNJR gig got him the recognition he craved in New York City, which led to a series of highly successful concerts in the New York area, which in turn led to a lucrative job offer from WINS–New York City.[32]

Cleveland fans had mixed emotions as they bid adieu to the "King of the Moondoggers." Although they would miss him, they could at least be proud that for a change Broadway was about to take its cue from the midwestern city on Lake Erie. (More cynical Clevelanders probably thought that New York was stealing Freed simply to get even because that year the Indians were finally ahead of the Yankees in the race for the pennant.)

On September 7, 1954, Alan Freed debuted his "Moondog Rock 'n' Roll House Party" on WINS, which also syndicated the program throughout the United States.[33] His wild approach to rhythm & blues captivated New York audiences as readily as those in the Midwest. The Moondog kingdom quickly spread northward and southward along the Eastern Seaboard. Its subjects now included millions of white and black listeners. Significantly, Freed still described the music he played as rhythm & blues, not rock & roll, and the media still referred to him as an R&B disc jockey. But just when the "King of the Moondoggers" seemed unstoppable, a foe rose up from the streets of New York claiming to be the real "Moondog." Louis Hardin's plan of attack was simple: he asked the New York State Supreme Court to order Alan Freed to cease and desist from using the "Moondog" name. Though no one realized it at the time, Hardin's lawsuit was the beginning of an important new chapter in the history of rock & roll.

Louis Hardin was a blind street musician who dressed like a Viking, wearing a horned helmet, homemade robes, and flowing cape. Arriving in New York City in the mid-1940s, he staked out a claim to the corner of 6th Avenue and 54th Street. By the time Alan Freed arrived in town, "Moondog" Hardin was already a local legend, playing percussion instruments and many of his own compositions for passersby and patrons of nearby Carnegie Hall.

The eccentric Hardin didn't take kindly to the notion of a rival Moondog. He got himself a lawyer and sued Freed for infringing on his Moondog name and turf. If the colorful street musician looked and sounded strange, there was nothing crazy about his lawsuit. Indeed, he had a very strong case. Hardin had been using the "Moondog" moniker since 1947, whereas Freed didn't adopt it until 1951. The clincher was Freed did not begin billing himself as "Moondog" until after he had played "Moondog Symphony" on his Cleveland radio show. Significantly, the composer and performer of that weird, obscure song was none other than—that's right!—Louis "Moondog" Hardin. Case closed. The judge ruled in favor of Hardin and ordered Freed to pay the street musician $5,700 in damages. More important, Freed had to stop using the "Moondog" name immediately.[34]

Freed was, to put it mildly, outraged. He had been on WINS radio for only two months, and now he was being forced to find a new signature name. The "King of the Moondoggers" was dead. Long live . . . What? That was the question. Freed and some drinking buddies went to a local bar to try to figure out an answer. "Alan was having a few drinks and bemoaning the fact that he had to come up with a new name," recalled Morris Levy, the president of Roulette Records and one of Freed's business associates. "To be honest with you, I couldn't say if Alan said it or somebody else said it. But somebody said 'rock and roll.' Everybody just went, Yeah. Rock and roll." It made sense. All Freed had to do was shorten the name of his program from "The Moondog Rock 'n' Roll House Party" to "The Rock 'n' Roll Party."[35]

Freed and Levy then launched a preemptive strike to head off any other Louis Hardins who might be lurking in the shadows of New York's civil courts. As protection against future lawsuits, Freed and Levy devised a plan to copyright the phrase "rock 'n' roll." Although ultimately the strategy proved unworkable, it gave Freed one additional reason to publicize the new name. And publicize it he did. From that point on, Freed took advantage of every available opportunity to apply the name "rock 'n' roll" to his program, the music he played, and his live concerts. An air check from early 1955 reveals that Freed's approach, as usual, was anything but subtle: "Hello, everybody! Yours truly, Alan Freed, the ol' King of the Rock and Rollers, all ready for another big night of rock and rolling. Rock 'n' roll records are the big beat in popular music today. Let 'er go . . . and we'll be here til nine o'clock, reviewing the Top 25 rock and roll favorites of the week. So welcome to Rock 'n' Roll Party number one!"[36]

Freed also changed the name and description of his R&B concerts. Instead of "Moondog Balls" or "rhythm & blues jubilees," they became "rock 'n' roll" concerts and dances. Only the names changed; the performers and music remained the same. But, according to Freed, both were now "rock 'n' roll." Freed unveiled his new approach in January of 1955 when he hosted his first "Rock 'n' Roll Jubilee Ball" at St. Nicholas Arena in New York City. To promote the show, the disc jockey mailed hundreds of letters to his fan club members. "Dear Fellow Rock 'n' Roller," began Freed, who then went on to promise that the upcoming concert would feature "sensational Rock 'n' Roll artists." The deejay neglected to explain that these "rock 'n' roll artists" were the same "rhythm & blues" artists who had always performed at his concerts.[37]

At long last—in late 1954 and early 1955—Freed was applying the term "rock 'n' roll" to the music. It was the perfect phrase at the right time. The music being played by Freed and other R&B disc jockeys was no longer just rhythm & blues. It now also included songs by R&B-influenced country artists like Bill Haley and His Comets and R&B-influenced pop artists such as the Crew-Cuts. Equally important, audiences were no longer just African Americans. White teenagers were now tuning in and turning on by the millions. The new name—rock & roll—sidestepped the racial stigma attached to rhythm & blues. Lastly, the fact that Freed's stage was now New York City meant that rock & roll was in the spotlight for the entire nation to see.

Alan Freed exaggerated his contributions to the birth of rock & roll music. Despite his claims, he clearly was not the "Father of Rock & Roll" or the "King of Rock & Roll." Nor did he invent the name. Freed does have to be given credit, though, for applying the phrase "rock & roll" to the music—not back in 1951 as he insisted, but in late 1954 after the music had already emerged. Even if the ol' King of the Moondoggers did not coin the term *rock & roll*, he certainly did much to popu-

larize it. Alan Freed became the new music's champion and top promoter.

By the end of 1954, rock & roll had arrived. The rise of the new
sound was intertwined with the rise of a new youth culture, as well as
the emergence of the civil rights movement on the national scene. As
Brown vs. Board of Education struck down segregation in public education and activists questioned Jim Crow laws, black and white rock &
rollers began integrating the pop charts. Although nobody knew it at the
time, events were beginning to unfold in various parts of the country
that would change popular culture even more. In Chicago, Chess
Records had just signed Chuck Berry to a contract. In Memphis, a
young Elvis Presley had just walked into Sun Records to record a song
for his mother's birthday present. And in Hollywood a movie had just
gone into production that would spotlight the new sound. Rock & roll
music was about to explode onto the national stage, sending shock
waves across Eisenhower's America.

3

ROCK AROUND THE CLOCK

Rock & Roll Goes National

The consciousness of the potential rock & roll audience was raised in the spring of 1955 by a movie called *Blackboard Jungle*. Frank Zappa, who became one of rock's most innovative musicians in the late 1960s and '70s, vividly recalls watching the film as a youngster: "When the titles flashed, Bill Haley and His Comets started blurching, 'One . . . Two . . . Three O'Clock . . . Four O'Clock, Rock!' It was the loudest sound kids had ever heard at that time. . . . Bill Haley . . . was playing the Teenage National Anthem and he was LOUD. I was jumping up and down. *Blackboard Jungle*, not even considering that it had the old people winning in the end, represented a strange act of 'endorsement' of the teenage cause." Like many adolescents, the young Zappa knew intuitively that something important was happening when he heard Haley singing "Rock Around the Clock." The song quickly became rock & roll's anthem, sounding a clarion call for teenage action. Music historian Arnold Shaw called it "the 'Marseillaise' of the rock revolution."[1]

Blackboard Jungle arrived in movie theaters at a time when most Americans were feeling guardedly optimistic about the future. In January 1955, families across the country crowded around their TV sets and watched proudly as a presidential press conference was filmed for the first time. Although Americans still feared the communist threat, they were confident that the current president and former World War II hero, Dwight Eisenhower, would defend and protect them from all internal and external threats. They also felt secure knowing that the Senate voted unanimously to continue its investigation of communism to guard against internal threats. They felt even safer in February when they heard the news that the United States had stockpiled over 4,000 nuclear weapons as compared to only 1,000 for the Soviet Union.

America's fears of possible war were offset by all sorts of good news. The economy was booming in 1955 as Americans rushed out to buy brand new homes in the suburbs, shiny automobiles with powerful engines, color television sets, fancy appliances, and a variety of other glitzy consumer goods. Popular culture added to their enjoyment. Sports fans cheered on the Brooklyn Dodgers as they finally defeated the New York Yankees in the World Series. They marveled at undefeated heavyweight champ Rocky Marciano as he successfully defended his crown against two tough challengers. While parents were watching new TV shows such as *Gunsmoke, The Lawrence Welk Show,* and *The $64,000 Question,* kids had their own favorite programs, especially *Davy Crockett, the King of the Wild Frontier,* made famous by actor Fess Parker in Disney movies and TV shows. Throughout 1955, Crockettmania swept the country, causing a run on coonskin caps and Davy Crockett T-shirts. The Crockett craze was proof that huge profits could be had by targeting the burgeoning youth market.

While youngsters were focusing on the "King of the Wild Frontier," teenagers were tuning in to hear the latest rock & roll hits. The new sound had begun integrating the pop charts long before Rosa Parks sparked the Montgomery Bus Boycott, Martin Luther King Jr. formed the Southern Christian Leadership Conference, or the Greensboro Four staged their sit-in at the Woolworth lunch counter.

In 1955, "Rock Around the Clock" became the primary vehicle for introducing hundreds of thousands—if not millions—of white youths to rock & roll. Haley and His Comets had actually recorded the song a year earlier, but the record was only moderately successful. When it resurfaced in 1955 as the theme for *Blackboard Jungle,* it rocketed all the way to the number 1 spot on the pop charts and remained there for eight weeks. Remarkably, the song was a fixture on the charts for over six months. By the end of 1955, rock & roll had arrived.

Many rhythm & blues artists didn't think rock & roll was all that new. "We were playing rhythm and blues for a long time," notes legendary R&B band leader Dave Bartholomew (who went on to produce and co-write most of Fats Domino's hit records), "and all of a sudden because white people are doing it, it's being called rock & roll. But it was still just rhythm & blues." R&B singer Ruth Brown agrees: "At what point did rhythm and blues start becoming rock 'n' roll? When the white kids started to dance to it." Bo Diddley is even more blunt: "Rhythm and blues became rock & roll when white boys began to play it."[2]

Such assessments are only partly correct. By 1955, rock & roll was more than just R&B. The new sound mixed varying amounts of black R&B, white country & western, white pop, and a smattering of other musical styles. Yet the very fact that such a musical hybrid was attracting racially mixed audiences by the mid-1950s suggests that both the music industry and American culture were changing. Industry insiders began noticing a shift in 1953. Although R&B had accounted for only 5 percent of total record sales in 1953, its trajectory was clearly headed upward. R&B labels reported all-time high sales in 1953 and predicted 1954 would even be better. The sudden surge could be explained in part by the expanding market among white teenagers as they gobbled up almost every R&B record they could get their hands on—from R&B originals done by black artists such as the Orioles, the Drifters, and the Chords to R&B-influenced hits by white artists like the Crew-Cuts and Bill Haley and His Comets.

In April 1954, *Billboard* magazine reported that audiences at R&B concerts staged by disc jockey Alan Freed were approximately one-third white. R&B disc jockeys across the nation noticed a similar trend, estimating that 20 to 30 percent of their listeners were now white. Percentages soared even higher in 1954 and early 1955. The audiences at Alan Freed's "Rock 'n' Roll Jubilee Ball" (held at New York City's St. Nicholas Arena on January 14–15, 1955) were reputedly between 50 and 70 percent white. Freed later confessed that only then did he have the "first inkling . . .that white people enjoyed rhythm and blues."[3]

The "big beat"—as Alan Freed sometimes described the new sound—was rapidly becoming a national craze. "The R&B beat has now captured a solid part of the pop music field and is even moving into hillbilly wax," explained a music trade writer in the autumn of '54. "Everyone knows how many tunes have started this year in the R&B field and then broken thru pop, but this is only part of the story. Almost 20 percent of the records being made these days with pop artists have a rhythm and blues beat, sound, or arrangement. The pop a&r [arrangement and repertoire] men have jumped on the R&B style for only one reason of course—to sell records. The kids have indicated that they want the music with a beat, and the large pop firms are sharp enough to go along with the trend."[4]

By the time Bill Haley and His Comets' "Rock Around the Clock" debuted on the pop charts in May of 1955, young audiences were primed for rhythm & blues–influenced music. The stage had been set by the media, as well as by the numerous rock & roll hits that had landed on the pop charts in 1953, 1954, and early 1955.

THE MEDIA AND ROCK & ROLL

Throughout 1955, the media played a major role in promoting the rock & roll phenomenon. Alan Freed continued to lead the charge, as both the name he applied to the music and his nightly radio program on New York's WINS caught on with increasingly more fans. His high-profile position as the host of a nightly radio show in the biggest market in the country offered the perfect podium for proselytizing. Freed's constant use of the term "rock 'n' roll" kept the new sound on message, and America took notice. The deejay's ratings and the music's new identity both took off, soaring higher and higher. When Freed's station began billing him as "America's #1 Rock 'n' Roll disc jockey," *Billboard* and other music trade magazines followed suit. Within a short time, the entire industry began viewing Freed as a rock & roll deejay rather than a rhythm & blues deejay.[5]

Disc jockeys across the country were soon jumping on the rock & roll bandwagon. By mid-1955, "Jumpin' George" Oxford (who gained a following as an R&B deejay on KSAN–San Francisco) was introducing his nightly radio show like this: "Hi. Old Jumpin' George here on KSAN 'til 5 o'clock tryin' once again to *rock* you and *roll* you to satisfy your soul, you hear?" Later on in the program, the erstwhile R&B disc jockey introduced Chuck Berry's "Maybellene" with this explanation: "This is old Jumpin' George saying you can call it *rhythm & blues* or *rock & roll* but here is one that is a hit under any name—Chuck Berry's 'Maybellene.'" Additional evidence of how R&B was evolving into rock & roll can be found on a promo that Jumpin' George did for an upcoming concert billed as "The Jumping George Rock & Roll Jubilee." The disc jockey assured listeners that they would be seeing in person "some of the greatest rock & roll stars of the day." Significantly, Jumping George's list of "rock & roll stars" included R&B performers such as the El Dorados and LaVern Baker along with white pop star Gloria Mann, who covered the Penguins' R&B hit, "Earth Angel."[6]

Television began showcasing rock & roll in 1955. Pop artists such as Perry Como, the Fontane Sisters, and Pat Boone made numerous appearances on network TV singing bland versions of R&B songs, but more authentic rock & rollers could also be found on the small screen. In June, Bill Haley and His Comets accepted an invitation to sing "Rock Around the Clock" on Milton Berle's popular television show. Not to be outdone, Ed Sullivan decided to spotlight the new music on his Sunday evening variety show. A news release on November 12 reported "Big-league TV is set to 'rock 'n roll' via an appearance booked this week for Dr. Jive (Tommy Smalls), local rhythm and blues disc jockey, for the Ed Sullivan CBS-TV show." Sullivan's plan was to have Dr. Jive host a fifteen-minute segment featuring LaVern Baker, Bo Diddley, and the Five Keys—R&B artists who were now being billed as rock & roll singers. Things didn't turn out exactly as Ed Sullivan planned, though. Hoping to reach a broader audience, Sullivan's staff instructed Diddley to sing Tennessee Ernie Ford's recent number 1 hit, "Sixteen Tons," instead of his own self-titled R&B song, "Bo Diddley." The singer reluctantly agreed and even practiced Ford's song for two hours using lyrics printed on cue cards. But when Bo took the stage for his live performance, he launched into a rocking version of his signature hit. Sullivan's people were furious and rushed the singer as soon as he left the stage to find out what had happened. "Man, maybe that was 'Sixteen Tons' on those cards," replied the R&B singer calmly, "but all I saw was 'Bo Diddley.'"[7]

Movies also helped promote rock & roll and the new youth culture. The controversial film *Blackboard Jungle* helped make Bill Haley and His Comets' "Rock Around the Clock" the most popular and important rock & roll hit of 1955. The record sold millions of copies after it was showcased in the dark docudrama that focused on one of the era's most pressing social concerns, juvenile delinquency.

Blackboard Jungle was certainly not the first motion picture to deal with teenage angst. Two years earlier, the tremendous success of Stanley Kramer's *The Wild One* had firmly established the box office appeal of films about the era's emerging youth culture. The 1953 film starred Marlon Brando as the leader of a rebellious motorcycle gang that terrorized a small town in California. At one point, Brando's character, dressed in tight jeans, a black leather jacket, and motorcycle cap, is asked, "What are you rebelling against?" He replies nonchalantly, "What've you got?" *The Wild One* dealt with a subject that was on a lot of people's minds in the mid-1950s: juvenile delinquency. "We are entering a critical period," warned a children's court judge in Buffalo, New York, in 1951, "a period which could bring disaster to the community's young people." The judge, like many adults, was concerned about the high rates of juvenile delinquency that had been plaguing America since World War II.[8]

The Wild One, which was based on a real incident that had occurred in Hollister, California, in the summer of 1947, brought those concerns to the big screen. The movie glorified rebellious youth, making Brando's character a popular icon for American teenagers who were soon wearing motorcycle caps and leather jackets everywhere. American capitalism quickly co-opted this fashion symbol of teenage rebellion. Many middle-class and working-class youngsters could not afford the real thing, so they bought mass-produced motorcycle jackets made out of cheap plastic that cracked after a few wears.

Not surprisingly, other films about troubled youth soon followed. One of the most successful was *Rebel Without a Cause* (1955). This time the misunderstood youth was not the leader of a working-class motorcycle gang; instead, he was a middle-class teenager from a well-to-do suburban high school. The film propelled a moody young actor named James Dean to instant stardom. Many young moviegoers could identify with Dean's troubled character, viewing him as a confused kid trapped in a meaningless adult world. Dean's cool, detached demeanor caught on as teenagers across the country copied his look and attitude. The film's director, Nicholas Ray, remembers the first time he met Elvis Presley: "[The King of Rock & Roll] got down on his knees before me and began to recite whole pages from the script. Elvis must have seen *Rebel* a dozen times by then and remembered every one of Jimmy's lines." Elvis even patterned his famous curled lip after Dean's pouty sneer.[9]

When *Rebel Without a Cause* hit movie theaters in the fall of 1955, *Blackboard Jungle* was already riveting the nation's attention on the growing problem of teenage alienation. Released on March 25, 1955, *Blackboard Jungle* stunned moviegoers with its bleak depiction of juvenile delinquency. The movie was filmed in black and white, creating an illusion that audiences were watching an old-fashioned newsreel about a contemporary urban problem. The film's title underscored the urgency of the situation, as did the script's frequent use of emotionally charged words such as "animals" and "jungle" to describe the deviant youth culture found in urban schools. Perhaps not coincidentally, the movie's title evoked memories of an earlier muckraking success—Upton Sinclair's seminal novel *The Jungle*, which exposed the horrendous problems associated with immigrant lifestyles and the meat-packing industry in turn-of-the-century America. The overall effect was chilling. Audiences came away convinced that, for good or bad, a new youth culture was on the rise.

Although not the first Hollywood movie to deal with American teenagers, *Blackboard Jungle* was the first to make use of rock & roll. Director Richard Brooks wrote the screenplay based on Evan Hunter's novel of the same name, and he hoped the new music would add authenticity to his film about troubled youths in an urban high school. Only one "rock & roll" song was used in the entire movie, but it proved to be a brilliant choice—"Rock Around the Clock" by Bill Haley and His Comets.

The song had been written a few years earlier by Max C. Freedman, a middle-aged Tin Pan Alley veteran whose biggest success up to that point had been as a lyricist for tepid pop hits such as Bing Crosby's "Sioux City Sue" (1946) and the Andrews Sisters' "Heartbreaker" (1947). Freedman was hired in 1953 by an aspiring Philadelphia music promoter named Jimmy Myers to write a song for Bill Haley, whose career was taking off after the success of "Crazy Man, Crazy." After Myers added his own professional name, Jimmy DeKnight, to the songwriting credits, he offered the new composition to Haley. Due to bad blood between Myers and Dave Miller, the owner of Haley's Essex record label, Bill was not allowed to record the song. But Haley liked it so much that he immediately added it to his stage act. The version by Haley and his group sounded very much like an earlier cover that they had done of Jimmy Preston's R&B classic "Rock the Joint." The Comets' guitarist even reprised almost note for note the guitar solo he had done on the Preston cover.

Essex Records' roadblock forced Jimmy Myers to shop the song around to other record companies. Sonny Dae & the Knights recorded a pop version of the song that became a minor regional hit, and Myers himself recorded a big band version of the song under the name of Jimmy DeKnight and His Knights of Rhythm, but the record went nowhere. Disappointed but not dispirited, Myers refused to give up. Opportunity knocked the following year when Haley's contract ran out with Essex. Myers helped Haley land a new record deal with Decca Records. Not surprisingly, one of the first songs Haley recorded was "Rock Around the Clock." Included as the "B" side of Bill Haley and His Comets' first Decca release ("Thirteen Women" was the "A" side), "Rock Around the Clock" barely managed to make it onto the pop charts, holding down the number 23 spot for one week in 1954.

Jimmy Myers was still not ready to give up on the song, though. "When I found out they [Decca Records] were getting rid of it, I loaded up the trunk [of my car]," explains Myers, "and went out for six or eight weeks. Every time I saw a radio antenna I drove off the road into the radio station. Usually they'd put it right on the turntable. By the time I got back to Philadelphia off the road, it was selling. Then I shot out about two hundred copies to every name I could get in Hollywood."[10] He struck pay dirt with one of those names.

Film producer Richard Brooks flipped when he received his copy. He knew instantly that he had found the right sound for his upcoming movie, *Blackboard Jungle*. The song and the film seemed made for each other, and Brooks knew exactly how to get the most mileage out of the record. He cranked up the volume as much as he could, knowing the loud sound itself would have moviegoers reverberating with feelings of rebellion and menace (figure 3.1).

Audiences were awed by the movie's explosive beginning. As the theater went to total darkness, the film began. At first only drums could be heard, sounding very much like a patriotic drum march. Then a disclaimer flashed on the screen:

> We, in the United States, are fortunate to have a school system that is a tribute to our communities and to our faith in American youth. Today we are concerned with juvenile delinquency—its causes and

Figure 3.1. *Blackboard Jungle* **featured Bill Haley and His Comets' "Rock Around the Clock." The 1956 film helped establish rock & roll's rebellious image. (Richard Aquila Collection)**

its effects. We are especially concerned when this delinquency boils over into our schools.

As the disclaimer rolled on, drums became even louder, morphing into an angry-sounding jungle drum beat:

The scenes and incidents depicted here are fictional.
However, we believe that public awareness is a first step toward a remedy for any problem.
It is in this spirit and with this faith that BLACKBOARD JUNGLE was produced.

For a split second, the screen faded to black. Then, the audience heard an amplified rim shot on drums. Suddenly the huge speakers in the theater exploded with a thunderous sound as Bill Haley shouted out:

"One . . . Two . . . Three O'Clock . . . Four O'Clock, Rock!" Simultaneously, the title—*BLACKBOARD JUNGLE*—appeared on the screen. And audiences' jaws dropped open with surprise. This was unlike anything anybody had ever seen or heard before.

"Rock Around the Clock" was used only in the opening credits and then again at the end of the movie. No other rock & roll song was heard in the film. But Haley's wild and raucous sound set a perfect tone for *Blackboard Jungle*. Loud and foreboding, it heralded a new youth culture threatening to turn American society upside-down. The song created an ominous mood as the movie's opening sequence depicted a subway train entering an urban ghetto. Against a backdrop of high-rise buildings and children playing almost naked in the streets, an aspiring teacher named Richard Dadier (played by Glenn Ford) makes his way toward the local school. The viewers are shown male students in a school yard, flaunting social convention by dancing with each other. A woman walks by the fenced-in school yard, and some of the boys reach through the bars like animals desperately trying to seize their prey.

Tension builds, foreshadowing the violence to come. The fact that this is an all-male school suggests a prison filled with dangerous inmates. As the plot unfolds, the audience witnesses a near rape of a female teacher, gang fights, muggings, switchblades, and teenage tough guys talking casually about sex, smoking in school, bad-mouthing teachers, and testing the limits of adult authority. The teachers' responses reinforce the notion that these young hoodlums are extremely dangerous. Even the idealistic Mr. Dadier describes his students as a "class of screaming, wild animals" and he calls the school "my jungle."

Blackboard Jungle's advertising campaign warned that juvenile delinquency was undermining public education: "A drama of teenage terror," proclaims one ad. "They turned a school into a jungle!" The movie dramatized many of American society's greatest fears in the 1950s. The fictional teachers at this inner-city vocational school are forced to deal with juvenile delinquents who come from a variety of working-class backgrounds, including blacks, Puerto Ricans, Italians, Irish, and Jews. Violence is always just below the surface, threatening to erupt at any moment. In one scene, Dadier and a fellow teacher are stalked in a back alley by a gang of youths who eventually attack, leaving the two teachers badly beaten.

The line between adults and troubled youths is often marked by music. Jazz is used as the background music when adults are on the scene, while the new rowdy rock & roll sound used in the intro is associated only with the youth gangs. At one point, a teacher (Richard Kiley) is forced by unruly youths to play some of his valuable jazz records in class. Originally, he had brought his jazz collection to school because he thought his "cool" records might help him get through to students. Gang leader Artie West (played magnificently by Vic Morrow) makes it clear that the idealistic young teacher has made a big mistake. Taunting the naïve teacher, Artie says in a threatening way, "Haven't you heard music is soothing for the savage beasts?" When Kiley's character reluctantly agrees to play one of his most valuable records, Artie and his boys become even more aggressive, making it clear that they want nothing to do with the adults' jazz music. One gang member asks sarcastically, "Ah, how about some bop?" as the kids around him smash all the jazz records.

Of course, in good 1950s fashion, the movie has a happy ending. Mr. Dadier eventually wins over most of his students, including a black youth (Sidney Poitier) who initially was the most troubled, but not before the teacher has a climactic showdown with Artie West, during which one of Artie's fellow hoods pulls a switchblade and is stopped by a friendly student who spears him with an American flag. (You've got to love the patriotic 1950s!)

Blackboard Jungle had more than enough messages for everybody. Audiences not only learned about problems involving youth, race, ethnicity, violence, and public education, but they also learned about the power of rock & roll. Not everyone came away with the same lesson. While many young people were impressed by the new sound and its potent message, many older Americans didn't like what they were seeing and hearing.

Adults in the 1950s—like their counterparts in other eras—often were uncomfortable with change. Many were convinced that the young people's music was no match for their own. "Nothing more than an exhibition of primitive tom-tom thumping," explained the conductor of the BBC Symphony Orchestra, "rock and roll has been played in the jungle for centuries." An article in New York's *Daily News* called the music a "barrage of primitive jungle-beat rhythm set to lyrics which few adults would care to hear." A writer for *Encyclopedia Britannica* also condemned the new sound: "The rowdy element [in pop music this year] was represented by 'Rock Around the Clock.' The rock 'n' roll school [of music] concentrated on a minimum of melodic line and a maximum of rhythmic noise, deliberately competing with the artistic ideals of the jungle itself."[11]

Some adults believed *Blackboard Jungle* and its rock & roll soundtrack incited teenage riots. When teen audiences began dancing in the aisles or on seats in movie theaters across the country, violence sometimes did break out. In one instance, moviegoers began throwing broken seats at each other. Authorities often made the situation worse, banning dancing or demanding that young people behave less enthusiastically. After a showing in Minneapolis, a group of young moviegoers took to the streets and committed various misdemeanors. When a similar event occurred in Hartford, Connecticut, a psychologist warned that teenage violence was a "communicable disease" being spread by a "cannibalistic and tribalistic sort of music." After witnessing a riot when the movie was shown in Washington, D.C., another adult came up with a similar conclusion: "It's the jungle strain that gets 'em all worked up." Even "Mr. Rock & Roll" himself, Alan Freed, was troubled by the alleged riots associated with "Rock Around the Clock" and *Blackboard Jungle*. "Hollywood is to blame," he explained. "It was unfortunate" that Haley's song was used in "that hoodlum-infested movie . . . [that] seemed to associate rock 'n' rollers with delinquents." An article in *Time* magazine even suggested that the communists were using the movie and music as proof that the American way of life was inferior.[12]

While Freed and other adults were condemning *Blackboard Jungle* for different reasons, many young people loved rock & roll's new rebellious image. The fact that adults hated the music probably made it that much more attractive. "Rock Around the Clock" became a rock & roll battle cry for the young. At Princeton University an undergraduate cranked up the volume on his record player and blasted the song out his dorm window. When fellow students followed his lead, the sound of Bill Haley and His Comets was soon reverberating across Princeton's limestone quad. "About midnight [students] gathered on the campus," reported a story in a music trade magazine, "set fire to a can of trash and paraded through the streets until an assistant dean dampened their hilarity."[13]

Other news stories reinforced the adults' belief that "Rock Around the Clock" was trouble. On July 3, 1955, a twenty-five-year-old disc jockey in Buffalo, New York, climbed up on a billboard to do a remote broadcast high above one of the city's busiest streets. Asking young drivers below to honk if they wanted him to keep playing "Rock Around the Clock," the young deejay played the song repeatedly as young motorists rushed to the area. "The antics of a disc jockey atop a sign about 75 feet above Shelton Square Sunday afternoon caused an ear-shattering traffic jam," reported the *Buffalo Evening News*, and it "brought out a fire aerial-ladder truck and four police cars and landed the WWOL employee in jail."[14]

The exposure "Rock Around the Clock" got from *Blackboard Jungle*, combined with all the media attention, helped the song become one of the year's biggest hits. Haley's record debuted on the pop charts on May 5, 1955, quickly shot up to number 1, and stayed there for eight weeks. "Rock Around the Clock" was on the charts for a total of twenty-four weeks, becoming a bestseller not just in the United States but around the world. (To this day, it remains, along with Bing Crosby's "White Christmas," one of the best-selling records of all time. Not only did "Rock Around the Clock" wind up selling well over six million copies, but it became a Top 40 hit again in 1974 after it was featured as the theme song on TV's popular sitcom, *Happy Days*.)

Old and young listeners might have disagreed about the value of "Rock Around the Clock," but two things are clear: "Rock Around the Clock" did more than any other previous song to popularize the new sound, and the record forever etched into the public's mind the alleged connection between rock & roll and leather jackets, switchblades, and teenage rebellion.

POP MUSIC AND THE ROCK & ROLL CRAZE

The music industry aggressively promoted rock & roll throughout 1955. Some record companies tried to duplicate the success of Bill Haley and His Comets by signing similar country-influenced singers. A young country singer named Bonnie Lou scored a Top 20 hit with "Daddy-O," which plugged into teenage slang. Boyd Bennett and the Rockets did even better. Bennett was thirty-one years old when Haley hit it big in

1955. Born in Muscle Shoals, Alabama, Boyd was raised near Nashville, Tennessee. Like Bill Haley, he grew up listening to country music. After learning how to play the guitar, he started performing out in the streets or near local bars and restaurants, passing the hat for donations. Following World War II, he moved to Kentucky, working as a disc jockey and performing in local nightclubs. By the early 1950s, Boyd Bennett and his band, the Rockets, were playing throughout Kentucky, Ohio, and Indiana. Their sets included a little of everything, including country and pop. Their growing local reputation earned them a recording contract with Sid Nathan's King Records in Cincinnati, and they achieved minor success with a few country music releases in 1954.[15]

When Boyd Bennett's country music career floundered, he took notice of the growing popularity of the new rock & roll sound. The success that Bill Haley and His Comets, a former country & western group, had in 1955 with "Rock Around the Clock" convinced Bennett and the Rockets to give rock & roll a try. In a manner befitting their name, the group blasted all the way up to number 5 on the pop charts in 1955 with "Seventeen," a country-influenced rock & roll song they had written expressly for the young audience.[16]

Some record companies turned to pop artists who could appeal to the young audience. Veteran orchestra leader Eddie Howard, already famous for Top 10 hits such as "On a Slow Boat to China" (1948) and "Sin (It's No Sin)" (1951), returned to the pop charts in 1955 with "The Teenagers' Waltz." Younger pop artists also arrived on the scene. The Cheers—a teenage-group from the West Coast—made it all the way to number 6 on the charts in 1955 with a song about a popular teen fashion, "Black Denim Trousers." Though the group was never heard from again, one of their members, Bert Convy, later found success as an actor and TV game show host. The Three Chuckles had a minor hit with "Times Two, I Love You." The song stalled at number 67 on the charts, but the group's lead singer, Teddy Randazzo, exhibited enough potential to get signed as a solo artist. He appeared in several rock & roll films and earned a few minor hits in the late 1950s and early '60s, including "The Way of a Clown" (1960). Later, he found even greater success as a composer: "Goin' Out of My Head" became a smash hit for both the Lettermen and Little Anthony and the Imperials; "Pretty Blue Eyes" was a hit for Steve Lawrence; and "Hurt So Bad" became a major hit for Little Anthony and the Imperials, the Lettermen, and Linda Ronstadt.

Another young group, the Hilltoppers (who named themselves after the sports teams at their alma mater, Western Kentucky University), likewise found success in 1955. Their version of the Platters' "Only You" made it all the way to number 8, and over the next few years they followed up with several other minor hits. Their leader, Billy Vaughn, went on to become the music director at Dot Records, where he supervised most of Pat Boone's later hits. During the 1950s and '60s, Vaughn also earned numerous instrumental hits of his own, including two Top 10 hits in 1955, "Melody of Love" and "The Shifting Whispering Sands."

THE COVER-RECORD PHENOMENON

Despite the few attempts to develop new artists with youth appeal, major record companies continued to view cover records as the fastest and easiest way to tap into the tremendous profits being generated by the rock & roll craze. Throughout 1955, record companies scrambled to keep pace with the new fad. The Crew-Cuts' 1954 cover of the Chords' "Sh-Boom" sent shock waves through not just the music industry but also throughout American society and culture. The white pop group proved once and for all that there was a huge white market for black rhythm & blues. In the process, the Crew-Cuts established a pattern for subsequent covers: Every time a rhythm & blues song done by a black artist on a small independent label began to climb the pop charts, it was quickly imitated by a white artist or group that recorded for a major record company. And even though the copycat record lacked the aesthetic quality of the original, it usually wound up the bestseller.

By early 1955, all the major record companies were trying to cash in on rhythm & blues' growing popularity. Even RCA Victor and Columbia, which previously had been reluctant to record R&B songs, jumped on the bandwagon: "The thinking of both the Victor and Columbia recording heads," reported a music trade magazine, "was that if this was what the kids wanted, this is what they were going to get."[17] Throughout 1955, the majors peppered the record charts with a barrage of cover songs. The McGuire Sisters made it all the way to number 1 with a pop-style rendition of the Moonglows' "Sincerely." The tepid remake showcased pop harmonies that sounded straight out of the 1940s backed by a full orchestra. Other than melody, not much was left of the Moonglows' original, which featured creative, street-corner harmonies and vocal gymnastics that duplicated the sounds of saxophones and other instruments. The Fontane Sisters, a white pop group that appeared frequently on Perry Como's TV show, also had a number 1 hit with their formulaic pop version of the Charms' R&B song "Hearts of Stone."

Pop diva Georgia Gibbs, who began her singing career with big bands back in the 1930s, likewise turned to R&B for material. In April 1955, she made it all the way to number 4 on the pop charts with her rendition of LaVern Baker's "Tweedle Dee." Gibbs's version was pure pop fluff. Her sweet, perky voice replaced Baker's earthy vocal, while blaring trumpets and a full orchestra were substituted for the sensual saxophone and R&B combo found on the original R&B hit. Gibbs followed up with an even bigger hit. Her 1955 remake of Etta James's "The Wallflower" shot up to number 1 on the pop charts. Georgia Gibbs's cover ran roughshod over the original. James's R&B song was rather controversial. It opened with a lusty male voice agreeing to a woman's apparent sexual demands. Etta James's suggestive R&B vocal sustained the sexual tension throughout, while repetitive sounds by backup singers and throbbing sax riffs added to the sensuality. The song's ending did not disappoint, climaxing with intimate vocal interaction between James and her man. Gibbs's cover record set out in a totally different direction, following a much safer path toward pop music success. It begins with a baritone male voice so over the top that it sounds like a cartoon character. A big band then kicks in, making it perfectly clear from the outset that the sweet-sounding Gibbs is singing about dancing, not sex. During a piano-plunking musical bridge, the white pop singer shouts out awkwardly to an apparent dance partner, "roll-roll-roll/rock-rock-rock!" The whole thing then bounces along to a big finish, replete with loud brassy instruments and Gibbs shouting "Rock!" Even the title of the song was changed to emphasize the new approach. Etta James's "The Wallflower"—which used words like "roll" and "rock" in its lyrics to suggest sexual intercourse—became Georgia Gibbs's "Dance with Me, Henry (the Wallflower)" that used "roll" and "rock" as synonyms for dancing (figure 3.2).

The cover records by Georgia Gibbs are just the tip of the iceberg when it comes to bad remakes of R&B songs. Most of the subsequent covers were just as bad, if not worse. Perry Como—that's right, veteran

Figure 3.2. R&B singer Etta James had a number 1 R&B hit in 1955 with "The Wallflower." That same year Georgia Gibbs covered it as "Dance with Me, Henry," which made it to number 1 on the pop charts. (Robert Pruter Collection)

pop crooner Perry Como!—had a smash hit with a mellow rendition of Gene and Eunice's R&B record, "Ko Ko Mo," while a new crooner on the pop scene named Pat Boone found tremendous success with bland versions of R&B songs such as the Charms' "Two Hearts," Fats Domino's "Ain't That a Shame," and Little Richard's "Tutti Frutti" and "Long Tall Sally." Even Gale Storm, the perky star of TV's *My Little Margie*, got into the act. She made it to number 2 on the charts with an incredibly bad remake of "I Hear You Knockin'," done originally by New Orleans R&B singer Smiley Lewis. The actress growled out Lewis's lyrics unconvincingly if not embarrassingly, while in the background a studio musician gamely plunked out piano riffs trying in vain to capture the New Orleans piano sound of Fats Domino.

Amazingly, the deep pit of bad cover records in 1955 seems almost bottomless. Here's a list of the most commercially successful covers in the approximate order that they peaked on the pop charts (the original artist is in italics, followed by the cover artist):

**February
1955**

"Sincerely"	*Moon-glows*	McGuire Sisters
"Hearts of Stone"	*Jewels*	Fontane Sisters (who actually covered an R&B cover by the Charms)
"Earth Angel"	*Penguins*	Gloria Mann

**March
1955**

"Ko Ko Mo"	*Gene and Eunice*	Perry Como
"Earth Angel"	*Penguins*	Crew-Cuts
"Pledging My Love"	*Johnny Ace*	Theresa Brewer

April 1955

"Tweedle Dee"	*LaVern Baker*	Georgia Gibbs
"Ko Ko Mo"	*Gene and Eunice*	Crew-Cuts

"Two Hearts"	*Charms*	Pat Boone

May 1955

"The Wallflower"	*Etta James*	Georgia Gibbs (the cover was called "Dance with Me, Henry [Wallflower]")

June 1955 No covers peaked this month

July 1955

"A Story Untold"	*Nutmegs*	Crew-Cuts

August 1955

"Why Don't You Write Me"	*The Jacks*	Snooky Lanson

Sept. 1955

"Ain't That a Shame"	*Fats Domino*	Pat Boone

Oct. 1955 No covers peaked this month

Nov. 1955

"At My Front Door"	*El Dorados*	Pat Boone

Dec. 1955

"I Hear You Knockin'"	*Smiley Lewis*	Gale Storm

Of all the cover artists, Pat Boone deserves special mention. Obviously, he wasn't the first white pop star to record black rhythm & blues, but Pat became the most successful. His first ten hit records included nine covers of R&B songs.[18] And before the decade was over, Pat Boone would have more hit records on the rock charts than any other artist except Elvis Presley.

Probably no one was more surprised by Boone's success with R&B songs than Pat himself. Boone was a Bing Crosby–style crooner when he signed his first recording contract with Randy Wood's Nashville-based independent label, Dot Records. The record executive convinced his young pop singer to give R&B a try in early 1955. "[Randy] built the company. He also owned a record store in Gallatin, Tennessee, called Randy's Record Shop. And he did a lot of innovative things, including advertising Randy's Record Shop on 50,000-watt clear-channel radio at night, which went all over the country and various parts of the world. [All of this] was from a little record store out in the country outside Nashville, Tennessee. So, he had great influence, and he had great instincts," explains Pat Boone. "When R&B began to rumble, there were a few records that started to happen that were covers of R&B hits. Randy quickly realized there was a whole wealth of material, and that if people liked those early R&B cover records, they might like more. And, here I came at just that moment."[19]

The first R&B song that Randy Wood asked Pat Boone to record was the Charms' "Two Hearts (Two Kisses)." Since Pat didn't listen to rhythm and blues, he had never even heard of the record. "But from the title," he recalls, "I imagined that the song would be something in waltz time, like Perry Como might do. Then Randy played me the record."[20] Was Pat Boone ever surprised! Wood instructed his young singer to listen to the song over and over again until he was ready to perform it. Eventually, they went into the studio and Pat gave it a shot. The resulting cover was more of a commercial success than an artistic one. Pat Boone rushes through the vocal, sounding awkward with the song's tempo, heavy beat, and unfamiliar style. Parts of it—like his hiccupping lead vocal or the background singers shouting "Whoop de dooh wha!"—are so bad they almost sound good. Many white teenagers loved it in 1955, sending the record to number 16 on the pop charts. His next release, an equally awkward cover of Fats Domino's "Ain't That a Shame," did even better, making it all the way to number 1.

Randy Wood and his young star followed up with a series of cover records that became hits in 1955 and 1956. Boone's versions of Little Richard's "Tutti Frutti" and "Long Tall Sally" were undoubtedly the worst of the batch. (Nowadays, it's painful to listen to those songs as Boone tries to croon his way through lyrics like "awop bop a lu bop, a bim bam boom.") His voice was better matched to slower-paced R&B

songs. Boone does an excellent job, for example, on classic R&B ballads such as the Flamingos' "I'll Be Home" and Ivory Joe Hunter's "I Almost Lost My Mind." "It was crazy for us," recalls Boone. "We were having million-seller hit records. It was also great for the original artists, because they now had a chance to be exposed to a far wider audience than they had ever known before."[21]

Pat Boone undoubtedly did help popularize the original R&B songs. But, back in the 1950s, many R&B performers and their supporters resented the tremendous commercial success of Boone and other cover artists. As cover record after cover record outdistanced the original on the pop music charts, critics were soon complaining about the gross unfairness of the practice. Disc jockey Alan Freed called white copycat records "anti-Negro" and refused to play them on his nightly radio show.[22]

In 1955, R&B singer LaVern Baker, whose song "Tweedle Dee" was overshadowed on the pop charts by Georgia Gibbs's cover version, was so outraged that she demanded legal action. In February, she asked her congressman, Michigan Representative Charles Diggs Jr., to consider new copyright legislation that would protect singers from "modern-day pirates." Baker explained that Gibbs's cover of "Tweedle Dee" on Mercury Records "duplicated my [original] arrangement note-for-note"— yet the old Copyright Act of 1909 protected only ownership of songs, not arrangements. "After an investigation of the facts," Baker pointed out, "you might see some wisdom in introducing a law to make it illegal to duplicate another's work. It's not that I mind anyone singing a song that I write, or have [had] written for me by someone, but I bitterly resent their arrogance in thefting my music note-for-note."[23]

Though LaVern Baker's legal arguments got nowhere with Congress or the courts, her moral indignation attracted considerable support among fans, critics, and even some music business executives. In August 1955, Alan Freed's employer, WINS radio in New York City, announced that the station would no longer be playing cover records that merely duplicated the originals. WINS program director Bob Smith was careful to distinguish between traditional "cover" records (which he defined as different-sounding versions of songs by various artists) and "copy" records (which allegedly duplicated note-for-note the arrangements and stylistic phrasings of singers). "When an original disk is followed by 'copies,'" explained Smith, "WINS will play only the originals."

This policy would apply to all types of music, including pop, R&B, and country & western. Smith emphasized that this new policy did not extend to traditional cover records, which have long been an important part of the record business and are "regarded as completely ethical by all."[24]

The WINS program director was correct when he said cover records were a tradition in the music business. Music publishers had always tried to have as many different versions of a song as possible, since it meant more royalties for the copyright holder. Frequently, covers were done by a variety of artists representing various musical styles in order to maximize sales on all the record charts. Hank Williams's 1951 composition "Cold Cold Heart" is a perfect example. Hank had a hit with the song on the country & western charts. Williams's record, along with pop versions by Tony Bennett, the Fontane Sisters, Eileen Wilson, and Tony Fontane, all made the pop charts. And R&B covers were done by Dinah Washington and Eddie Johnson.

But if WINS's program director was correct in pointing out that covers were a longtime staple of the music industry, he was either disingenuous or misinformed when he suggested that duplicate cover records were a new development. For one thing, the cover records of 1955 were hardly exact copies of the R&B originals. Few listeners would ever confuse Pat Boone's version of "Ain't That a Shame" with Fats Domino's. Nor would they think they were listening to Smiley Lewis when they heard Gale Storm's pop rendition of "I Hear You Knockin'." If these covers were trying to duplicate the originals, they failed miserably.

Even if some tone-deaf listeners did confuse the covers and the originals, duplicate records were not a new development in 1955. Stealing arrangements note-for-note happened all the time in the music industry. In 1953, for example, Mitch Miller complained that Mercury Records and Coral Records had issued covers that stole his musical arrangement of Joan Weber's "Let Me Go, Lover." The two record companies shrugged off the allegation and added that Mitch Miller had a lot of nerve complaining since he previously had produced covers that were exact copies of other labels' original recordings.[25]

If cover records were not a new phenomenon, then why all the fuss over these particular covers in 1955? Arguably, the 1955 covers were unique in two ways. For one thing, these covers were co-opting a new musical style, thereby infuriating R&B producers, performers, fans, and critics. Even more important, the covers of 1955 had a racial subtext. Major record companies were "whitening" black rhythm & blues to make it more acceptable to mainstream (i.e., white) audiences. Race was an extremely sensitive topic in 1955. The civil rights movement was picking up momentum. The Supreme Court's ruling in *Brown vs. Board of Education* (1954) overturned the notion of "separate but equal" in public education, while the Montgomery Bus Boycott in 1955 challenged other patterns of segregation.[26] White covers of black R&B songs became popular at that exact moment in history. No wonder many black artists and their supporters were furious. They viewed the 1955 covers as the latest examples of institutionalized prejudice in America.

Obviously, to a large extent, the 1955 covers were racially motivated, but one has to be careful not to exaggerate the role of race in this particular case. White and black artists had been covering each other's songs since at least the Jazz Age in the 1920s. By the 1950s, not only were whites covering black R&B artists, but black singers were also commonly recording covers of white pop songs or country & western originals. The Orioles, an R&B group from Baltimore, had a smash pop hit in 1953 with a cover of "Crying in the Chapel," a country & western ballad originally done by Darrell Glenn. Fats Domino found success with "Blueberry Hill," which was a hit in 1940 for Gene Autry, Glenn Miller, and Kay Kyser. Clyde McPhatter and the Drifters redid Bing Crosby's "White Christmas." Tab Smith recorded an R&B version of Tony Bennett's "Because of You." The Four Buddies remade the Four Aces' "It's No Sin." And the Moonglows—managed by Alan Freed—covered Doris Day's "Secret Love." Freed's enthusiastic promotion of the Moonglows' cover of Doris Day's song makes his later condemnation of white covers of black songs questionable, to say the least.

Furthermore, white pop singers of the 1950s were not just covering black artists. They also recorded R&B-influenced songs initially done by whites. For example, two white pop acts—the Fontane Sisters and Dorothy Collins—found success in 1955 with cover versions of "Seventeen" and "My Boy-Flat Top," both of which had been originally recorded by Boyd Bennett.

Even black R&B artists covered R&B songs in the 1950s. Otis Williams and the Charms went to the top of the R&B charts in 1954 with their rendition of the Jewels' "Hearts of Stone." Lloyd Price did a version of Fats Domino's "Ain't That a Shame" two years before Pat Boone did. Little Esther remade Big Mama Thornton's "Hound Dog," the Hollywood 4 Flames copied the Five Keys' "The Glory of Love," the John Godfrey Trio covered Billy Wright's "Hey Little Girl," and Savannah Churchill redid Faye Adams's "Shake a Hand."

For many record buyers, race was probably not even an issue. Not only were many whites buying records made by black artists, but numerous blacks were also color blind when it came to record purchases as evidenced by the fact that Pat Boone's covers of "Ain't That a Shame" and "At My Front Door" were hits on the rhythm & blues charts in 1955.

It would be inaccurate to suggest that race did not have any impact on record sales. Racial attitudes of Americans undoubtedly help explain why white artists' cover records of 1955 were commercially more successful than the black artists' original versions. This was a time when black faces were not often seen on television or in movies. These subtle forms of segregation extended to the music business, where the pop charts were overwhelmingly white and most radio stations programmed only music performed by white artists. This racial climate undoubtedly made it easier for whites to sell records to the white audience than blacks.

At the same time, race was not the only reason for the commercial success of cover records. The white versions were generally more familiar-sounding to most white listeners, who were accustomed to the traditional white pop sound and style. "Having been raised on the polish and varnish, the velvet and satin of big orchestras and syrupy crooning," explains Arnold Shaw, who worked in the music business in the 1950s, "only a small percentage [of young white listeners] were ready for the raw and exuberant earthiness of rhythm and blues. The attraction was there but also the edginess. And so along came white producers at the major companies to give them something that caught the lusty quality of the originals but wrapped it in a glossy plastic."[27]

Cover records also had built-in marketing advantages over R&B originals that were released on small, independent labels. The pop versions were issued by major record companies with better record distribution and pressing capabilities, as well as larger budgets for advertising and promotion. The major labels also had elliptical connections to an extensive network of disc jockeys who promoted covers over originals. "Exposure was the name of the game," insists Arnold Shaw, and there were "seven hundred R&B deejays versus ten thousand pop jockeys." As a result, R&B artists "were not played on the pop turntables."[28]

Another economic reality all but guaranteed the cover records' success on the pop charts. White cover versions were generally issued on 45-rpm records, a technological innovation that was taking the music industry by storm in the mid-1950s, whereas many of the R&B originals were still being released on the older 78-rpm record format. Although RCA and Columbia were marketing three-speed record players by 1952, white audiences with more disposable income were far more likely to make the switch from 78s to 45s. The owner of one of Chicago's most successful R&B record shops, for instance, reported in January 1955 that five out of every six R&B records he sold were 78s. "Independent [record] producers could evolve formulas for predicting when a song would cross over into the white market on the basis of the demand for the song at the 45-rpm speed," explain music historians Reebee Garofalo and Steve Chapple. "Of course, to go into a separate 45-rpm pressing, an R&B record would have to show evidence of strong sales potential. The dual technology had the effect of diverting the white audience from many R&B artists."[29]

White cover records overshadowed R&B originals for yet another reason. Many Americans feared that R&B records would undermine cultural standards or be too vulgar for mainstream audiences. The 1950s decade was a time of strict conformity. Television censors monitored closely what was beamed into the homes of millions of Americans. The Motion Picture Production Code made sure offensive language and indecent material would not appear in Hollywood films. The record industry towed the line with cover records. White pop versions frequently "cleaned up" the lyrics of sexually suggestive songs or made other changes to make R&B songs more acceptable to general audiences.

Pat Boone, for instance, consciously avoided certain types of lyrics and songs. "I was a clean-cut guy. [Although] I was doing this dreaded, feared rock & roll music, I became known for changing some of the words if I thought they might be offensive, and not even doing some songs—like 'Rock with Me, Henry, All Night Long'—which somebody had to do because it was a big R&B hit. I turned it down, and Georgia

Gibbs wound up doing it as 'Dance with Me, Henry' and that made it acceptable."[30] Not only did Pat avoid risqué R&B songs, but he even balked at recording lyrics that were grammatically incorrect. When he covered Fats Domino's "Ain't That a Shame," he initially tried to switch the lyrics to "Isn't That a Shame," but relented when his record company refused to go along with it. In concerts, though, Pat frequently introduced the song as "Isn't That a Shame."[31]

Arnold Shaw has suggested that "the contrast between white covers and the black originals was a matter of image as well as sound." Once again, Pat Boone is a perfect example. He was promoted as an All-American boy who was patriotic, religious, and devoted to his wife and daughters. Even his style—from his preppy sweaters to his white bucks—projected safe, positive images in an era concerned about juvenile delinquency, communist subversion, and integration. "I made the music seem safer," admits Boone. The same can be said of other cover artists, such as the Fontane Sisters and Gale Storm, who looked and sounded like respectable and proper young ladies. Cover artists, concludes Shaw, "contributed an aura of respectability to songs that the music establishment thought belonged in the ghetto and some, even, in the gutter."[32]

In effect, the cover records of 1955 won out over the R&B originals for a variety of economic, social, and cultural reasons. What covers lacked in artistic integrity and quality, they made up for in commercial success. But the cover-record phenomenon was short-lived. The advent of Elvis Presley in 1956 sent young listeners clamoring for the real thing. Though covers never faded away completely, record buyers became more discerning. After mid-1956, cover versions would succeed only if they actually sounded better than the original.

Nowadays, it is fashionable to simply condemn the cover records of 1955 as racist or inferior imitations. The truth is far more complicated. Cover records actually played a very important role in popularizing early rock & roll. Pat Boone points out an obvious reason why cover records were so popular in the mid-1950s: "That's simple, because America—the ears, the sensibilities, and even the deejays in radio—weren't ready for the raw earthiness of the original R&B. . . . [On] pop radio, the records were 'How Much Is That Doggie in the Window' and show tunes from Broadway, Eddie Fisher singing 'I'm Walking behind You' and 'Oh, My Papa.' It was a different vanilla world, and R&B just could not get played or heard on pop radio." Boone insists that cover versions, which he readily admits were "very vanilla versions" of R&B songs, helped introduce large audiences to the new sound. "And, so R& B began to cross over [to the pop charts]," explains Boone, "but there had to be that transition period and some transition type of records."[33]

Pat Boone is absolutely correct. In the beginning, cover records did make R&B more accessible to white audiences who were unfamiliar with the new sound and style. In the process, they helped pave the way for the coming of rock & roll by broadening the base for the new music. Boone understands the important role that he and other cover artists played in the history of rock & roll. "Well, I've often referred to myself as the midwife at the birth of rock & roll, sort of a catalyst," he says. "If you make the mistake of comparing my record of 'Tutti Frutti' to Little Richard's record, you'll say 'well, it's like night and day. The original is earthy and real and gritty and raw, and Pat's version sounds like a pop record.' Well, sure, if mine had sounded like [Little Richard's], it wouldn't have gotten played, either, because pop radio just wasn't ready for Little Richard when he first happened along, or Chuck Berry, or Fats Domino." The cover records helped change things. "Once my versions of their songs were accepted," says Boone, "then the deejays would start playing the original records, and the audiences began to appreciate the originals. And so the time of the cover record may have been, I think, two or three years at the most, and then it was finished."[34]

Audiences were not the only ones who benefited from cover records. Obviously major record companies and their cover artists made a ton of money. Ironically, the small, independent labels that produced the original R&B records also profited from cover versions. In most cases, independent record companies owned the publishing rights to the R&B songs, so they earned royalties on each record sold, regardless if it was the original or a cover version. "In '55 when I was [working] at . . . E. B. Marks Music, I was constantly approached by indie record companies that wanted to slice, lease, or sell their copyrights," explains Arnold Shaw. "These companies were interested in cash advances but also in my getting cover records. For the songwriters, as well as for their publishers, covers meant augmented income."[35]

The black artists who recorded the original songs were the ones hurt the most by cover records. Dave Bartholomew, the legendary record producer who wrote and produced many of the biggest hits for New

Orleans's R&B stars like Fats Domino, Smiley Lewis, and Lloyd Price, insists that cover records sometimes "killed the artists." When Gale Storm covered Smiley Lewis's "I Hear You Knockin'," for example, "he died of a broken heart."[36] No doubt similar stories could be told about LaVern Baker, the Chords, Joe Turner, the Penguins, the Teen Queens, Jesse Belvin, the Charms, Gene and Eunice, the Gladiolas, the Clovers, Little Richard, the Moonglows, the Nutmegs, Ivory Joe Hunter, and a host of other R&B artists whose styles and sounds were shamelessly appropriated by white cover artists. "Black artists have always been the ones in America to innovate and create and breathe life into new [musical] forms," explains Johnny Otis, an R&B band leader of Greek descent who had a Top 10 hit in 1958 with "Willie and the Hand Jive." "What happens is black people—the artists—continue to develop these things and create them and get ripped off and the glory and the money goes to white artists. This pressure is constantly on them to find something that whitey can't rip off."[37]

With hindsight, it seems obvious that the original R&B artists were cheated out of potential record sales, as well as the fame they would have acquired had their versions and not the covers become the hits. But we have to be careful here, because there is no guarantee that in the absence of cover records the original R&B songs would have gotten any air play or been hits on the pop charts. Pat Boone is probably correct when he says that the nation in 1955 was not yet ready for the real thing—earthy R&B songs done by black artists. Other things also have to be considered before we totally condemn cover records and artists. The success of cover songs sometimes created better opportunities for the original artists. Covers that made it big on the pop charts brought fame and recognition to the black R&B singers who wrote or recorded the original versions. The black artists could then tour more and sell more records on the R&B charts, and perhaps even on the pop charts. For example, a 1955 Combo Records' advertisement for Gene and Eunice's "Ko Ko Mo" was an obvious attempt to capitalize on the success of cover versions by Perry Como and the Crew-Cuts. The ad began: "This is it! The original 'Ko Ko Mo.'" It then went on to quote a newspaper critic as saying "the flurry of 'covers' on this disk indicates the kind of excitement it has stirred up in its first few weeks." An Atlantic Records advertisement for a new LaVern Baker song in 1956 used a similar tactic. The ad refers to Baker as "The Tweedle Dee Girl," a title that had even greater name recognition because Georgia Gibbs's cover version of Baker's "Tweedle Dee" had made it all the way to number 2 on the national pop charts in 1955.[38]

Some black R&B artists were actually able to cross over onto the pop charts because cover records paved the way for their entry. Pat Boone insists that R&B artists such as Little Richard were actually "thrilled" to be covered: "It was their hope that someone would cover their records." Boone recalls going to a New Orleans club to see Fats Domino: "When he heard I was in the audience," explains Pat, "he called me on stage and he said to the crowd, 'I want you all to know something. You see this ring?' He had a big diamond ring on every one of his fingers, and he pointed to the most prominent of his diamond rings and he said, 'This man bought me this ring with this song,' and the two of us sang 'Ain't That a Shame' together."[39]

One other silver lining can be found in the dark cloud of cover records. Although the rhythm & blues originals usually sold fewer copies than the cover versions, in the long run the originals became the recognized classics. Nowadays, it is Little Richard, Smiley Lewis, the Chords, and LaVern Baker—and not Pat Boone, Gale Storm, the Crew-Cuts, or Georgia Gibbs—who are honored in rock & roll history. Obviously, the original artists can't take belated kudos to the bank, but at least they have finally been recognized for their contributions to early rock & roll. The irony of this cosmic justice was not missed by Fred Parris, who wrote and sang lead on the Five Satins' pathbreaking doo-wop ballad "In the Still of the Nite" (1956). Black R&B groups like his, he explained, were the true "pioneers" of rock & roll, but unfortunately, "pioneers always get kicked in the ass."[40]

R&B ARTISTS CROSS OVER

Although Fred Parris's summation was accurate more often than not, the fact remains that more and more black artists were beginning to cross over onto the pop charts in 1955. Mercury was one of the first record companies to consciously capitalize on the new "rock & roll" name tag as a way to sell R&B records to a larger audience. An ad in a trade magazine in March of '55 proclaimed: "MERCURY ROCKS 'N ROLLS WITH 2 SMASH HITS!"—Dinah Washington's "That's All I

Want from You" and Red Prysock's "Rock 'n Roll." The ad promised "3 MORE" rock & roll songs were "COMING UP": Delores Ware's "There's a Whole Lot of Fish in the Sea," the Griffins' "Sing to Me," and the Honeytones' "Too Bad." Blend Records tried a similar approach with a music trade ad that announced "THE WEST COAST IS ROCKIN'" with Bob Williams and the Chromatics' "Rockin' Beat."[41]

Not only did numerous African American artists begin to appear on the pop charts in 1955, but some—notably Fats Domino, Chuck Berry, and the Platters—went on to record Top 10 hits with amazing consistency.

By the time rock & roll arrived on the scene, Fats Domino was already a huge success on the rhythm & blues charts thanks in large part to his personal charm and contagious New Orleans brand of R&B. The New Orleans Sound blended elements from rhythm & blues, boogie-woogie, Dixieland, ragtime, jazz, country music, and pop with blues from the nearby Mississippi Delta. Instead of guitars, it often featured a rolling bass, highlighted by a rhythm section and horns, set against a boogie-woogie style piano. The eclectic style reflected New Orleans's exotic mix of French, Spanish, English, Native American, African, Cajun, and Creole cultures.

Most people associate the New Orleans Sound with the music of Fats Domino, but to fully understand it one must recognize the contributions of legendary New Orleans musician Dave Bartholomew, as well as the musical traditions of New Orleans. Bartholomew, a talented producer, arranger, trumpet player, bandleader, and songwriter, was a driving force behind the New Orleans Sound that helped shape early rock & roll. He worked with most of New Orleans's top R&B performers, including Lloyd Price, Smiley Lewis, Shirley and Lee, Huey "Piano" Smith, Frankie Ford, and Chris Kenner. But he's best known for producing and co-writing most of Fats Domino's biggest hits, including "Ain't That a Shame" (1955), "Blueberry Hill" (1956), and "I'm Walkin'" (1957). Together, Domino and Bartholomew created a unique sound that not only influenced the rise of rock & roll but also transformed the entire pop music scene.

The New Orleans Sound was a potent Creole concoction that emerged during the late 1940s and early '50s. It can be heard on early rhythm & blues hits by Dave Bartholomew, Lloyd Price, Smiley Lewis, Fats Domino, and other New Orleans artists. Its many layers fit together like a jigsaw puzzle, creating a multitextured, full sound. Music historian Rick Coleman notes that every Fats Domino record featured "at least three layers of rhythm . . . including piano triplets, some variation of Bartholomew's bass line played by various instruments, horns riffing in the background, and the drums usually delivering a pounding 2/4 backbeat, which made the rhythms virtually irresistible." Music scholar Jonathan Kamin likened the layered New Orleans beat to "African polyrhythms."[42]

The New Orleans Sound emerged from both musical and cultural traditions. "That is true. We have a New Orleans sound," explains Dave Bartholomew. "If you have a birthday, we'll throw a party for you, and we'll have somebody do what's called a *second line*. The second line is actually uninvited guests. Like you have a club [in New Orleans] and you get out there and have a parade and the other people standing around they join in." Bartholomew adds, "That is actually called a second line—uninvited guests, and they got a handkerchief out, they started with an umbrella, and you go on from that. We just always had in mind that we just love to party."[43] Fats Domino's music exemplifies the New Orleans Sound, as well as the call-and-response pattern and distinct rhythms associated with African music. His vocals and music served as the "first line," which was then answered by his band's "second line" of echoing rhythms. Audiences—like second-line participants following a New Orleans jazz band—joined in through dancing and singing.

The New Orleans Sound was crafted in the J&M studio, a tiny New Orleans recording studio, owned and operated by Italian American Cosimo Matassa. Located on Rampart Street, across from New Orleans's famed Congo Square, J&M was actually just the backroom of a music and appliance store. The studio was about the size of "an ordinary motel room," recalls producer Bumps Blackwell. Given the studio's small size and unsophisticated recording equipment, Bartholomew and the musicians had to work hard to get a quality sound. "At that time, [J&M] was the only studio in town, if you really want to call it a studio," says Bartholomew. "We got some great sounds out of it, but it was very small . . . and we worked like dogs in it to get the sound we got. And, it still sounds good today." Bartholomew recalls with amazement the creative things they had to do to get a good sound: "One time, the drums would be in one corner; the next time they would be in the middle of the floor. The saxophone player would be moved around. It was just one of those type of things but we wanted to work and be successful, so that's what we did."[44]

The trademark New Orleans Sound is evident not just on Fats Domino records but on all the early R&B records Bartholomew produced. A good example is Lloyd Price's "Lawdy Miss Clawdy," which became a number 1 hit on the rhythm & blues charts in 1952. The record featured Price on lead vocal, backed by the Dave Bartholomew Band with a young Fats Domino on piano. Later covered by numerous rock & rollers, including superstars like Elvis Presley and Paul McCartney, Price's R&B classic "Lawdy Miss Clawdy" is now considered one of the greatest songs from the early days of rock & roll.

That New Orleans Sound is also evident on Smiley Lewis's 1955 R&B classic "I Hear You Knockin'." Bartholomew explains the story behind that record: "There was a skit back then that a [New Orleans] comedian used to do—his name was Lollipop Jones. . . . He was with this lady and she told him, 'Look, I'm sick and tired of this small-time stuff.'. . . So she said, 'Well, I'm leavin', I'm going to get a job at the Apollo, I'm gone and I'm not comin' back.' So when she went to the Apollo Theater she was a failure. And, when she came back, she was knockin' on the door, and he said, 'I hear you knockin' but you can't come in.'"[45] Audiences laughed loudly at the retort, since it contrasted sharply with the response on "Open the Door, Richard," a popular song of the day. The music behind Smiley Lewis on "I Hear You Knockin'" was provided by the legendary Dave Bartholomew Band. That band played backup on most of the hits coming out of New Orleans in the 1950s, including songs by Smiley Lewis, Lloyd Price, Little Richard, Shirley and Lee, and the Spiders, as well as Fats Domino.

Domino personified the New Orleans Sound. The last of eight children, Antoine "Fats" Domino was born in New Orleans's Lower Ninth Ward on February 26, 1928. Though his family was poor, Antoine always received encouragement and support from his parents and other family members. He grew up speaking Creole French and absorbed traditional Creole values of working and playing hard. When he was ten, Antoine began taking piano lessons from his brother-in-law, Harrison Verrett. The youngster was immediately hooked and developed a love for all types of music, particularly blues and boogie. In 1947, he joined a band formed by his friend Billy Diamond, and they began playing local clubs. Somewhere around that time, Diamond gave the chubby piano player his nickname. "I call him 'Fats,'" explained Diamond, because "he's gonna be famous someday, just like Fats Pichon and Fats Waller." Domino hated the name at first, but soon realized it could help his career. Diamond remembers telling Domino, "I saw the dream because of Fats Waller. Don't be 'Antoine,' be 'Fats,' because 'Fats' is an outstanding name, you know what I mean? Like 'Minnesota Fats,' 'Fats Domino' is a classic."[46] (figure 3.3).

Domino's big break came in November 1949, when Dave Bartholomew and Lew Chudd (the owner of Imperial Records in Los Angeles) discovered him playing at the Hideaway Club, a small joint off the beaten path in New Orleans. Chudd had recently hired Bartholomew as both a recording artist and talent scout in an effort to pump up his label's rhythm & blues catalog. When they heard people talking about the high-energy, roly-poly piano player who was knocking audiences dead at the Hideaway, they decided to check it out for themselves. From the moment they walked into the tiny, smoke-filled bar, they knew they were onto something. The large, enthusiastic crowd cheered Fats's every move and went absolutely wild when he played his signature song, "The Junker's Blues," an old folk song about a drug addict that had been recorded by Champion Jack Dupree in 1941. Chudd offered him a deal on the spot.[47]

A few days later, Dave Bartholomew arranged the young piano player's first recording session at Matassa's J&M studio. Dave was convinced that Domino's "Junker's Blues" could be a hit if he changed the lyrics and title. "That was actually a tune . . . sung by guys who were in jail," recalls Bartholomew. "It was actually a thing like 'When the Saints Go Marchin' In.'" The song was retitled "The Fat Man" to take advantage of Domino's nickname, as well as a popular radio show. "During that time, there was a radio show, a detective show by the name of 'The Fat Man.' So, that's where I got the name from," explains Bartholomew. It took only a few takes for Fats to nail the song. He began with a rolling, boogie-woogie piano intro and then launched into an infectious vocal. Listeners flipped when Fat imitated a mouth harp, wailing "wah wah wah wah" over and over again in a falsetto voice. The record shot to the top of the R&B charts, heralding the arrival of a new star as it created an iconic image for "Fats" Domino.[48]

Figure 3.3.   Fats Domino. (Richard Aquila Collection)

The team of Domino and Bartholomew followed up with a string of hits on the R&B charts, including a number 1 record, "Goin' Home" (1952). Like many rhythm & blues artists, Bartholomew insists that back in the 1950s there was very little difference between R&B and rock & roll. "Let's get it straight," he says, "they changed the name to rock & roll, but it's always been rhythm & blues. But, when the whites got involved they started calling it rock & roll." Bartholomew's comment offers insights into the origins of rock & roll. Significantly, the R&

B songs he recorded with Fats Domino and his own band in the early 1950s sound exactly the same as the music that people were calling "rock & roll" by the late 1950s. "It's exactly the same music with the Big Beat," he emphasizes. "We would perform and try to get the people to dance. That was the main thing."[49]

By the time rock & roll arrived on the national scene, Fats Domino was well positioned to cross over onto the pop charts. He already had two Top 30 pop hits to his credit: "Goin' Home" (1952) and "Goin' to the River" (1953). The door to Fats's pop success was thrown wide open when Pat Boone covered Domino's "Ain't That a Shame" in 1955. Although Boone's bland version became the number 1 hit on the national charts, Fats Domino's original still managed to make it into the Top 10. In the process, it introduced the veteran R&B singer to a much larger audience.

Fats Domino and Dave Bartholomew seized the opportunity and began aiming their music directly at the growing white, teenage market, as well as the older, more traditional pop audience. "What we actually wanted to do was to have everybody enjoy our music," explains Bartholomew. Knowing they already had the R&B market, they now wanted to bring in white teenagers and their parents. "I think Fats Domino and I was actually the first team to actually do what we call cross-over music. We love rhythm & blues completely, and started playing rock & roll where everyone could understand it [R&B]."[50]

A few weeks after Fats Domino made his debut on the national pop charts, he was joined by another singer destined to become one of rock & roll's all-time greatest stars. Chuck Berry wasn't exactly the kind of guy central casting would have sent over to play the part of an early rock & roller. After all, what could a black man who turned thirty in 1956 have in common with white teenagers? The answer to that question can be found in his approach to music (figure 3.4).

Chuck's sound was influenced as much by country & western and traditional pop as it was by blues or rhythm & blues. "Working for my father in the white neighborhoods [of St. Louis] I never heard Muddy Waters. I never heard Elmore James. I heard Frank Sinatra, I heard Pat Boone . . . and I said why can't I do as Pat Boone does and sing good music for white people," said Chuck Berry in a later TV documentary, "and that's what I shot for, writing 'School Day'—nice, nice music, and it caught on. I wrote about schools, and half of the people have cars, I

Figure 3.4.   Chuck Berry. (Robert Pruter Collection)

wrote about cars . . . and [people remember love, so] I wrote about love.
So I wrote all three, and I thought I hit pretty good [the] capacities of
people."[51]

Berry's recollection is not completely accurate. We know that as a young adult he often listened to Muddy Waters, Elmore James, and other great blues and R&B artists; he even played their music at the start of his career in local neighborhood bars. At the same time, Chuck's statement makes it clear that he was paying close attention to white pop singers such as Sinatra and Boone. His later career offers evidence that he consciously wrote and recorded songs that would appeal to the broader pop market.

Born in 1926, Berry grew up in St. Louis where he and his family listened to all types of music on the radio, including pop and country & western. As a youth, he sang in choirs at church and school, and by the time he was in high school he was practicing on an old acoustic guitar. His breakthrough came when he saved up enough money to buy an electric guitar. "I found it was much easier to finger the frets of an electric guitar," he recalled, "plus, it could be heard anywhere." Within a short time, he could replicate the riffs played by his favorite guitarists, including bluesman T-Bone Walker, R&B guitarist Carl Hogan, and jazz guitarist Charlie Christian.[52]

By the early 1950s, Berry was married, had started a family, and was juggling jobs, school, and music to get ahead. During the day, he worked for his father as a carpenter's helper around St. Louis; after work, he went to community college studying to become a hairdresser; and three nights a week, he played in local bars as part of a trio that included drummer Ebby Harding and pianist Johnnie Johnson (who later would play piano on most of Berry's biggest hits). In 1953, they became the regular band at St. Louis's popular Cosmopolitan Club due to their ability to pull in large crowds that included both blacks and whites. To satisfy the audiences' diverse tastes, the trio developed a repertoire that included blues, R&B, traditional pop, and even country & western. The integrated crowds went wild as Berry moved effortlessly from one genre to the next. "Listening to my idol Nat Cole prompted me to sing sentimental songs with distinct diction. The songs of Muddy Waters impelled me to deliver the down-home blues in the language they came from, Negro dialect," explained Berry. "When I played hillbilly songs, I stressed my diction so that it was harder and whiter. All in all, it was my intention to hold both the black and white clientele by voicing the different songs in their customary tongues." Years later, a bemused Berry recalled the initial reaction of black audiences to him singing country & western: "Some of the clubgoers started whispering, 'Who is that black hillbilly at the Cosmo?' After they laughed at me a few times, they began requesting the hillbilly stuff and enjoyed trying to dance to it. If you ever want to see something that is far out, watch a crowd of colored folk, half high, wholeheartedly doing the hoedown barefooted."[53]

Chuck's big break came in 1955 when he went up to Chicago and stopped by a blues bar to hear one of his favorite singers, Muddy Waters. Decades later he vividly recalled going up toward the stage to meet his idol, who was signing autographs. "It was the feeling I supposed one would get from having a word with the president or the pope," explained Berry. Chuck told Muddy that he loved his music, and he asked for advice about making a record. Berry recalls that the famed bluesman, though still signing autographs, took the time to reply: "Yeah, see Leonard Chess. Yeah, Chess Records over on Forty-Seventh and Cottage." That small piece of advice launched Berry's career. Chuck never forgot that his idol was the one who gave him the lead that changed his life.[54]

Before heading back to St. Louis, a nervous Chuck stopped by Chess Records. Leonard Chess agreed to see him and asked for an audition tape, preferably of original material. Berry rushed back home excited about the possibilities. For the past few years he had been writing new lyrics to old songs and this was an opportunity to write new ones from scratch. Within a week, Berry was back in Chicago at the Chess office with tape in hand. It included four original songs: "Wee Wee Hours," "Thirty Days," "You Can't Catch Me," and "Ida Red" (based loosely on "Ida May," an old folk song recorded by Woody Guthrie and country artists such as Roy Acuff and Bob Wills). To Berry's surprise, Leonard Chess liked the country-influenced "Ida Red" the best. The singer remembers that Chess "couldn't believe that a country tune (he called it a 'hillbilly song') could be written and sung by a black guy." Chess arranged to have Berry return on May 21 for a recording session and to sign a contract.[55]

When the big day arrived, Berry and the rest of his trio were joined in the studio by Willie Dixon on stand-up bass. "The first song we recorded was 'Ida May,'" says Berry. "Leonard suggested that I should come up with a new name for the song, and on the spot I altered it to 'Maybellene.'" Berry later insisted that he named the song after a cow in a children's story he remembered from third grade. Piano player Johnnie Johnson remembers it differently. He maintains that Chess thought the original title sounded too country. Just then, Leonard looked down and saw a mascara package in the studio and quickly suggested that they change the title to "Maybellene," modifying the spelling so the cosmetic company wouldn't sue. Leonard also wanted a bigger beat to appeal to teenagers. Thirty-six takes later, "Maybellene" was immortalized on tape. Convinced it could be a hit, Leonard Chess took a dub to New York City for Alan Freed to play on his syndicated radio show. To encourage airplay, Chess credited the song to "co-writers" Chuck Berry, Alan Freed, and another disc jockey, Russ Fratto.[56]

"Maybellene" began attracting attention the moment it was released. A trade magazine named it "Buy O' the Week" for July 30, 1955, reporting "trade in this disk has been unusually high. Now in both the R&B and pop categories, it is clicking as few records have this summer." "Maybellene" debuted on the national pop charts on August 20 and soon shot up to the number 5 spot. The record contained all the elements later associated with Chuck Berry's biggest hits. Powered by an electric guitar and big beat, the up-tempo song featured a humorous story line about romance, cars with powerful engines, a car chase, and lyrics aimed at teenage interests. "The kids wanted the big beat, cars, and young love," explained Leonard Chess. "It was a trend and we jumped on it."[57]

Some music critics later dismissed "Maybellene" as just "a formula song" that was "rather basic and unimpressive." But audiences loved it in 1955. They were attracted to the song's story line, danceable beat, and references to souped-up V-8 Fords and young romance. The record was an interesting mix of rhythm & blues, country & western, and pop. Some listeners loved the R&B-influenced sound; others were attracted to the humorous pop-style lyrics; still others were so intrigued by the country influences that they began referring to Berry as "the black Hank Snow." "Maybellene" became one of the hottest records of 1955, spawning unsuccessful covers by the Ralph Marterie Orchestra and the Johnny Long Orchestra and even several R&B "answer" songs, including John Greer's "Come Back, Maybellene." "Maybellene" made Chuck Berry a star. Emcees at concerts were soon introducing him as Chuck "Maybellene" Berry, and *Cashbox* closed out the year by giving him the "Most Promising Male R&B Vocalist Award."[58] In the years ahead,

Berry would more than live up to that potential. His songwriting skills, performance style, and ability to play his guitar "like ringin' a bell" eventually would make him one of the most successful artists in rock & roll history.

While Chuck Berry's up-tempo songs became the gold standard for teenagers who wanted to dance fast to the new rock & roll sound, the smooth harmonies of the Platters appealed to those who wanted to dance slow. The Los Angeles–based African American group originally was signed to Federal Records in 1953 and consisted of Tony Williams (lead singer), David Lynch (tenor), Herb Reed (bass), and Alex Hodge (baritone). By the time the Platters reached the national pop charts in 1955, they were on a major record label (Mercury), Paul Robi had replaced Alex Hodge, and Zola Taylor had been added as a contralto. The final lineup of four guys and a girl produced some of the smoothest harmonies on the pop charts in the 1950s.

The Platters' specialty—slow, romantic ballads—gave them wide appeal. The Platters' first big hit was "Only You," which reached number 5 on the pop charts in 1955. Later in the decade, they would achieve even greater success with number 1 hits such as "The Great Pretender" (1956), "My Prayer" (1956), "Twilight Time" (1958), and "Smoke Gets in Your Eyes" (1959). Although the Platters' sound and style were closer to traditional white pop than rock, the rock & roll audience embraced them anyway. Not only were Platters' songs well-crafted pop tunes, but perhaps more important they were perfect for slow dancing or romancing, whether it was at record hops or parties or in back seats of cars.

The Platters, Chuck Berry, and Fats Domino were not the only African American artists crossing over onto the pop charts in 1955. Chuck Miller made it to number 9 on the charts with "House of Blue Lights." Johnny Ace did almost as well, scoring a Top 20 hit with "Pledging My Love." Two black R&B groups, the Five Keys and the Charms, had Top 30 hits with "Ling Ting Tong." Other R&B acts also made the Top 100 pop charts: the Turbans released "When You Dance" at the end of the year, and it climbed all the way to number 33 in early 1956; the Royal Jokers' "You Tickle Me Baby" came in at number 77; the Robins' "Smokey Joe's Café" peaked at number 79; and the Drifters' "White Christmas" reached number 80. Significantly, both the Robins and Drifters would later find greater success with the help of two white songwriters and producers, Jerry Leiber and Mike Stoller. Atlantic Records in New York City was impressed by the success that Leiber and Stoller had had on the West Coast with the Robins, so they signed Leiber and Stoller as independent producers. When Jerry and Mike moved east, they brought along most of the Robins, changed their name to the Coasters, and cranked out numerous hits for the group such as "Yakety Yak" (1957) and "Charlie Brown" (1959). Leiber and Stoller worked similar magic with the Drifters. After several personnel changes, Leiber and Stoller guided the group to several big hits in the late 1950s and early '60s, including "There Goes My Baby" (1959) and "Save the Last Dance for Me" (1960).

Even black artists such as the Penguins, LaVern Baker, the Moonglows, the El Dorados, the Jacks, and the Charms who lost out to white cover versions of their records had at least a modicum of success on the mainstream pop charts. The Penguins made the biggest splash. Naming themselves after the Kool cigarette trademark, the Los Angeles–based R&B group hit it big with "Earth Angel." The lead singer starts things off by asking plaintively, "Earth Angel, Earth Angel, will you be mine?" The rest of the group then chimes in with all the requisite oohs and ahhs in the background. The record helped establish the musical formula for later doo-wop ballads: instrumentation was simple, driven forward by piano triplets. Wayne Stierle, the owner of Candlelite Records in the 1970s, recalls how the "tortured ballad" sent "chills" up his spine when he first heard it back in the '50s. "This recording inspired many vocal groups to form, and it gave hope to all those already working on an act, or a sound that might be outside the norm," says Stierle. "It was a landmark recording and a rock 'n' roll milestone that set the standard for the basic form of what would be the 'vocal group ballad' sound from 1955 through 1963."[59]

The Penguins' doo-wop ballad climbed all the way to number 8 on the pop charts in 1955, and today it is recognized as one of the all-time greatest hits in rock & roll history. But back in 1955, the Penguins' record had to share the glory with two cover versions: the Crew-Cuts' inferior record topped the Penguins' original by reaching number 3 on the charts, while Gloria Mann's even worse version made it to number 18.

While the Penguins and other R&B singers were crossing over to the pop charts, some R&B artists found the going more difficult. Bo Diddley, who had a number 1 hit on the R&B charts in 1955 with his self-titled song "Bo Diddley," appeared regularly at rock & roll concerts, but just couldn't crack the national pop charts. Other R&B artists tried, albeit unsuccessfully, to capitalize on the new rock & roll craze with records such as Red Prysock's "Rock 'n Roll," Babs Gonzales's "Rockin' & Rollin' the Blues," or Bob Williams and the Chromatics' "Rockin' Beat."

Significantly, none of these R&B artists changed their sound or style. The only difference is that they were now being marketed as rock & roll singers, not R&B singers. The very fact that these erstwhile R&B artists were now appealing (with varying degrees of success) to white audiences suggests that a sea change had occurred by late 1955. The pop charts, which previously had been the realm of mostly white artists, were now admitting black performers in increasingly larger numbers. In effect, cultural integration was actually taking place in the pop cultural world of music at the very moment when Rosa Parks, Martin Luther King Jr., and others were struggling to make integration a reality in American society.

By the end of 1955, rock & roll had gained a foothold in American popular culture. By then, the new sound had an identifiable name, it was being promoted throughout the media, and it boasted seminal hits such as "Rock Around the Clock," "Earth Angel," "Sh-Boom," "Ain't That a Shame," and "Maybellene," as well as identifiable stars like Bill Haley and His Comets, Pat Boone, Fats Domino, and Chuck Berry. The music was touted as a new sound for a new generation. But, despite its successes, one thing was still missing—a rock & roll star who embodied what the music was all about. Bill Haley was too old for most teenagers to relate to; Chuck Berry and Fats Domino were the wrong color for race-conscious America of the 1950s; and cover artists like Pat Boone were not authentic enough for millions of teenagers eager for the real thing. The burgeoning rock & roll audience would not have long to wait. A charismatic, nineteen-year-old southern white boy would soon step forward to pull the sword from the stone to become the "King of Rock & Roll."

II

The Coming of Elvis (1954–1956)

4

I WAS THE ONE

Rock & Roll Personified

Elvis Presley made it all the way to the number 1 spot on the record charts in early 1956 with "Heartbreak Hotel." The record's flip-side—"I Was the One"—also became a Top 20 hit. The ballad about romance gone wrong begins with Elvis telling his listeners, "I was the one" who taught her how to kiss and love. And it ends tragically as Elvis sings, "Who learned a lesson when she broke my heart? I was the one."[1] The passage of time now gives "I Was the One" an eerie quality that explains perfectly the coming of Elvis Presley and foreshadows his end. Elvis just as easily could have been singing about his relationship with teenagers in the 1950s. He was the one who introduced many young people to rock & roll. He was the one who taught them how to love the new sound. And ultimately he was the one who had his heart broken when musical trends changed in the late 1960s and early '70s.

Elvis Presley stepped almost godlike onto the American stage in 1956. He seemingly came out of nowhere. One day he was unknown, then there he was the next day singing his songs and shaking his hips on television in the national spotlight. Before the year was out, Elvis was rock & roll incarnate. Like the music itself, Presley was an American original. The rock & roll Adonis had it all: good looks, personality, sexy moves, lots of talent, and a fresh approach. Guys wanted to be like him. Girls just wanted him. One young female put it succinctly: "He's just a great big beautiful hunk of forbidden fruit."[2] (figure 4.1).

When Elvis sang "I Was the One" in 1956, it was no idle boast. For millions of teenagers, he was indeed "the one"—the undisputed "King

Figure 4.1. Early publicity photo that captures the young Elvis's smoldering good looks. (Photo by "PoPsie" Randolph L.L.C.; courtesy of Michael Randolph, executor to the estate of William "PoPsie" Randolph)

of Rock & Roll." Elvis Presley's rise to fame and fortune reveals much about life and culture in cold war America.

LET THERE BE ELVIS!

Unlike rock & roll music which evolved slowly over years, Elvis Presley exploded onto the pop music scene like the Big Bang. As is usually the case with most overnight success stories, the twenty-one-year-old Presley's rise to the top actually was a long time in the making. By some accounts, Elvis may have even begun charting his course when he was just a little boy.

The coming of Elvis is now shrouded in myth, befitting a cultural hero who changed the trajectory of pop music history, if not the entire youth culture of post–World War II America. The story begins with small-time record producer Sam Phillips, who owned and operated Sun Records, an indie label in Memphis, Tennessee, that specialized in rhythm & blues. Long before Phillips ever met Presley, he supposedly told his receptionist, Marion Keisker, "If I could only find a white man who had the Negro sound and the Negro feel, I could make a billion dollars."[3] Legend has it that Phillips's wish became a reality one hot, humid morning in the summer of 1953 when an eighteen-year-old Elvis Presley innocently walked into Sun Studios at 706 Union Avenue to record a disc for his mother's birthday. When Sam heard the primitive recordings, he immediately knew that he had found his "white man" with the "Negro feel." The rest of the story—as the saying goes—is history.[4] But did it really happen that way?

The Elvis legend certainly sounds good. The story has all the ingredients for a great movie, replete with a prescient adult waiting for opportunity to knock coupled with a deserving young lad whose devotion to his mother and belief in the American Dream enable him to fulfill his destiny of becoming rock & roll's first superstar. Horatio Alger couldn't have written a better script! There's only one hitch, albeit a huge one: there is no proof that the story actually happened.

When Elvis went into Sun Studios in June of '53, he supposedly was recording a present for his mother's birthday. Problem is, Gladys Presley was born on April 25. Given his well-known devotion to his mother, Elvis probably never would have waited several weeks to

record and deliver her birthday gift. Most likely, Elvis was not as innocent as the story suggests. His going into Sun Studios that morning was
not just a coincidence motivated by his desire to give his mother a gift.
Nor was it just Sam Phillips who controlled the flow of events. Presley
was also a prime mover. He knew exactly what he was doing when he
walked through that front door. The young Elvis was determined to be
a recording star. He was hoping to be discovered when he walked into
Sun Studios on that sunny morning in June 1953. His high school girlfriend, Dixie Locke, later recalled that Elvis always "had a plan, he
knew that he had a talent, there was something in his life that he was
supposed to do."[5]

Elvis's obsession with music began as a child in Tupelo, Mississippi.
From the moment he was born on January 8, 1935, music was always in
the air around him. His parents, Gladys and Vernon Presley, sang
whenever and wherever they could—in the local church, at revival
meetings, or at home doing chores, relaxing, or putting their baby to
sleep. Little Elvis took to it like a duck takes to water. "When Elvis was
just a little fellow," recalled his mother, "he would slide off my lap [in
church], run down the aisle and scramble up to the platform of the
church. He would stand looking up at the choir and try to sing with
them. He was too little to know the words, of course, but he could carry
the tune." Music was part of Elvis's life. Gospel songs could be heard in
local churches, blues drifted out of juke joints, and country & western
tunes and pop songs could be found on jukeboxes or on the radio.[6]

Young Elvis loved music for its own sake, but he probably also valued it as one of the bonds that his family shared. Elvis grew up in an
insular family that shielded him from the outside world. As an only
child (his twin brother, Jesse, died at birth), he was always very close to
his mother and father. "The three of us formed our own private world,"
admitted Vernon Presley. Together, they went for walks, visited kinfolk,
and went to church and outings. They were inseparable.[7]

Elvis spent the first two years of his life in Tupelo. Though dirt poor,
the Presleys at least had a small house to themselves. Living conditions
worsened when the family relocated to a one-room apartment in a poor
area of Memphis in 1948. The situation improved a few months later
when they moved into a two-bedroom apartment in Lauderdale Courts,
one of Memphis's housing projects for low-income families. The
cramped living quarters and hard economic times drew the family even

closer together. Looking back at those early days, Gladys was aware that the hardships affected her little boy. "Elvis would hear us worrying about our debts, being out of work and sickness," she later explained, "and he'd say, 'Don't you worry . . . when I grow up, I'm going to buy you a fine house and pay everything you owe at the grocery store and get two Cadillacs—one for you and Daddy and one for me.'"[8]

Always the obedient son, Elvis loved his "Mama" and "Daddy" dearly. "We were always happy," said Elvis, "as long as we were together." He was particularly close to his mother. Gladys watched over her son like a mother hen, constantly checking his whereabouts, walking him to and from school, helping him cross the street, always making sure he said his prayers, and constantly reminding him to be polite to elders and to remember his manners. Even when Elvis was in high school, his parents hovered over his every move. A neighbor recalls that Elvis's parents always treated him "like he was two years old. Mrs. Presley . . . just lived for Elvis. Years later he called her every night when he was touring and Mrs. Presley couldn't go to sleep until she heard from him."[9]

The Presleys enjoyed singing together. The youngster sang with his parents in church, joined them for group singing at revival meetings, and sang gospel music with them at home.[10] The Presleys' love of music wasn't limited to religious songs. The three of them enjoyed country & western and even some pop. Elvis and his parents often went to concerts to hear local country & western singers; every Saturday night they listened on the radio to Roy Acuff, Ernest Tubb, Bill Monroe, and other country music stars on the *Grand Ole Opry*; and they always enjoyed singing songs around the house. Writer Ernst Jorgensen believes that Elvis's family played a major role in shaping the youngster's musical tastes. "It was [Elvis's] father whose lovely baritone voice could be heard around the Presley house throughout Elvis's childhood, singing gospel and country songs," points out Jorgensen. "His parents were the ones who gave him his first guitar; his uncles gave him his first few lessons."[11]

With this pedigree, no wonder Elvis became obsessed with music. "I liked all types of music when I was growing up," said Elvis. "When I was in high school, I had records by Mario Lanza and the Metropolitan Opera. I just loved music."[12] Gospel music was a special favorite. The young Elvis loved the showmanship of the Sunshine Boys; he was touched by the Blackwoods' gospel harmonies; he was moved by black spirituals done by the Soul Stirrers and the Original Gospel Harmonettes. But most of all, he loved the overall sound and style of a Memphis gospel group called the Statesmen. It doesn't take much of an imagination to understand the effect that the Statesmen had on Elvis's style. The Statesmen featured "some of the most thrillingly emotive singing and daringly unconventional showmanship in the entertainment world," notes Elvis biographer Peter Guralnick. Wearing brightly colored clothes that might have been purchased in Elvis's favorite store—Lansky's (the Memphis store where all the "cool cats" shopped)—the gospel group combined emotional harmonies with a high-energy performance style guaranteed to get audiences leaping out of their seats. As lead singer Jake Hess's vocals careened up and down the musical scale, bass singer Jim "the Big Chief" Wetherington kept the rhythm driving forward by shaking his legs and jiggling his hips. The Big Chief "went about as far as you could go in gospel music," recalls Hess. "The women would jump up, just like they do for the pop shows." [13]

At the same time, Elvis was never locked into any one musical style. He was attracted to a variety of singers whose distinctive styles helped them connect with audiences. Dean Martin was a particular favorite. Dino's phrasing techniques and penchant for slurring lyrics is evident on numerous Elvis recordings from early ones such as "I Don't Care if the Sun Don't Shine" to later hits like "Are You Lonesome Tonight." Elvis also loved the interpretive styles of pop stars such as Bing Crosby and Eddie Fisher, country artists like Hank Williams, and R&B performers such as Arthur "Big Boy" Crudup and Wynonie Harris. [14] Eventually, Elvis would incorporate all these diverse styles into his own music.

When Elvis was ten, he sang in public for the first time in a talent contest at the Tupelo state fair. Although he had to stand on a chair to reach the mike, the game youngster made it through Red Foley's "Old Shep." He didn't win, but he did well enough to win a consolation prize. His parents bought him a cheap guitar for his eleventh birthday and arranged lessons. But usually the shy boy simply went off on his own and messed around, plunking away at the strings, doing the best he could, dreaming of the day when he could really play and sing.

The same way that some boys fantasize about becoming star athletes, Elvis dreamed about being a singer. Whenever possible, he gravitated in that direction. Along with hanging out with local musicians, he attended concerts the way sports fans went to ballparks. Being a spectator not only was fun, but it also offered the chance to take part in the event and learn from the pros. Growing up, Elvis played and sang whenever and wherever he could—for family friends, schoolmates, church groups, neighbors at Lauderdale Court apartments, and, of course, for his mother, who always encouraged him.[15]

Elvis viewed singing as a way to win praise. Music was the perfect sanctuary, the ideal vehicle for a kid who was shy and different, yet who believed in his heart that he was special. Music was something that Elvis could accomplish as an individual, something at which he could shine. His upbringing made him feel like a loner, and he found it difficult to fit in with the crowd. Elvis was at best an average student who was never going to impress anyone with his intellect or high grades. His shyness made it hard to meet new friends. He frequently seemed overly polite, always saying "Yes, ma'am" and "Yes, sir" to adults. And he clearly was a "mama's boy." Gladys wanted to know every move he made: where he was, who he talked to, what he was doing. The son was the center of his mother's universe, and the mother was the sun in her boy's galaxy, nourishing his love, hope, and dreams.[16]

Elvis's mother and his upbringing convinced him that he was different. He knew he did not fit in with the crowd. Perhaps his family's often desperate financial situation contributed to a sense of inferiority. Elvis was "unbelievably insecure," insists record producer Sam Phillips. "He tried not to show it, but he felt so *inferior*. He reminded me of a black man in that way; his insecurity was so *markedly* like that of a black person."[17]

Elvis had good reason to feel insecure around other kids, because they picked on him unmercifully. According to Red West, who went to school with Elvis at Humes High School, a tough school in a low-income section of Memphis, Elvis was always the brunt of jokes and pranks. "Elvis had his hair real long in those days," recalls West. "The rest of us had crew cuts. I remember once when all the guys were gonna get him and cut his hair. I helped him escape from that. He had trouble with his hair when he was playing [foot]ball. He just played one year and the coach told him to cut his hair or get off the team. That's about what it boiled down to. He wore the loud clothes, the pink and the black. He was just different. It gave the people something to do, to bother him." Elvis never forgot the cruel treatment he received at Humes High. Years later, Elvis confided to a Las Vegas audience: "[I] had pretty long hair for that time and I tell you it got pretty weird. They used to see me comin' down the street and they'd say, 'Hot dang, let's get him, he's a squirrel, he's a squirrel, get him, he just come down outta the trees.'"[18]

No wonder Elvis always identified with others who were outside the mainstream. He had a particular fascination with truck drivers, possibly because they seemed to be loners just like him, or maybe because his dad was one. Or perhaps because of how they looked. "How I happened to wear sideburns," explained Elvis, "was, my Dad was a truck driver and I admired him and other truck drivers I knew. Most wore sideburns and mustaches. So when I was sixteen, I grew sideburns to look as much like them as possible."[19]

Elvis was also fascinated by blacks on Beale Street, the main road through Memphis's largest African American neighborhood. He admired how they acted and looked, especially the individualistic and often outrageous way they dressed, and Elvis dreamed about the day when he, too, could buy flashy outfits at Lansky's clothing store on Beale Street. For similar reasons, he was attracted to gospel singers and other musical artists who were different. He loved movies about loners and rebels. James Dean, Marlon Brando, and Tony Curtis were special favorites. He combed his hair like Curtis and copied James Dean's look, demeanor, and facial expressions (very likely, Elvis spent hours in front of a mirror practicing the Dean sneer until he got it down pat). Elvis even memorized Dean's lines in *Rebel Without a Cause*. "I've made a study of . . . Jimmy Dean [and] I've made a study of myself," Elvis later admitted, "and I know why girls, at least the young ones, go for us. We're sullen, we're brooding, we're something of a menace." Elvis added, "I don't understand it exactly, but that's what the girls like in men. I don't know anything about Hollywood, but I know you can't be sexy if you smile."[20]

If Elvis was hoping to attract attention with his appearance and mannerisms, he was not disappointed. The brightly colored cat clothes that he favored, along with the sideburns and long, greasy, slicked-back hair attracted lots of attention. Adults gawked, while most teenagers laughed or taunted him. "He was just so different," remembers Elvis's high school sweetheart, Dixie Locke. "To watch him you would think, even then, he was really shy. What was so strange was that he would do anything to call attention to himself, but I really think he was doing it to prove something to himself more than to the people around him. Inside, even then, I think he knew that he was different. I knew the first time I met him that he was not like other people."[21]

Elvis wanted desperately to be noticed and truly believed that he was destined for greatness. Record producer Sam Phillips suggests that Elvis was always convinced "that he was destined to produce something great." Like the comic book heroes he enjoyed reading about, Elvis knew he would triumph in the end. "I always felt that someday, somehow, something would happen to change everything for me," he admitted after making it big in 1956. Music gave Elvis the chance to be in the spotlight and the chance at fame, fortune, and glory. Just as important, it offered Elvis a way not only to win approval from his father and beloved mother but also the chance to help them out financially. He bought his parents a Cadillac and new home just as soon as the money came flowing in.[22]

Elvis thrived in front of an audience, regardless of whether it consisted of his parents, relatives, or strangers. High school buddy Red West remembers the first time he saw Elvis perform at their high school talent show. "I never even knew he sang, but I was to get a surprise." Elvis walked purposefully but shyly toward the mike. He began by strumming a few chords and then began singing "Old Shep," the same song that he had done at the state fair a few years back. Elvis then did two other songs, one a love ballad that really seemed to move the crowd. "When he finished the show," recalls West, "the kids went crazy; they applauded and applauded. They just went mad. He was an easy winner. At first Elvis just stood there, surprised as hell. He seemed to be amazed that for the first time in his life someone, other than his family, really liked him." Red West added, "I'll never really know when Elvis got bitten by the bug of loving the applause of the audience, but my guess is that it happened right then in Humes High School. At last, it seemed, he had found a way to make outsiders love him." Red West believes that moment on stage in the Humes High School talent show was a real turning point for Elvis. It was the first—and maybe the only—time that Elvis made a mark in high school. "As shy as [Elvis] was, he had a definite magic on stage," says West. "After the show, he just seemed to go back to being ordinary old Elvis. But on stage, he had control." Presley's memory of the talent show is quite similar to Red West's, although Elvis remembers singing a different first song: "I wasn't popular in high school. I wasn't dating anybody. I failed music— only thing I ever failed. And then they entered me in this talent show and I came out and did my first number, 'Til I Waltz Again with You,' by Teresa Brewer. And when I came on stage I heard people kinda rumbling and whispering and so forth, 'cause nobody knew I even sang. It was amazing how popular I became after that."[23]

Music gave Elvis the chance to be in the spotlight and offered him the opportunity to follow his dreams. "I don't regard money or position as important," said Elvis years after he had made it big. "But I can never forget the longing to be someone. I guess if you're poor, you always think bigger and want more than fellows who have most everything from the minute they're born."[24]

By the time Elvis graduated from high school, his dream was clear in his mind. He knew exactly what he wanted: Elvis was smart enough to develop a plan, determined enough to follow through on it, and naïve enough to believe he would succeed. His mother made him believe he was special, and Elvis believed in his destiny. Ability, focus, determination, street smarts, and blind luck would account for his success.

When Elvis Presley, fresh out of high school, first walked into Sun Studios on that summer morning in 1953, this was not just a young man wanting to make a simple birthday record for his mother as legend has it. Nor was it a whimsical act or a mere coincidence. When Elvis's truck pulled up to that Memphis intersection at Union and Marshall, it was carrying a young man on a very specific mission.

As the truck slowed to a stop, Elvis looked past the large brick building on the corner that housed Taylor's Fine Food restaurant, and his eyes focused on his destination, if not his destiny. Just to the left of Taylor's stood a small red-brick store with a painted white front. In between two large windows stood a glass door framed in white. Above the entire width of the door and windows was a large white sign that read: "The Legendary Sun Recording Studio, 706 Union." The sign was decorated with the company logo—a bright yellow semicircle featuring the word *SUN* superimposed on sunbeams and musical notes with a rooster below suggesting that it was a rising sun.[25]

Sam Phillips opened his recording studio in 1950. His business card advertised not only his new recording service but also his eagerness. It

read: "We record anything—anywhere—anytime." Phillips was not exaggerating. He was willing to lug his recording equipment to bar mitzvahs, birthday parties, political rallies, or any other place with paying
customers. But all those bookings were just to pay the bills. His real
goal was to record local African American blues artists, hillbilly singers,
and other authentic artists who otherwise would just be playing in
Memphis honky-tonks. "I didn't have to look it up to know [blues sing-
er] B. B. King was talented," said Phillips. "I knew what I wanted. I
wanted something *ugly*. *Ugly* and honest. I knew that these people
were disenfranchised. They were politically disenfranchised and eco-
nomically disenfranchised, and, to tell the truth, they were musically
disenfranchised."[26]

Phillips was willing to record any promising singer, regardless of
musical style or appearance. "As word got out," noted a local Memphis
newspaper, "Sam's studio became host to strange visitors." These artists
might have looked weird to local observers, but they sure could sing.
Phillips began by recording Memphis blues artists such as Howlin'
Wolf, Rosco Gordon, and B. B. King (who was also a disc jockey on
Memphis's all-black radio station, WDIA). Whenever possible, he
leased the masters to indie companies. His first real taste of success
came in 1951 when he recorded Jackie Brenston's "Rocket 88," which
featured Ike Turner and his Kings of Rhythm as backup. The song was
released on Chess Records and became a number 1 hit on the rhythm
& blues charts in 1951. Its hard-driving beat and lyrics about cars and
sex have led many contemporary critics to view it as a rock & roll
prototype, if not the first rock & roll hit ever. In 1952, Phillips launched
his own Sun Record label. Within a year he found success on the R&B
charts with Rufus Thomas's "Bear Cat" and Little Junior Parker's "Fee-
lin' Good."[27]

The rise of Sun Records can be attributed in large part to Sam
Phillips's drive, determination, and vision. But, as is often the case, the
times also make the man. Sun's success was intertwined with the economic and social changes occurring not only in Memphis but in many
other cities in post–World War II America as well. By the 1950s, Memphis was becoming one of the South's thriving economic centers. It was
an agricultural hub for trading in cotton, hay, corn, sugar cane, sweet
potatoes, and other crops. After the war, new industries related to
chemicals, rubber, machinery, and furniture also opened up shop in

Memphis. Like a magnet, the city began attracting thousands of new workers. Between 1940 and 1950, Memphis's population mushroomed from 293,000 to 396,000. The boom times brought more spending power to all segments of Memphis society, including its large black community (which comprised about 40 percent of the city's population). Entrepreneurs took note. Memphis radio stations such as WDIA and WHBQ aimed their programming not just at Memphis's growing black population but at other blacks who lived within earshot as well. In the early 1950s, WDIA estimated that its 50,000-watt signal could reach one-tenth of the entire black population of the United States and that audience earned over $1 billion annually. By 1949, Memphis had a thriving local music business, including a record-pressing plant and record distribution company. Sam Phillips was not operating in a vacuum when he opened his independent record company in the early 1950s. Like other savvy businessmen, he was hoping to tap into the economic trends and demographic changes that were transforming the city of Memphis.[28]

In 1953, a group called the Prisonaires had a modest rhythm & blues hit on Sun Records entitled "Just Walkin' in the Rain" (which later became a number 2 hit for pop singer Johnny Ray in 1956). The Prisonaires' original version probably played an important role in convincing the young Elvis to give Sun Studios a try. The group's name was literal. When they recorded "Just Walkin' in the Rain," they really were serving time in the Tennessee State Prison. The record became a hit on Memphis radio stations, causing the local newspaper to run a story about how Sam Phillips had been willing to give the unknown singing group a chance on the Sun label. Although there is no way to know for certain whether the young Elvis ever read that story, there is no doubt that its message would have resonated with him if he had. If Sun Records could help the unknown Prisonaires have a hit, why not him, too?[29]

Even if the teenage Elvis missed the newspaper story about the Prisonaires, he still would have been aware that Sun Records was recording local talent. An avid listener of Memphis radio stations, he was familiar with local hits by Sun artists such as B. B. King, Junior Parker, and Rufus Thomas. He knew that Sam Phillips had given them their big break. As the teenage Elvis drove back and forth on Union Avenue, he could not possibly have missed the brightly colored sign above the studio that proclaimed "The Legendary Sun Recording Studio, 706 Union."

At that time, Sun Record's claim to legendary fame was more wishful thinking than reality, but that probably never occurred to the young man as he approached the record studio storefront on that summer morning in 1953. Most likely, all Elvis was thinking about was that his moment of truth had arrived. He was finally walking into a real recording studio. He was following his dream. Even if he only had a vague plan of action, Elvis was deliberately taking the next logical step on his career path. He wanted to be noticed by Sun Records—just like he wanted to be noticed by everyone else. The young man was too naïve to realize what a long shot this was. He believed in the American Dream and he believed in his destiny. Plus, he had heard about other people in his neighborhood making records, so probably to him it didn't seem like a long shot! Whatever he was thinking at the time, he later realized his plan had worked. Years later, Elvis said, "That was the best five bucks I ever spent."[30]

Exactly what happened when Elvis entered 706 Union Avenue that morning is not totally clear. The most convincing scenario was pieced together by Elvis biographer Peter Guralnick after he interviewed most of the individuals who were either there or had firsthand knowledge. According to Guralnick, the eighteen-year-old Elvis walked through that door into the reception area of Sun Records just several weeks after graduating from high school. Sitting there at the reception desk was Marion Keisker. More than just a secretary, Keisker had enjoyed some local success as a radio personality, and she had helped Sam Phillips establish his recording service and record company. Keisker never forgot that morning. She remembers her first impression of Elvis: he seemed shy and tentative and had long greasy hair. He was carrying a small guitar and mumbled something about wanting to make a record. She told him he could make a two-sided acetate for $3.98 plus tax, and for another dollar he could get a tape as well. He thought a moment and opted for the cheaper option. She then asked him, "What kind of singer are you?" He replied, "I sing all kinds." She responded, "Who do you sound like?" He looked at her and said matter of factly, "I don't sound like nobody."[31]

After plunking down his money, Elvis was introduced to Sam Phillips, who quickly positioned the nervous teenager in front of the mike and recorded two ballads selected by the young singer. Elvis did reasonably well on his first try, an earnest but uninspired version of the 1948 pop hit, "My Happiness." His second effort—singing the Ink Spots' 1941 hit "That's Where Your Heartaches Begin"—was less successful. The boy's voice quivered as he sang, and his guitar-playing was primitive at best. Elvis himself later admitted that his guitar playing "sounded like somebody beating on a bucket lid." If Elvis was hoping to be discovered that day, he was deeply disappointed. Sam Phillips showed little interest, although when Keisker put together a file on the young customer she did note "Good ballad singer. Hold."[32]

Throughout the fall of 1953, Elvis kept returning to Sun Records, always asking Miss Keisker if she knew of any band looking for a singer. The answer was always no, but she'd keep him in mind. By early winter, the recent high school grad was probably getting desperate. In January 1954, he paid another $3.98 to record a second acetate (tepid versions of Joni James's pop hit, "I'll Never Stand in Your Way" and Jimmy Wakely's country & western song, "It Wouldn't Be the Same Without You") perhaps in the hope that Sam Phillips would finally take interest. But again, nothing happened.[33]

For the next several months, Elvis continued to drop by Sun Records whenever he could. He always asked Marion Keisker if she knew of anyone looking for a singer and undoubtedly he was always hoping his very general question would lead to something very specific with Sun Records. Finally, opportunity knocked—or more accurately—phoned. On June 26, 1954, Elvis answered the call. It was Marion Keisker. She asked if he could drop by the studio that afternoon. "I was there by the time she hung up the phone," he later recalled. When he got there, Elvis learned that Sam Phillips had recently received a demo for a song called "Without You." Phillips thought that Elvis's voice might be a perfect fit for the plaintive ballad. The young man was probably so excited that he could hardly breathe. For almost a year, he had been waiting for his big break, dropping by the Sun office whenever he could, staying in touch with Marion Keisker, and recording two demos. As the words sank in, the young singer must have been thinking that his plan had worked. If Elvis thought all of this seemed too good to be true, he was right. When Sam Phillips gave him his chance to record "Without You," the boy just could not pull it off. Phillips asked him to try other songs. Nothing clicked. "I guess I must have sat there at least three hours," Elvis later told the local newspaper. "I sang everything I knew—pop stuff, spirituals, just a few words of [anything] I remembered." None of it, though, was up to Phillips's high standards. Yet Sam was not ready to give up on the boy. The amateurish singer clearly had a passion for the music, and his individualistic style and fresh approach rang true.[34]

Phillips was intrigued enough to ask Scotty Moore, a guitar player and leader of a local country & western combo who did some playing on Sun Records, if he would jam with Elvis just to see if anything developed. Scotty remembers the first time he heard Elvis Presley's name: it sounded like something "out of science fiction." But Moore was willing to give it a go. He invited Elvis over to his house on the Fourth of July (how's that for a perfect beginning for a man who would become an American icon?) along with Moore's bass player, Bill Black. They practiced some chords and took a shot at every song Elvis knew, including country & western hits by Eddie Arnold and Hank Snow, as well as pop standards made famous by artists such as the Ink Spots, Billy Eckstein, and Jo Stafford. Scotty's report back to Sam Phillips was hardly enthusiastic. The kid wasn't bad, but he wasn't anything special either. Scotty felt Elvis had a nice enough voice and maybe even sounded a little like Dean Martin on the ballads, but nothing bowled him over. Bill Black was more blunt: "Well, [Elvis] didn't impress me too damn much." Sam Phillips was not yet ready to give up, though. He invited the three of them to come to Sun studios the next day for a recording session.

On the night of July 5, they showed up at around 7 p.m. Phillips got them set up behind the mikes, and they started right in. For the next few hours, they played continuously. But, nothing caught Sam's attention. Scotty and Bill played just about everything Elvis knew, including pop stuff like Bing Crosby's "Harbor Lights" and Ernest Tubb's country hit "I Love You Because." Then, all of a sudden it happened. During a break around midnight, Elvis and Bill Black began fooling around with "That's All Right, Mama," an old rhythm & blues number written and recorded by Arthur "Big Boy" Crudup. Elvis later said, "this song popped into my mind that I had heard years ago, and I started kidding around with [it]." Scotty explains what happened: "All of a sudden, Elvis just started singing this song, jumping around and acting the fool, and then Bill picked up his bass, and he started acting the fool, too, and I started playing with them. Sam, I think, had the door to the control booth open . . . and he stuck his head out and said, 'What are you doing?' And we said, 'We don't know.' 'Well, back up,' he said, 'try to find a place to start, and do it again.'"[35]

Phillips was blown away by the impromptu performance. This was exactly the kind of original sound he was looking for. It evoked rhythm & blues, but this was no mere imitation. Sam was familiar with the original and this was nothing like it. Crudup's version was slower paced and had a bluesy electric guitar and drums. Elvis's take was faster and had a lighter feel backed by the country-style picking of Scotty's lead guitar and Bill's slap bass. The phenomenal result was neither rhythm & blues nor country. More than a blend of the two, it sounded fresh, exciting, and authentic. Phillips got it all on tape. Sam was convinced "That's All Right, Mama" could be released as a record but realized they were not done yet. After several unsuccessful attempts to record a suitable song for the B-side of the record, Elvis, Scotty, and Bill finally satisfied Sam with their up-tempo version of Bill Monroe's "Blue Moon of Kentucky." Compared to the original, which showcased Monroe's bluegrass vocal and a slow, waltz-like beat, Elvis's version was high octane. Not only did the young singer and his band transform the song to a 4/4 time, but Elvis's high-energy vocal captured the feel of wild and uninhibited rhythm & blues.

Elvis, Scotty, and Bill had begun their musical journey in the Sun Studio by producing a countrified version of an R&B song, "That's All Right, Mama." They ended by injecting a rhythm & blues feel into a classic country song, "Blue Moon of Kentucky." Sam Phillips was ecstatic and quickly got a demo copy of the record into the hands of his close friend Dewey Phillips (no relation), the popular disc jockey who worked at Memphis's WHBQ.[36]

THE SELLING OF ELVIS PRESLEY

At first, Dewey Phillips was not sure what to make of this Presley kid. He listened very carefully to the record Sam had given him, but he was puzzled by the sound. It wasn't rhythm & blues, but it wasn't country music either. Because it didn't fall into any one musical category, Dewey wasn't sure that the song would appeal to any one audience. But, because Sam was a close friend, he agreed to give the record some airplay on his top-rated *Red, Hot, and Blue* radio show. Nobody was more surprised than Dewey himself by his listeners' response. The switchboard lit up like a Christmas tree as kids kept calling in wanting to hear "That's All Right" again and again and again.

After a few days, Sam Phillips dropped off the record at other Memphis radio stations, where disc jockeys got similar responses with one big difference: at least two of the stations were spinning "Blue Moon of Kentucky" as the A-side. Elvis and everyone else at Sun Records couldn't believe it. It looked like they might actually have a two-sided hit on their hands.

Sam Phillips moved fast to take advantage of the sudden demand. The record was pressed at a local plant and shipped out as fast as possible. Sam also sat down with his hot new group and worked out business arrangements. Everybody agreed that Scotty Moore should act as the group's manager, since he already had some experience managing his own country & western band, the Wranglers. Scotty would get 10 percent right off the top. The remaining profits would be split three ways: Elvis would get 50 percent and Scotty Moore and Bill Black would each get 25 percent. This arrangement suggests that at least in the beginning, everyone viewed this as a group effort (although they also recognized that Elvis, as the lead singer, should be getting more money). The label on the first record reflected this thinking. It listed Elvis Presley as the vocalist and just beneath his name in slightly smaller print were Scotty and Bill. (Later releases changed the name to Elvis Presley and the Blue Moon Boys.)[37]

The more airplay "That's All Right"/"Blue Moon of Kentucky" received on local stations, the more the record caught on with local teenagers. Within a few weeks, kids all over town had turned the nonsensical last line sung by Elvis on "That's All Right"—"Ta dee da dee dee dee"—into a catch phrase. Elvis, Scotty, and Bill couldn't believe all the attention they were getting. They even got some bookings at a local club and were hired as the opening act for a Slim Whitman concert at Memphis's Overton Shell Park.[38]

The performance at the Overton outdoor amphitheater marked a turning point for Elvis. It was the first time he was appearing before a huge crowd. Plus, it was a big event in Memphis, and the insecure Elvis knew it. Everything seemed to be happening so fast. Barely a year out of high school, Elvis had a low-paying job as a truck driver delivering products for Crown Electronics. But he also had become somewhat of a local celebrity because his record was getting a lot of airplay on Memphis radio. He must have been in awe when he saw ads listing him as a performer at the upcoming Overton show (even though one billed him as "Ellis Presley"). Elvis was extremely nervous when the local paper interviewed him just before the concert. The editor's son conducted the interview. Years later, he recalled that the young singer "look[ed] like the wrath of God. Pimples all over his face. Ducktail hair. Had a funny-looking thin bow tie on. . . . He was very hard to interview. About all I could get out of him was yes and no."[39]

The resulting article published in the *Memphis Press-Scimitar* provides an interesting glimpse of the young Elvis on the eve of his first major performance. The contours of the myth of how Elvis was discovered were already beginning to take shape:

> IN A SPIN—Elvis Presley can be forgiven for going round and round in more ways than one these days. A 19-year-old Humes High graduate, he has just signed a recording contract with Sun Record Co. of Memphis, and already has a disk out that promises to be the biggest hit that Sun has ever pressed. It all started when Elvis dropped into Sun's studios one day to cut a personal record at his own expense. Sam Phillips, president of the company, monitored the session and was so impressed with the unusual quality in the young man's voice that he jotted down his name and address. Some time later, Phillips came across a ballad which he thought might be right for Presley's voice. They recorded it; it didn't click. But they tried again; this time with "Blue Moon of Kentucky," a folk standard, backed by "That's All Right, Mama."
>
> Just now reaching dealers' shelves, the record is getting an amazing amount of plays on all Memphis radio stations. "The odd thing about it," says Marion Keisker of the Sun office, "is that both sides seem to be equally popular on popular, folk and race record programs. . . ." Elvis . . . has been singing and playing the guitar since he was about 13—just picked it up himself.

The publicity photograph that accompanied the newspaper article shows a thin, teenaged Elvis with greasy slicked-back scraggly hair and long sideburns. He's wearing a light-colored cowboy-style suit with two stitched pockets and a white shirt with a thin, clip-on bow tie. The shot reveals a determined look on the young singer's face. His pursed lips suggest that Elvis had already perfected the sneer that he would later make famous. Most surprising, Elvis appears to be wearing dark eye shadow, which gives him an almost menacing appearance.[40]

The publication of the newspaper article on July 28, 1954, probably added to the stress that Elvis felt as he counted down the hours until the Overton concert. Not only would this be the first time he would be singing before a big crowd, but he was also on the same bill as the famous country & western star Slim Whitman. Elvis was terrified that he would embarrass himself before a hometown audience—but he was also determined to prove that he could make it as a successful singer.

Elvis's date with destiny arrived on July 30, 1954, when he took the stage and stepped in front of the mike on the stage of the Overton Park amphitheater. For a moment, Elvis, with Scotty and Bill standing next to him, just stared out at the huge audience. "We were scared to death," Scotty later recalled. "All those people—and us with these three little funky instruments." They launched into "That's All Right, Mama," bringing the audience up to its feet. Scotty remembers that Elvis was so nervous that he was up on the balls of his feet and shaking his leg in time to the music. "To his shock—and horror," notes Scotty, "the young girls in the audience went crazy, yelling, and applauding. He couldn't see what the audience saw. Because he was wearing baggy pants that were pleated in the front, his attempt to keep time with the music created a wild gyrating effect with his pants' legs. From the audience's angle those movements seemed exaggerated against the backdrop of the Shell, which had a tendency to amplify whatever was on stage, visually as well as acoustically."[41]

The same thing happened when Elvis performed the next song, "Blue Moon of Kentucky." As soon as Elvis and the boys were done, they ran off backstage. At first, Elvis wasn't sure how to interpret the audience's response. "I was scared stiff," he later admitted. "It was my first big appearance in front of an audience, and I came out and I was doing [my first song], and everybody was hollering and I didn't know what they were hollering at." Elvis quickly figured it out. "I came off-stage, and my manager told me that they was hollering because I was wiggling my legs," he explains. "I went back out for an encore, and I did a little more, and the more I did, the wilder they went."[42] Most likely, Elvis wasn't that surprised, since he had frequently marveled at how enthusiastically fans reacted whenever the bass singer of the Statesmen jiggled his legs at all-night gospel sings. In any event, the audience's reaction to Elvis at the Overton was an epiphany for the young singer. Elvis had found his performance style.

Throughout the rest of the summer, Elvis's record could be heard all over Memphis, blaring out of car radios as young drivers cruised the streets, blasting out of jukeboxes in diners and teen hangouts, and playing on record players at home in teenagers' bedrooms. Sam Phillips loaded up his old car with copies of the record and barnstormed throughout the South, peddling the product to disc jockeys, jukebox operators, retailers, and distributors in Tennessee, Texas, Louisiana, Georgia, and Mississippi. He even got a copy off to a friend at *Billboard* who reviewed it on August 7: "Presley is a potent new chanter, who can sock over a tune for either the country or the r&b markets." By August 28, "Blue Moon of Kentucky" had cracked into the *Billboard* country & western regional charts. [43]

The record was doing well enough to get regional bookings for Elvis, Scotty, and Bill. Along with a regular gig at a local Memphis club, they played anywhere they could within a seventy-five-mile radius—including high schools, Elks Clubs, Lions Clubs, hospitals, and churches in Tennessee, Mississippi, and Arkansas. Regardless of the location or size of crowd, Elvis loved performing and worked hard to develop his style. Scotty and Bill gave him tips on how to hold his guitar, how to stand in front of the mike, and how to deal with audiences. Elvis seemed to get better every time out. "His movement was a natural thing, but he was also very conscious of what got a reaction," noted Scotty. Elvis would "do something one time and then he would expand on it real quick." [44]

By the end of the summer, Sam Phillips was devoting most of his time to promoting Elvis's record and career. He even landed a guest shot for Elvis, Scotty, and Bill on the *Grand Ole Opry* in October. The *Opry* was a country variety show patterned after a barn dance. Broadcast live from Nashville's Ryman Auditorium, a half-hour segment of the program was syndicated each week on NBC radio. Anybody who was anybody in country music appeared on the *Opry*. Elvis, Scotty, and Bill were excited about performing on the Ryman stage—the same place where Red Foley, Jimmie Rodgers, Roy Acuff, Hank Williams, Gene Autry, and other country greats had performed. Unfortunately, the audience that witnessed the trio's performance—older and more traditional in their musical tastes—wasn't quite sure what to make of the wildly dressed young Elvis and his two-piece backup band. The trio was not invited back. [45]

Sam Phillips turned next to country music's second-most popular syndicated radio program, the *Louisiana Hayride*. Broadcast live from Shreveport's KWKH radio, the program reached all of Louisiana and parts of Texas and Arkansas. Elvis and his band (now known as the Blue Moon Boys) performed well enough to land a contract, and for the next year they made regular guest appearances on the *Hayride*, while they continued to release new songs on the Sun label. The modest but guaranteed income from the *Hayride* (and the resulting publicity from the radio appearances and new record releases) allowed Elvis, Scotty, and Bill to quit their day jobs and concentrate on playing at clubs throughout the South. [46]

The people who witnessed those early performances never forgot them. A young Buddy Holly and his high school friend Jerry Allison—who together would later form one of rock & roll's pioneering groups, the Crickets—caught Elvis's act in Lubbock, Texas. From that point on, recalls Allison, all Buddy wanted to do was to sing like Elvis. [47] Bob Luman, who became a successful country singer in the late 1950s and '60s and had a Top 10 hit on the rock charts in 1960 with "Let's Think about Living," had a similar experience when he saw Elvis perform in Kilgore, Texas. "This cat came out in red pants and a green coat and a pink shirt and socks, and he had this sneer on his face," remembers Luman. "He stood behind the mike for five minutes, I'll bet, before he made a move. Then he hit his guitar a lick, and he broke two strings. I'd been playing ten years, and I hadn't broken a *total* of two strings. So there he was, these two strings dangling, and he hadn't done anything yet, and these high school girls were screaming and fainting and running up to the stage, and then he started to move his hips real slow like he had a thing for his guitar." [48]

It was at another one of these performances—in New Boston, Texas—that Elvis caught the eye of "Colonel" Tom Parker, a former carnie pitchman who was promoting country artists such as Eddie Arnold and Hank Snow. Everything about Elvis impressed Parker, from the high-energy records that were climbing up the country charts to the frenzied way that audiences—particularly the girls—were responding to the young performer. Even Elvis's appearance caught Parker's attention. The Colonel took notice of how Elvis looked at their first meeting: the unusual young man was sporting loud "cat" clothes—a rust-colored suit, pink socks, and a purple and black polka-dot tie. Colonel Tom came away convinced that this kid, who was now being billed as "the Hillbilly Cat," had market potential—lots of it. [49]

By the end of 1955, Colonel Parker had wrested Elvis away from his previous business manager, Bob Neal, arguing that Neal was incapable of getting big bookings for the rising young singer. Neal knew in his heart that Parker was right, and he wasn't surprised that Elvis wanted Parker's help. From the very beginning, Neal was aware of Elvis's volcanic ambitions. According to Neal, the young singer always "talked not in terms of being a moderate success. No—his ambition and desire was to be big in movies and so forth. From the very first he had ambition to be nothing in the ordinary but to go all the way." [50]

Before 1955 was out, Colonel Tom Parker persuaded Sam Phillips to sell Elvis's contract and the rights to all previously recorded material to RCA Records for $35,000 and $5,000 in back royalties. That now sounds like a horrible deal. But in 1955, it was a fabulous offer. Prior to that, no recording contract had ever been sold for such a large sum of money. Not surprisingly, Phillips jumped at the chance. He knew that his small, independent record company lacked the resources and connections to take Elvis's career to the next level. RCA could do the job, though, and Sam didn't want to stand in Elvis's way. Furthermore, the sale would provide Phillips with the capital needed to keep Sun Records going. That money allowed him to sign and promote other artists such as Carl Perkins, Jerry Lee Lewis, and Johnny Cash. Not only did Sun Records benefit immediately from the RCA deal, but Sam benefited greatly in the long run. He used some of the profits from the sale to invest in the Holiday Inn motel chain, which was just getting started in 1955. That alone guaranteed Phillips's financial future. No doubt that helps explain why Sam was later able to tell an interviewer who asked him if he ever regretted selling Elvis's contract: "If I've been asked [that question] once, I must have been asked a thousand times. . . . No, I didn't, I do not, and I never will." [51]

Elvis Presley never forgot all that Sam Phillips had done for him. Sam was the guy who got him started. He was Elvis's mentor, producer, business manager, and all-around ticket to the music business rolled up into one. Yet, for all he was, Sam Phillips was *not* the one who discovered Elvis. That honor, according to Elvis himself, belonged to Marion

Keisker. "One thing I got to say about Elvis—he never forgot that lady," insists Red West. Later on in his career, "[Elvis] would pick up magazines and newspapers all saying about how he got started. And all the stories had Sam Phillips as being the man who discovered Elvis. Well, Elvis told me I don't know how many times that Marion Keisker was the one who really did the job." Elvis never forgot that Marion Keisker was the one who kept his telephone number; she understood that Sam Phillips was looking for a white singer with a black sound; she was the one who encouraged Sam Phillips to call. "That woman was the one who had faith, she was the one who pushed me," said Elvis. "Marion did it for me."[52]

ELVIS AND RCA

RCA Records took a big gamble investing so much money in a virtually unknown singer. There was no guarantee that Elvis Presley would make it so big. Granted, Presley seemed like a comer to many people who knew music trends. But Elvis's success had been confined to the small country & western field. He had yet to make the national pop charts (figure 4.2).

There were signs, though, that Presley's popularity was about to explode nationwide. Elvis's live performances were whipping audiences into a frenzy wherever he went. He'd come out on stage dressed in flamboyant cat clothes—he was partial to black and pink in those days. He'd step in front of the mike and pause for a moment, giving the audience time to take in the sight of this rebellious-looking young man with greased-back hair and athletic good looks. Sporting pegged pants and a wild sport coat, he'd give the audience a slight smile with a sneer on his lip and then launch into rousing rocker, gyrating his hips, shaking his legs, and bouncing on the balls of his feet. All the while, he banged out a beat on his small guitar, often snapping strings as he went along. Bob Neal, who booked most of Presley's early shows, remembers, "You'd see this frenzied reaction, particularly from the young girls."[53]

A concert in Jacksonville, Florida, epitomized the crowd's reaction to Elvis. Just as the rising young star finished his set before a sell-out crowd of about 14,000 young people, Elvis leaned into the mike and said playfully, "Girls, I'll see you all backstage." Pandemonium broke

Figure 4.2.   Early RCA recording session with Elvis backed by the Jordanaires. Sitting to the far right is guitarist Scotty Moore. On the left is Bill Black with his stand-up bass. Drummer D. J. Fontana has his back to the camera. (Photo by "PoPsie" Randolph L.L.C.; courtesy of Michael Randolph, executor to the estate of William "PoPsie" Randolph)

loose! Elvis was whisked backstage by security guards. But enthusiastic fans would not be denied. Noticing an open, overhead window, dozens if not hundreds of determined females came tumbling in and pushing their way into the dressing room area. Elvis, his guards, and anyone else back there scrambled for cover. Excited girls grabbed desperately at the singer, tearing his pink shirt and ripping his white sport coat to pieces. They made off with his belt, his shoes, and anything else they could get their hands on. Elvis jumped up on top of one of the showers for cover, and when it was finally over, he said somewhat sheepishly, "What'd I do?"[54]

Presley was being more than just a bit disingenuous. His body movements, facial expressions, and comments were often aimed at getting the crowd riled up. Some parts of the performance were rehearsed.

One example involves Elvis's bass player, Bill Black. Like many bass players in country bands, Bill provided comic relief during concerts. Elvis and Bill perfected one routine that never failed to excite girls. Right in the middle of the performance, Bill would walk over to Elvis's mike and say innocently, "Roses are red and violets are pink." Elvis would look puzzled and reply, "No, no, man. Roses are red, and violets are blue." Bill would then crack a lascivious smile, reach into his back pocket, pull out a pair of pink panties, and hold them up to the audience, while saying slyly: "I know Violet's are pink 'cause I got them right here."[55]

Presley's live performances fueled record sales, which led to praise from the music business. By the time RCA purchased his contract, Elvis was clearly on a roll. A popular country & western music magazine named him the year's "Best New Male Singer." Shortly thereafter, Elvis attended a convention of the nation's top country disc jockeys. Accolade after accolade was heaped on the new artist. The deejays voted his recent release, "Baby, Let's Play House," one of the year's top hits. Elvis was named the thirteenth most played artist on country radio. Then, to top it off, they voted Elvis the "Most Promising Country & Western Artist" in the country. "That was the first time I ever saw Elvis, although I had heard about him before that," recalls country performer Minnie Pearl. "Believe me, they had him on display."[56]

Elvis's new record label knew that the "Hillbilly Cat" was an up-and-coming country & western singer. The real question for RCA was whether they could turn their new singer into a successful pop performer. They paid big bucks to purchase Elvis's contract, because they hoped that the young country artist could cross over to the pop charts, and maybe even the R&B charts. Initially, RCA had stood idly by as other major labels jumped on the rock & roll bandwagon. The tremendous surge in sales of rock & roll records in 1954 and 1955 convinced RCA officials they no longer could wait. They saw Elvis as their best chance to get on board. "Although Sun has sold Presley primarily as a c&w artist," noted one trade magazine, "[RCA] plans to push his platters in all three fields—pop, r&b, and c&w."[57]

As 1955 drew to a close, RCA had high hopes for their new singer. Elvis Presley was equally optimistic. After all, he had a string of country hits behind him; he was set to record on a major label; he had perhaps the shrewdest manager around in Colonel Tom Parker; and he was scheduled to appear for the first time on national TV. Elvis was not going to be disappointed. Neither he nor RCA could possibly have imagined, though, exactly how good a year 1956 was going to be.

5

MONEY HONEY

Presleymania Sweeps the Nation

On March 24, 1956, Elvis Presley made his final appearance on CBS's *Stage Show*, the TV variety program hosted by big-band leaders Tommy and Jimmy Dorsey. "Well, we're gonna get things started out with a young fellow who's making his sixth appearance on *Stage Show*," announced Jimmy. "He's that dynamic singer of songs who incidentally leaves for Hollywood tonight for a screen test. We wish him a lot of luck. Here he is . . . Elvis Presley!"

A confident if not cocky Elvis steps dramatically on stage from behind a curtain. Dressed in a light-colored, sharkskin suit with a black shirt and white tie, the young singer immediately grabs the attention of both the in-house audience and millions of viewers watching live across the country. His greased-back hair is combed up in a huge pompadour and appears to have blond highlights due to the reflected spotlight. With his porcelain skin and dark eye shadow complementing his contrasting clothes, he stands out vividly against the black backdrop. As he steps behind the microphone the spotlight remains solely on him, leaving his three-piece backup band in the shadows. For a brief moment, he stares at the audience. He then begins to strum his guitar as he launches into "Money Honey," a rhythm & blues hit recorded a few years earlier by Clyde McPhatter and the Drifters. The appreciative audience cheers as Elvis sings playfully "[It's] money, honey, if you want to get along with me." The rest of the song explains that money is more important than anything else in life, including women and love.[1]

Elvis's performance is riveting. Although he copies the Drifters' version almost note-for-note, he puts his own mark on it through a high-octane approach. Presley alternately smiles and sneers as he delivers the lines, blending an expressive R&B approach with country-influenced hiccups. He elicits the biggest response from the audience during the musical bridge. He shakes his hips and wiggles his legs, flanked by Scotty Moore on lead guitar, Bill Black on bass, and D. J. Fontana on drums, who form a half-circle around the energetic singer. At the end, Elvis bows dramatically all the way down to the floor and then strides two steps back to the mike. Cradling his guitar, he sneers for a split second and then winks at the cheering audience.

Presley's performance of "Money Honey" is a perfect example of the raucous rock & roll that was sweeping the nation in 1956. It showcases Elvis's unique blend of rhythm & blues and country & western music. And it demonstrates how early rock & roll could be both conflict and consensus. Some viewers condemned the singer's nonconformist appearance and uninhibited performance style, but most could relate to the song's main message. "Money Honey" mirrored the era's consumer culture, offering evidence that young people wanted cash and material goods as much as anybody else in 1950s America. Indeed, "Money Honey" could have been the theme song for the Presleymania that was sweeping the nation and helping the economy in 1956. "When I met [Elvis], he only had about a million dollars' worth of talent," explained his manager, Colonel Tom Parker. "Now he has a million dollars."[2]

THE MARKETING OF ELVIS PRESLEY

As 1956 began, RCA and Colonel Tom Parker were relying on a multifaceted game plan to promote Elvis Presley. The major record company had the production team to get the most out of the young singer's raw talent, as well as the vast marketing resources needed to distribute records nationally and the media skills to mount a major media campaign. The Colonel, with his years as a carnie pitchman and musical promoter, knew exactly what he had to do. Not only did he want to hook audiences on his young star, but he had to get them so excited that they would be willing to empty their wallets for a piece of Elvis.

Colonel Parker realized that the latest craze in entertainment—television—was the perfect vehicle to move Elvis into the national spotlight. Americans were turning on and tuning in to TV sets by the millions. In 1948, only 0.4 percent of all American homes had television sets. That figure rose to 9 percent in 1950, and 34.2 percent by 1952, and then shot up to 64.5 percent in 1956. The Colonel knew that TV could launch Elvis's singing career nationally. That's why within a three-week period in late November and early December 1955, Parker negotiated—almost simultaneously—Presley's new contract with RCA Victor and arranged a television booking for Elvis on *Stage Show*, a CBS variety program hosted by big band leaders Tommy and Jimmy Dorsey. Jackie Gleason, who produced the Dorseys' variety show on CBS, jumped at the chance to book the up-and-coming singer, who he felt was a "guitar-playing Marlon Brando."[3]

Events moved quickly. Like a snowball careening down a steep mountain side, Elvis's career rapidly gained mass and momentum. On December 2, RCA Records rereleased Presley's last hit single on Sun Records, "I Forgot to Remember to Forget" (which was still on the country charts), along with four additional songs done originally for Sun Records. The following day, a full-page ad appeared in *Billboard*. Striking in its simplicity, it featured a black and white, full-length action photo that looked like a stop-action frame from an Elvis concert. His uninhibited performance style leaps off the page: here's Elvis with his legs spread in a defiant stance, his pelvis thrust forward. He's banging on his guitar, eyes closed, and screaming out lyrics with abandon. A headline with white type set against a black background appears directly over Elvis's head. It explains that the dynamic-looking performer below is "the most talked about new personality in the last 10 years of recorded music." The image alone makes the statement appear self-evident. If people had not been talking about Elvis, they certainly were now. Next, the record company scheduled Presley for his first RCA recording session on January 10 in their Nashville studio. Meanwhile, news stories reminded the public about Elvis's upcoming debut on the Dorseys' TV show.[4]

The first of Elvis's four appearances occurred on January 28, 1956. It was neither earth-shattering nor career-changing. The Dorsey Brothers'

Stage Show was not exactly must-see TV. It consistently trailed its network competition in the Nielson ratings. Furthermore, Elvis Presley—despite RCA's publicity blitz—was hardly a big draw. True, he had done well on the country & western charts, but he had yet to hit it big on the national pop charts. On the night Elvis appeared, the *Stage Show* auditorium was not even half full. Well-known Cleveland disc jockey Bill Randle had the honor of introducing the young singer. His description of what was about to happen was right on the mark: Here, he said, is "a young fellow who, like many performers, Johnny Ray among them, come[s] up out of nowhere to become, overnight, very big stars." Randle added, "We think tonight he will be making television history for you: Elvis Presley, and here he is!" The older audience wasn't quite sure what to make of this young singer who looked like a juvenile delinquent. Elvis, backed by Scotty and Bill, did two songs: the first was a medley of Joe Turner's "Shake, Rattle, and Roll" and "Flip, Flop, and Fly;" the second was Ray Charles's "I Got a Woman." The applause was tepid as he left the stage.[5]

Over the next three weeks, Elvis, Scotty, and Bill did three more guest shots on the Dorsey Brothers' show—each time the response was a little bit better than the time before. On February 4, Elvis did two rhythm & blues hits: Arthur Gunter's "Baby, Let's Play House" and Little Richard's "Tutti Frutti." On February 11, he sang two new songs that he had just recorded for RCA: Carl Perkins's "Blue Suede Shoes" and "Heartbreak Hotel." On his last *Stage Show* appearance in February, Elvis reprised "Tutti Frutti" along with "I Was the One."

Gleason and the Dorsey Brothers were pleased enough to invite the young singer back for two more appearances. Elvis couldn't have been happier. After he performed his new single, "Heartbreak Hotel," during his third appearance on the Dorseys' show, the record began to sell. It debuted on the national pop charts on March 3. Clearly, the television exposure was paying off. Presley showcased the song once again during his March 17 appearance on *Stage Show*. He also tossed in "Blue Suede Shoes." The following week, Elvis appeared for the last time on the Dorseys' show. This time he paired "Heartbreak Hotel" with Clyde McPhatter and the Drifters's rhythm & blues hit, "Money Honey."[6]

The national exposure worked. By March, Elvis Presley was the hottest entertainment property around. Neither RCA nor Colonel Tom Parker was about to let up now. RCA brought Elvis back into the studio to cut several more songs, enough to assemble his first album, entitled simply *Elvis Presley*. The album included five songs originally recorded for Sun Records and five new ones. The album's packaging was as important as the music inside. If a picture is worth a thousand words, the album cover said it all: there in black and white was a close-up of the intriguing new star, banging on his guitar, eyes shut, mouth wide open, screaming out the lyrics to one of his wild songs. Framing the black-and-white photo in bright pink and green was his name: Elvis Presley. The message was simple but complex, outrageous, maybe even revolutionary. The "King of Rock & Roll" had arrived. And this was just the beginning (figure 5.1).

Colonel Tom Parker threw his marketing campaign into high gear. Along with arranging Elvis concerts across the country, he hired the William Morris Agency to help him land a movie deal and more appearances on television. Everything Colonel Parker touched seemed to turn to gold—with one glaring exception. When he booked Presley for a two-week engagement at the New Frontier Hotel in Las Vegas, the result was anything but a resounding success. Elvis and his group (which now included drummer D. J. Fontana, along with Scotty and Bill) were the closing act for headliner Freddie Martin and his big band, plus comedian Shecky Greene. The marquee billed Elvis as an added attraction, calling him the "Atomic Power singer." They didn't realize how right they were. Americans of the cold war era were about to become as anxious about this new singer as they were about atomic energy. Both had explosive power.

Elvis's problem in Las Vegas stemmed not from him but from his audience. Unlike the young crowds Elvis normally played to, the Las Vegas one was middle-aged and didn't have a clue about what they were seeing or hearing. "They weren't my kind of audience," admitted Elvis. "It was strictly an adult audience. The first night especially I was absolutely scared stiff [but] afterwards I got a little more relaxed and I finally got 'em on my side." Elvis's band remembers it differently. Scotty Moore says, "We didn't even know we were failures." Bill Black adds, "For the first time in months we could hear ourselves when we played out of tune. After the show our nerves were pretty frayed, and we would get together in pairs and talk about whoever wasn't around to defend himself." Drummer D. J. Fontana offers the most succinct explanation: "I don't think the [older] people there were ready for Elvis. [He] was

Figure 5.1.   Cover of Elvis's first album. (Richard Aquila Collection)

mostly for teenagers, kids. We worked [right after Freddie Martin's Big Band], and here we were with three little pieces making all that noise, and they were eating $50 and $60 dollar steaks. We tried everything we knew. Usually Elvis could get them on his side. It didn't work that time. The Colonel did [one] show for teenagers on Saturday, and it was just jam-packed, with everybody screaming and hollering."[7]

Unfortunately, that Saturday matinee was the exception. All the rest of the time—for two times a night for two weeks—the older crowds just sat quietly and watched as this odd-looking "Hillbilly Cat" screamed out his songs and shook to the beat. Critics were not kind. *Newsweek* likened Presley in Las Vegas to "a jug of corn liquor at a champagne party." *Variety* issued a damning verdict: "Elvis Presley, coming in on a wing of advance hoopla, doesn't hit the mark here [in Las Vegas]. . . . The loud braying of the tunes which rocketed him to the big time is wearing, and the applause comes backed edged [only] with a polite sound."[8]

Ironically, Elvis's defeat at the New Frontier Hotel eventually turned into a win. While in Vegas, Elvis discovered a song that would guarantee his national celebrity if not notoriety. Scotty Moore remembers that Elvis and the band spent off hours hanging around casinos and bars. "One night [we] all went to check out the other acts on the strip. Performing at the Sahara lounge were Freddie Bell and the Bellboys. They had a [very minor] hit in 1953 with a song titled 'Hound Dog' that also had been a hit for R&B singer Big Mama Thornton. When [we] heard them perform that night, [we] thought the song would be a good one for [us] to do as comic relief." Scotty adds that even though Elvis was familiar with Big Mama Thornton's version, he liked Bell's rendition better. Freddie had changed the lyrics and quickened the tempo of the song, so it was Bell's version that Elvis began performing in his shows.[9]

Presley's Las Vegas stint turned out to be a tiny bump on the road to success. His upward trajectory was soon powered by two more television appearances, this time on the Milton Berle show. The first took place on April 3, 1956. Performing live on board the USS *Hancock* at San Diego Naval Station, Elvis brought the audience (made up mostly of young sailors and their dates) to their feet with a rousing rendition of "Blue Suede Shoes." But as wild as Elvis's first appearance on Berle's show was, it was just the warm-up.

Elvis's second appearance two months later was destined to go down in both television and rock & roll history. By the time Elvis returned to Berle's stage, he was the hottest singing sensation in the country. During the first five months of the year, Elvis racked up five Top 40 hits, including two that went all the way to number 1 on the pop music charts—"Heartbreak Hotel" and "I Want You, I Need You, I Love You." In January, February, March, and April, the "Hillbilly Cat" from Memphis wowed TV audiences with almost weekly appearances on CBS's *Stage Show* and Milton Berle's higher-rated show on NBC. Elvis's good looks and frenetic singing style catapulted him into the public spotlight as he introduced TV audiences to rhythm & blues–influenced songs such as "Heartbreak Hotel," "Tutti Frutti," "Money Honey," and "Blue Suede Shoes."[10]

But nothing that came before prepared TV viewers for what they were about to witness when the singer took the stage on Milton Berle's television show on June 5, 1956. The young Elvis—sporting a "D.A." hair-do (so-named because of its alleged resemblance to a duck's rear end) and "cat clothes" (i.e., bright-colored clothing associated with African American hipsters)—swaggered up to the microphone. The image was striking on black-and-white television. His light skin contrasted sharply with his dark, slicked-back hair and long sideburns. Elvis's "cool" clothes added to the contrast. He wore what appeared to be black shoes with white socks, a two-tone black-and-white shirt open at the collar, and black slacks paired with a light-colored sport coat. The coat's window-pane pattern, broad shoulders, and tapered waist recalled the hip zoot-suit look from the 1940s.[11] (figure 5.2).

Standing before a TV audience for the first time without his trademark guitar, the handsome but wild-looking young man launched into a frenzied version of the song he had discovered just a few weeks earlier in Las Vegas—"Hound Dog." Most viewers had never heard the song before (even though it had been a number 1 hit on the R&B charts for Big Mama Thornton in 1953). Viewers were mesmerized nationwide as the young performer screamed out raw lyrics and danced uninhibitedly to the primitive beat. Audiences were stunned, even shocked by the intensity of the performance, not to mention lyrics that featured slang words like "ain't" and a nonsensical story line about a "hound dog just crockin' all the time." What was going on here?

Some viewers thought Elvis's movements were lascivious, if not outright lewd, particularly when at one point the young Presley slowed the pace of the song, bumping and grinding to the sexy beat. A writer in the *San Francisco Chronicle* insisted the performance was "in appalling taste." Another in the *New York Herald Tribune* said Elvis was "unspeakably untalented and vulgar." Jack Gould, the TV critic for the *New York Times*, elaborated: "Attired in the familiar oversize jacket and open shirt which are almost the uniform of the contemporary youth who fancies himself as terribly sharp, [Elvis Presley] might possibly be classified as an entertainer. Or, perhaps quite as easily, as an assignment for a sociologist." After dismissing Presley's singing voice as amateurish, Gould condemned the performer's suggestive moves on stage. "He is a

Figure 5.2.   Elvis's controversial performance on Milton Berle's TV show, 1956.
(Richard Aquila Collection)

rock-and-roll variation of one of the most standard acts in show business," explained Gould, "the virtuoso of the hootchy-kootchy that heretofore has been primarily identified with the repertoire of the blonde bombshells of the burlesque runway." Gould concluded, "Mr. Presley has no discernible talent." Ben Gross of the *New York Daily News* concurred. "[Popular music] has reached its lowest depths in the 'grunt and groin' antics of one Elvis Presley," pointed out Gross. "The TV audience had a noxious sampling of it on the Milton Berle show the other evening. Elvis, who rotates his pelvis, was appalling musically. . . . What amazes me is that Berle and NBC-TV should have permitted this affront."[12]

The commotion over Presley's performance on Berle had barely died down when Elvis was scheduled to appear on Steve Allen's television show three weeks later. Not wanting to offend viewers or sponsors, Allen decided to tone down Elvis the way he knew best—by incorporating the singer into a comedy skit. Many fans couldn't believe their eyes when they tuned in Allen's show on the night of July 1. They witnessed a decidedly tamer version of Elvis Presley, wearing a white tie and black tuxedo and singing calmly to a live basset hound. Steve Allen, relieved that he had figured out a way to get Elvis past NBC's censors and unrelenting critics, later insisted that the skit was merely "a way of saying something comic." Elvis's fans were furious, however, and the next day they picketed outside of the RCA studios, demanding the return of the "real Elvis."[13]

Looking back now, it is hard to believe that Elvis had actually performed "Hound Dog" live on TV before recording it. Such timing would never happen today, because new acts are vetted and marketed in far more sophisticated ways. Not surprisingly, given the public response, Elvis rushed into the studio the morning after appearing on the Steve Allen show to record the song, which then rocketed to the top of the music charts.[14]

The Presley recording made it clear to everyone that neither Elvis nor rock & roll could be contained. Elvis had been shocked and hurt by the vicious critics who panned his performance on Berle's program. He dwelled on the criticism and even had problems sleeping. But he refused to back down. "I don't feel like I'm doing anything wrong," he told one interviewer.[15] If anything, Elvis was now more determined than ever to sing and perform his music exactly the way he wanted. The young rock & roller pulled out all the stops on the recorded version of "Hound Dog," demonstrating to fans and foes alike that his uninhibited approach would not be denied. From the opening drum roll to the climactic finish, Elvis screamed and shouted his way through the song with wild abandon. The result may be the greatest song in rock & roll history. The record captures the very essence of rock & roll—its youthful ebullience, its wild behavior and rebellious nature, and, of course, its preoccupation with sex.

If some adults were bothered and bewildered by the loud noise and nonsensical lyrics, a lot of young people were bewitched. Teenagers knew intuitively that Elvis and "Hound Dog" offered them something new, something very important. The young, uninhibited performer had arrived to lead teenagers into the promised land of rock & roll.

Elvis's star continued to rise during the summer of '56. Along with "Hound Dog," two other Presley records shot up to the number 1 spot on the *Billboard* charts: "I Want You, I Need You, I Love You" and "Don't Be Cruel." Like a big train from Memphis roaring down the tracks, Presley picked up momentum. He seemed to be everywhere at once. Colonel Tom Parker landed him a movie deal with legendary Hollywood producer Hal Wallis that guaranteed seven pictures. When Elvis arrived in Hollywood on August 17 for his first acting job at Twentieth Century Fox Studios, he was beside himself. Ever since he was a kid, he had wanted to make movies just like his idols, James Dean and Tony Curtis. He was thrilled when Wallis compared him not only to the rebel Dean but also to Marlon Brando. And he was excited that his first film, tentatively entitled *The Reno Brothers*, was going to be a historical drama set in the Civil War era. The icing on the cake was that the producers did not want him to sing in the movie. This was a role for a real actor. "I want to become a good actor, because you can't build a whole career on just singing," explained Elvis. "Look at Frank Sinatra. Until he added acting to singing he found himself slipping downhill."[16]

Presley's enthusiasm was short lived. A revised script was shoved into his hands the moment he arrived on set. This one called for him to sing four songs. The first, "Love Me Tender," didn't seem too bad. The pretty ballad was based on an old folk song called "Aura Lee." Elvis's intimate and sexy rendition turned out so well that it convinced the producers to change the name of the movie to "Love Me Tender." The other three songs Elvis had to perform were written for the movie and were pure schmaltz, typical of the kitsch fillers found in musicals of the 1950s. Elvis was unhappy, but he knew the show must go on, so he did the best he could (a pattern we would see all too often in later Presley movies). The overall results weren't all that bad. For one thing, the movie riveted the nation's attention on the young star. When it opened at New York City's Paramount Theater, a huge fifteen-foot cutout of Elvis holding his guitar and dressed as his Clint Reno character was placed upright over the movie marquee. Passersby and crowds found it impossible to ignore the towering Elvis figure or the marquee blasting its message: "ELVIS PRESLEY in LOVE ME TENDER, starts Thurs Nov 15 at N.Y. Paramount." The movie became a box office smash, and the title song was released as Elvis's new single and immediately became a number 1 hit. Equally important, Elvis's fans—if not film critics—gave him rave reviews.[17]

While Elvis was making it big in 1956 on the record charts, on TV, and at the box office, Colonel Parker was working tirelessly behind the scenes to market the entertainment industry's hottest new property. The former carnie pitchman hawked Elvis every way he could think of: he sent out news releases and offered inside tips to teen magazines, gossip columnists, and anybody else who could keep Elvis's name in front of the public. The press couldn't get enough. Elvis's face adorned hundreds of movie and fan magazines, while headlines such as "Is he a new JAMES DEAN?" and "HOW IT FEELS TO BE ELVIS" or "MOVIELAND'S NEXT GREAT LOVER" lured millions of readers.

The Colonel didn't miss any opportunity to make a buck. He employed H. G. Saperstein, who marketed merchandise related to TV shows like *The Lone Ranger*, *Lassie*, and *Ding Dong School*, to promote Elvis products. He also brought in Howard Bell, who helped promote Walt Disney's *Davy Crockett* and *Mickey Mouse* merchandise. The results were phenomenal, a capitalist's dream: fans could buy Elvis socks, shirts, skirts, sweaters, hats, charm bracelets, bubble gum cards, pencils and pens, bookcases, bookends, combs, soft drinks, even Elvis glow-in-the-dark pictures. One of the best-selling items was Elvis lipstick, which came in Tutti Frutti Red, Heartbreak Pink, Cruel Red, Love-Ya Fuchsia, Tender Pink, or Hound Dog Orange. Within a few months, over 450,000 units were sold—each one allegedly "individually autographed." Another company offered Elvis Presley flasher buttons (which changed shape and pictures when moved). Still another marketed an Elvis look-alike doll. Its advertisement promised that for only $3.98 fans could get the thrill of a lifetime. Just imagine, tempted the ad, "Elvis Presley for YOURSELF. He'll be your companion—morning, noon, and *nighttime*, too."

Stores couldn't set up displays fast enough as enthusiastic teenage consumers rushed into Macy's, Sears, Grants, Kresge's, Woolworths, and thousands of neighborhood five-and-dime stores across the country. Even though Presley was only getting about three cents on the dollar for every item sold, by the end of 1957 he was pulling in about $55 million from the sale of Elvis products. "It's nothing new," Saperstein explained to *Newsweek*. "It happened with Valentino, Theda Bara, and Clara Bow. We are each of us insecure in our way. We like to identify ourselves with people who are somebody." Elvis products allowed teenagers to join a new rock & roll consumption community. The product was the price of admission; the payoff was proof that you were part of your generation's newest and hottest fad. [18]

The marketing of Elvis Presley cut across various media. Elvis seemed to be the only thing people were talking about—in newspapers and magazines, on the big screen in movie theaters, the small screen in people's living rooms, and up and down the aisles in grocery stores, department stores, and anywhere else they sold records or Elvis paraphernalia. Presleymania took on an even greater urgency after Elvis appeared on one of TV's most popular shows, Ed Sullivan's *Toast of the Town*: twice in the fall of 1956 and once in January 1957.

Sullivan's CBS variety program dominated Sunday night television, always capturing the lion's share of the viewing audience. At first, the staid host wanted nothing to do with the controversial young singer, explaining to *TV Guide*: "I wouldn't have him on my show at any price. [Presley] is not my cup of tea." But as the Presley bandwagon picked up momentum during the spring and summer of '56, Ed jumped on board. In July, Sullivan announced that he would be paying Elvis a record-setting $50,000 for three appearances on his show in the fall and winter (the fact that Scotty Moore, Bill Black, and D. J. Fontana were going to be paid only the union rate of $78.23 per show clearly demonstrated to the Blue Moon Boys who the real star was). Sullivan admitted that he had booked Elvis for commercial reasons but guaranteed that his show's high standards would remain intact. "In signing Presley, I'm stringing along with the kids. I think he has some kind of tone in his voice that scores with them, the same as Frank Sinatra had," he explained. But he made it clear that he would not tolerate what had happened on Steve Allen's and Milton Berle's shows. "I can tell you now that he'll sing no suggestive lyrics for us. As for his gyrations, the whole thing can be controlled by camera shots." When Steve Allen found out about Sullivan's remarks, he wise-cracked that he was going to offer Ed $60,000 to appear three times on his show. But the stiff, humorless Sullivan would not be "permitted to bump, grind, wiggle, waggle, or smile."[19]

As things turned out, Ed Sullivan wasn't even around for Presley's debut on September 9. The host wound up in the hospital after a car accident and was replaced by actor Charles Laughton. Elvis and the Blue Moon Boys began with "Don't Be Cruel" and "Love Me Tender," the latter of which was from Presley's up-and-coming movie. When they returned later in the show, Elvis did "Hound Dog," as well as a raucous version of Little Richard's "Ready Teddy." At the end of the performance, the teenagers in the studio audience went wild, screaming and cheering. The pompous, puffy-cheeked Laughton looked straight into the camera and said wryly: "Well, what did someone say? Music hath charms to soothe the savage beast?" No doubt, Ed Sullivan was pleased as he watched from his hospital bed. Later, he had even more reason to be happy when he found out that the show scored the highest Trendex rating ever recorded, demonstrating that it had captured 82.6 percent of the television audience.[20]

Elvis's second appearance on Ed Sullivan's *Toast of the Town* on October 28 was a similar success. On January 6, 1957, he appeared for the third and final time on the popular CBS show. Despite the fact that the cameras shot Elvis only from the waist up, the singer's performance was nothing short of a grand triumph. Elvis's first set was a fast-paced medley of his hits, including "Hound Dog," "Love Me Tender," "Heartbreak Hotel," "Too Much," and "When My Blue Moon Turns to Gold Again." Later in the show, he returned for a touching rendition of the spiritual "Peace in the Valley." When it was over, Ed Sullivan rushed to his side. Holding up his hand to stop the screams and cheers, Sullivan told the audience: "I wanted to say to Elvis Presley and the country that this is a real decent, fine boy, and wherever you go, Elvis . . . we want to say that we've never had a pleasanter experience on our show with a big name than we've had with you." On stage, Elvis was clearly touched by

Sullivan's earnest pronouncement; backstage, Colonel Tom Parker was beside himself. The former carnie pitchman couldn't have planned it better himself. He understood that Sullivan's heartfelt endorsement would convince viewers once and for all that despite Elvis's wild looks and outrageous performing style, he was a fine young man, indeed.[21]

Most likely, nobody was more shocked than Elvis himself about how far he had come in just one year. If his appearance on the Dorsey show back in January 1956 had launched his national career, his appearance on the Sullivan show in January 1957 was proof that he had arrived. Elvis Presley had become an American icon. In the twelve months in between the two television appearances, Elvis had racked up eighteen hits on the *Billboard* charts, including six number 1 records. His first album became a bestseller. His first movie was a box office smash. Elvis lipsticks, Elvis clothing, Elvis jewelry, and a variety of other Elvis paraphernalia were selling like crazy. Presleymania was sweeping the nation. The twenty-one-year-old Elvis could only shake his head in wonder. "I don't know what it is," he confided to one reporter. "Only the other day, Daddy looked at me and said, 'What happened, El? The last thing I remember is that I was working in a little ol' paint factory and you were driving a truck.'"[22]

BACKLASH

The phenomenal actions of Elvis fans nationwide resulted in equally hysterical reactions on the part of those who hated rock & roll in general or Elvis in particular. Across the nation, people from all walks of life denounced Presley as an untalented, indecent, and unpatriotic threat to American society, culture, and freedom. Critics blasted his working-class demeanor and tastes. They accused him of inciting riots, encouraging sexual deviancy, and promoting juvenile delinquency. Some suggested that Presley was a communist and/or the Anti-Christ come to undermine youth and the country's entire social fabric. One anti-Presley group conducted a "motivational research study" of 100 teenagers and concluded that Elvis fans were often rebels and misanthropes. They compared Presley to Peter Pan, insisting he was a "symbol of destruction" for young people who did not want to grow up. A noted psychologist told the Associated Press that the "'need to be needed' accounts for two controversial phenomena among humans—an Elvis Presley worshipper and a hardened criminal." In early 1957, a cover story in *True Strange Magazine* entitled "The Strange Cult of Rock and Roll" noted the similarities between rock & roll and frenzied primitive cults that might be found "deep in the Belgian Congo," in the "Australian Bush," or on "some south sea island." Chicago's Catholic Cardinal Stritch evidently agreed, because he denounced the "tribal rhythms" of rock & roll in a pastoral letter. [23]

Racism and fears of miscegenation and juvenile delinquency fueled many of the attacks. Media critic Tom Engelhardt suggests that Elvis personified two of the greatest fears of 1950s America—the rise of juvenile delinquency and the emergence of blacks. "The two . . . merged in the 'pelvis' of a Southern 'greaser,'" writes Engelhardt. Presley "dressed like a delinquent, used 'one of black America's favorite products, Royal Crown Pomade hair grease' (meant to give hair a 'whiter' look), and proceeded to move and sing 'like a negro.'" Engelhardt adds, "Whether it was because they saw a white youth in blackface or black youth in whiteface, much of the media grew apoplectic and many white parents alarmed." [24]

Whites were not the only ones troubled. Some members of the African American community shuddered at the thought of Presley crossing the racial divide. Concerned black adults—like their white counterparts—were intent on saving young girls from the lascivious rock & roll singer. African American disc jockey and Memphis personality Nat D. Williams was disgusted by the sight of seeing young "black, brown and beige teen-age girls" screaming and out-of-control at an Elvis concert. Williams wondered, "How come cullud girls would take on so over a Memphis white boy?" [25]

Beginning in 1956 and picking up momentum in 1957, Elvis became the prime target of self-appointed guardians of American culture. Parents, ministers, priests, rabbis, teachers, principals, and assorted other adults fervently believed that "Elvis the Pelvis" had to be stopped in order to save young people, the nation, and perhaps all of Western civilization. In Ottawa, girls were suspended from a Catholic school for attending an Elvis concert. A high school principal in San Francisco expelled two girls for winning a "Why I Love Elvis" contest. Some radio stations refused to play Presley records. A Nashville disc jockey burned 600 Elvis records in a public park. A used car dealer in Cincinnati promised to break fifty Elvis records for every car he sold that day (he quickly sold five). A columnist for the *Toronto Telegram* started an organization for his readers called the "Elvis Suppresley Club." A high school principal in Wichita Falls, Texas, told the press, "We do not tolerate Elvis Presley records at our dances, or blue jeans or ducktail haircuts." And the editors of *Music Journal* condemned Elvis for his "leering, whining, moaning" and "filthy performances."[26]

Even some young people joined the anti-Elvis forces. Catholic schoolgirls in St. Louis decried Elvis as a false king and burned him in effigy as they publicly prayed acts of contrition for "excesses committed by teenagers." Many young males hated Elvis for no other reason than girls loved him. They spit at him, threw eggs at him when he performed, and even tried to pick fights with him. Elvis later admitted to a reporter that he had been involved in several scuffles caused by "somebody hittin' me or tryin' to hit me." Presley explained, "I mean I can take ridicule and slander, and I've been called names, you know, right to my face and everything. That I can take. But I've had a few guys that tried to take a swing at me and naturally you just can't stand there. You have to do something."[27]

Two male students at Yale University came up with a less violent way to combat Elvis's growing popularity. To counter the ubiquitous "I Love Elvis" buttons popping up across the country, they began marketing "I Love Ludwig" buttons to promote Beethoven. To help the cause, a music store in Manhattan put up a sign that read "Combat the Menace! Get Your Ludwig Button." Within a few weeks, the Yalies claimed to have 20,000 supporters. Supposedly, even famous musicians such as Issac Stern and Eugene Ormandy were seen wearing Ludwig buttons. Before 1957 was out, some teenagers began sporting "I Hate Elvis" buttons. Never one to miss an opportunity to make a buck, Colonel Parker decided to take advantage of the anti-Presley movement when he began selling "I Hate Elvis" buttons at concerts right alongside the more common "I Love Elvis" variety. At a Detroit concert, a group of Elvis fans refused to let a young girl take her seat until after she removed her "I Hate Elvis" button.[28]

Elvis was perplexed and hurt by all the venomous attacks. After all, his parents had raised him to be a good Christian, to always do the right thing, and to always be polite to everyone he met. He wasn't trying to be obscene on stage nor did he think he was undermining the morals of young people. "I can't really understand [the criticisms]," he said in August 1956. "I can tell you this, though. I don't scheme up any actions for the songs I sing, like I've heard some people tell. I sing the way I do, and act the way I do, because it comes natural to me when I'm singing. I wouldn't do it if I thought it wasn't the right thing to do, or if I thought someone was being hurt by it." Over the next several months, he continued to proclaim his innocence. "Some people seem to have the idea that I'm a controversial influence on the young folks," he said in a January interview distributed to disc jockeys across the country. "Whatever I do, I always want to do my best for the teenagers. I certainly never wanna do anything that would be a wrong influence. When I sing, I just . . . I just sing from my heart." A few months later, he assured an interviewer, "I certainly don't mean to be vulgar or suggestive, and I don't think I am. . . . That's just my way of expressing songs. You can't stand there like a statue."[29]

When a reporter asked Elvis if it was true that the Mexican government was banning him because his singing "lacked esthetic values and is pornographic," the singer was defiant. "Pornographic? I don't rightfully know what that means. But if it means obscene, it just ain't true," he insisted. "That's something I've had to fight all the time. People claim I do bumps and grinds. Why, I never did a bump or grind in my life. I've been to the burlesque show. I know what bumps and grinds are. But I'd never do them. I couldn't live with myself if I did. Why, I'd never think of putting on an obscene show for teenagers! If I thought I was, I'd quit. If you sow the bad seed, you've got to reap the result. I'd never be a party to putting on a dirty show."[30]

Elvis was just as adamant when he responded to charges that he caused juvenile delinquency. "I don't see that," he said, "because if there is anything I have tried to do, I've tried to live a straight, clean life, not set any kind of a bad example." When a reporter asked him if he thought his rambunctious fans had lost their morals or manners, he immediately responded, "No, they haven't. They're growing up, you know, and they're having a nice time and nobody's gonna stop that." Elvis suggested that all of this was just good, clean American fun. "I mean the only way they gonna stop that is for the United States to turn Communist." Elvis emphasized that his fans weren't bad, they were just trying to have a ball while they were still young. "I know I don't blame 'em and I don't see why anybody else should."[31]

Presley defended his fans on numerous other occasions, always care-ful to point out that these teenagers were not hoodlums. "Sure, they get a little enthusiastic, but I've never had a destructive crowd. They've never torn up the seats or ruined the theater or anything like that," he explained. "Adults don't understand those kids. When you're young, you've got a lot of energy and enthusiasm. You've got to blow it off somehow. That's what kids do when they see my shows. Later, when they grow up, they'll lose a lot of that energy and they'll act like grown-ups."[32]

Not all adults condemned Elvis. Many parents, teachers, ministers, and others acknowledged that the young singer might be different, but he certainly was not a threat to teenagers or anybody else. In early 1957, journalist Fred Sparks summed up the pro-Elvis arguments in a column syndicated by the Scripps-Howard chain. "I like Elvis Presley," he be-gan. "I am bored to illness by the eggheads, long-hairs, tea-cup tipplers, self-appointed moralists and arty snobs who are running around this country . . . saying: 'Elvis Presley must go. . . . He's a bad example for our young people.'" Sparks went on to praise Elvis, comparing him to Will Rogers, Carl Sandburg, and American folk heroes. Sparks insisted that if Elvis is indecent then "so are half the bestseller books, three quarters of the paintings in the nation's galleries, Helen Hayes, and one-piece bathing suits." Nor are Elvis's "leg-wiggles and mouth-twist-ings" that much different from square dance callers or ballerinas. Sparks added perceptively: "Most of the songs he has single-handedly rocketed to the hit parade stratosphere are also happy hollerings of Americana. I'm positive the words of 'You're Nothing but a Hound Dog' and 'Heartbreak Hotel' will be picked over by historians as mad, jolly mutterings of our golden era just like long hairs today treat as holy these medleys of our depression: 'Brother, Can You Spare a Dime?' and 'Let's Have Another Cup of Coffee.'"[33]

Others in the media likewise praised Elvis Presley. Reporters wrote often about how Elvis was charitable, polite, earnest, soft-spoken, and basically just a fine, young man. After James Gregory, the editor of *Movieland and TV Time*, met the young singer for the first time, he reported back to his readers: "I'd like to assure you that [Elvis is] one of the nicest, brightest, most well-mannered young men I've ever met."[34]

Regardless of whether people loved Elvis or hated him, one thing is certain: nobody was ignoring Presley. In just one short year, Elvis

Presley had gone from being a little-known country singer to the hottest act in America. The *Tupelo Daily Journal* called him "the young prince of rock 'n' roll . . . who is a guitar playing Pied Piper."[35] Before he was through, Elvis would be elevated to the undisputed "King of Rock & Roll."

ELVIS PRESLEY AND AMERICAN CULTURE

Elvis was not the inventor of rock & roll or even its first star. But he certainly did more than any other artist to popularize the new sound. His inimitable style and unique blend of R&B, pop, and country music helped him land an incredible 101 hits on the Top 40 record charts—including eighteen number 1 hits—between 1956 and his death in 1977. (Perhaps even more astonishing, he earned four additional Top 40 hits after his death, including "A Little Less Conversation," an electronic remix of an earlier Elvis recording that became a worldwide dance hit in 2002.)

As Elvis racked up hit after hit, several themes emerged. He sang about teenage love on songs such as "Heartbreak Hotel" and "Love Me Tender." He focused on teen interests ("Blue Suede Shoes") and traditional values ("Money Honey" and "Old Shep"), as well as teenage bravado and defiance ("Baby Let's Play House" and "Hound Dog"). Elvis could rock with the best rhythm & blues shouters, and then croon out a slow ballad à la Dean Martin that sent chills up girls' spines.

Presley was undeniably the biggest star of rock & roll's first decade. The big question is: *why* was he so phenomenally successful? There are the obvious reasons: teenagers loved his music; they thought Elvis was cool; he had matinee-idol looks and was sexy; and he was outrageous—from his slicked-back hair and long sideburns to his wild clothes and uninhibited performances.

Audiences probably responded so enthusiastically to Elvis for the same reasons that had first attracted Sam Phillips: this kid was *different*. He sounded different, looked different, and performed in a different way. Presley had an authentic feel for the music and a knack for connecting with young audiences. He spoke directly to their interests, their values, and their desires. "I watch my audience, and I listen to them," explained Elvis, "and I know that we're all getting something out of our systems, but none of us knows what it is."[36]

Elvis may not have understood, but many females knew exactly what *it* was: Elvis was the best-looking and sexiest guy they had ever seen. His bedroom eyes, the sneer on his lip, the dark wavy hair, long sideburns, extraordinary good looks, and sexy moves attracted women like a magnet. Sonny West, a high school friend who later became part of Elvis's entourage, recalls the incredible effect that Elvis had on Sonny's date at an Elvis concert. According to Sonny, the young lady had a "demeanor and looks" that suggested "that when someone invented virginity and apple pie, they must have had her in mind." A half hour into the concert, "she was behaving totally out of character—like a sex-starved little nymphet." Sonny had no doubts that Elvis caused the girl's transformation. There Elvis was onstage, remembers West, "straddling the microphone in the most suggestive of manners. His groin gyrated inches from the upright stand, and he was shaking in convulsive movements as if possessed by an alien spirit. When he sang quietly he sobbed. When he sang loudly, he commanded his worshippers." West's date was not the only female in the audience under Elvis's spell. Sonny remembers that most of the females in the audience were whipped into a sexual frenzy. "Every time [Elvis] moved, it seemed like a couple of hundred gals were getting it off."[37]

Many observers were impressed by Presley's close relationship to women. "Elvis seems to come alive only when a girl is around," said reporter Kay Gary. And it was not just a sexual thing. Young girls and older women alike were attracted by his charisma, charm, and constant flirting. Gary recalls seeing Elvis flirting with numerous young women in a restaurant. "He stood chest-to-chest with one, running his fingers lightly around the blouse ruffles. And she stood still and said nothing while he talked to her in a low voice." Elvis's sexuality hit women on several levels. Linda Thompson, who became Elvis's girlfriend in the early 1970s, insists that she never met a man as "dichotomous" as Elvis. "On the one hand, he exuded untamed sexuality," she explains. "On the other, he was like a pious little choirboy." Other women were similarly attracted to his childlike innocence. Actress Natalie Wood noted his "wonderful little-boy quality." His wife, Priscilla Beaulieu Presley, explained: "Elvis brought out this mothering quality. . . . We'd all baby him. Then you'd see him on stage and he looked so strong and so virile, it was like *Oh My God*. But there was this child that was still in him."[38]

If some fans loved Elvis for his looks and charisma, others were turned on by his unique sound. It epitomized how rock & roll was a hybrid of black rhythm & blues, white country, and traditional pop. Sam Phillips explained that Elvis "has a white voice, [and] sings with a negro rhythm which borrows in mood and emphasis from country style." Other white singers like Bill Haley and Pat Boone had copied rhythm & blues before, but Elvis was no mere imitator. He lived it and felt it. That authenticity came through loud and clear in his music. Elvis's version of Big Mama Thornton's number 1 R&B hit, "Hound Dog," is a perfect example. No mere cover version, Elvis made the song his own—much to the chagrin of the song's writers, Jerry Leiber and Mike Stoller, who initially thought it sounded "terribly nervous, too fast—and too white." Only after the royalties came pouring in did the two songwriters realize how wrong they had been. Elvis's rendition might not have been as bluesy as Leiber and Stoller liked, but it clearly appealed to white teenagers in a way that Big Mama Thornton's version never could. Elvis's "Hound Dog" had a youthful energy, subversive-sounding lyrics that suggested sex, and an explosive sound that virtually assaulted the listener. Elvis had transformed Leiber and Stoller's R&B song into pure rock & roll. And the more adults were turned off by it, the more young people tuned in. "I happened to come along at a time in the music business when there was no trend. I was lucky," he said modestly. "The people were looking for something different. I came along just in time." Elvis and his unique sound became the personification of rock & roll.[39]

Elvis's unusual appearance attracted attention as much as his sound. An early photograph taken of Elvis and fellow performers on radio's *Louisiana Hayride* clearly shows the contrast. Almost all the males are dressed in western garb, including cowboy hats, western suits, and cowboy shirts and ties. And there's Elvis way off at the end of the line with his hands in his pockets looking like he just stepped off Beale Street in Memphis, sporting pegged pants, a flashy sport coat, no tie, and an open shirt with the collar turned up. [40] Elvis's appearance was as shocking and as different as his music. His overall look and outrageous clothing sent a visual message of nonconformity, if not outright rebellion. For 1950s America accustomed to conformity and the buttoned-down look of Madison Avenue, Elvis's slicked-back hair and long sideburns were a frontal assault on the status quo. For a population accustomed to oatmeal-colored khakis, drab olive greens, and the muted colors associated with the World War II era and the Great Depression, the bright colors and wild clothing styles favored by Elvis—neon pink, bright chartreuse, polka dots, stripes, plaids, fitted sport coats, and pegged pants— were nothing short of stunning. Even in high school, Elvis was different. "If he had a regular haircut like the rest of us, he probably wouldn't have been bothered [by classmates]," explains high school friend Red West. "But I guess the other kids thought he was trying to show off or something. That hair has always been his crowning glory. I have never known any other human to take more time over his hair. He would spend hours on it, smoothing, mussing it up and combing it and combing it again."[41]

Elvis acted as cool as he looked. His uninhibited stage performances caused pandemonium. "He really knew how to manipulate an audience," notes Red West. "He knew exactly when to hit them with fast tunes that whipped them up, and he knew exactly when to hit them with ballads and love songs. If any audience doesn't warm to him immediately, he uses every trick in the business." For Elvis, that meant talking playfully, sometimes coyly, to audiences, using suggestive moves, and dancing wildly to the beat, rocking on his heels, rolling his hips, and shaking his legs. Audiences went crazy. Girls screamed in delight. Couples wound up dancing in the aisles. That response was evident right from the very beginning. "As the featured entertainer at the grand opening of a new business arcade," noted a reporter in 1955, "[Elvis] played to a wildly enthusiastic audience of more than 3000 who couldn't restrain themselves and started dancing and jitterbugging." Adults were shocked at the explicit sexuality of his performance style. But the young singer just shrugged it off, saying innocently, if not disingenuously, "People say I'm vulgar. They say I use my hips disgustingly. But that's my way of putting over a song. I have to move. When I have a lot of energy, I move more. I lose three to four pounds a performance. I've always done it this way."[42]

Despite Elvis's protestations, many in conservative 1950s America viewed him as a subversive nonconformist. Critics condemned his "suggestive" and "vulgar" approach to music; church leaders damned his lewd songs and performances; parents feared his rebellious look and

deportment would lead their children astray; and paranoid conservatives in the wake of McCarthyism hinted that Presley might be part of a
communist plot to undermine American values and democracy. Ironically, even the communists were scared of Elvis, calling him a "weapon
in the American psychological war to infect a part of the population
with the philosophical outlook of inhumanity . . . to destroy everything
that is beautiful."[43]

While Elvis was hardly the threat to civilization that his critics made
him out to be, his overall sound, style, and appearance certainly pushed
the limits of American society and culture. Many young people viewed
Presley as a refreshing antidote to crewcuts and other conservative
styles of 1950s America. His mixture of black rhythm & blues and white
country and pop suggested cultural integration at a time when segregation was the unofficial, if not official, law of the land. His sexy songs and
uninhibited performance style challenged accepted norms. And his outrageous appearance was in blatant defiance of the era's clean-cut, buttoned-down look.

But if many teenagers viewed Elvis as a rebel, they also knew in their
hearts that he was no wild-eyed radical. The rock & roll hero believed in
God, respected his parents, was always polite to adults, and loved his
country from its purple mountain majesties down to its apple pie, hot
dogs, and cars. Most of Elvis's young fans weren't seeking a cultural
revolution; they just wanted to have fun. And Elvis was showing them
the way.

Fans could relate to Elvis's puckish sense of humor that ranged from
witty to sophomoric. He could play the clown on stage, as he did aping
fear on the *Milton Berle Show* in 1956 when Irish McCalla, the stat-
uesque star of TV's *Sheena Queen of the Jungle*, held a knife to his
throat. Or he could play the role of a trickster, poking fun at the Establishment and social conventions. When one reporter asked him a serious question about his contribution to American culture, Elvis dead-
panned, "Like income taxes, you mean?" On another occasion, he displayed his ostentatious jewelry to an audience, explaining, "I just
wanted to show you all this because you paid for it."[44]

Fans loved Elvis in part because in many ways he was just like them.
He talked like them, joked like them, and enjoyed the same junk foods
and lifestyles. The only big difference was that Elvis was actually experi-
encing the kind of phenomenal success that most young people could

only dream about. Still, Elvis did it in a way that fans could relate to. The singer's legendary generosity is a perfect example. Many fans appreciated the way Elvis gave countless gifts to people in his life. After all, if they suddenly came into a lot of money the way Elvis had, they liked to think that they would be doing the same thing, too. That's why Presley's legion of fans smiled and nodded approvingly when they read in newspapers and magazines that Elvis not only purchased a house for his parents and a pink Cadillac for himself, but he also bought his friends cars, jewelry, and clothes. He even gave presents to perfect strangers. "Money's meant to be spread around," explained Elvis. "The more happiness it helps create, the more it's worth."[45]

Elvis was a success in part because he was all things to all people. Marion Keisker noticed it at once. "This boy has something that seems to appeal to everybody," she said shortly after Elvis signed with Sun Records. She was right in more ways than she knew. Elvis was a walking, talking, singing Rorshach inkblot. Fans saw in Elvis what they wanted to see: good looks, a new style, sex, rebellion, wildness, or alternately traditional values and conservative beliefs. Perhaps the one thing that everyone could agree on was that Elvis was unique. He had a different look, a different sound, and a different style. Even his name was distinct.[46] Elvis Presley was an American original. That, in itself, explains his phenomenal success.

While much of Elvis Presley's success can be attributed to his good looks, talent, performance style, and other personal qualities, the times and external forces also helped make the man. The rising power of the modern media played a major role in shaping Presley's destiny. Elvis's chances for success were greatly enhanced when Sam Phillips sold his contract to RCA Records, one of the nation's leading record companies. RCA enabled Elvis to record with talented producers and musicians and to use state-of-the-art recording equipment and studios, and it provided him with large advertising budgets and all the connections he needed to become a national star. Extensive media exposure on national television, on radio, in movies, and in print riveted public attention on the young singer and powered his rising star. And, of course, Elvis's astute manager, Colonel Tom Parker, guided Elvis's rise to the top through shrewd deals, innovative promotions, and comprehensive marketing campaigns. "Without Colonel Tom there would never be an Elvis Presley," noted Sonny West. "They are both part of a whole."[47]

Elvis Presley plugged into American culture on a variety of levels. His success and mystique were intertwined with the dichotomies and tensions that could be found in 1950s America. Elvis reflected the era's conflict and consensus, change and continuity, affluence and anxiety. He embodied the changing times when it came to race, gender, and youth. At the same time, he also represented the staying power of traditional American values involving family, capitalism, patriotism, and religion.

For many listeners, Elvis was a culture hero who symbolized rock & roll, the new generation, and a new way of life on the 1950s horizon. Taking black songs and making them respectable for whites, Presley helped complete the transformation of R&B race music into rock & roll. In the process, he became rock & roll's answer to James Dean—a role model for alienated youths. Elvis wore his cool persona and a seemingly everpresent sneer like nonconformist badges as he sang wild rock & roll songs, thrust his pelvis to the beat, and appeared in outrageous clothes, a D.A. style haircut, and long sideburns.

Unlike Dean's rebel without a cause, Elvis was a man with a mission. He introduced millions of young people to the new world of rock & roll. And audiences couldn't get enough of his unrestrained vocals and physical movements that radiated sexual electricity. The rock & roll Adonis looked amazing on stage, wiggling his hips, shakin' to the beat, and rockin' up a storm. Whether he was dressed in wild pink shirts, all black, or his notorious gold-speckled suit, Elvis suggested that uninhibited pleasure was what the music was all about. Implicit in his music and performance style was a questioning of 1950s conformity. The music's driving beat, the jive talk, the uninhibited sexuality, and the cat clothes were all indictments of 1950s segregation policies and consensus behavior. "It wasn't just the way Elvis looked, it was the way he moved that made people crazy, pissed off, driven to screaming ecstasy, and profane revulsion," explains Bruce Springsteen. "Elvis was the first modern 20th-century man, the precursor of the sexual revolution, of the civil rights revolution."[48]

Yet Elvis was not just a cultural rebel. Paradoxically, the young man from Memphis also represented traditional beliefs. He personified the American myth of success. His career was a classic rags-to-riches tale: poor country boy strikes it rich in the big city. Elvis dramatically proved that even a southern boy from humble origins could escape from poverty if he worked hard and had faith in God, country, and motherhood. His 1962 hit "Follow That Dream" summed up in less than two minutes what Elvis represented throughout his career. He never gave up. He pursued his dream until he caught it. The reward was all the fame, fortune, and glory America had to offer. Horatio Alger could not have created a better American archetype.

Elvis transcended mere material success. He embodied American democracy and the notion of equal opportunity. The young Elvis personified Thomas Jefferson's agrarian myth—the idealized American with roots in the soil, untainted by the corrupting influences of civilization and cities. Elvis was down to earth, pious, respectful, capable, yet modest. "Some people can't figure out how Elvis Presley happened," he explained. "I don't blame them for wondering that. Sometimes I wonder myself."[49] Such humility struck a responsive chord. In true American fashion, success had pursued the man, until the man caught it. Like Andrew Jackson, Abe Lincoln, and others from the pantheon of American folk heroes, Elvis made it big, but he remained the common man.

Presley reflected other traditional values. Family, community, and God were always integral parts of Elvis's identity. "The happiest times I've ever had have been with my family," he explained. "In fact, I can't wait to get home every once in a while to be with my mother and daddy. And we all have fun together. We sit around and watch television, go to movies, go for drives on Sunday afternoons. Different things." Presley always made it clear that he was extremely religious. He sang "Peace in the Valley" on one of his first TV appearances and later recorded an entire album of sacred songs. "I believe in God, I believe in Him with all my heart," he said. "Being religious means that you love God and are real grateful for all He's given, and want to work for Him. I feel deep in my heart that I'm doing all this."[50]

Of course, piety and profits traditionally went hand in hand in America. Elvis was no exception. Presley made a ton of money and became a glitzy symbol of American capitalism and conspicuous consumption. He bought big-ticket items like houses and cars, and anything else that caught his eye, including clothes, jewelry, toys, sports equipment, TVs, radios, record players, and movie-making equipment. He frequently paid his friends' way at amusement parks and movie theaters. Newspapers reported that Elvis bought cars for every day of the week (he was so fond of his pink Cadillac that he bought a pink suit to go along with it). When questioned about all the automobiles, he joked, "I was thinking about a Presley used car lot." The more money he made, the more he spent. And the more he spent, the more Americans loved him. After all, wouldn't they do the same if they could? It was like a fairy tale. Imagine a little boy in a toy store who could afford any toys he wanted. That was Elvis. His innocent approach to consumption ("Aw shucks, I'm just havin' some fun") was charming not greedy. His ability to fulfill every wish smacked of Aladdin's lamp. And his propensity for lavishing Cadillacs and gifts on friends and strangers recalled the Good Samaritan and Robin Hood.[51]

Elvis made it to the top of his chosen profession. That achievement alone, in the eyes of Americans who valued excellence, made Presley worthy of adulation. He was the undisputed "King of Rock & Roll"—a talented performer and singer, innovative yet traditional. Elvis had it all: good looks, sex appeal, charisma, a sense of humor, humility, ambition, ability, and luck. Plus, he was colorful and Americans always liked exciting heroes. Elvis knew exactly what he wanted to do, and he accomplished it with a flourish. His fourteen consecutive million-sellers and legions of fans stand as testimony to his greatness. His shining star lit the way for others who followed, from early rock & rollers like Jerry Lee Lewis and Buddy Holly to later superstars such as the Beatles, Bob Dylan, and Bruce Springsteen. Perhaps Buddy Holly put it best: "Without Elvis Presley, none of us could have made it."[52]

Elvis had universal appeal. Unruly teens emulated his look and style. Less rebellious fans loved him as a teen idol. Mothers saw him as a son. Country & western fans cheered him as a good ol' boy. Religious fans welcomed him as a fellow traveler. He was a rocker, a pop singer, a country artist, a blues singer, a sacred music artist, a matinee idol, a TV and movie star, and a friend everyone thought they knew. His wide appeal made him a legend in his own time. And Elvis's career reflects those years. If his music had roots in the biracial culture of the rural South, his success was tied to new developments in post–World War II America, including the rise of new media, mass advertising, and sweeping demographic change. The mass movement of southern blacks and whites to northern cities, along with the rise of post–World War II youth culture, set the stage for Elvis's drama.

The mixed response to the coming of Elvis says a great deal about 1950s America. Reflecting the era's anxieties and conformity, cultural conservatives bombarded Presley with "Elvis the Pelvis" jokes and other boorish remarks. Other fearful adults blasted Elvis as a threat to morality, segregation, religion, traditional music, and social order. Still others had no idea what to make of the odd-looking singer. But many young people understood intuitively. They greeted Elvis as a rock & roll prophet who could deliver them from the sins and constraints of 1950s conservatism. Presley became a culture hero, representing the new youth culture, as well as traditional beliefs involving God, love, family, and country. He symbolized tradition and innovation, opportunity, racial harmony, freedom, individualism, capitalism, and the pursuit of happiness.

Elvis changed America. "Television and Elvis gave us full access to a new language, a new form of communication," explains Bruce Springsteen, "a new way of being, a new way of looking, a new way of thinking about sex, about race, about identity, about life; a new way of being an American, a human being; and a new way of hearing music. Once Elvis came across the airwaves, once he was heard and seen in action, you could not put the genie back in the bottle. After that moment, there was yesterday, and there was today, and there was a red hot, rockabilly forging of a new tomorrow, before your very eyes."[53]

As the "King of Rock & Roll," Elvis Presley personified the myths and beliefs of his subjects. His songs and style reflected the dreams, interests, and values of the American people. When all is said and done, it is impossible to fully explain all the reasons why Elvis made it so big. Perhaps the most succinct explanation can be found on a Coasters' record from 1957 entitled "What Is the Secret of Your Success?" Written by Jerry Leiber and Mike Stoller (who also composed "Hound Dog"), the song suggests a simple but obvious answer: "Some cats got it and, uh, some cats ain't."[54]

By the end of 1956, Elvis Presley was the undisputed "King of Rock & Roll." Thanks to records, radio, television, movies, and other media, millions had witnessed Elvis's ascension to the throne. Like the young King Arthur drawing the sword from the stone, the lad from Memphis established his claim to the crown through an equally unforgettable act. Elvis Presley walked onto the national stage and unleashed an uninhibited performance style that left American culture "all shook up." Nobody had ever seen or heard anything quite like this before. The man who would be "King of Rock & Roll" had arrived. Neither popular music nor America would ever be the same.

III

After Elvis: The Growth of Rock & Roll (1956)

6

THE GIRL CAN'T HELP IT!

Rock & Roll and the Media

The ascension of Elvis Presley to the heights of pop music stardom would not have happened as quickly or as completely without the aid of national media. Movies, television, radio, newspapers, magazines, and books all played an important role promoting not just Elvis but also rock & roll in general. For professional and commercial reasons, the media were attracted to the new teenage craze like moths drawn to light. A good example is a motion picture released by Twentieth Century Fox in December, 1956. Entitled *The Girl Can't Help It*, the film featured Tom Ewell as theatrical agent Tom Miller, who is hired by former gangster Fats Murdock (Edmond O'Brien) to turn his girlfriend, a blonde bombshell named Jerri Jordan (Jayne Mansfield), into a successful rock & roll singer. Film historian Douglas Brode describes the movie as "a light comedy which attempted to tread a delicate balance between satirizing the newly popular rock 'n' roll and exploiting the phenomenon to the hilt."[1] (figure 6.1).

The movie begins with an introduction filmed in black and white. Ewell, dressed in a tuxedo with tails, steps forward onto a small stage to address the viewers. A drum set, saxophone, banjo, and cello are suspended behind him. "Ladies and gentlemen," he says bowing politely, "the motion picture you are about to see is a story of music." He explains it is filmed in the "grandeur of Cinema-Scope." He does a double-take and then pushes out the screen on each side, widening the

Figure 6.1.   Publicity shot of Jayne Mansfield for the 1956 movie, *The Girl Can't Help It*. (Richard Aquila Collection)

picture so it shows a wider stage with a harp on the left and piano on the right. And, he adds, this movie is filmed in "glorious life-like color by

DeLuxe." When he repeats the sentence, the film is transformed instantly from its original, drab black and white into amazing color. "Our story is about music," he continues, "not the music of long ago but the music that expresses the culture, the refinement, and the total grace of the present day." Suddenly, a jukebox lights up and a record blasts, drowning out Ewell's voice. Credits flash on the screen as Little Richard screams out lyrics to the title song: "The girl can't help it if she was born to please." Background singers shout in agreement.[2] As the credits roll, young couples bathed in bright pink, green, and blue lights dance passionately to the song.

Compared to other early rock & roll films that were B-movies at best, *The Girl Can't Help It* is a virtual extravaganza. Not only is it filmed in color and Cinemascope, but it spares no expense when it comes to sets, costumes, performers, or production crew. Jayne Mansfield's wardrobe budget alone cost $35,000. Along with the stars already mentioned, the supporting cast included well-known actors Henry Jones and John Emery and established pop stars Julie London and Ray Anthony. The movie was written and directed by Hollywood veteran Frank Tashlin, music was conducted by the accomplished Lionel Newman, and the title song was written by well-known composer and performer Bobby Troup. Of course, this movie—like earlier rock & roll flicks—showcased rock & roll singers to attract young audiences. It featured a lineup of fourteen different rock & roll acts singing seventeen songs.

One movie poster features Jayne Mansfield bending over in a tight, low-cut dress, ogled by Tom Ewell. A smaller picture in the left-hand corner shows the couple kissing. Across the top are pictures of rock & roll stars who appear in the film, including Eddie Cochran ready for action with his guitar, Little Richard singing while banging his foot on his piano, and Gene Vincent strumming on his guitar. A roster of all the rock & roll singers in the film completes the poster, listing Fats Domino, the Platters, Gene Vincent and His Blue Caps, and other lesser-known performers. The headline on the poster says it all: "It's got the Heat! And the Beat!"[3]

The Girl Can't Help It is probably the best rock & roll movie of the 1950s. The film actually had a plot, even subplots. "As the story unfolds," writes rock & roll singer and movie buff Marshall Crenshaw, "we get a hilarious look at the sleazy machinations of the jukebox and record businesses."[4] Though hardly Oscar quality, the movie at least keeps the viewers' attention with Ewell, O'Brien, Jones, and Mansfield turning in excellent performances.

No viewer will ever forget Jayne Mansfield walking down the street, strutting her stuff to the beat of Little Richard's sexy "The Girl Can't Help It." Men can't avert their eyes as she wiggles by, dressed in a tight black dress with a slit up the front and a plunging neckline. A man delivering ice watches in awe, as his ice melts; a milkman looks down at her cleavage from his perch on the steps of an apartment building, and as she turns toward him to enter the building, he gapes at her incredible hourglass figure while milk erupts from his bottle; inside, a resident bends over to pick up his morning paper and milk, and when he sees her shapely legs climb the stairs, his glasses shatter.

Some of the rock & roll performances are equally memorable. Captured forever in brilliant color by DeLuxe are a very young-looking Fats Domino, smiling and charming his way through "Blue Monday"; a frenetic Little Richard decked out in pegged pants and drape suit coat shouting out the lyrics to "The Girl Can't Help It"; Eddie Cochran doing his best Elvis imitation on "Twenty Flight Rock"; a wild-looking Gene Vincent and His Blue Caps unleashing a show-stopping performance of "Be Bop-a-Lula"; or the Platters harmonizing to a doo-wop ballad and displaying choreographed moves with the four guys dressed in light green tuxes and red-plaid bowties and the lone woman wearing a stunning emerald gown, all set against a matching green backdrop (figure 6.2).

The Girl Can't Help It is just one example of many media attempts to cash in on the new rock & roll phenomenon that had the nation abuzz in 1956. Just as the girl in the film couldn't help it that she was born to please, rock & roll couldn't help it that media were attracted to the new sound. The emergence of Elvis Presley created a media feeding frenzy, as print journalism, books, radio, movies, and television served up tons of information about the young singer and the new rock & roll sound. Throughout the rest of the decade, the audience for rock & roll would expand considerably as a variety of media riveted public attention on the coming of the King and his Court.

Figure 6.2. The Platters were one of the most successful vocal groups of the 1950s. (Photo by "PoPsie" Randolph L.L.C.; courtesy of Michael Randolph, executor to the estate of William "PoPsie" Randolph)

PRINT MEDIA PROMOTE ROCK & ROLL

It is hard to tell whether Elvis Presley or the media benefited more from the symbiotic relationship they developed in the 1950s. Presleymania was aided and abetted by all the attention Elvis got in print and electronic media. But the media profited by serving up large helpings of Elvis stories to a public hungry for information about the young Hillbilly Cat. As Elvis's popularity soared, rock & roll went along for the ride.

Newspapers, magazines, and books zeroed in on the rock & roll craze. Local papers across the nation followed Elvis's every move. Here's how a San Diego paper described a Presley concert: "[Presley] followed a woman vocalist, an acrobatic dance team, a comedian, and a xylophone player. The audience stomped their feet [and yelled] 'We want Elvis.' And then he appeared. The boys cheered and whistled. The

girls screamed, jumped, and clapped." A Minneapolis newspaper reported a similar response as "Elvis Presley, young bump and grind
artist, turned a rainy Sunday afternoon into an orgy of squealing in St.
Paul auditorium." Presley was more subdued in Jacksonville, Florida. A
newspaper pointed out that a local judge advised Elvis before his first
show "to 'keep it clean' or face court charges." Noting all the media
attention the singer was getting, the reporter added, "Presley . . . spent
his spare time between performances posing for magazine, television
and newspaper photographers and answering reporters' questions."[5]

Magazines also tracked Elvis. In 1956 alone, he was the sole subject
in eleven different magazines. He appeared on the cover of numerous
others ranging from *TV Guide* to *Photoplay*. On May 14, 1956, *Time*
reported: "He is Elvis Aaron Presley, a drape-suited, tight-trousered
young man of 21 and the sight and sound of him drive teenage girls
wild." A few months later, *Life* magazine ran a nine-page spread—
"Elvis: A Different Kind of Idol." A December issue of *Cosmopolitan*
educated readers with a feature story entitled "What Is an Elvis
Presley?" Not a week went by without *Time* and *Newsweek* spotlighting
the new singer.[6] Throughout 1956 and beyond, the press followed his
every move, focusing on Elvis's music, love life, clothes, cars, houses,
personal habits, or anything else that could attract readers. A letter to
the editor of *Life* magazine in 1956 suggests the reason behind the
extensive press coverage: "Sirs: We want to thank you for that picture
spread you had about our 'dream baby'—Elvis . . . The 'cats' here in
Philly are wild about Elvis. He's the 'king,' the supreme ruler."[7]

News stories were not limited to Elvis. *Life* magazine ran a piece in
1955 about the new "frenzied teenage music craze" that was causing "a
big fuss" around the nation. Other stories focused on the growing popularity of the new sound. "Economists have long predicted that the flood
of new babies born during the recent war would one day make themselves felt as a greatly inflated teen-age market," noted a music industry
trade magazine in January 1956. As proof of the growing popularity of
the new teen-oriented music, the magazine cites recent releases such as
"Teen-Age Prayer," "Teen-Age Heart," "Teen-Age Meeting," and
"Nina, Queen of the Teeners." Some stories attacked rock & roll. *Time*
gave it a particularly scorching review on June 18, 1956, as the country
was in the midst of Presleymania. The music is too loud, declared the
magazine, while rock & roll lyrics are "nonsense" or "moronic." Another

Time article that same year complained that rock & roll did for music "what a motorcycle club at full throttle does for a quiet Sunday afternoon."[8] Very likely, those kinds of criticisms by adults only added to the music's popularity among teenagers.

Regardless of whether they came to praise or bury rock & roll, print journalists realized that stories about Elvis and the new music boosted circulation. That's why both general circulation magazines such as *TV Guide, TV Radio Mirror, Movieland and TV Time, Popular TV, Photoplay,* and *TV Movie Screen,* as well as more specialized teen-oriented magazines like *Movie Teen, Dig, Teensville, Teen Hop, Hep Cats, Juke Box Stars, Modern Teen, Rock and Roll Round Up, Sixteen Magazine, Teen Life,* and *Teen* were soon spotlighting rock & roll. For example, *TV Guide* ran a cover story entitled "The Plain Truth about Elvis Presley." *TV Radio Mirror* put Elvis and Ed Sullivan on the cover, promising the inside scoop not only about Elvis's TV appearance but also an exclusive on "The Girl Who Got to Presley." *Private Lives*—a magazine devoted to gossipy stories about Hollywood stars and celebrities—featured a story about Elvis that asked the question, "Ants in His Pants?" Magazines also spotlighted Pat Boone, Bill Haley, Alan Freed, and any other rock & roll heroes who could help sales.[9]

Books likewise promoted rock & roll. Publishers realized that teenagers were eager to buy and read anything that was even remotely linked to the new music. Cheap paperbacks soon arrived on the scene, including James Gregory's *The Elvis Presley Story* and Ernie Weatherall's *Rock 'n Roll Gal* (the cover featured a young blonde in a tight sweater and short shorts pressing her body up against a muscular teenage boy with Elvis-style hair). In the end, it almost didn't matter if the books, stories, or articles about rock & roll were positive or negative. In either case, they called attention to the new music and helped spread the popularity of the new sound.

RADIO AND ROCK & ROLL

Radio provided even greater exposure for rock & roll. Unlike print media, radio was instantaneous, allowing audiences to hear their favorite songs and singers and not just read about them. The rise of rock & roll was intertwined with the growing popularity of Top 40 radio in the mid-1950s. The new music arrived on the scene just as radio stations were searching desperately for a way to survive. The coming of television in the decade after World War II threatened more traditional forms of entertainment like radio, movies, and print journalism with extinction. Here's how quickly television took over: in 1946, there were only 10,000 TV sets in the United States; by the end of the decade, there were over a million; and by 1952, there were 27 million. Four years later, 64.5 percent of all American homes had one or more TV sets. Network radio witnessed an immediate impact as their advertising revenue plummeted from $134 million in 1948 to $103 million by 1952. Those ad dollars were heading toward TV. Radio knew it had to change with the times or become extinct. [10]

Luckily, radio was not totally without ammunition for its battle against television. For one thing, it had easy access to the audience. A 1953 survey found that 96 percent of all American homes owned at least one radio; 13 million Americans owned portable radios; and 71 percent of all automobiles had radios. What's more, 66 percent of all respondents reported that they listened to the radio every day. Radio had other advantages. By the late 1940s, improved recording techniques that made use of magnetic tape recorders allowed for better quality and cheaper transmission of recorded sound. Disc jockeys who played recorded music like Martin Block in New York, Al Jarvis in Los Angeles, and Dave Garroway in Chicago were also growing in popularity by the 1940s. The U.S. government's decision to award more radio licenses in the fifteen years following World War II gave birth to numerous locally owned stations across the country as the total number of stations mushroomed from 973 in 1945 to 4,306 by 1960. Throughout the 1950s, these new stations were desperately looking for ways to attract larger audiences at a time when many listeners were turning to television. [11] And then, along came rock & roll. To say the radio industry took notice would be an understatement.

Rock & roll would become one of radio's biggest weapons in the war against television. By the early 1950s, network radio was cutting back programming, substituting prerecorded material for live entertainment, and even slashing advertising rates to survive. Programmers began scurrying about looking for new ways to compete. Radio pioneer Bill Gavin explains one of the most important solutions they hit on: "Hundreds of radio stations . . . had been making handsome profits [before the coming of TV] without a network [affiliation], simply by identifying with the preferences and concerns of their local listeners. In doing so, radio spawned a new breed of broadcast entertainer, the disc jockey."[12]

Through disc jockeys and radio, rock & roll strengthened its grassroots connections to audiences across America. Deejays became the high priests of the teenagers' new musical religion. Riding the airwaves, they accompanied kids to and from school, they spoke to them in cars, on the beaches, at parties, and even in the privacy of young listeners' bedrooms. Disc jockeys became cultural middlemen offering young audiences admission into the world of rock & roll. They talked in slang kids understood. They hosted record hops and emceed openings of bowling alleys, drive-ins, soda shops, Laundromats, and other local businesses. And they welcomed young people to their radio shows each day and night. They introduced listeners to all the latest hits and newest releases and provided behind-the-scenes tidbits about the rock & roll scene. All the while, radio was selling not just products of advertisers but rock & roll itself.

The first wave of "rock & roll" disc jockeys actually predated the birth of the music. These pioneering deejays were spinning the hits even before it was called rock & roll. Some of the biggest names from the early 1950s included George "Hound Dog" Lorenz in Buffalo, John R. (aka John Richbourg) and Gene Nobles in Nashville, Hunter Hancock in Los Angeles, "Jumpin'" George Oxford in San Francisco, Dewey Phillips in Memphis, Tommy "Dr. Jive" Smalls in New York City, "Jocko" Henderson in Philadelphia and New York City, Robin Seymour in Detroit, and, of course, Alan Freed in Cleveland and New York. These early rock & roll deejays all shared a love of rhythm & blues–influenced music. They also had their own styles and idiosyncratic approaches for putting together daily radio programs. They selected their playlists, programmed their own shows, and took a free-form approach behind the mike, developing close ties to their audiences as they introduced them to the new sound.

Danny Neaverth, who became one of the most popular disc jockeys ever in Buffalo, New York, remembers growing up in Buffalo where he listened to George "Hound Dog" Lorenz on WKBW radio in the mid-1950s. Though white, Lorenz was a devotee of African American culture and rhythm & blues. His live radio program frequently originated from the ZanziBar located in an all-black neighborhood in Buffalo.

Tuning in, listeners would hear Lorenz scream, "The Hound's aroun'—Ah-Owoooo!"[13] (figure 6.3).

Neaverth vividly recalls the impact Lorenz had on him: "The Hound Dog was a gruff guy, a white guy playing black music. Wow, what a neat thing! And he knew all of the groups and he was in a black night club at night performing on WKBW, 50,000 watts up and down the eastern seaboard." Neaverth then begins talking in a gruff, throaty voice to mimic the way the Hound sounded. "Oh, ho man, the Hound Dog's around," says Neaverth, "Oh yeah. Hey, Daddy, we're playing all the great songs. Oh yeah yeah yeah yeah." According to Neaverth, the great thing about George Lorenz was that he knew everything there was to know about the music he was playing. He often knew the artists personally, and he loved the music. In addition, he was a great pitchman. Neaverth again imitates Lorenz's gruff, gravelly voice: "'Wild Irish Rose' wine man, wine, oh ho ho. The Hound loves it all the time. Get some wine. It's fine. Yeah." The Hound was a real character, says Neaverth. "While the songs were playing, he'd be beating on the table to keep the rhythm of the music and it was very exciting at the time." Neaverth recalls going to school and telling his friends, "Did you hear this guy called the Hound Dog, man, he's playing some great music. I don't know who those people are. He's playing something by the Drifters or, I remember, 'Annie Had a Baby.' That was really racy. Holy mackerel, what kind of song is that? Better not tell your Mom and Dad you're listening to that stuff." Years later, Neaverth still smiles when he thinks about those days. "That was my introduction [to rock & roll]," he says, "[The Hound] was introducing me to something new I hadn't heard before."[14]

Disc jockeys like George "Hound Dog" Lorenz not only introduced white teenagers to black music, but they influenced young listeners in other ways as well. Cultural historian William Graebner suggests that the Hound's tremendous popularity can be attributed to two factors. First, Lorenz "was an iconoclast in an age of conformity, an inspiration for those youths, mostly working class, who felt trapped by an unyielding dominant culture." For example, Graebner cites a fan who remembers an incident that occurred in a Buffalo diner. The fan recalls the Hound walking in wearing purple "drapes" (i.e., peg-legged pants). "When we saw him, we put Elvis's 'Hound Dog' on the jukebox," said the fan. "There was this square sitting at the counter, and, looking at the

Figure 6.3.   Pioneer disc jockey George "Hound Dog" Lorenz spent most of his career in Buffalo, New York, where he introduced local teenagers to R&B music and early rock & roll. (Courtesy of Buffalo Stories Archive/The Steve Cichon Collection)

Hound's clothes, he says, 'What's this, a centennial or something?' The Hound says [to us], 'He just doesn't understand, does he?'"

The second reason for Lorenz's great success was related to race. "Lorenz was at the center of a complex set of relationships between white and black cultures," explains Graebner. "Though white, Lorenz was responsible for transmitting the energy and sexuality of black culture to white teenagers. Besides programming black music, he regularly referred to himself as 'the big round brown Hound,' used a 'jive, hip talk' adapted from black language patterns. . . . His ZanziBar broadcasts attracted interracial audiences. . . . [The] Hound Dog represented the possibility of an interracial community based on a shared black youth subculture."[15]

Disc jockeys like the Hound often became as popular or even more popular than the recording artists themselves. "The singing stars and bands appeared on the radio, or on stage, and then were gone," explains music writer Ben Fong-Torres. "The deejay was there, day after day. A song was two or three minutes. The deejay stayed with his listener for three or more hours, in the background accompanying homework, or in the foreground providing gossip, information, and contest prizes. Hyped up and corny or warm and comforting, the deejay amounted to a friendly adult voice. They were accessible by phone, at local hops, and at big concerts."[16]

The second wave of rock & roll disc jockeys arrived on the scene in the mid- to late 1950s, around the same time that Elvis Presley was introducing millions of people to the new music. The new generation included deejays such as Dick Biondi, Jack Carney, Russ "Weird Beard" Knight, B. Mitchell Reed, Perry Allen, Joe Niagara, Casey Kasem, Arnie "Woo Woo" Ginsburg, Russ "the Moose" Syracuse, and Tom Shannon, to name just a few. Part of their success can be attributed to the rise of a new radio format—Top 40 radio—that took the nation by storm in the mid- to late 1950s and early '60s.[17] Top 40 not only made these deejays regional or national celebrities, it also launched rock & roll to even greater heights of popularity.

The origins of Top 40 are linked to the radio careers of three individuals from the 1950s: Todd Storz, the owner and operator of KOWH in Omaha, Nebraska; Gordon McLendon, who operated several Texas radio stations; and Bill Stewart, who programmed stations for both Storz and McLendon. Storz told a magazine reporter in 1957 that he hit on the idea for Top 40 when he was in the army and spent lots of time in bars and restaurants off base. "The customers would throw their nickels into the jukebox and come up repeatedly with the same tune," he explained. "Let's say it was 'The Music Goes Round and Round.' After [the customers were] all gone, the waitress would put her own tip money into the jukebox. After eight hours of listening to the same number, what number would she select? Something she hadn't heard all day? No—invariably she'd pick 'The Music Goes Round and Round.'"[18]

By the late 1950s, other versions of Storz's story were making the rounds. Sometimes, he was sitting in a bar or diner by himself and other times he was with his program director, Bill Stewart, or a group of disc jockeys trying to figure out how to attract more listeners. Another variation had Storz deciding after he read a marketing report by a local researcher. Regardless of when or how it took place, the tale always ended the same way with Storz deciding to showcase only the forty songs that people wanted to hear repeatedly. "Todd Storz was the genius behind [Top 40], saying, 'Hey, people go into a saloon and they play the same forty records over and over again,'" explained Dick Clark. "So, it was all seat-of-the-pants knowledge, grapevine knowledge. You picked what you thought was going to be a hit."[19]

In 1951, Todd Storz instructed his program director at KOWH, Bill Stewart, to implement the Top 40 format. By the end of the year, the Omaha station's listening share of the audience jumped from 4 percent to 45 percent.[20] Eventually, Storz's success allowed him to buy additional stations in Kansas City, Minneapolis, Miami, and New Orleans. Wherever he went, he switched to Top 40, always with the same success.

Not surprisingly, the Top 40 format spread rapidly across the country as radio stations searching for new ways to bolster ratings eagerly adopted the new formula. Each step along the way, station managers and programmers tweaked the formula in hopes of even greater success. Gordon McLendon, for instance, added the "instant news" concept by having roving reporters out on the streets phoning in news whenever it happened. Others tried news at twenty minutes before and after the hour unlike the traditional on-the-hour news feed provided by the networks. Between 1952 and 1955, the formula took shape as a distinct Top 40 sound came into being. "Top 40 programming," explain music historians Steve Chapple and Reebee Garafalo, "meant strictly limiting the station playlist to mainstream market pop singles, repeated station identifications, jingles, weird sound effects, extensive use of echo chambers, integration of hourly news broadcasts into the music format, and the use of promotional gimmicks and contests for the audience." Many of these gimmicks, admit Chapple and Garafalo, had been around for many years, but the "Top 40 concept put them all together."[21]

Though the formula sounds rigid, it did not preclude variations or individualism. If anything, the personality of each disc jockey became more important than ever. Todd Storz pushed his deejays to connect even more to audiences. Every disc jockey has "to use his own talent," he explained. "If he sings, let him sing. He is left completely free to talk as he feels best."[22] The "personality jock" became the star of Top 40. Arnie "Woo Woo" Ginsberg introduced Top 40 to Boston listeners when he hosted a popular show on WBOS in 1956 and later on WMEX. He attracted a huge following with his rapid delivery and use of numerous sound effects, including a train whistle that was the source of his nickname. Peter Tripp found success on the airwaves in Kansas City and New York City, where he gained fame as radio's "curly-headed kid in the third row." His best-known stunt came in 1959 when he stayed awake for 201 hours and 10 minutes straight to benefit the March of Dimes.

One of the most memorable and successful personality deejays who got started in the mid-1950s was Dick Biondi, whose numerous stops in the 1950s and beyond included Top 40 stations in Buffalo, Chicago, and Los Angeles. Billing himself as the "Wild I-tralian," "The Big Mouth," or "The Screamer," Biondi attracted legions of fans with his energy, humor, and high-pitched, squeaky voice. He related to listeners by telling personal stories, by dedicating songs to local high schools, and by making frequent appearances at record hops and high schools throughout the listening area. Biondi poked fun at everybody and everything—advertisers, fellow deejays, the songs he played, his listeners, himself, even his boss. During his stint at WKBW in Buffalo, New York, in the 1950s and early '60s, Biondi repeatedly joked about his boss on the air. He crossed over the line one evening when he made fun of the station manager on the air for coming into work immediately after his honeymoon. The furious boss stormed into the studio and ordered the deejay to knock it off. No sooner did the boss leave than Biondi clicked on the mike and told listeners: "Hey, my boss just left the studio. Can you imagine him coming in here the day after his honeymoon? He's driving down Main Street in a gray Impala, so if you see it, throw rocks at it . . . it'll serve him right!" Biondi later told an interviewer, "Wouldn't you know it, some kid put [a stone] the size of an orange . . . right through the windshield, and the next morning I was gone."[23]

Biondi's wild personality and constant jokes got him fired from twenty-five radio stations. Station managers were not always amused by his antics, but teenagers loved Biondi and cheered him on wherever he went. Radio programmer Mike Joseph insists that Dick Biondi was the best deejay in rock music history. His qualities were perfect for Top 40 radio and the new rock & roll sound: "his energy . . . his presentation, his appeal to the younger generation. He had absolute magnetism in the markets where I worked with him and saw him operate. . . . He fit with the format [and] sounded like a rock jock should."[24]

A segment of one of Biondi's programs on Buffalo's WKBW offers a glimpse of the disc jockey's phenomenal style: "This is the wild I-tralian Dick Biondi from the Big 'KB. How about that boss of mine? I want to take a moment real quick here to remind you that coming up on January 30, we're going to be down at St. Mary's Hall in Reading, Pennsylvania. I'm really looking forward to that. Remember the last time we were there? We had Freddy Cannon, we had the Shirelles, we had the Jordan Brothers, also the great Little Anthony and the Imperials. Want to remind you to get your tickets at Ripley Clothes 709 Penn Street in Reading. I want to thank Ripleys because they gave me a nice red jacket the last time I was down there." Then he does a quick cut to a canned promo: "This is Dick Biondi from 'KB, the Big One in Buffalo." He follows with a canned jingle: "Big Weather Is Here on WKBW." Biondi then does the weather, which he announces direct from "Action Central." Later in the show, he introduces WKBW's "Pulse-Beat News."[25]

That snippet from Biondi's show demonstrates the role played by personality disc jockeys in Top 40 radio of the 1950s and early '60s. In just thirty-seven seconds of airtime, Biondi manages to establish his wild personality, insult his boss, plug a concert, showcase his close ties to audiences, demonstrate that listeners in faraway Pennsylvania could hear Buffalo's powerhouse station, and remind audiences that he personally knows big-time rock & roll artists and joins them for concert appearances. All the while, he's emphasizing his close ties to fans as he speaks to them in a conversational tone, even telling them a personal tidbit about the red jacket he got as a gift. If all that wasn't enough, Biondi also manages to cram in two mentions of his own name, three mentions of his station's call letters, and two promos/jingles, as well as references to WKBW catch phrases such as "the Big 'KB," "Big Weather," and "Action Central."

Top 40 deejays like Dick Biondi not only became folk heroes to young audiences but they also helped spread the popularity of rock & roll. They reinforced its grassroots appeal and underscored the fact that the rock & roll scene was like nothing that had come before. By the time Elvis appeared on the national stage in 1956, Top 40 was firmly in place. The format had grown remarkably in just a few years, from twenty stations in 1955 to hundreds by the end of the decade. Of course, Top 40 was not designed specifically to help rock & roll. Indeed, many radio programmers could care less about the types of songs they were playing. "I do not believe there is any such thing as better or inferior music," insisted Todd Storz. "If the public suddenly showed a preference for Chinese music, we would play it." Repetition was the only thing that mattered. One of Storz's station managers explained it this way to disc jockeys who were reluctant to play the same songs over and over: "About the time you don't like a record, Mama's just beginning to learn to hum it. About the time you can't stand it, Mama's beginning to learn the words. About the time you're ready to shoot yourself if you hear it one more time, it's hitting the Top Ten."[26]

The notion of playing just the hits was not that new. After all, programs such as *Your Hit Parade* (which began on radio and then shifted over to television) and radio's *Lucky Lager Dance Time* had been doing exactly that since the mid-1930s and early '40s respectively. What made Top 40 seem new was its frenetic pace and its overall sound, established by the rapid-fire delivery of its deejays, jingles, sound effects, and contests, as well as by the revolutionary rock & roll hits it was playing. "We all stole from Storz," admitted one station owner. "We were losing our ass after TV came in, but we all heard about Storz. . . . [So] we got those forty records and we played the #1 tune on the hour and the #2 on the half hour. People complained like crazy but we played the hell out of that rock and roll, and it worked."[27]

Top 40 not only promoted rock & roll, but it reinforced the music's close ties to audiences. This was cultural democracy at work. After all, hits were often sung by performers not much older than the teenagers in the audiences; the records were being introduced by deejays with close ties to their audiences; and the songs were not just being handed down from the top but were also bubbling up from the bottom. Stations were playing the songs listeners wanted to hear. Radio programmer Mike Joseph, who worked at numerous Top 40 stations during the 1950s and early '60s, understood that stations couldn't succeed unless they were literally on the same wavelength as their audiences. "I follow the audience flow of the market around the clock. The type of listener, the age, the nationality of every single person in the market, around the clock," he explained to writer Ben Fong-Torres. "And I program my music accordingly."[28]

With teenagers cheering on and tuning in, Top 40 and rock & roll became two of the biggest success stories of the 1950s. Top 40 radio offered young listeners a fast-paced format that featured entertaining hosts introducing all the top hits, catchy jingles, and exciting contests. The deejays became celebrities in their own right. They hosted dances and other public events, promoted concerts, and had legions of dedicated fans. Some teenagers would show up at local record hops just to see their favorite disc jockey in person. "You were as important as the artist you were playing," explains Tom Shannon, who began his long and successful radio career as a Top 40 deejay at WKBW–Buffalo. "If [teenagers] listened to you, they attached themselves to you."[29]

The deejays' celebrity status resulted in part from the exalted role they played as middlemen between rock & roll singers and audiences. Like priests, they stood just a bit closer to the gods. Tom Shannon notes that WKBW became "the font of information" for young people. Its deejays, therefore, were like "the Oracle of Delphi because [they] were on 'KB and [supposedly] knew everything about rock & roll." Disc jockeys "were the ones who had the information, the ones who knew . . . where these artists were and where they came from."[30] Yet deejays couldn't be successful unless they could relate to audiences. Shannon points out that there was always a close connection between 'KB disc jockeys and young listeners. They talked to teenagers who called into their shows; they took requests; they dedicated songs to local groups and organizations; and they frequently mentioned local high schools on the air. WKBW disc jockeys also did record hops, bar mitzvahs, church socials, dances, and other personal appearances wherever they could—not just in Buffalo, but throughout 'KB's vast listening area, sometimes traveling north to Canada or south to Baltimore to do record hops or other local events.[31]

These roving Top 40 disc jockeys became important ambassadors for rock & roll. Their grassroots connections to listeners combined with their position as musical middlemen helped them spread the new sound to more and more people. Media personality Casey Kasem, who began his career in the 1950s as Top 40 deejay Casey at the Mike, explains: "It wasn't unusual for a deejay who believed in a song to play it a half dozen times in an evening. . . . As a result, many deejays were responsible for breaking hit records across the country." Disc jockeys had tremendous influence over their listeners. "If a deejay says something, young people will believe it because after all it's the same disc jockey that's playing their favorite music," says Kasem. Listeners "feel that they have a lot in common [since] a disc jockey comes into [their] home on a daily basis." For many listeners, deejays became virtual friends who could be counted on. For instance, the Sensations' "Please Mr. Disc Jockey" (1956) featured a young girl asking a deejay to intervene in her love life. "Please," she sang to her on-the-air friend, "tell him I love him from me."[32]

By the mid-1950s, Todd Storz's Top 40 stations and copycat stations were attracting between 50 and 70 percent of the listening audiences in their cities. The phenomenal success of Top 40 radio not only enabled radio to survive the coming of television, but it brought radio to new levels of popularity as well. In the mid-1950s, radio listenership began to climb back up, and by 1958 it was up 25 percent over its pre-television peak in 1947. "Radio's revenues are higher today than they ever were even in radio's so-called heyday, and are expected to total $700 million for [1958]," reported *Time*. The magazine noted sadly that "1958's radio is not 1947's radio. The radio is no longer in the living room but in the kitchen, on a bedside table, in the car. 1958's audience listens with half an ear, usually while doing something else." Another big change was that local radio had replaced network radio. "Radio's new and lusty child is the local station," complained *Time* magazine. "With some honorable exceptions, the locals' standard fare consists of the so-called 'Top 40' tunes (mostly rock 'n' roll), news-headline teasers, whooped-up contests and giveaways, voices of home-town deejays that every housewife learns to know and like during her lonely hours spent over dishes, ironing board and stove."[33]

That *Time* magazine story inadvertently suggests the extremely profitable relationship that developed between radio and rock & roll during the 1950s. The switch to Top 40 and rock & roll helped radio stations pull in advertisers and listeners. It also enabled rock & roll to expand its market. Millions of additional teenagers nationwide could now listen to rock & roll. But significantly, teenagers were no longer the only members of the rock & roll audience. As the *Time* article implies, housewives (and other adults) across the country were also now tuning in by the millions.

Top 40 was a product of the 1950s. It was born of necessity to survive the onslaught of television. It thrived on the entrepreneurial spirit of the day that witnessed businessmen, merchants, local advertisers, and budding media moguls looking for new ways to tap into the postwar prosperity. It took advantage of the country's postwar desire for new products and new approaches. And it capitalized on the coming of rock & roll to attract a new demographic of young listeners.

As Top 40 spread across the country, it expanded the audience for rock & roll and introduced millions of white Americans to black-influenced music and culture. Paradoxically, Top 40 depended upon local advertisers and hometown audiences for its existence, but it promoted a nationwide hit list. From sea to shining sea, Americans began listening to the same tunes, the same records, the same artists, and even the same itinerant disc jockeys who crisscrossed the land like rock & roll gypsies. In large part because of Top 40 radio, rock & roll became a cultural binding force for the new generation of teenagers who came of age in post–World War II America.

TELEVISION AND ROCK & ROLL

Television—like radio—promoted rock & roll by showcasing popular singers. The ratings boost that Ed Sullivan, Steve Allen, and the Dorsey Brothers all experienced after booking Elvis Presley convinced variety shows that rock & roll was ready for prime time. A headline in a major trade publication in April 1956—"Networks Eyeing Rock 'n' Roll as

Powerful Audience Factor"—announced the change in attitude. "Rock 'n' roll and television were made for each other," explains Professor Karal Ann Marling. "In dancing blips of light, television registered the bobbing hanks of hair, the swinging jackets, the swiveling hips." The details weren't as important as the overall image. "On the little living room screen, motion—new, exciting, and visually provocative in its own right—was the distilled essence of Elvishood," suggests Marling.[34]

Throughout the mid-1950s, TV became a showplace for rock & roll, as Ed Sullivan, Perry Como, Milton Berle, Steve Allen, and other variety show hosts booked the latest rock & roll acts making the pop charts. Each week, millions of viewers were introduced to the various forms of rock & roll, from the rebellious sounds of wild rockabilly artists like Gene Vincent and Eddie Cochran to the calmer, more pop-influenced musical stylings of Pat Boone and the Crew-Cuts. Despite the era's segregation, even African American artists were spotlighted. Viewers throughout the nation, including the South, could see black groups such as the Five Keys or Frankie Lymon and the Teenagers moving in choreographed steps to their latest hits, or Fats Domino singing with a broad smile on his face as he effortlessly plunked out piano triplets.

Rock & roll popped up elsewhere on TV. Weekly amateur hours such as *Arthur Godfrey's Talent Scouts* and Ted Mack's *Original Amateur Hour* featured amateur singers, dancers, jugglers, and other performers who competed for prizes. Pat Boone, the Chordettes, and the McGuire Sisters are just a few of the many hit artists on the 1950s rock & roll charts who got their start on amateur hours. Of course, not everyone who tried out made it on the air. Two of rock & roll's earliest stars—Elvis Presley and Buddy Holly—both flunked auditions for Godfrey's program. Rock & roll could also be heard on television programs that focused exclusively on popular music. The best example is NBC's longtime staple *Your Hit Parade*, which began on the radio in 1935 and became one of television's most popular programs throughout the 1950s. Every week, the show's regulars—pop singers such as Snooky Lanson, Dorothy Collins, Russell Arms, and Gisele Mackenzie—performed the top seven songs in America as determined by a formula worked out by the producers. The program assured viewers: "*Your Hit Parade* survey checks the best sellers on sheet music and phonograph records, the songs most heard on the air and most played on the automatic coin machines . . . an accurate, authentic tabulation of America's taste in popular music."[35] How this allegedly scientific survey was actually done was never made clear. *Your Hit Parade* sailed merrily along until the rise of rock & roll. Then it was sunk by the widening gap between traditional-sounding pop and the new rock & roll sound. Not only was it painful for older viewers to have to experience rock & roll songs on one of their favorite TV shows, but young audiences cringed when they heard a pop artist like Snooky Lanson trying to sing "Hound Dog." Low ratings caused cancellation of the show in early 1959.

Whenever possible, television tried to present viewers with a non-threatening version of rock & roll. Steve Allen had Elvis wearing a tux singing "Hound Dog" to a pooch; Ed Sullivan ordered his cameramen to show Elvis only from the waist up; and Sullivan frequently interviewed rock & rollers after they performed to assure viewers these were not juvenile delinquents but just typical American boys. Fats Domino recalls that the owner of his record label got him booked on the Sullivan show by comparing Fats to the popular Louis Armstrong. When it came time to perform, Sullivan allowed only Fats Domino and his piano on stage; the rest of Fats's R&B group had to play behind the curtain. That way there would not be a group of black males on stage who might appear threatening to some white viewers. Fats reluctantly went along with it, because he understood the power of Sullivan's show. "The next day [after the Sullivan appearance]," Fats explained, "we sold over a million records on 'Blueberry Hill.'"[36]

Television was literally offering rock & roll a national stage. And the more rock & roll the audiences saw, the more they began to accept these often strange-looking singers and their new musical style. The Platters are a perfect example of rock & roll performers who benefited from television exposure. Their popularity increased dramatically after they began appearing on national TV. They even became the first black R&B rock group to reach the top of the national pop charts when "The Great Pretender" made it to number 1 in early 1956. By decade's end, they would earn fifteen Top 40 hits, including four number 1 records.

All of this television exposure expanded the market for rock & roll. In February 1956, a trade magazine reported that the new music "seems lately to have achieved a certain measure of respectability." Everyone seemed to be jumping on the rock & roll bandwagon. An Ice Capades show called the "Rock and Roll Ice Review" opened at the Roxy Theater in New York, Hollywood was making movies about rock

& roll, a rock & roll–sounding jingle was featured in a Pall Mall cigarette commercial, a Top 10 review including rock & roll songs opened at Carnegie Hall, and television shows regularly spotlighted the new sound. The article concluded: "Television, as well as radio, has played an increasing part in bringing Rock and Roll and R&B talent into the home."[37]

ROCK & ROLL ON THE BIG SCREEN

Hollywood didn't need television, radio, magazines, or newspapers to find out about rock & roll. Movie producers and directors learned firsthand in 1955 about the music's commercial value. The use of Bill Haley's song "Rock Around the Clock" in the opening credits of the film *Blackboard Jungle* not only attracted millions of young viewers to movie theaters across the country but it helped make the song the number 1 record in the country. The following year, Hollywood looked on with envy when Hal Wallis cast the new singing sensation, Elvis Presley, in the movie *Love Me Tender*. Though many wondered about the rock & roller's acting ability, nobody questioned the results as the movie attracted huge crowds and millions of dollars in profits for the studio.

Most rock & roll flicks found success by parading numerous rock & roll performers in front of young audiences. *The Girl Can't Help It* was unusual in that it was filmed in color and Cinemascope, but it was typical because it offered viewers the opportunity to see a variety of rock & roll stars performing on the big screen. That formula was used by numerous low-budget films in 1956. Moviegoers could head to their neighborhood theatres to see rock & rollers appearing in black-and-white, B-movies such as *Rock Around the Clock*; *Rock, Pretty Baby*; *Shake, Rattle, and Rock*; *Don't Knock the Rock*; *Rock, Rock, Rock!*; and *Hot Rod Girl* (which promised viewers "Chicken-Race! Rock 'n' Roll! Youth on the Loose!").

Rock, Rock, Rock! was the most interesting of the rock & roll B-movies that arrived in 1956. The film introduced audiences to a pretty ingénue named Tuesday Weld (who later played Thalia Menninger on TV's *The Many Loves of Dobie Gillis* before going on to star in numerous movies). It featured two other individuals who later became stars in their own right: Valerie Harper, who gained fame in the 1970s as Rhoda

Morgenstern on TV's *The Mary Tyler Moore Show* and its spin-off, *Rhoda*, played one of the teenagers. And a then-unknown singer named Connie Francis performed the vocals for Weld's singing parts. (Connie would not have her first hit record for another two years.) The plot of *Rock, Rock, Rock!*—like those found in most 1950s rock & roll flicks— was thin at best. Tuesday Weld plays a desperate teenager trying to save money to buy a dress to wear to a rock & roll dance at her school. All the while, she has to please her boyfriend and avoid interference from parents and other adults. Of course, the storyline is not what attracted young people to the box office. The real lures were the rock & rollers on screen.

The movie poster for *Rock, Rock, Rock!* suggests how all these films were marketed. The viewer's attention is immediately drawn to the center of the poster where a girl's legs are exposed up to her thighs when her dress twirls upward as she jitterbugs with her boyfriend. Superimposed in large red letters across their bodies are the words "Rock, Rock, Rock!" On the left, smirking and pointing at the couple, is an older-looking man identified as "The King of Rock 'n' Roll Alan Freed." The bottom of the poster is equally provocative, suggesting interracial romance. On the right is a seductive-looking Tuesday Weld with her long blonde curls falling softly on her shoulders. In the left-hand corner, facing her and looking very cool as he snaps his fingers, is Frankie Lymon, the young African American lead singer for Frankie Lymon and the Teenagers. The text boasts: "The greatest rock 'n' roll music played by biggest rock 'n' roll groups this side of heaven!" Separate boxes spotlight major performers such as Chuck Berry, LaVern Baker, and Frankie Lymon and the Teenagers, while smaller print advertises the Moonglows, the Flamingos, and the Johnny Burnette Trio, plus lesser-known singers and "Alan Freed's 18 piece ROCK 'N' ROLL BAND." The poster promises, "21 New Hit Songs. 21." Dynamic images get across the vitality of the new music: the dominant picture is a couple dancing to a fast beat; other pictures show a teenage crowd dancing wildly to the music or depict singers Chuck Berry and LaVern Baker performing their hits.

Teenagers who saw the film were not disappointed. They were wowed by disc jockey Alan Freed as he introduced singer after singer. Many thought that Chuck Berry stole the show. "You know, gang, you all remember 'Maybellene' about the young man with the guitar who couldn't catch her with his car," Alan Freed says by way of introduction, "well, here he is to tell us all about it with a brand new automobile. Chuck Berry and 'You Can't Catch Me.'" The camera then cuts away to show the rock & roll singer crouched over, ready to spring into musical action. Dressed in a white tux with matching white shoes and contrasting black lapels and bowtie, Berry suddenly explodes in an eruption of sound and motion, his legs twitching and feet flying to the beat. He uses comical facial expressions and over-the-top body movements to pantomime the lyrics, all the while cradling his guitar sensually, even kissing it at one point. Berry closes the song with his signature duck walk, allowing audiences nationwide to witness it for the first time. Movie critics were left breathless. "Chuck Berry is certainly one of the foremost song stylists of the day, regardless of category," wrote one reviewer. "His gestures, body movements, and facial expressions act out the lyrics of 'You Can't Catch Me' in the film so completely that if the sound went dead, the viewer would not be lost. One can virtually see the words." Another reviewer had similar praise for the singer's act: "Chuck Berry . . . mimes the lyrics of the tune with hands, feet, face, and body movements, all but making a humorous ballet of it. His performance alone is worth the price of admission."[38]

Although rock & roll movies never came even remotely close to being nominated for an Academy Award, they usually did achieve their more modest goals: rock & roll movies made money for their producers; they provided exposure for rock & roll stars; and they portrayed rock & roll in exemplary ways, suggesting that rock & roll singers and music were safe and as American as apple pie.

The arrival of Elvis Presley on the pop music scene in 1956 sent shock waves across America. As Presleymania took the country by storm, movies and other national media did their best to capitalize on the rock & roll phenomenon. In the process, they provided momentum to the Presley bandwagon and all but guaranteed the popularity of rock & roll.

7

THE ROCK AND ROLL WALTZ
Pop Music's New Fandango

In 1956, a thirty-four-year-old veteran pop singer named Kay Starr, with numerous pop hits to her credit, including "So Tired" (1948) and "Wheel of Fortune" (1952), earned a place in rock & roll history with a record entitled "Rock and Roll Waltz." Nothing about the schmaltzy pop ballad—except for its title and lyrics—had anything to do with the new teenage music. Her major record label, RCA/Victor, was betting that the mere reference to rock & roll was enough to sell millions of records to teenagers caught up in Presleymania. The RCA execs hit the jackpot big time when the record shot up all the way to number 1 on the national pop charts (figure 7.1).

The song tells the story of a teenage girl who comes home after a date and catches her parents dancing in the living room to a rock & roll song. "And while they danced, only one thing was wrong," she sings. "They were trying to waltz to a rock and roll song." The bemused protagonist thought it looked cute and encouraged her teenage listeners to give it a try. "A one, two, and then rock / A-one, two, and then roll," she sings, "It's old but it's new / Let's do the rock and roll waltz."[1]

Starr's smash hit illustrates how the pop music industry was trying to cash in on the rock & roll craze of 1956. By the end of the year, almost every record exec, A&R (arrangement and repertoire) man, promoter, distributor, songwriter, song plugger, or anybody else who dreamed about having a hit record was practicing their own version of the rock &

Figure 7.1. Pop singer Kay Starr had a number 1 hit in 1956 with "Rock and Roll Waltz," a traditional pop song that alluded to the new teenage music. (Courtesy of Music Library and Sound Recordings Archives, Bowling Green State University)

roll waltz. At times, it seemed like every resident of Tin Pan Alley was capitalizing one way or another on the new teenage sound. There were cover records, bandwagon records, and songs about the new youth culture, as well as numerous attempts to record new pop rock artists with the potential to connect with teenage audiences.

COVER RECORDS

The Presley phenomenon of 1956 convinced both large and small record companies that enormous profits could be made selling rock & roll records to teenagers. Major record companies continued to produce cover versions of R&B songs as a way to take advantage of the expanding youth market. Georgia Gibbs did a pop version of LaVern Baker's "Tra La La." Don Cornell covered the Moonglows' "See Saw." Some pop singers became serial coverers. Pat Boone had extraordinary success in 1956 with cover versions of Ivory Joe Hunter's "I Almost Lost My Mind," Joe Turner's "Chains of Love," the Flamingos' "I'll Be Home," and Little Richard's "Tutti Frutti" and "Long Tall Sally." The Diamonds scored with copycat versions of the Willows' "Church Bells May Ring," the Clovers' "Love, Love, Love," the G-Clefs' "Ka-Ding-Dong," and Frankie Lymon and the Teenagers' "Why Do Fools Fall in Love?" The Fontane Sisters chimed in with pop renditions of the Teen Queens' "Eddie My Love" and Fats Domino's "I'm in Love Again."

Several R&B songs were targeted by multiple artists. The G-Clefs' "Ka-Ding Dong" was copied by the Diamonds and the Hilltoppers.[2] The Teen Queens' "Eddie My Love" was redone by the Chordettes and the Fontane Sisters. Clyde McPhatter's "Seven Days" was covered by the Crew-Cuts and Dorothy Collins. And Frankie Lymon and the Teenagers' "Why Do Fools Fall in Love?" was rerecorded by the Diamonds, Gloria Mann, and Gale Storm. The Jayhawks' "Stranded in the Jungle" was covered by both a white pop group, the Gadabouts, and a black R&B group, the Cadets.

All of these records—like the initial wave of covers in 1954 and 1955—brought rock & roll, as well as rhythm & blues, to the attention of a much broader audience. There was one big difference, though. The covers of 1956—unlike earlier ones—did not always outsell the originals. Although the Presley phenomenon encouraged major record companies to continue issuing cover records as an easy way to profit from the rock & roll craze, a funny thing happened on the way to the bank. All of a sudden, the demand for covers plummeted as teenagers began demanding the real thing.

In April of 1956, Frankie Lymon and the Teenagers broke the monopoly that cover records had on the pop charts when their original recording of "Why Do Fools Fall in Love" reached number 6 on the

Billboard charts, beating out inferior pop versions by Gale Storm, the Diamonds, and Gloria Mann. From that point onward, cover records usually weren't successful unless they actually sounded better than the originals. For example, in 1956 Little Richard's original version of "Long Tall Sally" triumphed over Pat Boone's tame version. Same thing with Fats Domino's "I'm in Love Again," which came in at number 3 compared to the Fontane Sisters' inferior remake that peaked at number 38.

Cover records were far from done, though. Boone's 1956 version of the Flamingos' "I'll Be Home" became a number 4 hit, while the original didn't even chart. The Fontane Sisters' rendition of the Teen Queens' "Eddie My Love" reached number 11 on the charts, while the original stalled at number 14, tying it with another cover by the Chordettes. Despite the continued success of some cover records, a sea change clearly had occurred. Cover records faded fast after 1956, and the phenomenon was all but dead by 1958. By the mid-1950s, African American culture was on the rise. There were impressive civil rights victories such as *Brown vs. Board of Education* and the Montgomery Bus Boycott. Jackie Robinson broke the color barrier in baseball. *Amos and Andy* became the first all-black program on television. And black R&B music gained in popularity as it morphed into rock & roll. With all this racial change in the wind, it is not surprising that white teenagers were becoming more receptive to black rock & rollers. An Atlantic Records' advertisement in the autumn of '56 said it all: "Covers—Shmovers. Atlantic has the [real] HITS."[3]

The cover-record phenomenon offers an interesting glimpse of American life and thought in the years following World War II. Cover records reveal racial attitudes; they reflect how Americans thought and acted; and they provide evidence of both continuity and change in 1950s America. Covers suggest that popular music is often a cultural battleground. Every time a new style representing oppositional subcultures appears—whether it was rock & roll in the early 1950s or later developments such as the British rock invasion, the folk-rock craze of the mid-1960s, or rap music of the 1980s and '90s—the dominant culture responds with a safer, more homogenized version. In the process, the dominant culture both changes and is changed by the new subculture.

The cover records of the mid-1950s were clearly bad imitations of authentic R&B-influenced music. Yet they played an important role in expanding the market for early rock & roll by attracting many new listeners who weren't ready for the real thing. In the process, they contributed to cultural integration. Though the R&B originals usually sold fewer copies than the cover versions, in the long run the originals became the recognized classics. Pat Boone's 1956 cover of Little Richard's "Tutti Frutti" is a perfect example. Though Boone's tepid remake initially climbed higher on the rock charts, peaking at number 12 as compared to Little Richard's number 17, the exciting R&B original is now considered the definitive version. Listening to Little Richard screaming out "Wop bop a lu bop a bim bam boom" as compared to Pat Boone crooning the same nonsense syllables speaks volumes about the role of cover records in rock & roll history.

BANDWAGON RECORDS

Kay Starr's "Rock and Roll Waltz" was the music industry's most successful attempt to jump on the rock & roll bandwagon. But throughout 1956, numerous other "bandwagon" records also tried to go along for the ride. Some songs—following the lead of "Rock and Roll Waltz"—simply alluded to the new sound. Georgia Gibbs's "Rock Right," Archie Bleyer's "Rockin' Ghost," Don Cornell's "Teenage Meeting (Gonna Rock It Up Tonight)," and Sunny Gale's "Rock and Roll Wedding" worked "rock" into the title. Perry Como's "Juke Box Baby" was a bit more subtle with its vague reference to teenage girls' love of rock & roll. Pop star Guy Mitchell made it all the way to number 1 on the charts with "Singin' the Blues," a bouncy number that referenced the latter half of the rhythm & blues equation. Gogi Grant's cover of a country & western song, "Wayward Wind," also made it to number 1 on the charts. Although the song did not refer specifically to rock & roll, it picked up on one of early rock's most successful formulas by mixing country music with a big beat.

Most bandwagon records pandered shamelessly to teenage interests in 1956. Gloria Mann's "Teenage Prayer" and the Chordettes' "Teenage Goodnight" found success by addressing the young audience directly. Sonny James's number 1 hit, "Young Love," suggested teenage romance was unique. Another song aimed at young love—"Too Young to Go Steady"—became a Top 30 hit for pop music veteran Nat "King" Cole. Pop singers mined other areas of teen culture with varying degrees of success. The Rover Boys, named after the famous children's book characters, earned hit records with teen-oriented ballads such as "Graduation Day" and "From a School Ring to a Wedding Ring." Patti Page's minor hit "My First Formal Gown" climbed the pop charts as teenage girls were dreaming about junior proms. And Eddie Fisher's "Dungaree Doll" and Julius LaRosa's "Lipstick, Candy, and Rubber Sole Shoes" found success by alluding to popular teen products.

Some bandwagon records redirected a longtime staple of Tin Pan Alley—the novelty song—toward new, teen-oriented subjects. Two minor novelty hits took advantage of rock & roll's name: Buddy Hackett's "Chinese Rock and Egg Roll" and Barry Gordon's "Rock Around Mother Goose." Nervous Norvous (aka Jimmy Drake) had a smash hit with "Transfusion," a comedy record about a teenage boy who drove his hot rod with wild abandon. Young listeners loved the song's twisted humor about a reckless young driver involved in numerous crashes. The sounds of screeching tires and car crashes, coupled with memorable lyrics about drinking, high-speed driving, and blood transfusions at the hospital (where the banged-up driver coolly tells the doctor, "shoot the juice to me, Bruce") helped the record race all the way up to number 8 on the charts. His follow-up, "Ape Call," advised teenage males if they wanted to be "cool cats" and win the girl, they needed to do what men have done throughout history—"Go ape!" To emphasize the point, the record was punctuated by ape calls that sounded straight out of Tarzan movies from the 1930s.

Jim Lowe's novelty hit, "Green Door," also struck pay dirt. It piqued the curiosity of many teenagers as Lowe described all the music and laughter that could be heard behind the mysterious door and wondered about what was really going on. The record made it all the way to number 1, powered by a big rock & roll beat and numerous allusions to partying, drinking, and other wild types of behavior that appealed to teenagers. A trade magazine noted that there was a clear lesson in the success of novelty records like Lowe's "Green Door" and Buchanan and Goodman's "The Flying Saucer": "both the pop and r&b fields have been richer for the free exchange of materials that now takes place between them."[4]

"The Flying Saucer (Parts 1 and 2)" became the most interesting novelty hit of the year. A trade magazine described the record as a "sampler" of excerpts from fifteen different hit songs. The music publishers who owned rights to the originals immediately filed a lawsuit claiming copyright infringement. Ironically, even more publishers and record companies were upset that their hits were not included. One executive complained, "If you're not on the 'Flying Saucer,' you're nowhere." The music trade concluded that the record "has revived sales interest in at least one of the old rock and roll disk hits excerpted on the record [i.e., the Penguins' 'Earth Angel']," and the sales of other songs sampled on "Flying Saucer" such as Little Richard's "Long Tall Sally" have likewise "spurted ahead since the disk hit the market."[5]

Buchanan and Goodman's record—inspired by Orson Welles's radio drama *War of the Worlds*—managed to lampoon two different crazes at the same time: flying saucers and rock & roll. Bill Buchanan and Dickie Goodman set their make-believe news bulletin in the middle of a music program. The announcer on the record was an obvious parody of the era's best-known TV newsman, John Cameron Swayze. Snippets of popular rock & roll records were spliced into the dialogue. "We interrupt this record to bring you a special bulletin," begins the announcer. "The reports of a flying saucer hovering over the city have been confirmed. The flying saucers are real." What follows is a hectic and hilarious pseudo news report of flying saucers, alien creatures, and panic in the streets as reported by "John Cameron Cameron" and his intrepid crew of roving news reporters. At one point, a reporter asks a man on the street holding a guitar what he would do if a saucer were to land. A clip from Elvis's first big hit, "Heartbreak Hotel," answers, "Just take a walk down lonely street [to Heartbreak Hotel]." After the saucer lands, the reporter describes a professor who walks up to it and knocks on the door to see if there's any sign of life aboard. From inside comes a Smiley Lewis clip: "I hear you knockin', but you can't come in." When the alien finally emerges, John Cameron Cameron urgently tells listeners: "I believe we're about to hear the words of the first spaceman ever to land on earth." There's a pause, then the refrain from Little Richard's hit "Tutti Frutti" rings out: "A wop bop a loo bop, a lop bam boom!"[6] The comedy record is absolutely brilliant as it takes aim at television, radio, and, of course, rock & roll. The comedians' follow-up, "Buchanan and Goodman on Trial," joked about how they were being sued for copyright violation for using clips of rock & roll songs in their records.

Another novelty hit from 1956 took a less gentle approach to the new sound. Comedian Stan Freberg had a minor hit with "Heartbreak Hotel," a sharp parody of Elvis Presley's sound and style. As he makes his way through the original lyrics, he takes numerous cheap shots at Elvis such as, "Could I have a little more echo on my voice" and "ripped my jeans, third pair today."[7]

All of these novelty hits that poked fun at rock & roll and the youth culture succeeded on several levels. Not only did they make a ton of money for the record labels and artists, but they produced lots of publicity that promoted the new music. As they introduced rock & roll to numerous new listeners, they suggested that rock & roll was essentially just harmless fun.

POP ROCK PROTOTYPES

After the coming of Elvis Presley, the pop music industry continued to crank out hits by pop rock pioneers such as Bill Haley and His Comets, Pat Boone, the Crew-Cuts, and Boyd Bennett. Even before Elvis, those singers had demonstrated the ability to blend white pop with the new rhythms and beats associated with rhythm & blues. Elvis's arrival and the growing market for rock & roll assured their continuing success.

Bill Haley was an old-looking twenty-nine when Elvis arrived on the scene. Chubby with a receding hairline and a silly-looking spit curl in the middle of his forehead, Haley looked more like an appliance salesman than a rock & roll singer. Yet he and his band racked up hit after hit in the mid-1950s. They began their run on the national charts in 1953 with "Crazy Man, Crazy." Over the next two years, they earned seven additional Top 30 hits, including the seminal "Rock Around the Clock" (1955).

The group remained a fixture on the rock & roll charts in 1956 and throughout the rest of the decade. Just as Elvis was making his first appearance on national TV in January 1956, Bill Haley and His Comets debuted a song on the pop charts that was destined to become one of their greatest hits: "See You Later, Alligator." The record climbed all the way to number 6 on the pop charts as its refrain—"See you later, alligator; after a while, crocodile'"—caught on as the latest teenage expression. Riding the Elvis/rock & roll wave of 1956, Haley and his group followed up with several additional hits. Among them were three Top 30 hits: "R-O-C-K" reprised the "Crazy Man, Crazy" phrase employed in their first hit and was featured in the soundtrack of the film "Rock Around the Clock"; "The Saints Rock 'n Roll" was a rock & roll version of the spiritual "When the Saints Go Marchin' In"; and "Rip It Up" was a cover of Little Richard's hit. Haley and his group also cracked the Top 100 list with "Hot Dog Buddy Buddy," "Rockin' through the Rye," "Teenager's Mother," "Rudy's Rock," and "Don't Knock the Rock." Three of the songs are particularly interesting. "Rudy's Rock" was an excellent instrumental that showcased the Comets' sax player, Rudy Pompilli. The song, with its wailing sax, fast-paced guitar licks, and pounding drums, became a benchmark for other instrumental rockers.

"Teenager's Mother" and "Don't Knock the Rock" were tame in comparison, but they reflect the fact that not everyone in 1950s America appreciated the coming of rock & roll. Public attacks on rock & roll were common during 1956. Music industry insiders condemned the sound as a "mongrel music" that mixed pop and country music with rhythm & blues. Censors carefully inspected the lyrics on rock & roll releases. And many adults were appalled at Elvis Presley's gyrations on stage and were convinced that rock & roll was leading unsuspecting American youths down a dangerous path. After thousands of rock & roll fans jammed into Hartford's State Theater for an Alan Freed concert featuring several rock & roll performers, city officials were described as "hopping mad" over the teenagers' alleged rioting, drunkenness, and unruly behavior. Rock & roll seemed to be spinning out of control. After a teenage riot in Asbury Park, New Jersey, the mayors of Asbury Park and Jersey City banned rock & roll concerts. Similar concerns led to the banning of rock & roll in other cities across the nation, including San Jose, California; San Antonio, Texas; and Santa Cruz, California. A letter to the editor of the *Denver Post* concluded, "This hooby doopy, oop-shoop, ootie ootie, boom boom de-addy boom, scoobledy goobledy dump—is trash."[8]

Bill Haley and His Comets tried to come to rock & roll's rescue with their song "Teenager's Mother (Are You Right?)." Ironically, the song was the flip side of Haley's cover of Little Richard's raucous "Rip It

Up." Addressing mothers of teenagers, Haley asks if they can remember how much they loved the Charleston when they were young and whether they ever came home late from a date. In the last verse, he adds: "Now we won't say who's right or wrong, but here's the moral of this song / It can't be bad, what makes you glad, and you are only young so long."[9] The group's last hit of 1956, "Don't Knock the Rock" (which was from the soundtrack of the film of the same name), similarly defended rock & roll against its critics.

The fact that Bill Haley and His Comets championed rock & roll's cause did not guarantee them continued success in the rapidly changing world of rock. With newer, younger, and cooler rock & roll acts appearing almost daily, Haley and his group found it difficult to keep up. After 1956, they had only one more big hit. In 1958, they reached number 22 on the record charts with "Skinny Minnie," a danceable record with a big beat and humorous lyrics about a rather unusual young lady. The refrain said it all: "Skinnie Minnie, she ain't skinny / she's tall, that's all."[10]

Before their run on the record charts was over, Bill Haley and His Comets racked up fourteen Top 30 hits, including the groundbreaking "Crazy Man, Crazy" and the multimillion-seller "Rock Around the Clock." Their last big year was 1956, when the group chalked up numerous hit records, headlined live concerts, frequently appeared on TV shows, and were featured in two feature-lengths films, "Rock Around the Clock" and "Don't Knock the Rock." Bill Haley and His Comets might not have been the best-looking or most-talented rock & rollers around, and obviously they weren't the youngest ones either, but Haley and his group were among the first practitioners of the new sound.

Bill Haley introduced many white, middle-class teenagers to rock & roll. John Peterson is a perfect example. Peterson remembers what it was like growing up in Mason City, Iowa, in the 1950s. "We were hip beyond our years, called each other 'Daddy-O,' and exclaimed, 'Cool, man, cool!'" he says. One day Peterson went down to the local record store to buy his first rock & roll record. "I asked the teenagers there, whom I considered to be much older and wiser than I, what they recommended," he explains. "With some trepidation I ended up buying 'Rock Around the Clock,' by Bill Haley and His Comets. It was great!" He was also impressed by "the profound, 'See you later, alligator; after a while, crocodile.'" Peterson's discovery of the new music eventually led him to join a rock & roll band, and he later played keyboards with the Pete Klint Quintet, earning a minor hit on the national pop charts in 1967 with "Walkin' Proud." Eventually, John Peterson went to medical school and established a family practice in the Midwest. But, like many members of his generation, Dr. Peterson never forgot how important music was to his life back in the 1950s and '60s. "In the midst of hula-hoop contests, crew cuts, vanilla and cherry Cokes, Pez candy, and atom bomb drills in school," he says, "my life was accompanied by music—classical music and rock 'n' roll music."[11]

Bill Haley and His Comets helped spread rock & roll to numerous other youths across America. Their hit records made rock & roll more acceptable and safer for the masses, and established Haley as one of the founding fathers of rock & roll. Though Bill Haley's music now sounds terribly dated, in the mid-1950s it was nothing short of revolutionary. The commercial blend of country, pop, and R&B that Haley recorded with the Comets produced a sound teens could relate to and dance to. Young fans cheered wildly as Bill Haley and His Comets, dressed in glowing sharkskin suits, cranked out hit after hit between 1953 and 1958. Their enthusiastic response suggests that the young generation was desperately searching for a new sound that would set them apart from their elders, while the negative reaction of many adults to Haley's music reflects the conservatism of the 1950s. Bill Haley's contribution to early rock & roll was recognized in 1987 when he was inducted posthumously into the Rock and Roll Hall of Fame.

The coming of Elvis and the subsequent demand for rock & roll enabled two other pop rock groups to prolong their careers in 1956. The Crew-Cuts, who had helped spark the rock & roll craze with their number 1 hit from 1954, "Sh-Boom," were able to muster only a few more hits after Elvis's arrival. While Elvis was making his first television appearances in January 1956, the Crew-Cuts' "Angels in the Sky" was reaching number 11 on the pop charts. The song—a strange blend of 1950s white pop harmonies and R&B-inspired doo-wop—reflected the growing popularity of religion in cold war America. The lyrics beseech listeners desperate for love to talk to the angels and pray for God's help.[12] Before the year was out, they added two more Top 30 hits, a dreadful pop song entitled "Mostly Martha" and an equally bad cover of Clyde McPhatter's "Seven Days." The Crew-Cuts had their last Top 20 hit in 1957 with a bland rendition of Sonny James's "Young Love."

Boyd Bennett and the Rockets also rode the rock & roll craze. Although the thirty-two-year old Bennett never came close to duplicating the success of "Seventeen," which made it to number 5 on the charts in 1955, he and his group did crack the Top 40 in early 1956 with "My Boy Flat Top." The song—a blatant attempt to reach the youth market—showcased a young Adonis with the latest hairstyle, as well as hot rods, teenage slang, and rock & roll. Bennett's follow-up, a tame version of Carl Perkins's rockabilly hit "Blue Suede Shoes," barely dented the national charts.

The most successful of the early pop rockers was Pat Boone. In the years after Elvis's arrival on the national scene, Boone established himself as a major star with fourteen Top 10 hits, several best-selling albums, a hit TV show, and starring roles in movies, as well as a best-selling book of advice for teenagers, 'Twixt Twelve and Twenty (figure 7.2).

Historians and music critics have not been kind to Pat. They have dismissed him as a contrived pop singer, whose old-fashioned values and squeaky-clean looks left him out of touch with the rock & roll audience. James Miller, a former editor of Rolling Stone Magazine, describes Boone as a pop singer who watered down rock & roll for the masses. "Pat Boone was Al Jolson without the burnt cork or emotional intensity," explains Miller. "[He was] a low-key, clean-scrubbed, deeply pious spokesman for cultural uplift, filtering much of the blues and the rhythm out of rhythm and blues, and turning the new music into a winsome form of family entertainment." Rock & roll historian Reebee Garofalo is even more harsh, maintaining that Pat Boone "represents the epitome of cultural theft." Garofalo condemns Boone not only for his cover records but also for building his "career by sanitizing the [R&B] classics." Boone's "antiseptic versions of Little Richard's 'Tutti Frutti' and 'Long Tall Sally' alone would be enough to earn him the unyielding wrath of anyone who professes a love of rock 'n' roll," says Garofalo. "The 'white buck' shoes that became his signature only reinforced the racist implications of his 'white bread' delivery."[13]

The criticism and vitriol leveled at Pat Boone have been overly harsh and unfairly dismiss his contributions to early rock & roll. Granted, Boone's music was mainstream, his R&B covers sounded anything but authentic, and he did have a clean-cut appearance. But none of these negate his historical and cultural significance during the early days of

Figure 7.2. Publicity shot of Pat Boone in his signature white bucks. (Richard Aquila Collection)

rock & roll. While critics, journalists, and historians commonly write Boone off as just an imitator, Boone's fans saw him as the real thing.

They cheered him on as a rock & roll hero. And Pat's success helped spread the popularity of the new sound.

Boone deserves his rightful place in rock & roll history for a variety of reasons. His phenomenal success on the rock & roll charts is one obvious one. Boone must have been doing something right, because he sold more records in the 1950s than any rock & roller except Elvis. For millions of fans, Pat Boone was a bona fide rock & roll star. "Radio stations would have these contests between the various performers [to see who was the most popular rock & roll singer]," explains Boone. "It usually boiled down to contests between Elvis and me, who's the most popular. Elvis, I guess, won two out of three of the contests, but I would win at least a third of them."[14]

The fact that many teenagers viewed Pat Boone as a rock & roll superstar should not come as a surprise. It is important to remember that early rock & roll encompassed a variety of styles. The 1950s and early '60s were the glory days of Top 40 radio. Teenagers listening to a rock & roll station would hear a real mix, everything from R&B favorites by Little Richard and Fats Domino or rockabilly hits by Elvis and Carl Perkins to the latest pop rock hits by Pat Boone or Bill Haley and His Comets. Rock & roll fans would then rush out to local stores to purchase the latest releases by all of these different performers. Even Elvis collected Pat Boone records. "I think [Pat Boone's] undoubtedly is the finest voice out now, especially on slow songs," said Elvis. "You know, Boone was recording before I was—and I bought his records even back then." In 1957, Presley ran into Boone on a movie lot in Hollywood and serenaded him with an impromptu version of Pat's latest hit, "April Love."[15]

Boone always viewed himself as part of the rock & roll phenomenon of the 1950s. "I was just as much a part of the [rock & roll] scene as Elvis or Jerry Lee or Little Richard," insists Boone. "In fact, I was having more continued chart success than any of them. Because from '55 through '59 is one of the records I still hold in the record business of over 200 consecutive weeks I was never off the singles chart. Elvis dropped off; none of the others were on anything like that in consecutive weeks. . . . So, yes, I knew I was part of the scene and a very influential part of the [rock & roll] scene."[16]

While many contemporary critics dismiss Pat Boone as a contrived pop artist who sold a watered down version of rock & roll for the mass market, Boone points out that he always had a great deal of creative input in the recording process. "It was sort of a blend, a mixture of influence between myself and Randy Wood [owner and producer for Dot Records]," explains Boone. Sometimes Wood would insist that Pat had to do additional takes of songs; other times Boone would take the lead. Boone insists there was always an authentic quality to both his sound and style. "I was the raw thing, the real thing. I was a kid from Tennessee who lived like I lived because I thought it was right. And I sang what I sang because I liked it and I sang it my way. And so the image grew around that. It was not anybody trying to create an image. . . . Kids identified with me because I was like them. And it wasn't that I was trying to be like them. I really was."[17]

Even Pat's clean-cut image and the white bucks were not contrived. "It was certainly no plan by anybody. It wasn't a PR kind of creation. I was just me," explains Boone. "I was married. I was going to college. I was a regular churchgoer." He adds that when Elvis came along, the media quickly began making comparisons. "We had a lot of the similar background [and] upbringing," explains Boone, "both boys [were] from Tennessee and churchgoing families and all that, lower-middle income or lower income families." But Pat notes one striking dissimilarity: "Elvis wasn't married and [reporters] asked him a question early in our mutual career, 'When are you going to get married and settle down and have kids like Pat Boone?' And [Elvis] gave us that famous leer to the camera and said, 'Well, why should I buy a cow when I can get milk through the fence?' And that quote went around the world and of course that made me look like a saint. And that did draw a line between us, where I was the clean-cut guy." Of course, admits Boone, there was some validity to that generalization. Although Pat was singing rock & roll, he did change words of songs if he felt they were offensive. He even refused to record some R&B songs for moral reasons. For instance, he passed up the opportunity to cover Etta James's R&B hit "Roll with Me, Henry." Shortly thereafter, pop star Georgia Gibbs had a big hit with the song after she changed the title to "Dance with Me, Henry." "I couldn't even have done that," explains Pat with a chuckle, "I couldn't have sung 'Dance with me, Henry, all night long' [in good conscience]."[18]

Pat Boone's appearance was not a PR gimmick planned by his record company or publicity agent. On stage he just wore the clothes he normally wore, right down to the shoes on his feet. "I wore the white bucks on television because they were the only decent pair of shoes that I had," he explains. "I was just wearing what all the other high school and college kids were, virtually, in America. White bucks dirtied and cleaned up and dusted with white powder or just left scroungey. In fact, the shoe companies started putting out pre-dirtied white bucks so they looked like they had already been used and worn for a while." He adds, "Nobody thought about it. It wasn't premeditated. Immediately high school and college kids all over the country would say, 'Hey, that's the way I look. That's what I wear.'" Boone concludes that white bucks certainly "became my trademark, but not intentionally."[19]

Not only was Pat's clean-cut image authentic, but it resonated with some fans every bit as much as Elvis Presley's rebel image did with others. After all, the 1950s was a time of conformity and consensus, an era when most teenagers adhered to mainstream values. "When kids saw me on television the first time . . . I was still a kid," explains Boone. "I was in college. And so kids identified with that. They said, 'Look there's one of us. He dresses like us. He looks like us. He sounds like us. And, he's making it. Man, I want to be like that.'"[20]

Pat Boone's music plugged into the traditional values associated with Eisenhower's America. In 1956, Boone sang about marriage and romance on hits such as "I'll Be Home" and "Friendly Persuasion." And he came across as a clean-cut, All-American Boy on other hits such as "Gee Whittakers," which included tame lyrics such as "jeepers creepers," "aw shucks," and "doggone it."

Boone's success—like that of other artists on the rock & roll charts in the 1950s—provides evidence that rock & roll was a racial and cultural melting pot. As lame as Pat's covers of R&B songs might now seem to listeners, those hit records helped popularize the R&B sound. In the process, they helped rock & roll spread to millions of new listeners, both young and old. Pat believes that he, like Elvis, helped shake up the pop music industry. As an example, he cites his first hit, a 1955 cover of the Charms' R&B song "Two Hearts, Two Kisses." "It was unlike anything else that was happening then," he points out, "because that was the day of Perry Como and Patti Page and Nat Cole and Vic Damone." He followed up with covers of other R&B songs such as Fats Domino's "Ain't That a Shame" (1955), the Flamingos' "I'll Be Home" (1956), Little Richard's "Long Tall Sally" (1956), and Ivory Joe Hunter's "I

Almost Lost My Mind" (1956). "I did a bunch of R&B songs that introduced [that type of music] to a [larger] audience," Boone explains. "The
kids loved it and the parents were concerned. They were just about as
concerned about my influence on the young people through the music
as they were about Elvis."[21]

Despite Boone's reluctance to record songs that were not in keeping
with his values, he still came under attack for recording rhythm & blues.
He recalls getting letters and telegrams from churchgoers who believed that type of music was harmful to teenagers. "I was lumped in
with whichever other few performers were doing the R&B stuff," he
explains. On one occasion columnist Earl Wilson quoted Boone out of
context, implying that Pat did not want teenagers to dance to his music
because that would be sinful. Disc jockeys around the country then
threatened to stop playing Boone's records. "We had to put out that
fire," says Boone. "It was a volatile period because legislators and ministers, teachers, parents, all kinds of groups were actually burning records
and breaking them because they thought this whole thing of rock & roll
was going to be a bad influence on their kids."[22]

Boone's brand of pop rock was just as important historically as rockabilly or R&B-influenced rock. His hit records not only helped broaden
the base and popularity of rock & roll but they also offer snapshots of
1950s America, allowing us a glimpse of American attitudes toward the
family, romance, religion, and race. Pat's style and image established an
alternative to the Elvis model for rock & roll stars. Subsequent rock &
rollers did not have to be rebellious or behave wildly. They could follow
Boone's approach, which was in keeping with the consensus behavior of
1950s America. "Elvis and I were like salt and pepper," explains Boone.
"Some people can't take salt; some people can't take pepper." Boone
offered middle-of-the-road teenagers a safe choice in the world of
1950s rock & roll. "I was a good role model," he suggests, "[whereas]
Elvis they weren't too sure about. [Many teenagers] found him exciting,
but you know they weren't going to break rules and they weren't going
to have a chance maybe to live like Elvis. But most of them thought,
'Hey, I can live like Pat Boone.'"[23]

Pat Boone was the real thing. He was not just a slick, mass-produced
pop star disguising himself as a rock & roller. His clean-cut image was
not contrived. It simply reflected the 1950s consensus model that glorified traditional American values. Boone notes that years later *Rolling*

Stone sent out a reporter to do an exposé, hoping to "turn over the rocks and see what crawled out." The reporter found nothing. To the magazine's credit, says Boone, "they tipped their hat and put me on the cover of *Rolling Stone* and said, 'We haven't found many things that have stayed the same, remained consistent. And, like it or not, and a lot of us don't, but Pat Boone is what you see. What you see is what you get. He's not putting us on, so we tip our hat.' And, they called me 'The Great White Buck.'"[24]

Pat Boone and his pop rock style comprise an important chapter in the history of rock & roll. He admits that his "vanilla, white-bread versions" of R&B songs were not as good as the originals. But he insists that he should not be compared to the R&B artists but to the white pop artists like Perry Como, Vic Damone, and Patti Page, who dominated the national record charts in the 1950s: "I mean, that's what was happening on pop radio [back then], and my versions of R&B and rock & roll were shockingly different to anything else that was going on in pop radio then. And that's the comparison that needs to be made."[25]

NEW POP ROCKERS

The continuing success of Pat Boone combined with the sensational rise of Elvis sent shock waves throughout the pop music industry as record companies searched frantically for new pop rockers who could appeal to teenagers. The Diamonds were among the most successful newcomers in 1956 with covers of Frankie Lymon and the Teenagers' "Why Do Fools Fall in Love?," the Willows' "Church Bells May Ring," the Clovers' "Love, Love, Love," Eddie Heywood's "Soft Summer Breeze," and the G-Clefs' "Ka Ding Dong."

The Diamonds mixed traditional white pop harmonies with black R&B, but the group never seemed as contrived as the Crew-Cuts or similar white copycat singers who merely imitated doo-wop. The Diamonds were more self-effacing, and their cover records did not just duplicate the originals. Instead, they offered variations, often with a lighthearted touch that gave the records an edgy sound. A good example is the Diamonds' rendition of Frankie Lymon and the Teenagers' "Why Do Fools Fall in Love?" At first, the Diamonds follow the original almost note for note. Suddenly out of nowhere, they veer wildly off course as the lead singer holds a note for what seems like an eternity. All the while, the background singers chime in with equally humorous nonsensical syllables, poking gentle fun at the doo-wop genre. The Diamonds' sense of humor and infectious sound propelled their career forward. Bigger and better hits would follow: "Little Darlin'" would make it all the way to number 2 on the charts in 1957, and "The Stroll" would peak at number 5 in 1958.

The Diamonds were not the only pop rock act on the pop charts in 1956. Patience and Prudence—two sisters aged eleven and fourteen—found success with "Tonight You Belong to Me" and "Gonna Get Along Without You Now." Both records paired the girls' adolescent-sounding vocals with lyrics about young love and romance. Tommy Charles followed suit with two minor hits that also focused on teenage romance: "Our Love Affair" and "After School." The Mike Pedicin Quintet came out of the Philadelphia area with a sound similar to Bill Haley and His Comets and scored a minor hit with "The Large Large House." Another pop rock group, the Four Lovers, also made it onto the charts with a teen-oriented song, "You're the Apple of My Eye." (Two of the original members of the group, Frankie Valli and Tommy DeVito, later joined forces with Bob Gaudio and Nick Massi. In the early 1960s, they changed their name to the Four Seasons and went on to have a string of hits in the 1960s and beyond, including "Sherry," "Big Girls Don't Cry," and "Walk Like a Man.")

Elvis's phenomenal success in 1956 sent some record companies scurrying for young country singers with teenage appeal. ABC-Paramount Records had high hopes for George Hamilton IV, a good-looking young man from North Carolina who made it all the way to number 6 on the pop charts with a soft ballad about young love called, appropriately, "A Rose and a Baby Ruth." After several additional hits in the late '50s about teen romance and youth culture, he tacked toward country music and joined the *Grand Ole Opry*. Dot Records found brief success with Sanford Clark, an Oklahoma-born singer who grew up in Phoenix, Arizona. Clark scored a Top 10 hit in 1956 with "The Fool." The country-influenced song was powered by a chugging bass line and won over many teenagers with its sad tale about a young man with a broken heart. Capitol Records' Sonny James found even greater success with his number 1 hit, "Young Love," a country rock ballad about adolescent romance that also became a number 1 hit for actor Tab Hunter. After a few other releases aimed at the teen audience, James switched to the country music market, eventually becoming one of country music's biggest stars.

The most blatant attempt to cash in on Presleymania was a record entitled "Dear Elvis (Pages 1 & 2)" done "with love" by a female artist identified only as Audrey. It came out on the Plus record label, which described the release as a "madrigal with mimicry." The record plugged into three of the year's hottest trends: the subject was Elvis Presley; the approach copied the "break-in" sampling technique pioneered by Buchanan and Goodman's "Flying Saucer"; and the recording artist was allegedly a typical teenage girl, with whom millions of other teenagers presumably could relate.

Purporting to be a letter recited by a young teenage fan, the record begins: "Dear Elvis, I'm writing this letter / To me, you are the most." Audrey talks about starting up an Elvis fan club and parents who unfairly criticize the rock & roll idol. Snippets from recent hits such as Pat Boone's "I Almost Lost My Mind," the Platters' "Only You," and Tennessee Ernie Ford's "Sixteen Tons" are spliced in to emphasize major points. Audrey explains that even though many singers are now trying to copy him, Elvis will always be "the dreamiest." The record ends with audio clips of Elvis singing pointedly, "I wanna play house with you" and "We're gonna kiss and kiss . . . kiss some more."[26]

Audrey's "Dear Elvis" found only limited success on the pop charts and it certainly was not one of pop rock's most artistic moments, but it clearly indicates that by the end of 1956, the record industry had taken notice of the Presley phenomenon, as well as the commercial potential of teenagers and the growing market for rock & roll. In the years ahead, record companies would continue to seek out young talent to market as rock & rollers. Although the search would yield far too many young singers who were rock & rollers in name only, it would also discover many talented pop rockers, including Ricky Nelson, Connie Francis, Paul Anka, Del Shannon, Bobby Vee, and Gene Pitney, to name just a few.

By the end of 1956, pop rock had established itself as an important genre of rock & roll. But the best was yet to come. The title of Bill Haley's 1956 hit could just as easily have been applied to the future of pop rock—"See You Later, Alligator."

8

LET THE GOOD TIMES ROLL
R&B Goes Mainstream

The coming of Elvis Presley in 1956 threw open the pop music flood-gates to all types of rock & roll. Suddenly, black rhythm & blues artists found it easier to cross over onto the national pop charts. Veteran R&B duo Shirley and Lee are a good example. They rode the rock & roll wave all the way to number 20 on the pop charts with "Let the Good Times Roll," arguably the strangest-sounding hit of 1956. It begins with horns and drums playing a musical riff answered by a plinking piano— "BUM BUM, bum bum / BUM BUM, bum bum / BUM BUM, bum bum." All of a sudden, Lee jumps in, singing the first two verses on his own. "C'mon, baby, let the good times roll," he urges, "c'mon, baby, let me thrill your soul." As the listeners' ears perk up, Lee explains how he and his baby are going to "roll all night long."[1]

Then things get really weird. Shirley takes over and sings the third verse with one of the most unusual voices in rock & roll history. Sound-ing like a Munchkin holding her nose to get a higher pitch, she delivers some pretty suggestive lines of her own, asking Lee to "close the door" so they could "roll all night long." Listeners had never heard anything quite like it. "When Shirley sings, her natural voice goes simultaneously sharp and flat," explains rock critic Langdon Winner. "Each note is an average of tones, a half step up and a half step down. There is no strain or contortion of her vocal cords to achieve this effect. It simply comes out." The result is both "bizarre" and "alluring."[2]

The song's unique sound, suggestive lyrics, and obvious references to "rock" and "roll" appealed to teenagers. This was no sanitized, homogenized cover record. It was the real deal—earthy lyrics sung by identifiable black voices backed by a rocking New Orleans rhythm & blues band. The record typified the "New Orleans Sound," which legendary New Orleans producer Dave Bartholomew said was irresistible to listeners. Bartholomew explained that people just had to dance when they heard that big beat, adding "even other musicians were trying to learn what we were doing."[3]

"Let the Good Times Roll" became one of the most recognizable hits in rock & roll history. The record's distinct sound, teen-oriented lyrics, and danceable beat resonated with 1950s teenagers who were beginning to rethink mainstream attitudes toward race, sex, and traditional-sounding pop music.

In retrospect, Shirley and Lee's hit is a perfect metaphor for the growing popularity of rock & roll and African American artists. In just one year, the number of black singers on the national record charts almost doubled. In 1955, only seventeen black acts made the pop charts; twelve months later, there were thirty-two African American acts on the charts. R&B artists also found new opportunities as performers at rock & roll shows across the country.[4] When Shirley and Lee sang "Let the Good Times Roll" in 1956, they could just as easily have been referring to all the new prospects for black R&B artists on the national pop charts. The emergence of black artists guaranteed that rock & roll would be a racial and ethnic melting pot. The resulting blend would be an important step toward cultural integration—not just for popular music but also for the entire country.

POP-INFLUENCED R&B VOCAL GROUPS

Not surprisingly, the first R&B harmony groups to find sustained success on the pop charts often had a smooth pop style that sounded familiar to audiences raised on white pop music. The Orioles landed several hits on the national record charts with traditional pop-sounding records such as "What Are You Doing New Year's Eve" (1949) and "Crying in the Chapel" (1954). Billy Ward and the Dominoes followed up their first hit on the pop charts—the bawdy, novelty R&B hit of

1951, "Sixty Minute Man"—with more traditional pop stylings such as "Rags to Riches" (1953) and "St. Therese of the Roses" (1956). Otis Williams and the Charms also found success in 1956 with a traditional pop sound when they turned the tables on the cover syndrome and charted with their rendition of Cathy Carr's pop hit, "Ivory Tower." But, without a doubt, the most successful R&B group on the pop charts in the 1950s was the Platters. Comprised of lead singer Tony Williams, backed by David Lynch, Herb Reed, Paul Robi, and Zola Taylor, the Platters first hit the pop charts in 1955 with the romantic pop ballad, "Only You." Subsequent hits followed the same formula—slow, dreamy songs with lush orchestration that were perfect for dancing and romancing.

The Platters became one of pop music's biggest success stories of 1956. When the year began, their record "The Great Pretender" was already climbing the charts. Eventually, it rose all the way to number 1, making the Platters the first African American group to earn a number 1 hit on the *Billboard* record charts. Their follow-up, "(You've Got) The Magic Touch," did almost as well, coming in at number 4. They then demonstrated their own magic touch with their second number 1 hit of the year, "My Prayer." Before the year was over, they added two additional Top 20 hits, "You'll Never Know" and "It Isn't Right." The Platters would go on to have an incredible career, earning two more number 1 records, "Twilight Time" (1958) and "Smoke Gets in Your Eyes" (1959), as well as numerous Top 30 hits.

The Platters' excellent choice of material, well-produced records, smooth harmonies, and performance style that mimicked traditional white pop groups of the 1940s and '50s were the main reasons for their success. "When our first two records hit, 'Only You' and 'The Great Pretender,' it was like we were getting away with murder," says group member Paul Robi, "because people in the South did not know we were black."[5]

Mainstream audiences loved the Platters' pop harmonies and updates of ballads from the 1930s and '40s. And their popularity earned them guest spots on numerous TV shows and in movies, as well as offers to perform in many of the nation's top nightclubs. The Platters' middle-of-the-road pop sound and style were a perfect fit for the conformity demanded in cold war America. Parents saw them as nonthreatening and purveyors of good music that was safe for kids. And teenagers fell head over heels for the Platters' sentimental songs about love and romance. With the guys dressed in tuxedos and Zola in a gown, they offered up a visual style perfect for any formal occasion from weddings to junior proms.

R&B ROCK GROUPS

Despite their success on the rock & roll charts, the Platters hardly typified the new sound. More representative were R&B acts such as Shirley and Lee (who represented the R&B duo tradition) or R&B harmony groups such as the Cadillacs, Moonglows, and Five Satins (who typified the street-corner harmony sound later known as doo-wop).

Although there weren't many R&B rock duos during the mid-1950s, the few that did exist produced some of the most popular hits of rock & roll's first decade. Gene and Eunice got things started with their 1955 rhythm & blues hit "Ko Ko Mo." Their version of the song never crossed over to the pop charts, but two cover versions by the Crew-Cuts and Perry Como became Top 10 hits in 1955. Several R&B duos released records in 1956 with mixed results. Robert and Johnny took a shot with "You're Mine" and "I Believe in You," but didn't hit it big until "We Belong Together" became a Top 40 hit in 1958. Johnnie and Joe got good reviews in 1956 for "I'll Be Spinning," but they didn't find major success until the following year with "Over the Mountain, Across the Sea," which made it all the way to number 8 on the national charts and became one of rock & roll's all-time greatest hits.

Shirley and Lee had greater success in 1956 with "Let the Good Times Roll," in part because they arrived on the scene after Elvis Presley opened the pop music doors to black performers. Their Top 20 hit "was proscribed by many pop deejays for its alleged suggestiveness," recalls Arnold Shaw, who worked as a music publisher in the 1950s. "Lee, who wrote the rocker, sang in a sad-sack drawl that was an appealing foil for Shirley's piping little-girl voice."[6]

A guitar-playing R&B duo named Mickey and Sylvia did even better. By the time Mickey Baker met Sylvia Robinson in 1954, he had already gained fame as one of the most talented session guitarists in the rhythm & blues field. Sylvia had released several R&B songs on indie labels, but nothing had clicked yet. Shortly after they teamed up, they hit it big with "Love Is Strange" (co-written by Bo Diddley).[7] The song's hypnotic guitar riffs, Latin beat, and suggestive lyrics helped make it one of the outstanding records of the year. Released in December 1956, it debuted first on the R&B charts, and then within a few weeks crossed over onto the national pop charts. Not only did teenage dancers love the Latin beat, but audiences across the country were also attracted by Mickey and Sylvia's erotic banter about how she got her "lover boy" to come when called (figure 8.1).

DOO-WOP

R&B street-corner harmony groups—whose style was dubbed "doo-wop" in the 1970s—found even greater success in 1956. If the first wave of doo-wop on the pop charts back in 1954 and 1955 originated in black rhythm and blues, the second wave that hit in 1956 was clearly rock & roll. Frankie Lymon and the Teenagers led the way. The young singers—signed by George Goldner's Gee label in New York City—helped establish doo-wop as an integral part of rock & roll. The multicultural group consisted of five teenagers from the Sugar Hill section of Harlem. Two of them, Herman Santiago and Joe Negroni, were Puerto Rican; the other three, Frankie Lymon, Jimmy Merchant, and Sherman Garnes, were African American. Prior to auditioning for Goldner, the quintet had gone by a variety of names, including the Premieres, the Ermines, and the Coupe de Villes.

Goldner knew he had struck gold as soon as he heard them perform a song they had written called "Why Do Birds Sing So Gay?" He loved their harmonies, their enthusiasm, and their upbeat sound. But he knew he had to make some changes. The first thing that had to go was the song title. Goldner insisted on something that would appeal more to teenage listeners, so the group recorded a new version of the song—now entitled "Why Do Fools Fall in Love?" Goldner also changed the group's name first to The Teenagers and then to Frankie Lymon and the Teenagers. Not only would the new name showcase the talented twelve-year-old lead singer, but it would give the group appeal with young listeners who comprised the fastest-growing segment of the record-buying market. Lymon's lively lead vocal combined with the

Figure 8.1. R&B rock duo Mickey and Sylvia. (Robert Pruter Collection)

group's energetic harmony sound propelled "Why Do Fools Fall In Love" all the way to number 6 on the charts, beating out inferior covers by the Diamonds, Gale Storm, and Gloria Mann. In the process, it established doo-wop as a teenage sound (figure 8.2).

Frankie Lymon and the Teenagers were not the only doo-wop group competing against white cover records in 1956. The G-Clefs beat back

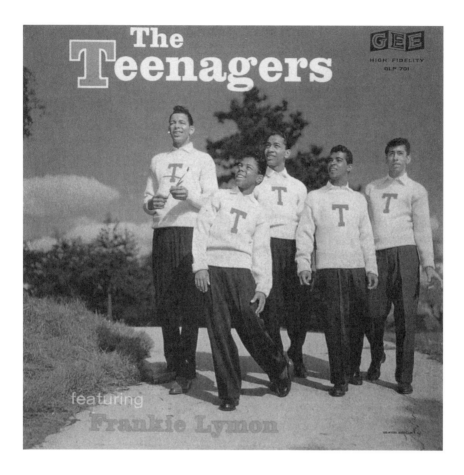

Figure 8.2. Frankie Lymon and the Teenagers became one of the most popular doo wop groups in early rock & roll. (Richard Aquila Collection)

two cover versions as their hit, "Ka-Ding Dong," climbed to number 24 on the charts, while versions by the Diamonds and Hilltoppers peaked at number 35 and number 38 respectively. The Moonglows' "See Saw" made it to number 25, while Don Cornell's cover reached only number 57. The Clovers' "Love, Love, Love" and the Diamonds' cover version both made it to number 30 on the charts. The fate of the Jayhawks' "Stranded in the Jungle" was less clear. While their original version came in at number 18 on the charts as compared to the Gadabouts' pop version that peaked at number 39, it eventually lost out to another version issued by the Cadets (a black R&B group that also recorded as the Jacks), which landed in the number 15 spot on the charts. The Teen Queens did not fare so well in their battle against covers. Their original version of "Eddie My Love" came in at number 14, as did the Chordettes' cover version. Both lost out to the Fontane Sisters' cover, which made it to number 11 on the charts.

As rock & roll became increasingly more popular in 1956, many R& B groups avoided covers completely. The Cadillacs, the Five Satins, the Six Teens, the Cliques, the Cleftones, the Willows, the Five Keys, and the Coasters all made the national pop charts with hits aimed at the young audience. The Cadillacs were one of the first R&B groups to cross over onto the pop charts without being covered. Like many groups in the mid-1950s, they were named after a car, giving them immediate appeal with teenagers in the midst of America's car culture. They came out of Harlem in 1955 and hit the national charts early the next year with "Speedoo," which was lead singer Earl Carroll's nickname. Audiences were wowed by the song's sound and message, as well as the group's on-stage choreography. The fast-paced beat was ideal for teenage dancing, while the suggestive lyrics focused on a cool guy called "Speedoo" because he didn't waste time with ladies.[8]

If songs like "Speedoo" showed teenagers the up-tempo side of doo-wop, other doo-wop hits reflected the romantic—even seductive—side of the genre. A perfect example is the Five Satins' sensual ballad "In the Still of the Nite." Not to be confused with Cole Porter's pop standard "In the Still of the Night," this doo-wop classic was written by the group's lead singer, Fred Parris. His pristine and plaintive vocal served as the focal point as the rest of the group sang in all their doo-wop glory one of the most famous vocal riffs in rock & roll history—"Shoo do in dooby doo / Shoo do in dooby do / Shoo do in dooby do."[9] Recorded in a church basement, the vocals and instrumentation sounded muffled but as smooth as the Five Satins' name. Tight harmonies, soaring falsettos, suggestive imagery, and a throbbing sax solo helped the song become one of the most erotic and requested records in rock & roll history. "In the Still of the Nite" made it to number 24 on the national pop charts when it was first released in 1956, and made the national charts again when it was rereleased in 1960 and 1961.

R&B ROCK GOES SOLO

The year 1956 provided opportunities for many R&B solo artists. Some, like "Big Joe" Turner, were veteran R&B singers who hoped to catch on with the new rock & roll audience. By the time rock & roll came along, Turner was already a giant in the rhythm & blues field with legendary R&B hits like "Chains of Love" (1951), "Chill Is On" (1952), "Honey Hush" (1953), and "Shake, Rattle, and Roll" (1954). Interestingly, that last R&B hit never made the national record charts because it was totally eclipsed by Bill Haley and the Comets' cover version. The song did call attention to Turner, though, and helped land him a role in the 1957 film *Shake, Rattle, and Rock*. Despite his enormous talent and his stylistic influences on early rock & roll, Big Joe was never able to make the transition to rock & roll. Born in 1911, he was simply too old for the new teen-oriented music. The closest he ever came to Top 40 hits on the national record charts were with "Corrine, Corrina," which made it to number 41 in 1956, and "Honey Hush," which peaked at number 53 in 1959.

Numerous other veteran R&B singers, including Wynonie Harris, Roy Brown, Ivory Joe Hunter, LaVern Baker, Faye Adams, Ruth Brown, Etta James, Dinah Washington, Roy Hamilton, and B. B. King, suffered similar fates, either because of their age or because their music, styles, and sounds were too close to old-fashioned rhythm & blues. For example, Wynonie Harris, nicknamed "Mr. Blues" because of the fifteen R&B hits he racked up between 1946 and 1952, was retired by the time rock & roll appeared in the mid-1950s. His manager explained Harris was lured back by the coming of the new teenage music. "What they call rock and roll today, Harris was singing ten years ago," he explained. "One only has to compare Harris' . . . 'Good Rockin' Tonight' with Elvis Presley's more recent version of it to see that."[10] But the old R&B singer's comeback went nowhere. Roy Brown, who wrote Harris's number 1 R&B hit, "Good Rockin' Tonight" (1948) and helped shape the New Orleans R&B sound in the late 1940s and early '50s, had his only Top 30 hit on the rock & roll charts in 1957 with a version of Fats Domino's "Let the Four Winds Blow." Similarly, Ivory Joe Hunter, who had over twenty hits on the R&B charts between 1945 and 1958, had only one big hit on the rock & roll charts. His seminal "Since I Met You Baby" climbed all the way to number 12 in 1956. LaVern Baker, one of the most popular female R&B singers of the 1950s with fifteen Top 20 hits on the R&B charts, was able to crack into the Top 20 on the national pop charts on only three occasions: "Tweedle Dee" (1955), "Jim Dandy" (1956), and "I Cried a Tear" (1958).

Other R&B artists fared better, either because they were closer in age to the rock & roll audience or because their music and sound appealed more to young audiences. One of the most talented R&B artists to take a crack at the burgeoning rock & roll market was Clyde McPhatter. His first taste of success came as the lead singer for Billy Ward and His Dominoes, one of the premier R&B groups of the early 1950s. McPhatter was one of the first R&B singers to introduce a gospel style to the music. In 1953, he formed his own group, the Drifters, and signed a contract with Ahmet Ertegun's Atlantic Records.[11] (After McPhatter left the group, the Drifters underwent several personnel changes and eventually found tremendous success in the late 1950s and early '60s with major hits such as "There Goes My Baby," "Save the Last Dance for Me," and "Under the Boardwalk.")

Even though Clyde McPhatter's early releases on Atlantic were successes only on the R&B charts, they were destined to become rock & roll classics. "Money Honey" is a perfect example. The 1953 release made it all the way to number 1 on the rhythm & blues charts, but it never cracked the pop charts during this pre–rock & roll era. Yet the song became a rock & roll classic after Elvis Presley did a cover of it in 1956. "Money Honey" showcases the twenty-one-year-old McPhatter at his best, with his tense and expressive vocal careening up and down the scale like a runaway roller coaster. The song's message—that money is the only thing that really matters—was in keeping with the era's emphasis on consumer goods and conspicuous consumption.

After McPhatter split with the Drifters in 1955, he found success on the rock & roll charts with "Treasure of Love" (1956) and "A Lover's Question" (1958). The latter reached number 6 on the national charts. "[A Lover's Question] used an arrangement very similar to those used by harmony gospel groups (such as the Dixie Hummingbirds)," explains music historian Charlie Gillett, "with a bass singer providing a vocal equivalent of a double bass rhythm while McPhatter wailed the melodic, plaintive lyric."[12] His only other Top 10 hit came in 1962 with the up-tempo "Lover Please."

While older and more established R&B singers found it difficult to catch on with the broader teenage audience, a new, younger generation of R& B artists—including Fats Domino, Chuck Berry, and Little Richard—found the transition much easier.

FATS DOMINO

When the twenty-one-year-old Elvis Presley hit it big, Fats Domino was twenty-eight and already had numerous hit records to his credit, including sixteen Top 10 hits on the R&B charts and three hits that crossed over onto the national pop charts. In 1956, Fats would prove once and for all that he was not just a rhythm & blues singer. Before the year was out, he earned six more hits on the national charts, establishing him as one of rock & roll's biggest stars.

Fats started the year fairly slow with "Bo Weevil," which stalled at number 35 on the charts. But as Presleymania swept the nation, Domino found his stride with a two-sided hit. "I'm in Love Again" climbed all the way to number 4, while its flip-side, "My Blue Heaven" (which had been a number 1 pop hit for both Paul Whiteman and Gene Austin in 1927), reached number 19. He followed up with another song aimed at the pop audience, "When My Dreamboat Comes Home" (a number 3 hit for Guy Lombardo in 1937), which peaked at number 14. He saved the best for last. In October, his cover version of "Blueberry Hill" (a pop classic originally recorded by Glenn Miller and Gene Autry in the 1940s and Louis Armstrong in 1956) began climbing the pop charts, eventually making it all the way to number 2 in early 1957. Dave Bartholomew, who produced all of Domino's hits, was extremely pleased with Fats's version of the song: "Blueberry Hill was actually recorded . . . before we did it by the late Louis Armstrong. It wasn't our tune. . . . But I put the bridge in that. Actually, what I was doing was complementing Fats' voice because I wasn't exactly sure that this was the right change we were playing. . . . So we did that and immediately it was a three-million seller. . . . We made it a standard. . . . I think that's one of those things that will live on and on and on and on."[13]

Throughout the rest of the 1950s and into the '60s, Fats Domino racked up hit after hit on the national pop charts. One of the few rock & rollers of the era with both million-selling singles and albums, Fats attracted large audiences wherever he performed. Bartholomew insists that audiences were attracted by the big beat in Domino's music. "The whites were just beginning to learn how to dance," he explains. "[By the late 1950s] they was learnin' on the Dick Clark show, and Fats Domino was dynamite during that time. And everybody wanted to see Fats. When we would get to the place, there'd be 3,000 or 4,000 people trying to get in at different gates. And we always had 10 or 15,000 people, because he was an original. And when they got there, we'd give them a show, give them something to go back and tell other people, because there was no other band doing what we were doing. . . . It was the New Orleans Sound. It was new, and they didn't know what the hell we were doing."[14]

Dave Bartholomew played a major role in Domino's spectacular success, co-writing, arranging, and producing most of Fats's hits. "Dave mostly did the arrangement to the music, but I wrote most of the things," said Fats. "I give Dave a lot of credit, because he knew just what I wanted." Bartholomew tells it differently. "Let's get this straight," he explains. "We didn't sit down and write songs together. There were just a few things Fats and I did together. . . . Most of my catalog was actually written by me because I ran Imperial Record Company. I was A&R man—arrangement and repertoire man—for Imperial for 35 years and I wrote for an awful lot of people." Bartholomew put the studio band together, did all the musical arrangements, and was in charge of the recording sessions. "I had final say," he points out. "I found Fats and I made Fats." Frank Fields, who played bass on most of Domino's hits, underscores the important role played by Bartholomew, noting "Fats' musical vocabulary didn't carry you too far." Bartholomew was the one who wrote the musical notations and created all the musical arrangements for the band. And he was the one who produced the records. "Every time you turn around, people get it ass backwards," says Bartholomew. "I was the producer [not Fats or Cosimo Matassa who owned the studio]. I did the arranging. I did the lyrics, except with Fats where we worked the lyrics out together. But I did all the music. Nobody but Dave Bartholomew."[15]

At the same time, Domino's role in the creative process should not be minimized. Fats wrote numerous tunes and lyrics; he collaborated with partners other than Bartholomew to write "I'm Ready" in 1956, as well as later hits such as "Be My Guest" (1959). Fats wrote some of his later hits such as "I Want to Walk You Home" (1959) totally on his own. Those closest to Domino in the recording process were often the ones most impressed by his talent. Bartholomew himself called Fats an "original" and predicted early on that he was "gonna be great someday." Drummer Earl Palmer insists, "Fats was a hell of a lot better musician than people give him credit for. He had a lot of original thoughts and they were all creative." Cosimo Matassa, who engineered Domino's recording sessions in his New Orleans studio, agrees. Domino "was creative," he says. "No matter what he does comes through. He could be singing the national anthem, you'd still know by the time he said two words, it was him. Obviously, unmistakably, and pleasurably him." Significantly, Domino usually got what he wanted in the recording studio. For example, Bartholomew did not like their take on "Ain't That a Shame." "There's not too much of a story there," he explains. "I wanted to explain more why it was a shame but Fats said 'no.' So we let it go like that. But it's good."[16]

Although the singer and the producer may not always have agreed on details, they teamed up to record some of rock & roll's greatest hits, including "Ain't That a Shame" (1955), "Blueberry Hill" (1956), and "I'm Walkin'" (1957). Domino's records offer fascinating glimpses of 1950s America. Songs such as "Blue Monday" (1956) and "I Want to Walk You Home" (1959) capture working-class attitudes and everyday speech patterns. "Ain't That a Shame" (1955), "Blueberry Hill" (1956), and "My Blue Heaven" (1956) reflect traditional attitudes toward romance. Domino's songs and performance style reflect 1950s conservatism in other ways. Dave Bartholomew points out that he and Fats always tried to stay within the proper boundaries. "Most of the parents [back then] thought we were helping the kids get out of hand," he explains, "but it wasn't us because we didn't go to that extent. . . . We had respectable rock & roll. You can't put that on the blacks. . . . All we did when you saw us is we had a suit on. We were very respectable."[17]

The era's attitudes toward race are intertwined with Fats Domino's music. On one level, Fats was able to transcend segregation. He frequently appeared on television and radio; he and his band played both white and black venues; they often performed before integrated audiences; and they earned the respect of music lovers regardless of color. "Everywhere we played—places like Biloxi, Mississippi, where it was real segregated—we was invited to [white] wedding receptions and

things like that," recalls Bartholomew. "I was always accepted everywhere because the band . . . didn't have any characters. We had gentlemen. So we were invited everywhere." Fats Domino and his band
played throughout the South and became a favorite at white colleges as
well as white country clubs. "What actually happened," says Bartholomew, "is our music carried us on and on to [greater] heights." Of
course, off stage, Fats Domino and Dave Bartholomew had to face the
same racial problems as other African Americans in 1950s America.
"Quite naturally, off the bandstand, we was always different," explains
Bartholomew. "You're still black. That even goes today. I don't know
what it will actually take [to change that], but it's gonna be bigger than
you or I to solve this problem."[18]

Though Fats Domino and other black rock & rollers did not cause
an end to racial discrimination in the 1950s, they certainly helped
undermine it. Domino's concerts were "ground zero for racial integration," insists music historian Rick Coleman. "Whites overflowed segregated boundaries to sit or dance next to blacks at Domino's shows and
bought his records by the millions," explains Coleman. "As the first
black rock 'n' roll superstar, Domino helped pave the way for integration, becoming the goodwill ambassador for a revolution."[19]

The very existence of black rock & roll stars like Fats Domino was
tantamount to cultural subversion. Racism was undermined every time
a white teenager cheered Fats Domino at a concert, enthusiastically
watched him on TV, listened intently to one of his songs on the radio, or
rushed out to buy one of his records. Domino chipped away at racism in
other ways. His 1956 hit "I'm in Love Again" included the line "eenie,
meenie, and miney moe / told me you didn't want me around no more,"
which was a mischievous variation on a well-known racist children's
rhyme. At concerts, Fats encouraged black and white audiences to
dance, often right next to each other. One of Domino's band members
went so far as to say, "Fats made integration. Fats was the Martin
Luther King of music. He brought white and blacks together, Indians,
everything."[20]

Dave Bartholomew suggests that the type of music that he and Fats
played brought blacks and whites together in subtle ways. "Let me tell
this to the world," he says proudly. "Our music for many many years
when I was jammin' all over the place, all over the world, the ladies and
gentlemen would be around and say, 'C'mon we gonna have Dave play.'

And this would be a lot of whites. I remember we were jammin' in France on the Riviera, and what we did, man, all the white musicians were there, man, and say, 'C'mon, let's get together.' So we always had a bond between us. We didn't think about color. The musicians would just get together and play." The music, says Bartholomew, gave them at least a little victory against racism.[21]

Fats Domino was one of early rock & roll's most popular stars. He did not have the good looks and charisma of Elvis Presley, the outrageous sound of Little Richard, or the acrobatics or poetics of Chuck Berry. But his inimitable style and common-man appeal made him a rock & roll legend. His charming persona and nonthreatening image made him an ideal vehicle to broaden the base of rock & roll. His warm, infectious vocal style and identifiable piano sound powered fast-paced rockers as well as ballads and pop standards. "One of the great piano players of all time," is how Dave Bartholomew describes Domino. "He made the triplet on the piano very famous. He was very authentic. He didn't copy anyone. He was original and still is." Bartholomew notes that Domino's vocals always had a folk music or country & western quality, sort of a blend between folk and rhythm & blues. "In other words, like when the people were in the cotton fields, having hard times, and they would sing and it would actually come from the heart. And that's what actually would come from Fats Domino's voice."[22]

Fats Domino and Dave Bartholomew are now recognized as two of rock & roll's founding fathers. Over the years, they have collected numerous honors. Most notably, they were inducted individually into the Rock & Roll Hall of Fame; they entered the Song Writers Hall of Fame as a team; and Fats Domino was awarded the National Medal of the Arts in 1998. At a ceremony in the Rose Garden, President Bill Clinton explained that Domino's "rich voice and distinctive piano style helped to define rock & roll, the music that more than any other creative force in America has brought the races together." Such official kudos only confirm what rock & roll fans have known for decades: the music of Fats Domino and Dave Bartholomew helped teenagers find their thrill on "Blueberry Hill."

CHUCK BERRY

As Presleymania swept across the United States in the summer of 1956, Chuck Berry's "Roll Over Beethoven" became a Top 30 hit. The record was not Berry's first appearance on the national charts. That honor belongs to "Maybellene," a number 5 hit in 1955. But even if "Roll Over Beethoven" wasn't Berry's first hit, it was nonetheless one of his most important. The record heralded the coming of rock & roll and offered a tantalizing glimpse of the singer's uncanny ability to write lyrics that appealed to both white and black audiences.

"Roll Over Beethoven" alludes to the changing music scene of 1956, referring specifically to disc jockeys, jukeboxes, and teenagers dancing like a "spinnin' top" to new "rockin' rhythm records." For good measure, it tosses in a reference to a current hit, "Blue Suede Shoes," popularized by both Carl Perkins and Elvis Presley. Coming on the heels of "Maybellene," the record guaranteed that Chuck would not be a one-hit wonder. Along with its bold declaration that old-style music had been replaced by the new rhythm & blues sound, it announced the arrival of a new style and a new day. Here was a black man telling the white establishment to back off and serving notice to everyone that the times were changing. "Roll Over Beethoven," he proclaimed, "and dig these rhythm and blues."[23]

Although "Roll Over Beethoven" was Chuck Berry's only hit on the national pop charts in 1956, he had three additional songs on the R&B charts—"No Money Down," "Too Much Monkey Business," and "Brown-Eyed Handsome Man"—which became well known to the rock & roll audience. Berry's penchant for writing teen-oriented lyrics would soon earn him a string of rock & roll hits about dancing, dating, cars, high school, and other teen interests. Before the decade was out, Chuck Berry would become one of the greatest rock & roll stars around with Top 10 hits such as "School Day" (1957), "Rock & Roll Music" (1957), "Sweet Little Sixteen" (1958), and "Johnny B. Goode" (1958).

In 1956, though, Chuck was still trying to establish his rock & roll credentials. His appearance and exciting performance style would contribute greatly to his success. Berry—like the title of one of his early songs—was a "brown-eyed handsome man." On stage he dressed in a flashy tuxedo or drape jacket with pegged pants. Tall and slim, his agile movements added a striking visual element to his distinctive sound. He won over audiences everywhere he played, beginning with his very first appearance at a rock & roll show at the Brooklyn Paramount in 1955. A music trade magazine reported, "When [Alan] Freed introduced Chuck Berry, the Chess artist tore down the house with a rollicking version of 'Maybellene.'"[24]

From that moment on, audiences could not get enough of his showmanship. They loved his facial expressions, acrobatics, dance steps, comedic moves, and sexually suggestive antics. Like other rhythm & blues performers, he cradled his guitar near his crotch and often played it at a right angle, aiming the phallic instrument directly at excited females in the audience who screamed wildly for more. Another crowd pleaser was the duck walk, which became Berry's signature move. Fans squealed in delight as the performer squatted down and began bobbing his head as he glided across the stage to the beat. Chuck later revealed that he invented the step out of necessity. He was appearing at the Brooklyn Paramount and his suit had so many wrinkles that it looked like seersucker. So he hit on the idea of squatting down and doing this funny little walk in order to hide the wrinkles from the audience. Berry was always determined to put on a good show. "To me, a gig was played for the purpose of entertaining the patrons," he explained. "I can never understand why any group would not terminate a song that has boredom showing from the audience." Chuck Berry learned that lesson under fire, trying to please unruly crowds in the St. Louis club where he began his career. He says, "The varied audience at the Cosmo Club gave me an early start at judging the state of the people to be entertained."[25]

The singer's dynamic performances complemented his seminal sound. Berry records typically opened with a blasting guitar riff. The song would then explode into a chugging rhythm and pounding back beat, establishing an identifiable sound for early rock & roll. Chuck's guitar style was inspired in part by the guitarist in Louis Jordan's R&B band. "Much of my material," notes Berry, "begins with Carl Hogan's familiar riff, like 'ba-doo-doo dah / ba-doo-doo dah." Berry adds that his guitar playing was also influenced by Les Paul's electrifying licks on pop hits such as "How High the Moon." [26]

Music historian Joe Stuessy credits Berry with making the guitar "the central instrumental ingredient in rock & roll." The resulting sound was a virtual duet between the singer and the instrument. "The statement-and-answer technique in which the guitar mimics the just completed vocal line is related to the two-bar or four-bar 'trade-offs' found in jazz," says Stuessy. Berry's style pointed the way for other rock guitarists. "The double-note playing in his solos, the alternating chords of his rhythmic accompaniments (similar to some rock piano styles) set models to be followed for years," explains Stuessy. [27]

Berry's approach incorporated call-and-response patterns traditionally found in African American music. Chuck's guitar provided a dominant rhythm that was answered by the boogie-style piano playing of Johnnie Johnson. Chuck says that by the mid-1950s he was "fluent enough picking the guitar to fill in full choruses without repeating licks. Johnny and I became so tight in feeling each other's direction that whenever I played a riff with any pause in it, he would answer it with the same melodic pattern and vice versa." [28]

In recent years, some people have suggested that Chuck Berry was not the sole composer of his hits. Rolling Stones' guitarist Keith Richards—who credits Berry as one of his biggest influences—says that Chuck undoubtedly wrote all the lyrics, but his piano player, Johnnie Johnson, may have helped with the music. At first, Johnson completely denied the theory, insisting he was simply in the studio when Chuck wrote songs. But the question lingered due to circumstantial evidence. Critic Michael MacCambridge claims that Berry's songs are written in "unusual keys for a guitar player" and that Berry had never written any songs before he made four demos with Johnnie Johnson for Chess in 1955. MacCambridge compares the Berry–Johnson dynamic to "the collaborative one used by the Beatles and the Rolling Stones and other groups in which multiple composers share songwriting credits." Adding credence to that theory is the fact that Johnson actually sued Berry in 2000, asking for songwriting credits and back royalties, but the suit was dismissed because of a statute of limitations. [29]

In any case, Chuck Berry crafted a hybrid sound that was successful both artistically and commercially. If Elvis Presley began in country and moved toward rhythm & blues, Berry started out in R&B and moved toward country. The two musical styles came together at the point where they intersected with pop. Berry points out, "The nature and backbone of my beat is boogie, and the muscle of my music is melodies that are simple." Pop melodies were just the beginning. Berry also relied on other pop music tricks to sell records, including referencing specific places, girls' names, or popular consumer goods.[30]

Berry's lyrics were particularly important to his success. Numerous critics view him as rock & roll's first poet laureate. "The lyrics of Chuck Berry's songs constitute some of the most exciting folk poetry in the rock field," suggests art historian Carl Belz. "They represent the folk artist's unconsciousness of art—particularly in his innocent notion that poetry should rhyme, and that all rhythmic spaces should be filled, even if filling them necessitates the slicing of words or the creation of new ones." Sometimes writing in the first person, other times as an observer, Chuck was a masterful storyteller with an uncanny ability to craft pointed lyrics that captured the essence of youth culture, as well as everyday life in 1950s America. Berry understood that white teenagers "helped launch black artists nationally into the main line of popular music," so he made a conscious decision to tap into that market. "Whatever would sell was what I thought I should concentrate on, so from 'Maybellene' on I mainly improvised my lyrics toward the young adult and some even for the teeny boppers."[31]

Unlike most performers from an R&B background, Berry had a talent for writing lyrics that plugged into white teenage interests, as evidenced by later songs such as "School Day" and "Sweet Little Sixteen." His 1956 hit "Roll Over Beethoven" glorified the new music that teenagers loved. By the time it was released, teenage rebellion was already a fixture in popular culture. Marlon Brando starred as a motorcycle gang leader in *The Wild One*, James Dean portrayed an anguished youth in *Rebel Without a Cause*, and Alan Freed's rock & roll shows were viewed by many adults as a prime cause of juvenile delinquency. In this context, Berry's "Roll Over Beethoven" defiantly proclaimed the arrival of rock & roll.

Chuck's early records recall daily life in 1950s America. "Maybellene" (1955) alludes to the popularity of V-8 engines, Fords, and Cadillacs; "Thirty Days" (1955) references crooked judges and courts; "Too Much Monkey Business" (1956) relates the daily hassles of going to school, working for a living, and dealing with salesmen; "No Money Down" (1956) talks about popular tastes in automobiles and buying products on credit.

Berry might have helped shape the times almost as much as his music reflected them. Arguably, the very presence of black rock &

rollers on the pop music charts and in the national spotlight promoted racial integration. "Democracy, one of the most important things taught (but not necessarily practiced) in our classrooms, was manifesting itself in the ballrooms," noted R&B band leader Johnny Otis. "A spontaneous integration occurred. Rock 'n' roll audiences became integrated." Of course, not everyone was pleased to see white teenagers cheering black singers. Sonny Curtis, who performed with Buddy Holly's group, the Crickets, remembers that as kids he and Buddy had to go out in the car late at night to listen to Chuck Berry and other African American singers "'cause it was considered 'race music.'" Mick Jagger has a similar memory: "I was crazy over Chuck Berry, Bo Diddley, Muddy Waters, and Fats Domino. . . . My father used to call it jungle music." The Rolling Stones' lead singer kept listening anyway. "It seemed like the most real thing I'd ever known." [32]

Berry was always aware of the role he and other rock & rollers were playing in bringing the races together. The African American singer never forgot his first appearance before a large, mostly white audience at the Brooklyn Paramount in 1955. "I doubt that many Caucasian persons would come into a situation that would cause them to know the feeling a black person experiences after being reared under old-time Southern traditions and then finally being welcomed by an entirely unbiased and friendly audience, applauding without apparent regard for racial differences." The singer never failed to be amazed by integrated audiences at rock & roll concerts: "We'd go in [to perform] and see the salt and pepper all mixed together." [33]

Some fans and music experts insist that Berry consciously chipped away at the racial barriers. Listeners often interpret lyrics to songs such as "Johnny B. Goode," "Jo Jo Gunne," "Brown-Eyed Handsome Man," and "Promised Land" as subversive attempts to further the cause of African Americans. Some writers even compare Berry to the legendary "trickster" of African folklore who employs humor and pranks to defeat his oppressor. Music writer Rick Coleman suggests that African American artists such as Chuck Berry, Fats Domino, and Little Richard were all "tricksters" who charmed "their way into white culture with harmless-sounding lyrics and seducing rhythms." [34] Historian Glenn Altschuyler likewise argues that Berry purposefully gave "voice to black culture and music." "Brown-Eyed Handsome Man," says Altschuyler, "played slyly with racial attitudes and even fears." Altschuyler explains that the opening lines of the song "seem to promise a racialized discussion as well, this time of economic oppression and sexual power."[35]

These experts are probably giving Berry more credit than he deserves. For the most part, Berry did not consciously write songs as social commentary on race relations. He makes it clear in his autobiography that he did not want to infuse race into "Johnny B. Goode." On the other hand, "Brown-Eyed Handsome Man" was a deliberate attempt to praise people of color if not African Americans. Berry wrote the song on his first tour in California. His bookings were mostly in Hispanic neighborhoods, so there were not very many whites in the audience. "The auditoriums were predominately filled with Hispanics and 'us,'" he explains. "But then I did see unbelievable harmony among the mix, which got the idea of the song started."[36]

Even if most of Berry's songs did not intentionally set out to undermine the era's racial status quo, some listeners certainly interpreted them that way. And Chuck's actions often spoke louder than his words. He did not suffer fools easily, regardless of their skin color. On concert tours, he sometimes stood up to white restaurant owners who refused to serve blacks, he questioned bigots who refused to allow him to play, and he resented anyone who treated African Americans as second-class citizens. During one performance in the South, for example, Berry was gleeful when he saw prejudiced white policemen grow angry because white teenage girls were displaying affection for black rock & roll singers. Years later, he still vividly recalled the scene: "Twice as many young whites as blacks rushed toward the stage, climbed on, and began socializing," he explained. "We knew the authorities were blazing angry with them for rushing on stage and at us for welcoming them, but they could only stand there and watch young public opinion exercise its reaction to the [racial] boundaries they were up against." Berry understood that rock & roll tours that included both white and black performers helped advance integration. And he was proud of the role he played in the process. At one point, Chuck confided to white rockabilly singer Carl Perkins, "You know, Carl, we might be doing as much with our music as our leaders are in Washington to bring down the racial barriers."[37]

Chuck Berry's tremendous popularity in the 1950s cannot be attributed to any one factor. It was the overall package that attracted teenagers. Sonically, Berry's music was quintessential rock & roll—a pounding beat, a piercing electric guitar, and driving rhythms that were perfect for fast dancing. Lyrically, the records were sometimes humorous, other times ironic, but always interesting, telling stories that teenagers could relate to about cars, schools, romance, and pressures from parents, teachers, police, and other authority figures. Visually, the charismatic rock & roller was sensational, combining dynamic stage performances with an undeniable message that reverberated throughout the land long after the amplifiers were turned off and the spotlights dimmed. As "Roll Over Beethoven" predicted, here was a black man and his R&B-influenced music making it big in a predominately white America.

LITTLE RICHARD

The year 1956 witnessed the arrival of another major African American rock & roll artist—Little Richard. To put it mildly, Little Richard (aka Richard Penniman) was not exactly the kind of artist who could be easily marketed in the conservative 1950s: he looked and sounded weird, he acted strange, he was black, and he was homosexual. Yet Little Richard became one of the most successful and important artists in rock & roll's first decade.

Born in Macon, Georgia, in 1932, the young Penniman's musical tastes ranged from rhythm & blues to gospel music and all the way back to jump blues. In his late teens, he put together an R&B band called the Upsetters. The name of the band was apt, recalls drummer Charles Conner, because "when we'd go into a place, we'd upset it! We were the first band on the road to wear pancake makeup and eye shadow, have an earring hanging out of our ear and have our hair curled in process." Conner points out that Little Richard was the only member of the band who was actually gay, "but he wanted us to be different and exciting." The band would take the stage playing a few warm up notes and all of a sudden, Little Richard would come charging out. Audiences were stunned by his appearance. He wore flamboyant colors, capes, ruffled shirts, and shimmering sharkskin suits with draped jackets and baggy pegged pants. And the only thing more outrageous than his makeup was his processed pompadour, which stood anywhere from six to twelve inches over his forehead.[38]

Little Richard's wild singing and performance style were in keeping with his look. "He sang with an intensity and frenzy and commitment that marked the outer limits of rock 'n' roll," explains music scholar Arnold Shaw. Little Richard shouted out lyrics and screamed in between beats for emphasis. "One night he might walk on top of the piano. Another night he might wander into the crowd. He'd prance and preen, then jump up and holler, egging the audience on, whipping them up, getting ready to play," notes music historian James Miller. When he got the crowd worked up, Little Richard would then "hit the piano, hammering out triplets, a picture of frenzy, sweat pouring down his face, his head shaking, his hair falling, the music rocking."[39] Only then would he start singing, launching a ferocious attack on the lyrics and melody.

Little Richard represented a risqué rhythm & blues tradition that dated back to at least the 1940s. He honed his sound and style to perfection playing in small bars in front of audiences that appreciated his weird appearance, histrionics, and wild songs. In 1955, Little Richard was signed by Art Rupe's Specialty Records. His first recording session—held in the same New Orleans studio where Fats Domino recorded all of his hits—was almost a disaster. Record producer Bumps Blackwell (who previously had worked with Quincy Jones and Ray Charles) was amazed when Little Richard walked into the studio. The singer was wearing a shirt that "was so loud it looked as though he had drunk raspberry juice, cherryade, malt, and greens, and then thrown up all over himself," recalls Blackwell. The producer was even more surprised when Little Richard began to sing. Instead of living up to his billing as an outrageous singer and performer, Penniman was almost sedate as he worked his way through eight songs. The studio musicians—the same ones that Dave Bartholomew used on Fats Domino records—were not impressed.[40]

The recording session went nowhere fast, so Blackwell took Little Richard down the street for lunch at a local blues bar. As soon as he walked through the door, Little Richard was instantly transformed. Bumps explains what happened: "We walk into the place, and the girls are there and the boys are there and he's got an audience. There's a piano, and that's his crutch. He's on stage reckoning to show Lee Allen [who headed up the bar band] his piano style. So *wow!* He gets to sing. He hits that piano . . . and starts to sing." Blackwell just stood there with his mouth open. He couldn't believe his eyes or ears as Little Richard screamed out obscene lyrics to "Tutti Frutti," a song that the flamboyant singer had written and had been playing in bars for years. "Awop-bop-a-loo-mop a good goddam / Tutti-Frutti, good booty / If it don't fit, don't force it / You can grease it, make it easy!"[41]

Bumps rushed Little Richard back to the studio and quickly brought in someone to tone down the lyrics. Little Richard didn't like the result but agreed to record it anyway. They wrapped up the session in fifteen minutes. Though the new version had tamer lyrics, it still sounded just as raw and just as defiant. It begins with Little Richard screaming out nonsensical syllables: "Awop-bop-a-loo-mop a bim bam boom!" followed by "I've got a gal named Daisy / she almost drives me crazy, whooo."[42]

At first, Little Richard was not convinced: "I didn't go to New Orleans to record no 'Tutti-Frutti.'. . . I never thought it would be a hit, even with the lyrics cleaned up."[43] Despite the singer's skepticism, the record took off like a shot. Even though Pat Boone's cover stole some of Little Richard's thunder and siphoned off potential record buyers, Little Richard's version did well enough to make it all the way to number 17 on the national record charts. "The white stations wouldn't play black records . . . and then they took Pat Boone and threw Pat Boone on me," Little Richard later explained. "But the white kids . . . they wanted to hear me. They would still bring me in their house, and they didn't want their Mama to know I was in the house. So, they'd put Pat Boone on top of their bed. And I was in the closet. But I was still in the same house."[44]

"Tutti Frutti" launched Little Richard's career as a rock & roll singer and established a pattern for subsequent hits. Given conservative attitudes of the 1950s, Little Richard knew he had to clean up his act if he wanted airplay on rock & roll stations. From that point on, he wrote and sang sexually suggestive songs, but the lyrics were never as explicit as those he had sung in R&B bars. Even still, censors kept a close watch on his songs. The NBC radio network, for instance, refused to play Little Richard's "Long Tall Sally" (1956) until censors aired it first. A trade magazine reported, "the censor exec finally just shook his head and . . . [said] 'How can I reject it when I can't even understand it?'"[45]

Looking back, it seems strange that Little Richard was able to get away with as much as he did in Eisenhower's America. After all, he was performing in the shadow of McCarthyism with public fears about communists, juvenile delinquents, minorities, and perverts lurking everywhere. Evidently, Little Richard was so outrageous and so far over the top that the general public just couldn't take him seriously. Rock writer James Miller theorizes that "Richard intuitively grasped the issues at play. Being black and being gay, he was an outsider twice over. But by exaggerating his own freakishness, he could get across: he could evade the question of gender and hurdle the racial divide." Miller notes that Little Richard all but confirmed this when he wrote in his memoir: "We decided that my image should be crazy and way out, so that adults would think I was harmless. I'd appear in one show dressed as the Queen of England and in the next as the pope."[46]

If adults overlooked Little Richard, teenagers did not. Indeed, for many members of the rock & roll audience, Little Richard epitomized what the music was all about. He screamed out his vocals, pounded his piano with abandon, and spewed forth sexually suggestive lyrics as he racked up hit after hit. In 1956, he scored with "Tutti Frutti," "Long Tall Sally," "Slippin' and Slidin'," "Rip It Up," and "Ready Teddy." The following year, he enjoyed success with "The Girl Can't Help It," "Lucille," "Jenny Jenny," and "Keep a Knockin'." His last Top 10 hit, "Good Golly, Miss Molly," came in 1958. Then, his career came to a sudden halt when the R&B rocker found religion. Little Richard's plane almost crashed while he was touring Australia and the Philippines. He recalls looking out the plane's window and seeing an engine on fire. Right there and then, he promised God that if he survived he would give up the "devil's music" and become a preacher. When the plane landed safely, Little Richard turned his back on rock & roll and enrolled in a divinity school run by Seventh Day Adventists. "If you want to live with the Lord, you can't rock 'n' roll, too," he explained to an Australian reporter. "God doesn't like it." (By the late 1960s, Little Richard had resumed his music career. Either the singer determined that God had changed his mind about the music, or Little Richard simply concluded that his debt to God was paid in full. In either case, he never again had another major hit record.[47])

Though his time at the top of the rock charts was brief, Little Richard left his imprint on the new music. The erstwhile R&B shouter personified the wilder side of rock & roll: defiance, sex, and freedom. His raucous style and suggestive songs became rock & roll archetypes, influencing contemporaries such as Elvis Presley, Jerry Lee Lewis, and Buddy Holly, as well as later rockers like the Beatles, John Fogerty, and Mitch Ryder and the Detroit Wheels. "When Jerry Lee [Lewis] hits the piano keyboard with his butt, bangs the keys with the boot of his heel of an outstretched leg and leaps on top [of the piano], it's Little Richard," insists music scholar Arnold Shaw. "When Presley chokes-gasps-gulps his words and swivels his pelvis, it's Little Richard. When the Beatles scream 'yeah, yeah, yeah' and gliss into a high falsetto, it's Little Richard." No doubt, the flamboyant singer would totally agree. Little Richard summed up his music and significance in his typical immodest way: "I call it the healing music—the music that makes the blind see, the lame, the deaf, and dumb hear, walk, and talk. The music of joy, the music that uplifts your soul. . . . I am the living flame, Little Richard is my name."[48]

BO DIDDLEY AND OTHER R&B ROCKERS

While Little Richard, Fats Domino, and Chuck Berry were establishing themselves on the pop charts in 1956, other black rhythm & blues singers were having a harder time making the transition to rock & roll. Otis Williams, the lead singer of the Charms, was able to muster only one minor hit, "That's Your Mistake." Sonny Knight's "Confidential" managed to creep into the Top 20, but his follow-ups flopped. Little Willie John did somewhat better. After he earned his first Top 30 hit on the national charts in 1956 with "Fever," he scored two additional Top 20 hits: "Talk to Me, Talk to Me" (1958) and "Sleep" (1960).

Bo Diddley—despite an innovative rock & roll sound rooted in Chicago rhythm & blues and the rural South—had an even tougher time trying to make the transition from R&B to rock & roll. Neither his number 1 R&B hit from 1955, "Bo Diddley," nor his R&B hit from 1956, "Pretty Thing," made the national pop charts. Even though Presleymania was taking the country by storm in 1956, Diddley's "Pretty Thing" went nowhere. One of the more interesting records of the year, it featured a spectacular drumbeat, as well as an innovative call-and-response between the lead vocalist and the harmonica player. Perhaps Diddley's earthy R&B vocal style, the song's African-influenced drum sound, or distinct blues harmonica were just too alien for most white teenagers. Or maybe it just sounded too southern (Diddley repeatedly sings about his "purdy thing") for white teenagers living mostly in other parts of the country. More complicated reasons might also explain why Bo was unable to make it big as a rock & roll star. Diddley's story suggests why many talented rhythm & blues artists had a hard time making it in rock & roll (see figure 8.3).

Like other R&B artists of the day, Diddley was a product of the changing times. When African Americans migrated northward during the World War II era in search of jobs in industrial cities like Chicago, they brought along blues music from the rural South. By the 1940s and early '50s, bluesmen like Muddy Waters and Howlin' Wolf could be heard on a regular basis in Chicago's loud and smoky blues bars. Their primal vocals, earthy lyrics, and blues-inspired electric guitar licks inspired a new generation of R&B singers such as Bo Diddley, who became prototypes for 1950s rock & roll.

Bo was born Ellas Bates on December 30, 1928, in Macomb, Mississippi. His last name was legally changed to McDaniel when he was adopted and raised by his mother's cousin, Gussie McDaniel. When he was seven or eight years old, he moved with her to Chicago, where he received a new nickname. There are all sorts of stories about how Ellas McDaniel became Bo Diddley. Some writers insist that "Bo Diddley" was a childhood nickname or that it was the name he used as a teenager when he boxed in a Golden Gloves tournament. Others suggest he was named after a one-stringed African instrument. Still others insist that the Chess brothers thought up the name when they signed him to his first contract with Chess Records. Setting the record straight, Bo says, "The Chess brothers didn't have nothin' to do with it. 'Bo Diddley' is a childhood nickname that the kids in grammar school gave me. I don't know where it came from. They just started calling me Bo Diddley." The name stuck, and he used it as a teenager when he fought in the Golden Gloves. [49]

Like many rhythm & blues performers, young Bo got interested in music at church. By the time he was in his teens, he was performing with local street bands. His lucky break came in 1955 when he was walking down the street at Cottage Grove and 48th, not far from his house on the South Side of Chicago. "There was this guy named Sonny at a back door, and he was throwing out old broken records and stuff in the garbage can because the garbage can was right outside the back

Figure 8.3.   Bo Diddley was one of rock & roll's Founding Fathers. (Robert Pruter Collection)

door," Diddley vividly recalled over forty years later. "When I saw him doing that, I said, 'Hey, man, you all make records in there?' And, he said 'Yes.' He told me to go around to the front door and come in and see Leonard or Phil Chess [the owners of Chess Records] and let them hear what I had. So I ran home the two blocks and got a little disk I had made on a Webco recorder that I had. They liked what I had, and that's the beginning of it."[50]

Bo Diddley made it big with his very first release on Chess Records, the modestly titled "Bo Diddley." The 1955 R&B classic epitomizes the prototypical rock & roll that came out of Chicago-style rhythm and blues. Its driving guitar, pulsating rhythm, and pounding beat make it sound fresh even today. One of his band members, Roosevelt Jackson, suggested the title. Bo explains, "I wrote the song, but it wasn't [originally] called 'Bo Diddley.' It was called 'Uncle John.' And then I changed the lyrics, because the lyrics were a little rough, you know." Though the record made it all the way to number 1 on the R&B charts, it never crossed over to the national pop charts. Still, Bo maintains his song was the first rock & roll record ever. "I'm only going by what Alan Freed did," explains Bo. "He was the one who first spoke the word 'rock 'n' roll' even though Bill Haley and the Comets and Louis Jordan [sic] sang 'Good Rockin' Tonight.' But it never was 'rock 'n' roll.' . . . But then Alan Freed came out and says, 'Here's a man, Bo Diddley, who's gonna rock and roll you right out of your seat. That's when the word was put together. Alan Freed did it."[51]

The record "Bo Diddley" established the artist's signature sound powered by frenzied electric guitar riffs and a distinct 4/4 rhythm pattern reminiscent of African rhythms. The "Bo Diddley beat"—also known as a hambone beat or alternately as "shave and a haircut, two bits"—was later featured on numerous rock & roll hits, including early hits such as Johnny Otis's "Willie and the Hand Jive" and Buddy Holly's "Not Fade Away," as well as later rock classics like the Who's "Magic Bus." But there was always more to Bo Diddley's music than just the hambone beat. His roots are planted deep in bayou country, and most of his songs echo the sounds of Mississippi blues and Chicago R&B. Bo makes it clear, though, that the distinction between rhythm & blues and rock & roll was an artificial one back in the mid-1950s. "Yeah, it was rhythm & blues. The name 'rock & roll' came up when my white brothers started doing it, playing guitars and this stuff other than country music," he explains. "And because we had that race crap going on, most people who owned everything didn't want to be connected with black music. . . . 'Rock & roll' came up because they had to separate the music, [so] the terms 'rock & roll' and 'rhythm & blues' became the same thing. But, in doing business, they had to have a different meaning. But it's basically the same thing, you know? Either they couldn't get or did not want black music being played on white radio stations." Bo adds, "I remember when they all invented this, because everybody was talking about it saying, 'We got to get some way to get this [rhythm & blues] stuff played.' Alan Freed came up with the word 'rock 'n' roll.' Well, it's all the same thing. It's just that rock & roll was for the white boys, and rhythm & blues was for black boys."[52]

Diddley's sound and dynamic performance style made him a favorite on rock & roll tours sponsored by Alan Freed and other promoters. Throughout the mid- to late 1950s, he and his band toured constantly with all the big rock & roll stars, including Fats Domino, Carl Perkins, Gene Vincent, and Mickey and Sylvia, bringing the new sound to young audiences throughout the country. Bo became an instant rock & roll icon with his unique cigar-box-shaped guitar and sharp clothes (ranging from cool, all-black outfits to hot cat clothes like a red plaid tuxedo). His acrobatic stage show featured him strutting about, jumping up and down, wiggling his body, and playing his guitar between his legs.

Given Bo Diddley's legendary reputation as a rock & roll pioneer, many people are surprised to learn that he did not have a hit on the national pop charts until 1959, when he reached number 20 with "Say Man." None of his other releases even made it into the Top 40. Many people—including Bo himself—were mystified by the talented rock & roller's inability to land hits on the national pop charts. Clearly, he had the talent to make it big. An energetic performer, Bo crafted a unique rock & roll style in the 1950s and '60s that combined elements from rhythm & blues music and African American culture. He could shout out excellent rhythm & blues–based hard-rockers, such as "Bo Diddley," "Pretty Thing," "Mona," and "I'm a Man"; segue into Latin-tinged material like "Crackin' Up"; and then turn around and delight audiences with humorous songs like "Say Man," "Pills," and "The Story of Bo Diddley." Some songs even plugged into pop culture trends: "Road Runner" alluded to the popular cartoon, while albums such as *Bo Diddley Is a Gun Slinger* picked up on the popularity of TV westerns in the late 1950s and early '60s.

If Bo Diddley had so much going for him, then why wasn't he able to make the pop charts with any consistency? There are several possible explanations. For one thing, Bo's primal sound was always closer to rhythm & blues than it was to rock & roll. Music historian Robert Palmer describes Diddley as "the most primitive of the early black rock & rollers, [he] built his hits on blues and folk materials from back country Mississippi and on the Latin-like 'hambone' beat."[53] Records like "I'm a Man" appealed more to fans of blues music and R&B than to white teenagers accustomed to traditional pop or melodic rock & roll. And, all too frequently, Bo Diddley records were too sexually suggestive for AM radio. For example, "Hey Bo Diddley" (1957)—based on the "Old McDonald" childhood rhyme—described Bo living on a farm with "women here, women there, women, women everywhere."[54]

Diddley's vernacular style, rooted in the black neighborhoods of Chicago's South Side, may have been too alien for the broader pop audience. For example, Diddley's biggest hit, "Say Man," was viewed by most white listeners simply as a funny, novelty record. What most white teenagers did not know at the time was that "Say Man" was actually based on a game of verbal insults known as "the dozens" on the streets of urban black neighborhoods. The creative repartee between Bo Diddley and maracas player Jerome Green that is featured on "Say Man" not only reflected African American urban culture, but it also foreshadowed the rise of rap music. While humor allowed "Say Man" to connect with white audiences, Diddley found less success with vernacular lyrics or allusions to African American culture on releases such as "Hush Your Mouth" and "Diddley Daddy." Other records such as "Who Do You Love?" were almost menacing in tone. Music historian Rick Coleman suggests that Bo's music was a virtual assault on the rigid social order of 1950s America: "Wild braggadocio—exemplified by the toasts, signifying, and dirty-dozens ancestors of rap heard in Bo Diddley's greatest hits—was a form of ego release in blues, r&b, and rock 'n' roll."[55]

Unlike Chuck Berry, Little Richard, and other black R&B singers who altered their singing styles or toned down their lyrics to reach a predominately white pop music audience, Bo Diddley refused to compromise his music or approach. Whereas Chuck Berry eagerly tacked toward white teenagers on songs such as "School Day" or "Sweet Little Sixteen," Diddley either was not willing or not able to make that move. And where Berry was happy to follow the Chess brothers' advice and change the title of "Ida Red" to "Maybellene" to reach a wider audience, Diddley refused to budge. Years later, he was still proud of the fact that the Chess brothers never told him what to do or how to do it. "They just had the tape recorder and they gave me the chance," he explained. "That is the thing I admire them for because they saw something in me; they saw a product and they got the product and put it out there and people bought it." Significantly, though, Chess Records never forced him to sing a particular type of music or aim his records at the rock & roll audience. "I had my own thing," Bo says. "They couldn't change me. . . . They just didn't know what to do with me. I was me, and they just had to accept me the way I was."⁵⁶

Bo's independence may have hurt him in more ways than he knew back in 1950s America. Given racial attitudes of the day, some whites did not have much tolerance for African Americans who stood up for their beliefs or rocked the boat. For instance, Bo's refusal to follow orders when he appeared on Ed Sullivan's TV show in 1955 infuriated the taciturn host. The show's producer didn't want to offend white viewers with Bo Diddley's raucous, self-titled R&B hit, so he ordered the singer to substitute Tennessee Ernie Ford's popular "Sixteen Tons." Diddley even practiced Ford's song during rehearsal. But when Bo took the stage for his live performance, he shocked the host and the producer by playing his own hit instead. Diddley later recalled that Ed Sullivan "got mad . . . Sullivan said that I was one of the first colored boys to ever double-cross him. Said that I wouldn't last six months." Bo was never invited back.⁵⁷

Racism held Bo Diddley back in other ways. Given the racial politics of 1950s America, the road to success was steeper for African Americans than for whites. Society as a whole and the music industry in particular were both more receptive to white performers. And the music industry all too often took unfair advantage of black performers, cheating them out of royalties or not living up to promises to promote their records and careers. Bo always insisted that he and other black artists of the 1950s never got all the royalties they were owed because of racism in the music industry. Discrimination also prevented African Americans from getting the credit they deserved. "Yeah, well, I stayed on the charts longer than Elvis Presley but I don't get credit for it, you know, but nobody ever mentions it," says Bo. "In America, we still got that same bullshit going on [today]. It's just dressed up. People should get credit for what they do. But credit shouldn't get snatched away from and hung on somebody else." Bo admits that Elvis Presley sold more records than he did but emphasizes that Elvis "was not the first [to sing rock & roll]. And a lot of people think he was because this is what they been told and read. But it's not the truth." Bo believes that African American artists did not get all the credit they deserved because of race. "[It was] bad news, baby. Bad news. It was a hurtin' thing. I never knew what all the crap was about. . . . This is America, and this is music and anything else. That type of hatred causes the downfall of everybody, not just one person. It's a bad disease, you know?"[58]

The fact that Bo Diddley was a large, handsome black man with a self-confident attitude and commanding stage presence made it that much more difficult for him to make it big nationally. The first wave of solo African American rhythm & blues singers who crossed over onto the pop charts were usually nonthreatening types such as the chubby, affable Fats Domino, the theatrical Little Richard, or the gimmicky Chuck Berry who could be both funny and ingratiating to white audiences. Bo Diddley was different. He was a virile, independent black man who insisted on doing his own thing on stage. He excited both white and black females in the audience with his bad boy image, good looks, athletic body, and fluid dance steps moving sensuously to the beat. The more that white teenage girls screamed, the less white teenage boys and parents wanted to see the charismatic African American singer.

Despite his lack of success on the pop charts, Bo Diddley left his mark on rock & roll. The "Bo Diddley Sound" helped define the new music. Recalling African-based polyrhythms, it became the archetype for rock & roll powered by frenzied electric guitars, pounding drums, and hypnotic beats. Diddley's other innovations included guitar riffs that made use of tremolo, reverb, and distortion, and a band that included some of the first female guitarists and musicians in rock & roll history.

Bo Diddley's appearance and style were as unique as his sound. Bo looked different with his thick, horn-rimmed glasses, square-shaped guitar, and cool "cat" clothes. At times, he seemed almost menacing, with his gravelly voice, macho songs, and high-voltage rhythm & blues. On other occasions, his mocking delivery and humorous lyrics had audiences laughing. When asked who influenced his music and style, Bo

Diddley says matter of factly, "Who influenced me? Huh? You can't read nowhere where anyone influenced Bo Diddley. I'm self taught."[59]

Bo insists that he set the pace for other performers, including Elvis Presley. "Elvis was a nice looking young man, and he played a little bit of guitar, but he took the wiggling and the stuff like that from me and Jackie Wilson," explains Diddley. "I was the one who started that, you know. And everybody used to say, well, I was the worst thing to ever hit the stage because I wiggled, you know. That means you were dirty, you know, because America wasn't ready for people wiggling and dirty and doing the rubber leg thing. I was the dude that started all of that. And Elvis copied me. And he went ahead with it, and they shut the door on me and kept me back." Bo does not blame Elvis at all for what happened. He understands Presley was just trying to be successful. Instead, he points the finger at the movers and shakers in the music business. "That's the part I hate about the black and white thing, you understand? I started something, and my white brother started doing it, and them guys said, 'We don't need him [Bo Diddley], can you do that, man?' Then they stick [Elvis] up there doing it, and then you never get a chance to see me up there doing it, you know . . . ? That was the thing that pissed me off—I did not get the recognition for what I created. And it hurts, you know?"[60]

Perhaps one of Bo Diddley's later recordings, "You Can't Judge a Book by the Cover" (1962), best sums up his career. You cannot judge Bo Diddley's music by simply looking at how well his singles did on the charts. But you can tell how important he was to rock & roll by looking at how his music influenced other artists, as well as by the caliber of performers who covered his songs. Despite the fact that Bo Diddley only had four relatively minor hits on the rock charts in the 1950s and early '60s, he had a major impact on the development of rock & roll. Numerous artists have covered his songs and copied his sound. The "Bo Diddley beat" powered numerous records during rock & roll's first decade, including Buddy Holly and the Crickets' "Not Fade Away" (1957), Johnny Otis's "Willie and the Hand Jive" (1958), and Dee Clark's "Hey Little Girl" (1959). Holly recorded a version of "Bo Diddley," and in the 1960s, the Rolling Stones did "Mona," Eric Clapton and the Yardbirds found success with "I'm a Man," and Quicksilver Messenger Service scored with "Who Do You Love." The British rock invasion of 1964–1965 solidified Diddley's reputation. Super groups like the Beatles, Rolling Stones, Animals, Yardbirds, and Who praised Bo Diddley as one of the founding fathers of rock & roll. One British group, the Pretty Things, even named themselves after Diddley's song. When Americans finally took notice, Bo's career took off in the late 1960s and '70s. In 1987, Bo Diddley was inducted into the Rock and Roll Hall of Fame. In 1998, he received a Lifetime Achievement Award from the National Academy of Recorded Arts and Sciences, and a similar one from the Rhythm & Blues Foundation. The following year, his 1955 classic, "Bo Diddley," was cited as a "recording of lasting qualitative or historical significance" by the Grammy Hall of Fame. And in 2004, *Rolling Stone Magazine* ranked him number 20 on their list of the Top 100 Artists of All Time.

Bo Diddley was pleased and honored by all the awards, but he was also quick to point out that the belated recognition did not make up for all the hard times and lost income. "I'm happy that I finally got the recognition. . . . Okay, I made it to the Hall of Fame, so I must have been doing something good in order to be recognized for that. But where is my . . . money?" he asks. "I've influenced so many cats that done build mansions, they done build this and that, and they got a heavy nest egg. . . . I was making the money, but I didn't get it [from the record company], you know?"[61]

Back in the mid-1950s, Bo Diddley never achieved the commercial success of other early rock & roll stars like Fats Domino, Chuck Berry, or Elvis Presley, but he is now recognized as one of rock & roll's all-time-greatest performers. His electrified rhythm and blues helped establish the boundaries of early rock & roll; his seminal sound influenced numerous performers; and his greatest songs—such as "Bo Diddley," "I'm a Man," and "Who Do You Love?"—became rock & roll classics. Bo Diddley's music speaks to the dreams of 1950s America, while his experiences and failures suggest the tragic racial realities of life in cold war America.

THE ROCK & ROLL MELTING POT

The emergence of black R&B performers on the national pop charts offers ample evidence of the cultural integration that was occurring in America by the mid-1950s. As the civil rights movement was picking up momentum with landmark cases such as *Brown vs. Board of Education* (1954) or through the Montgomery bus boycott (1955) and the rise of Martin Luther King Jr. and the Southern Christian Leadership Conference, R&B rock & rollers were also moving African Americans into the national spotlight.

The national success of black R&B artists in 1956 was frequently the result of whites and blacks working together behind the scenes. Indies such as Chess, Atlantic, Ember, Gee, Specialty, and other small labels that produced the R&B rock hits making the pop charts in the late 1950s were rock & roll melting pots. The racial and ethnic mix included white and black owners, songwriters, producers, studio musicians, and performers. Most listeners heard only the final product; they were totally oblivious to the behind-the-scenes multiculturalism and diversity that were responsible for the hits. For instance, listeners heard only the black-sounding voices of Frankie Lymon and the Teenagers and didn't realize that the group actually consisted of three blacks and two Puerto Ricans and that a white, Jewish middle-aged man named George Goldner was arranging and producing the songs. Or they heard Chuck Berry singing "Maybellene," not knowing how Leonard Chess helped shape the song.

Perhaps the best example of how early rock & roll was often a black and white amalgam involves an R&B group called the Coasters and two young white songwriters and producers named Jerry Leiber and Mike Stoller. Headquartered in New York City's Brill Building district—rock & roll's equivalent of Tin Pan Alley—Leiber and Stoller would turn the Coasters into one of the most successful acts in the history of rock & roll.

Jerry and Mike met as teenagers in Los Angeles and offer rock & roll evidence that opposites attract. Leiber was manic and never stopped talking; Stoller was laid back and quiet. "From the get-go, our energies were different," Leiber later explained. "Mike was cautious and I was impetuous." Initially, neither was that impressed by the other. Leiber remembers that Stoller had a goatee and was wearing a beret. "*A bebopper*, I thought to myself," Leiber recalled many years later, "Oh, shit, not one of them." Stoller was just as nonplussed. "The first thing that I noticed about Jerry was the color of his eyes. One was blue and one was brown. I'd never seen that before," said Stoller. "There was something intriguing about it, but it was strange—almost as strange as his request that we write songs together." The two teenagers argued for a while about whether they should become partners, and then finally agreed to do it. "And so began a six-decade argument with no resolution in sight," wrote Stoller in 2009. "It was 1950. We were seventeen."[62]

The main thing they had in common was a passion for African American culture and rhythm & blues. "The blues was the bottom line," said Leiber. "The blues was our bond. . . . The blues became the basis of a lifetime of work." As high schoolers, the two Jewish kids tried to talk like blacks, act like blacks, and sing, play, and compose music like blacks. According to Leiber, they even used to get into arguments over which of them was "the blackest." Jerry explains, "I felt black. I *was*, as far as I was concerned. And I wanted to be black for lots of reasons. They were better musicians, they were better athletes, they were not uptight about sex, and they knew how to enjoy life better than most people."[63]

With Leiber writing the lyrics and Stoller composing the music, the two found a modicum of success in the early 1950s peddling their songs to local R&B labels. They picked up valuable experience working with R&B legend Johnny Otis. Together they wrote and produced records for Little Esther, Big Mama Thornton, and other West Coast R&B artists. Leiber and Stoller's breakthrough came in 1953 when Thornton's recording of their composition "Hound Dog" (the same song later made famous by Elvis Presley) became a number 1 hit on the R&B charts. Leiber still recalls the lesson he learned during the R&B recording session. Big Mama Thornton ripped into the young songwriter when he tried to tell her how to sing the song. Leiber recalls the three-hundred-pound Thornton glared at him "like looks could kill and said, 'White boy, don't you be tellin' *me* how to sing the blues.'" It was at that precise moment, says Leiber, "when I found out I was white."[64]

In 1954, the two songwriters and fledgling producers started up their own R&B label, Spark Records, and found success writing and producing hits for the Robins, including "Riot in Cell Block #9" and "Smokey Joe's Café." Impressed by the young songwriters' ability to crank out authentic sounding R&B hits, Ahmet Ertegun purchased the master tapes for his New York City–based Atlantic Records, and he signed the two songwriters to an independent production deal. "It was the first of its kind," points out music historian Arnold Shaw, "and [it] initiated a development in which eventually creative control of recording was taken out of the hands of company A&R executives and vested in outside producers."[65]

Contrary to the famous dictum "Go west, young man," Leiber and Stoller struck gold when they headed east to work in the record industry based in New York City. Along with writing pop hits in 1956 for Ruth Brown and the Drifters, two R&B acts on Atlantic Records, they found success as independent producers for Atlantic Record's subsidiary label, Atco. Their first assignment was to write and produce songs for the Coasters (whose lead singer, Carl Gardner, and bass singer, Bobby Nunn, had previously been with the Robins). Leiber and Stoller hit pay dirt almost immediately when the Coasters earned their first hit on the pop charts in 1956 with "One Kiss Led to Another." Under the tutelage of Leiber and Stoller, the Coasters would go on to record some of the most memorable songs in rock & roll history, including "Searchin'" (1957), "Yakety Yak" (1958), and "Charlie Brown" (1959). The hits that Leiber and Stoller wrote and produced for the Coasters were truly inspired. Each told a story in which every member of the group played a role. The two-minute songs were actually "playlets" says Jerry Leiber, and groups like the Robins and Coasters were like "a little company of players, a vaudeville troop."[66] (figure 8.4).

Looking back at the Coasters' catalog of hits, it is difficult to know where Leiber and Stoller leave off and the Coasters begin. Not only did Leiber and Stoller write the songs and produce the records, but they often told the Coasters exactly how to sing them. "Jerry Leiber would actually transform himself into this character [in the song]. He would slink and dance around the office, singing the part he wanted Billy Guy or Carl Gardner [of the Coasters] to become," explained one eyewitness, "[Leiber] would become that guy he wanted them to imitate. . . . I had never really seen anybody transform himself into a black guy [like that]."[67]

Leiber and Stoller's contributions to the final product cannot be underestimated, yet the Coasters have to be given ample credit, too. After all, they were the ones who actually sang the songs and performed them in front of audiences. The Coasters' hit records were true collaborations between whites and blacks, songwriters and singers, producers and performers. "Leiber and Stoller were writing black music," insists the Coasters' Carl Gardner. "[These] two Jewish kids knew my culture better than I knew my culture. And, I said, how do they do that?" Over

Figure 8.4. This photo includes several legendary figures from the early days of rock & roll. Composers Mike Stoller and Jerry Leiber are at the piano. Behind them from left to right are: Herb Abramson of Atlantic Records; producer Jerry Wexler; the Coasters, one of the most successful R&B rock groups of the 1950s and early '60s; and Atlantic Records' owner, Ahmet Ertegun. (Photo by "PoPsie" Randolph L.L.C.; courtesy of Michael Randolph, executor to the estate of William "PoPsie" Randolph)

the years, some critics have charged that Leiber and Stoller were exploiting the Coasters by perpetuating stereotypes that portrayed blacks as fools, but Leiber and Stoller don't buy that. Jerry Leiber points out that the Coasters shared their sense of humor: "Of course, [the Coasters] had attitudes. If they thought we went too far they would stop us. . . . They would tell us no."[68]

Leiber and Stoller had a remarkable talent for blending black and white musical forms in a way that accurately reflected the interests and values of both the artists and the audiences. They weren't just mimicking African American culture, they were living it and making it accessible to millions of white listeners. The resulting sound was neither white nor black—it was cultural integration at work. "[Leiber and Stoller] were just like brothers to us," explains Charlie Thomas of the Drifters. "There was real prejudice back then, but these guys didn't believe in it, and we didn't believe in it either. . . . They did the best that any producers ever could do for a black group in those days. They were always respectful. They'd made sure we were respectable and had that class."[69]

Leiber and Stoller's collaboration with black R&B groups demonstrates how rock & roll emerged as a black and white amalgam by the mid-1950s. Cultural integration was occurring in a variety of ways. Not only were black artists integrating the national pop charts, but musical styles were also mixing as black and white artists got to know each other intimately as they worked closely in recording studios, shared the same stages, and even began traveling together on the same tour buses.

The rise of Elvis Presley in 1956 paved the way for the coming of numerous black rock & roll artists. Not only did Elvis introduce many white listeners to rhythm & blues–influenced music, but his infectious zeal for "cat music" also inspired rock & roll fans to try the real thing. The growing popularity of black artists on the pop charts in 1956 provides evidence of the social, cultural, and political changes that America was going through by the late 1950s. Opportunities for African Americans were opening up across the country as the civil rights movement expanded. Cultural integration became commonplace on the pop charts as white teenagers demanded the new rock & roll sound as sung by black artists.

Rock & roll audiences might not have been fully aware of all the political, social, cultural, and economic ramifications of the coming of rock & roll, but they got the big picture. They knew intuitively that rock & roll was a potent mixture of black music and white music. They understood that black rock & roll stars were gaining celebrity status and were being cheered on by white audiences at the very same time that most blacks in the United States were being denied equality and even the right to vote. It was obvious to rock & roll performers, producers, and fans alike that the new sound was not in tune with commonly accepted racial attitudes in the 1950s.

After 1956, even more R&B rock artists would arrive on the scene, including major artists such as James Brown, Jackie Wilson, Ray Charles, Sam Cooke, the Drifters, the Shirelles, the Impressions, and the Isley Brothers, as well as Motown stars such as Mary Wells, the Miracles, Temptations, Supremes, Four Tops, Marvin Gaye, and Stevie Wonder to name just a few. All of these R&B rock artists would play a leading role in transforming rock & roll into a cultural and racial melting pot. In the process, African American rock & rollers helped set the stage for the cultural integration of not just pop music but all of American society and culture.

9

DIXIE FRIED

The Growth of Southern Rockabilly

In 1956, Sam Phillips signed a young country artist named Carl Perkins to his Sun Record label. He was hoping that the good-looking singer/songwriter could be the label's next Elvis Presley. Perkins was about as raw and unschooled musically as a recording artist could be. His musical journey to fame and fortune has an undeniable mythical quality—the common-man hero who with the help of a wise old mentor rises from poverty on the wings of talent and determination.

Born to poor sharecroppers near Tiptonville, Tennessee, Carl Perkins grew up picking cotton sometimes up to fourteen hours a day. It was there out in the cotton fields where young Carl first heard the twin siren sounds of country music and rural blues. Whenever possible, he tuned his family's battered old radio to local stations just to hear the music. "I always loved the sound of the guitar, and finally got me this old one from a black man named Uncle John, who lived on the same plantation that my family did," Perkins later recalled. "I used to go over and listen to him play a simple blues-type thing. I loved the way he pushed the strings." Perkins adds, "I'd practice up on [country artists] Bill Monroe and Ernest Tubb's 'Walking the Floor over You,' and I'd add Uncle John's blues licks. That's where my style came from."[1]

By the mid-1950s, Carl was living in Jackson, Tennessee. During the day, he worked in a bakery. By night, he and his brothers played music in local honky-tonks. Billing themselves as the Perkins Brothers Band, they experimented with a variety of musical styles, including traditional country and the newest in rhythm & blues. Carl played guitar and sang lead. His musical hero was Hank Williams, whose unique country blues style had him riding high on the record charts.[2]

Like many young country musicians, Perkins's world turned upside down the first time he heard the music of Elvis Presley. He later recalled, "The first time I heard Elvis was when my wife was in the kitchen, and she said, 'Carl, that sounds just like y'all.'"[3] Perkins immediately packed up his car and headed for Memphis hoping that he, too, could make records on Sam Phillips's Sun label.

Perkins soon landed an audition. The man who had discovered Elvis liked what he saw and heard. No doubt, Sam Phillips was hoping that lightning would strike twice, because Perkins's sound evoked Presley's blend of country and blues. But the owner of Sun Records realized that Perkins was more pure country than Elvis. "[Carl] was a tremendous honky-tonk picker," Phillips said. "He had this feel for pushing a song along that very few people had. . . . I was so impressed with the pain and feeling in his country singing." Phillips had a gut feeling that this guy "could revolutionize the country end of the business."[4] Perkins might even have greater potential than Elvis, since the good-looking, twenty-two-year-old not only had a strong voice, but he was an excellent composer and musician as well. Phillips was particularly impressed by Perkins's fresh lyrics, catchy melodies, and sensational guitar playing.

"Dixie Fried" was one of the first songs that Perkins wrote and recorded for Sun Records. Recorded in the same studio where Elvis belted out "That's All Right Mama" and "Blue Moon of Kentucky," the Perkins song told the story of a good-ol' southern boy named Dan who stormed into a night spot on the outskirts of town. The wild young man soon got drunk and pulled out a razor, scattering customers in all directions. "All the cats knew to jump and hop," sang Perkins, "'cause [Dan] was born and raised in a butcher shop." Eventually, the cops showed up and hauled Dan off to jail, but throughout the ruckus, young Dan kept hollering to onlookers: "Rave on, children, I'm with ya. Rave on, cats . . . let's all get dixie fried!"[5]

Though "Dixie Fried" did not become a major hit, the song is a perfect example of a musical style known as rockabilly. Perkins called it "blues with a country beat."[6] The coming of Elvis not only paved the way for Carl but also for other rockabilly artists throughout the South.

By 1956, the country music field was a promised land for record executives searching frantically for the next Elvis Presley.

THE RISE OF ROCKABILLY

Rockabilly's musical roots ran deep in southern soil, nurtured by gospel, country, bluegrass, blues, and R&B. Jerry Naylor (who followed Buddy Holly as the lead singer of the Crickets) observes that rockabilly combined "a 'pushy,' fat rhythm guitar; the electrifying magnetism of a gutsy, rhythmic lead guitar; the blistering slap of an upright bass fiddle; plus all of these elements swimming in a man-made lake of 'tape-delay echo.'" Naylor adds, "The magic of rockabilly erupts as much in the detail of the music as in the lyrics of the song and the singer's performance."[7]

Most rockabilly artists were—like Elvis—southern white males who could mix country rhythms and blues beats with lyrics aimed at teenagers. Their songs often made use of rebellious images involving drinking, sex, and wild behavior. "It was 'cat music,' a secret language for the young seeking to break away from the adult music of their forebears," explains music historian Peter Guralnick. "It was called rockabilly, because it was not the clankety rock of Bill Haley and His Comets nor the hillbilly sound of Roy Acuff and Ernest Tubb but a fusion of the two."[8]

The sound was first recorded by Sam Phillips in his tiny Sun Studio in Memphis, Tennessee, but eventually it would spread to singers and studios across the land. "No one seems to know who actually coined the term *rockabilly*," says Jerry Naylor. "The only fact on which most everyone agrees is that Rockabilly music was born on the sweltering night of July 5, 1954, when [Elvis Presley] was nervously horsing around during a coffee break of a demo session at a tiny Memphis recording studio [Sun Records]."[9] Elvis first tried out the rockabilly sound on country audiences with varying degrees of success in 1954 and 1955. Then, he introduced rockabilly to an unsuspecting national audience on network TV in early 1956. The resulting Presleymania turned country music's "Hillbilly Cat" into rock & roll's first great superstar and encouraged other rockabilly singers and country artists to try their hand at rock & roll.

THE SUN ROCKABILLY STABLE

Sun Records in Memphis, Tennessee, became the launching pad for the new style. The artists who recorded there view Sam Phillips as the grandfather of rockabilly. Singer Charlie Feathers recalls how Phillips encouraged his move from traditional country music to the new sound. "I tried to play like [bluegrass legend] Bill Monroe. A lot of bluegrass is done fast. Years ago, people had the upright bass and fiddle around the house. They'd start poppin' that old bass. . . . Catgut strings had a unique sound. Gave plenty of bottom." Enter Sam Phillips and Sun Records. "Then somebody put cotton-patch blues with bluegrass and created rockabilly. Most beautiful music I ever heard in my life. Sun didn't have a studio suited to country. I think we got it goin' down here, man, 'cause we had the accent. But what really made those early [Sun] records was slapback echo, the slappin' bass, and no drums. What a sound! Right off the floor and onto the record."[10]

Rockabilly was the product of the early collaborations between Sam Phillips and Elvis Presley, Scotty Moore, and Bill Black. After Presley switched to the RCA label in late 1955, Phillips began looking for a new artist who might be successful with the rockabilly sound. In early 1956, he found his man, signing Carl Perkins to his Sun label (figure 9.1).

Carl became the first rockabilly artist to follow Elvis onto the pop charts. The two had a lot in common. Both grew up in or near Memphis, absorbing the region's eclectic musical sounds that mixed country & western, bluegrass, gospel, rhythm & blues, pop, and rural blues. Both got their start on Sun Records. Both dressed in flashy "cat" clothes. Both artists even made their debut on the national record charts on exactly the same day, March 2, 1956. Elvis's "Heartbreak Hotel" was released on RCA records, while Perkins's "Blue Suede Shoes" was on the Sun label. For several weeks, the two records vied for top-selling honors. Eventually, Elvis won. "Heartbreak Hotel" made it all the way to number 1, edging out Perkins's song, which peaked at number 2. The fact that Elvis released his own version of "Blue Suede Shoes" just four weeks after Perkins's song first made the charts no doubt cut into Perkins's sales. But, in the long haul, Perkins's original became the definitive and best-selling version of the song.

Perkins wrote "Blue Suede Shoes" at the end of 1955, but why he wrote it is a mystery. There are two different stories about how the song

Figure 9.1. Carl Perkins wrote and recorded the 1956 hit, "Blue Suede Shoes,"
one of the top rockabilly songs of all time. (Richard Aquila Collection)

came about. Johnny Cash, who was Perkins's close friend and a fellow
Sun recording artist, always insisted that he was the one who gave Carl
the idea. Cash remembers being backstage with Perkins at a performance in Amory, Mississippi. And he recalls telling Perkins that he had
a "feel for the 'bop' kind of song [that Elvis was having so much success

with]," so why didn't he record one? When Perkins replied that he had already tried but just couldn't come up with the right song, Cash suggested an idea based on a guy he had met in the air force. Cash then regaled Perkins with a story about his former sergeant, an African American named C. V. White. Sergeant White was always proud of his appearance. One day, he asked Cash how he looked. When Cash jokingly poked fun at the sarge's attire, White replied that Cash could say anything he wanted as long as he didn't step on White's blue suede shoes. Johnny laughed and pointed out that the sergeant's shoes were regulation army. White, with a mischievous gleam in his eye, responded, "Tonight when I get to town they're gonna be blue suede, man." Perkins laughed at the tale and agreed it was a "great idea for a bop song." Perkins, according to Johnny, immediately took out a pen and wrote the song within a very few minutes. [11]

Carl later insisted that the inspiration for "Blue Suede Shoes" came not from Johnny Cash but from an incident that he witnessed while he was playing in a night club in his home town of Jackson, Tennessee, on December 4, 1955. He saw a young couple dancing fast to one of his songs. All of a sudden, the couple stopped and the boy looked down at this feet. "I heard [him] tell [the] girl, 'Now, don't you step on my suedes,'" recalls Perkins. The boy's embarrassing remark clearly hurt the girl's feelings. "I thought, man, I don't own a pair of suede shoes, but if I did, I'd kick them jewels off, and I'd give them to her." When he got home that night, Perkins kept thinking about the incident. "That bothered me so much that I could not go to sleep that night," he explained. "I was living in a government housing project. I was up at three o'clock in the morning. The song had to be born that night. I kept thinking, 'Don't step on my blue suede shoes.' Then I thought of that old nursery rhyme: one for the money, two for the show, three to get ready, four to go. That's the way it got started." Perkins remembers rummaging around frantically for something to jot the song down on. "I couldn't find any paper to write on. We had two small babies at the time. I guess I didn't have any need for writing paper because all my people lived around here. So I took three Irish potatoes out of a brown paper bag and wrote: 'Don't step on my blue swade shoes.' I didn't even know how to spell suede." [12]

The next morning he called Sam Phillips and sang the song to him over the phone. Phillips like what he heard and booked some recording time in the Sun Studio for Perkins and his band. Just several weeks earlier, the Sun Records owner had sold Elvis's contract to RCA, and he realized that high-energy songs like "Blue Suede Shoes" could make Perkins the Sun label's newest rockabilly sensation. Phillips began to work his magic as soon as the recording session began. He convinced Carl and the band to make the song more up-tempo. He also suggested an important change in the lyrics. "I told Carl that [singing] 'Go man go' made it sound too country." Phillips recommended the line be switched to "Go cat go." Using the term *cat*—which was associated with black rhythm & blues—gave the song an entirely different appeal. "'Go cat go' made it into something altogether different and new," explained Phillips.[13]

The record was released on January 1, 1956, and rocketed up the charts. The energetic, fast-paced number was perfect for dancing, while the in-your-face defiant lyrics appealed to rebellious teenagers interested in cool clothes and the latest rock & roll sound. Within weeks, the record was a bona fide hit on all three *Billboard* charts—pop, country, and rhythm & blues. "Blue Suede Shoes" not only became Sun Records' first million-selling record, but it made Carl Perkins the first country artist to appear on the R&B charts. Elvis, whose own record "Heartbreak Hotel" was headed for the top of the charts at the same time as Perkins's, couldn't have been happier for Sun Record's newest star. He congratulated Carl, telling him that he loved the sound and energy.

If Elvis was elated by Perkins's success, the man who had purchased Elvis's contract for RCA was jealous. Steve Sholes, evidencing more than a little buyer's remorse, even called Sam Phillips to ask if he had signed the wrong Sun artist. Sam assured Sholes about Elvis's potential, and he reluctantly agreed to allow Elvis to do a cover version of Perkins's hit. But Sam insisted on certain restrictions that would prevent the cover from being released too quickly. He wanted to make sure that Elvis's version would not compete with Perkins's record on the charts.

On a crisp cold morning on January 30, 1956, Sholes brought Elvis into the RCA studios in New York City to cover "Blue Suede Shoes." Presley seemed hesitant as he approached the mike. Elvis may have even been thinking that he was stealing a song from a friend. That might explain why it took him ten takes to get the song to a level that Sholes thought was good enough for a record. But even then, Elvis's version seemed rushed and inferior to the original. The young rock & roller admitted to his producer that he didn't think he could ever outdo Perkins's record. Evidently, most listeners agreed because Perkins's "Blue Suede Shoes" not only outsold Elvis's rendition at the time, but it is now considered the definitive version.[14]

For the first three months of 1956, Carl Perkins was viewed by some fans as a potential rival for Elvis Presley. But then on March 22, disaster struck. En route to New York City for a scheduled appearance on Perry Como's TV show, the vehicle carrying Perkins and his band crashed into a truck when Perkins's manager fell asleep at the wheel. The band manager and truck driver were killed instantly. The other passengers, including Carl and his two brothers, Jay and Clayton, who played in the band, all wound up in the hospital in serious condition. Jay never fully recovered and died from a brain tumor in 1958. Clayton had a rough time bouncing back and later committed suicide. Carl was unconscious for three days, suffering a cracked skull, broken ribs, and a shoulder fracture. Perhaps worse, his morale was shattered.

Watching Elvis on TV as he recuperated in his hospital bed, Carl could only think about what might have been. "They were gonna give me a gold record," Perkins later mused. "Sam Phillips was already in New York. . . . He was gonna surprise me and announce to the world . . . that my record was number one on all three charts." Presley was particularly gracious in Carl's time of trouble. Elvis sent Carl a telegram saying, "If I can help in any way please call me." Then in deference to his friend, Elvis insisted on changing the set he was scheduled to perform on CBS's "Stage Show" just two days after Carl's accident. At the last moment, Elvis substituted "Money Honey" for "Blue Suede Shoes."[15]

Whether Carl Perkins would have been a major star and rival for Elvis is debatable. To this day, his fans still see him as the real thing, insisting that Carl not only had the looks and charisma to make it big, but in some ways he was even better than Elvis since Perkins was an excellent guitarist and wrote his own material. Elvis fans say no way, confident that no one else had the matinee-idol looks, charisma, sex appeal, voice, and stage presence to compete with the man who would be king of rock & roll. Even Perkins accepts the pro-Elvis argument. "I've been asked many times about how I felt about that [watching Elvis succeed while Perkins was laid up in the hospital]. I always admired

Elvis, I like what he did. I knew he had the same feel for the music that I did; we loved the same type of things. And nobody was topping anybody," insists Perkins. But Carl is also quick to admit, "I *did* lay there thinking, 'what if?'—but Elvis had the looks on me. He was hittin' 'em with his sideburns, flashy clothes, and no ring on his finger; I was married, with three kids. There was no way of keepin' Elvis from being the Man."[16]

Perkins was right about Presley and not just for the reasons he cites. One of the biggest differences between the two singers was that Elvis was rock & roll, while Carl was country. Sam Phillips understood this from the very beginning. The Sun Records owner viewed Elvis as an innovator who, by sheer charisma, could bring country and R&B into the pop mainstream. Perkins, on the other hand, was always too country. Phillips called him "one of the great plowhands in the world." And Phillips understood that Perkins's true potential was to "revolutionize the country end of the business."[17]

Equally important, Carl Perkins lacked Elvis Presley's confidence, determination, and sense of destiny. "I felt out of place when 'Blue Suede Shoes' was Number One," he later noted. "I stood on the Steel Pier in 1956 in Atlantic City . . . and the Goodyear blimp flew over with my name in big lights. And I stood there and actually cried. That should have been something that would elevate a guy to say, 'Well, I've made it.' But it put a fear in me." Perkins always felt inferior and doubted his ability to keep pace with Elvis and other rock & roll stars. When Carl had problems writing a follow-up to "Blue Suede Shoes," the disheartened singer turned increasingly to alcohol for help and told Sam Phillips that his creative juices were no longer flowing. Phillips encouraged him not to give up but to keep trying something different. But Perkins insisted that his attempts at originality only resulted in terrible music. Phillips pointed out that those were not mistakes but were legitimate attempts at original music. Not convinced, Carl replied, "It's just a big original mistake." A frustrated Phillips replied, "That's what Sun Records is. That's what we are."[18]

In any case, Perkins's career was short-circuited by the car crash. Following the accident, he never again had a major hit although he did record several excellent songs, including "Boppin' the Blues" (1956) and "Dixie Fried" (1956), as well as three others that were later covered by the Beatles: "Matchbox," "Honey Don't," and "Everybody's Trying to Be My Baby." "Carl Perkins' songs personified the rockabilly era," said county singer Charlie Daniels, "and Carl Perkins' sound personifies the rockabilly sound more so than anybody involved in it, because he never changed."[19]

Carl Perkins was a seminal figure in rockabilly history whose influence stretched far beyond his one glorious hit, "Blue Suede Shoes." His sound and style influenced later singers from Ricky Nelson in the 1950s, to the Beatles in the '60s, and John Fogerty in the '70s and beyond. And his humorous, down-to-earth approach to rock & roll tapped into the lifestyles and dreams of working-class audiences across America. "[Sam] Phillips, Elvis, and I didn't create rockabilly; it was just the white man's response to the black man's spiritualness," he later said modestly. "It was born in the South. People working those cotton fields as I did as a youngster would hear black people singing. . . . There's lots of cats that was doin' our things, and maybe better, that were never heard of—they're the ones that created rockabilly, the ones who never even got on record. We're just the lucky ones."[20]

On the afternoon of Tuesday, December 4, 1956, Carl Perkins joined three other singers for an impromptu jam session in the Sun Records studio. The session would be memorialized in rock & roll history as "The Million Dollar Quartet" because along with Perkins it featured Elvis Presley, Johnny Cash, and the still unknown Jerry Lee Lewis. Sam Phillips was shrewd enough to turn on the tape machine, thereby capturing the moment for posterity. Although the session was later released as a CD entitled "The Million Dollar Quartet," the title is somewhat inaccurate since Johnny Cash does not actually appear on tape. According to witnesses, he was in the studio when the jam session started but left before the recording began.

The songs they sang that day demonstrate the building blocks not just of rockabilly but also of rock & roll. Although Elvis was no longer on the Sun label, he clearly sounds at home as he bounces musical ideas off of the current Sun artists. He playfully performs some of his own songs for Carl and Jerry Lee, including "Love Me Tender," "Don't Be Cruel," and "Paralyzed." The three singers then plow headlong into a hodgepodge of material, moving effortlessly through a variety of songs, representing traditional pop, country, bluegrass, rhythm & blues, rock & roll, and spirituals. Along with providing listeners with a virtual primer on the roots of rock & roll, the session is significant for other reasons.

The recording demonstrates that Elvis and the others loved all types of rock & roll, from Chuck Berry's R&B-influenced rock style to Pat Boone's softer sound. At one point, Elvis tells his fellow rockabilly artists about how he had witnessed an amazing performance by the lead singer for Billy Wards's Dominoes. Though Elvis didn't get his name, he was blown away by the guy's performance. Elvis's comments demonstrate that he was an astute judge of talent. The dynamic singer turned out to be Jackie Wilson, who would become a rock & roll superstar in the late 1950s and '60s with a string of major hits, including "Lonely Teardrops" (1959), "I'll Be Satisfied" (1959), and numerous others in the 1960s.[21]

The Million Dollar Quartet jam session was one of the earliest recordings done by Jerry Lee Lewis, who would eventually become one of rockabilly's legendary artists because of his outrageous performance style and seminal hits such as "Whole Lot of Shakin' Going On" (1957), "Great Balls of Fire" (1958), and "Breathless" (1958). From the start, as evidenced in the Million Dollar Quartet session, the uninhibited Lewis sang with abandon. Unlike most rockabilly artists who played guitar, Lewis's weapon of choice was the piano. While Lewis would not earn his first hit for another two years, the final member of the "Million Dollar Quartet"—Johnny Cash—was about to join Presley and Perkins on the pop charts in 1956.

Not only was Cash never as exciting as the other three, but arguably he wasn't even a rockabilly singer. His plaintive sound was always more country & western than rock & roll. It was powered by Cash's sad baritone vocals and sparse musical accompaniment that often featured a chugging bass line that evoked the mournful sound of a freight train rushing through the night. "Johnny Cash and his Tennessee Two [group] punched out an unusually stark and distinctively rhythmic sound in the Sun Record studios," explains country music expert Michael Streissguth. "He [initially] wrote lyrics pulled from the joys and desperation of his own rural experience."[22]

Even when he smiled, Cash seemed depressed. He usually dressed in black or drab colors. He even wrote and recorded a song in 1971, "The Man in Black," that explained that he wore black to show solidarity with the weak, poor, and oppressed people of the world. His black hair, deep brown piercing eyes, and frequent scowl added to his dark demeanor. He looked every bit the poor country boy that he was. Born and raised in rural Arkansas, Johnny Cash was the son of sharecroppers. He grew up listening to the *Grand Ole Opry* on the radio and enjoyed Hank Williams, Ernest Tubb, Roy Acuff, and especially the Louvin Brothers. "Nothing in the world was more important to me than hearing those songs on the radio," he later said. "This was the music and these were the great artists who helped me learn how to later tell real *song-stories* from personal experiences and places and things I'd felt and seen." After he saw the Louvin Brothers in concert, he knew he wanted to be a musician. His friends didn't believe he could do it, but his mother encouraged his dream. "I had no doubt about it. And Mother knew it, too," he explained. "She had that same feeling—she'd say, 'J.R., you're gonna be a singer on that radio.'" By his early teens, he was singing and writing gospel and country songs and even performing regularly on KLCN radio in Blytheville, Arkansas. After a brief stint in the air force, he moved to Memphis in hopes of becoming a radio announcer. Instead, he wound up selling vacuum cleaners door to door. He also continued playing music and eventually hooked up with guitarist Luther Perkins (Carl's brother) and bassist Marshall Grant.[23]

Cash and his band, the Tennessee Two, auditioned for Sam Phillips and landed a Sun Records contract in 1955. Initially, Phillips had reservations about the country singer, but evidently he saw enough potential to tell Cash, "Go home and sing a little bit. Write me some songs like Elvis Presley is recording. Bring those back and we'll record them." Soon thereafter, Cash returned to Sun, and good to his word, Phillips recorded him. Since Cash's group lacked a drummer, Phillips came up with an unusual suggestion that resulted in what would later become Cash's signature sound. "Sam came up with the idea of weaving a strip of paper between the strings of Johnny's acoustic rhythm guitar and having him play his chords higher up on the neck," explains Jerry Naylor. "This gave the trio an eerie, almost brushstroke-like snare drum sound. . . . This 'paper trick' guitar rhythm sound—which everybody in early Rockabilly later tried to replicate—became one of Johnny Cash's 'secret weapons.'"[24]

Cash wondered what Phillips had seen in him and his little band. "Luther had a little secondhand Sears amplifier and a six-inch speaker. Marshall Grant had a bass that was held together with masking tape, and I had a little $4.80 guitar," Cash later recalled. "Phillips had to be a genius to get something out of that conglomeration." What impressed

Cash the most was how Phillips approached recording sessions. "Sam didn't have a clock in the studio," explained Cash. "He didn't let me feel like I was spending anybody's money by just singing new songs. After an hour or two, he'd say, 'OK, what else you got? Let's keep going till we get your best.' I loved that in a producer. That's what Sam did with all of us at Sun; he tried to find the uniqueness in each of us. He didn't try to simply make us sound like everyone else."[25]

After Phillips worked his magic on the group, a distinct Johnny Cash sound emerged. Unlike most country records of the day that featured fiddles and steel guitars, Cash's records sounded downright spartan. "The sound . . . consisted only of the string bass of Marshall Grant, the simple *boom-chicka-boom* picking of lead guitarist Luther Perkins, Johnny Cash's rhythm guitar with paper woven between the strings for a more percussive sound, and, of course, Cash's voice, deep and sonorous as a cavern," writes country music expert Paul Kingsbury. "Instantly recognizable, it could have been the bass part in a gospel quartet or the word of a biblical prophet." Though not the raucous rockabilly that audiences came to expect from Elvis or Carl Perkins, Cash's sound still struck a responsive chord among young listeners. Perhaps teenagers were drawn to the music's simplicity and honesty. "I think it was Johnny's integrity and his creative fire that made him so successful," suggests Kris Kristofferson, "but above all it was like he represented the truth."[26]

Young fans might also have been attracted to Cash's rebel image or his songs that spoke directly to teenage interests. His first Top 20 hit, the hypnotic "I Walk the Line" (1956), delivered a heartfelt message about staying loyal to one's true love. The song—powered by Perkins's guitar licks and Grant's slap bass—sounds like a train coming down the track. Cash's mournful vocal adds to the solemn declaration of fidelity. "It was different than anything else you had ever heard," explained Bob Dylan years later. "The record sounded like a voice from the middle of the earth. It was so powerful and moving. It was profound, and so was the tone of it, every line; deep and rich, awesome and mysterious all at once."[27]

After several hits on the rock & roll charts, Johnny Cash went on to become a country music superstar, hosting his own TV show and recording with many of the era's greatest artists, including Bob Dylan. In 1992, Cash was inducted into the Rock & Roll Hall of Fame. In his acceptance speech, Johnny explained that he grew up listening to country music and blues music, which influenced his singing and songwriting. He said modestly that he was explaining that background to show everyone present "that I might actually possibly belong in the Rock and Roll Hall of Fame." He added, "I'm extremely proud of it, and whether I belong here or not, I'm going to take it and show it off at home."[28]

Johnny Cash's music and style resonated with audiences from the 1950s until his death in 2003. "Truly he is what the land and country is all about, the heart and soul of it personified and what it means to be here; and he said it all in plain English," said Bob Dylan. "If we want to know what it means to be mortal, we need look no further than the Man in Black. Blessed with a profound imagination, he used the gift to express all the various lost causes of the human soul. . . . [Johnny Cash] rises high above all, and he'll never die or be forgotten, even by persons not born yet—especially those persons—and that is forever."[29]

Not all Sun rockabilly artists made it big. Indeed, the extraordinary commercial success of the Million Dollar Quartet was more the exception than the norm. Some Sun artists got only a small taste of success. Roy Orbison came to Sun Records at the suggestion of his friend Johnny Cash. Sam Phillips insisted that Orbison try his hand at rockabilly, and Roy earned a modicum of success in 1956 with a lightweight rocker called "Ooby Dooby." But Phillips's refusal to let him sing ballads eventually caused Orbison to move on to Monument Records in Nashville, where he found phenomenal success in the late 1950s and '60s with a string of hits, including powerful ballads such as "Only the Lonely," "Running Scared," and "Crying," as well as upbeat rockers like "Pretty Woman."

For every Elvis and Carl Perkins or even Roy Orbison, there were many other Sun rockabilly artists in the mid- to late 1950s who never came close to fame, fortune, and glory, including Warren Smith, Charlie Feathers, Sonny Burgess, Billie Lee Riley, and Van Story—but even they had their moments. Warren Smith, for example, found local success with several rockabilly songs, including the "Ubangi Stomp" (1956), which plugged into the era's racial stereotypes of hedonistic African natives doing wild dances.

Sam Phillips had lots of hits and even more misses with Sun Records, but his energy, recording genius, and keen eye for talent resulted in some of the finest rock & roll songs of the 1950s. Long after he retired, Phillips loaned his original RCA 70-D mixing board and one track Ampex 350 tape machine to the Rock & Roll Hall of Fame for an exhibit that would recreate his Sun Studio control room. "People are going to wonder how we got the sound we did out of the equipment we had. But you can overcome a lot of things with just a little pioneering spirit," he explained proudly.[30]

ROCKABILLY GOES NATIONAL

Along with encouraging Sun recording artists, Elvis's phenomenal success caused other country singers to try their hand at rockabilly. Gene Vincent was one of the first to hit it big. Vincent grew up listening to country music in Norfolk, Virginia. While in the navy, he began playing around with the guitar and singing for anyone who would listen. When he got out of the service, he returned home and by 1955 was performing regularly on a country music show on local radio.

Like many other country artists, Vincent's music career changed dramatically the moment he heard Elvis. He quickly put together a rockabilly group called "The Blue Caps" (named after the golf cap favored by President Eisenhower). In early 1956, they recorded a demo of "Be-Bop-a-Lula," which Vincent had co-written with local disc jockey "Sheriff" Tex Davis. They sent it off to a Capitol Records executive in Nashville and got an immediate response. Eager to find their own "Elvis," Capitol signed Gene Vincent and the Blue Caps to a long-term contract and hustled the group into a recording studio in Nashville. They struck gold with the first song they recorded—"Be-Bop-a-Lula." To this day, rock & roll enthusiasts still argue about the song's origins. Some claim it was written as an ode to a local stripper; others insist it was a cute take-off on the era's popular "Little Lulu" comic strip character. There is no debate, though, about the song's place in rock & roll history. The record debuted on the national pop charts on June 16, 1956, and remained on the charts for the next twenty weeks, peaking at number 7.

"Be-Bop-a-Lula" stunned listeners. Using the echo chamber effect made famous by Elvis Presley's "Heartbreak Hotel," Vincent sings excitedly about his sensuous girlfriend—a hot girl in "red blue jeans" who "yells more, more, more, more." The song climaxes as Vincent repeats breathlessly that "Be-Bop-a-Lula" is "my baby doll, my baby doll, my baby doll."[31] Audiences were shocked and awed by the song's blatant sexuality.

The group's appearance and performance style underscored the defiant nature of "Be-Bop-a-Lula." Gene Vincent had a menacing look topped off by a hostile, punk attitude. A noticeable limp—the result of a serious motorcycle accident—added to his quirky demeanor. Vincent and the Blue Caps looked like hoodlums about to steal hubcaps off a police car. On or off stage, they wore brightly colored "cat" clothes or black leather jackets, white T-shirts, and pegged pants. They played and sang with wild abandon, their blue caps frequently falling off to reveal slick, greased-back "D.A." hairdos. The swarthy-looking Vincent looked more like Brando's motorcycle gang leader in *The Wild One* than any clean-cut hero from a Pat Boone movie (figure 9.2).

Singer and rockabilly authority Jerry Naylor recalls the first time he saw Vincent's band perform: "Now, I'd witnessed Elvis in 1955 and thought *that* was the greatest performance I'd ever seen. But when

Figure 9.2.   Gene Vincent and the Blue Caps are best known for their 1956 hit, "Be-Bop-a-Lula." (Richard Aquila Collection)

Gene hit the stage, it was as if he took everything Elvis had done and moved it up by several degrees." Naylor could hardly believe his eyes. "[Vincent] had something freer about him, something more reckless, wild, lusty," insists Naylor, "and add to that his outlaw look, with signature T-shirt, blue jeans, greasy hair, and black leathers. Gene Vincent was an original rocker with a bad boy image."[32]

Gene Vincent and the Blue Caps' performance style is captured in brilliant color in the 1956 film *The Girl Can't Help It*. The scene begins with a long shot of a building in New York called the Beaux Arts Rehearsal Hall. As the camera zooms toward the front door, viewers hear "Be-Bop-a-Lula" coming from inside. The camera pans upward to an open window, a black shade is drawn halfway down with the words "NO. 1" written on the window. Through the open part of the window, the viewer can see the rockabilly group performing: Vincent is in the center, legs spread apart, cradling his guitar as he sings; to the left are his guitarist and drummer; on the other side are the bass player and another band member spread eagled playing a guitar. This is one weird-looking band. Vincent is dressed in gray pegged pants and a bright blue, multistriped shirt. He and the group are all wearing their signature blue caps. Gene moves to the beat as he sings praises to "Be-Bop-a-Lula." As he hits the last word at the end of a verse, the group screams in ecstasy as their blue caps fall off their heads. Vincent's hair cascades down his forehead as he continues singing and moving sensually to the beat. When he reaches the midpoint in the song, he shouts emphatically, "Let's rock!" The guitar break begins, as the camera pans back out to the street.[33]

Vincent's run on the rock & roll charts was brief but spectacular. Although he never had another Top 10 hit, he did record several interesting follow-ups, including "Race with the Devil" (1956), "Bluejean Bop" (1956), "Lotta Lovin'" (1957), and "Dance to the Bop" (1957) that appealed to rebellious youth and reflected teenage interests in hot rods, fashions, dancing, and romance. His main claim to fame, though, rests with "Be-Bop-a-Lula." Vincent's signature song became one of rock & roll's all-time greatest hits and all but guaranteed the artist's later induction into the Rock & Roll Hall of Fame. Many singers tried to emulate Elvis Presley in the early days of rock & roll, but nobody did it better than Gene Vincent. Presley's own band members couldn't believe their ears the first time they heard "Be-Bop-a-Lula." They were absolutely convinced that Elvis had recorded the song behind their backs. Even Elvis's own mother thought it was her son she heard singing on the radio. When Elvis finally met Vincent, he congratulated him on his hit record. To Elvis's surprise, Gene replied apologetically, "I wasn't trying to copy you. I wasn't trying to sound like you." Elvis smiled and said, "Oh, I know that, it's just your natural style."[34]

FEMALE ROCKABILLY SINGERS

Rockabilly was mostly a male domain, but female singers occasionally got in on the action. Jean Chapel came out of Kentucky and started her career on Sun Records in 1955 before moving to RCA, where she was billed as "the Female Elvis Presley." The pretty blonde performed live several times in Alan Freed shows but never had a hit record. In 1956, Sam Phillips's Sun Records tried to market Barbara Pittman as a rockabilly singer. Like Elvis, Pittman had grown up in Memphis. And, like Elvis, her style blended country music with R&B. But unlike Elvis, Pittman never got anywhere. She later suggested that Sun Records never properly marketed her perhaps because they didn't know how to deal with a female singer. "You see, I was always a well-endowed girl," she explained, "and the guys [at Sun Records] used to tell me that they didn't know how to fit a 42 into a 33 and 1/3 [record album]."[35]

More successful was Janis Martin from Sutherlin, Virginia. The country singer was signed to RCA records in 1956. The label immediately began billing her as "the Female Elvis" because of her vocal styling and lively stage performances. Her greatest success came in early 1956 with "Will You, Willyum," which peaked at number 50 on the national record charts. Powered by a driving piano, slap bass, drums, and electric guitar, the upbeat rockabilly song featured Martin alternately snarling like Elvis and cooing seductively while she describes her sexy boyfriend who thrills her to her "fingertips." She adds suggestively, "When I'm close to you, all I can do is say . . . will you, Willyum?" Although she had numerous bookings, Janis Martin's subsequent teen-oriented releases such as "My Boy Elvis," "Let's Elope Baby," and a cover of Roy Orbison's "Oooby Dooby" failed to chart.[36]

Perhaps the most blatant attempt to cash in on the Elvis phenomenon was the appearance of a female singer billed as "Alis Lesley." Discovered by an LA disc jockey who dubbed her the "Female Presley," Miss Lesley made her debut in Hollywood in September 1956, appearing on stage with several other rock & roll acts, including the Coasters and Gene Vincent. "If the stunt proves successful," predicted a trade newspaper, "it could result in a battle of the sexes among rock 'n' roll fans." The very absence of any further news stories suggests that Alis Lesley was no Elvis Presley.[37]

The most talented female rockabilly singer was Wanda Jackson, whose sexy appearance and glamorous style were as shocking as her approach to the new sound. Although she began her career in country & western music, she began experimenting with rock & roll in 1956 because of Elvis's phenomenal success. Born in Oklahoma, the young Jackson learned her love of country & western music from her father, a local country singer. The family moved briefly to California and then back to Oklahoma City, where Wanda began singing and playing the guitar at local talent contests. While in high school, she became a regular performer on Oklahoma City's KLPR radio. Country singer Hank Thompson heard one of her broadcasts and helped her land a recording contract. After she graduated in 1955, she began touring with Thompson.

Right from the start, Wanda Jackson was different. Even her onstage clothes did not conform to the cowgirl outfits usually worn by female country performers. Instead, she wore fringed dresses with rhinestone spaghetti straps, skimpy camisoles with corset waists, tight-fitting side-strap halter dresses that bared her shoulders, or lacy bustier dresses that anticipated Madonna's look by more than three decades. On one occasion, *Grand Ole Opry* host Ernest Tubb refused to let her take the stage until she covered her bare skin with an old western jacket.[38]

Like many country singers, Jackson's career changed dramatically because of Elvis Presley. Wanda first met Elvis on a country music package tour in 1955. They remained good friends even after Elvis became the hottest rock & roll star in the nation. Sitting around Presley's home in 1956, Wanda was stunned when Elvis advised her to try her hand at the new sound. "I'm just a country singer," she protested. "I am, too, basically," replied Elvis, "but, you can do this." Soon thereafter, Jackson gave it a whirl. Her first attempt at rockabilly came in 1956 with "I Gotta Know," a novelty song that that alternated wildly between a country ballad and rock & roll. A few months later, she took another tentative step toward rock & roll with "Hot Dog! That Made Him Mad."[39]

Wanda Jackson's efforts at rock & roll yielded few hits, even though some of her later releases such as "Fujiyama Mama" (1957) and "Let's Have a Party" (1960) were excellent rockabilly songs. Why she wasn't more of a commercial success is hard to explain. She certainly had at least as much talent as other country artists of the day who were able to cross over onto the rock & roll charts. Perhaps the times just were not right for a hard rockin' female singer. "Her records didn't really sell," admits Rick Kienzle on the liner notes of a recent Wanda Jackson compilation CD, "[maybe because] America was barely used to the idea of hip-shaking male rockers, much less rockin' gals."[40]

Jackson eventually drifted back toward conventional country music and found success with more traditional country songs such as "Right or Wrong" (1961) and "In the Middle of a Heartache" (1961). But she never abandoned rock & roll completely, recording rockabilly versions of Leiber and Stoller's "Kansas City" and "Riot in Cell Block #9" and Elvis Presley's "Hard-Headed Woman" in 1960, and Rod Bernard's "This Should Go on Forever" in 1961.

If the rise of female rockabilly singers demonstrates how ubiquitous the style had become by the end of 1956, the failure of those female artists to make it big suggests that rockabilly was mostly a guy thing. Most successful rockabilly artists were young white males singing about things that young males all over the country were interested in: girls, parties, girls, drinking, girls, cars, girls, and, of course, girls. In effect, the world of early rock & roll was just as sexist as the rest of 1950s America.

UP-AND-COMING ROCKABILLY ARTISTS

By the end of 1956, other rockabilly artists were beginning to make their move. Although none had made it big yet, they would soon become some of the biggest stars in the rock & roll universe. Eddie Cochran caught the public's attention with his dynamic performance of "Twenty Flight Rock" in the 1956 film *The Girl Can't Help It*. He would make it onto the national charts the following year with minor hits such as "Sittin' in the Balcony" and "Drive-in Show," before achieving superstardom with "Summertime Blues" in 1958.

By the end of 1956, other budding rockabilly singers were also getting started. In Memphis, Jerry Lee Lewis signed with Sam Phillips's Sun Records. In Clovis, New Mexico, Buddy Knox and Jimmy Bowen began recording at Norman Petty's studio. Nashville-based Brenda Lee—a twelve-year-old who had won a talent contest when she was just five years old and started singing professionally shortly thereafter—signed a recording contract with Decca. Another act based in Nashville, the Everly Brothers, were also on the verge of making it big. Don and Phil Everly had moved to Nashville in 1955 to launch their music careers. They spent most of the next year and a half writing songs and playing local clubs. After a false start on Columbia Records, the two would sign with Cadence Records in early 1957 and go on to become one of the greatest acts in rock & roll history.

Buddy Holly was likewise launching his career in the mid-1950s. The story of how he and the other members of his band, the Crickets, got started was not that much different from the stories of other rockabilly singers. The Crickets' particular brand of rockabilly is often referred to as the "Tex-Mex" sound, because it was born on the Texas plains north of Mexico. Featuring vocalist Buddy Holly on lead guitar, Jerry "Ivan" Allison on drums, Joe B. Mauldin on bass, and Niki Sullivan on rhythm guitar, the Crickets crafted a crisp rhythm & blues-based, Tex-Mex style recorded in Norman Petty's studio in Clovis, New Mexico. "We like to think that we play rhythm-and-blues, with country-and-western overtones," explained Buddy Holly, "and my personal favorites in this field (the boys agree with me on this, by the way) are Elvis Presley, Ray Charles, the Everly Brothers, and Eddie Cochran. We also like Little Richard."[41] (figure 9.3).

Buddy Holly and Jerry Ivan Allison first met in middle school. Buddy was in the eighth grade, "J. I." was in seventh. By the time they reached Lubbock Senior High School, the two were hanging out with other guys who shared their love of country & western music, including Don Guess, Bob Montgomery, Sonny Curtis, and Larry Welborn. The teenagers all played instruments and formed themselves into a variety of groups playing wherever they could. "When I first started playing any kind of music with Buddy," explains Allison, "he and Bob Montgomery [already] had a country band called 'Buddy, Bob, and Larry,' but [then]

Figure 9.3.   Early publicity shot of the Crickets. Standing on the ladder is Buddy Holly. In front from left to right are Joe B. Mauldin, Jerry "J. I." Allison, and Niki Sullivan. (Richard Aquila Collection)

we started a band with steel guitar. Don Guest played steel, Sonny Curtis played fiddle . . . we [went] around West Texas playing country shows and dances at that sort of thing."[42]

One of their classmates, Peggy Sue Gerron (who later married Allison and whose first name inspired the title of one of Buddy Holly's biggest hits), vividly recalls that Holly and his friends began as country singers: "Every time I heard [Buddy's band] play in school or at the used car lot or on top of the Hi-D-Ho Drive-In or in the skating rink . . . they were always country." Buddy admitted as much in an assignment he wrote for his sophomore English class in 1953: "I have thought about making a career out of western music if I am good enough."[43]

Eventually, Buddy Holly and Bob Montgomery paired off as a duo. Their music and sound were influenced not only by the country singers and pickers they listened to the most—such as Hank Williams, Bill Monroe and the Bluegrass Boys, the Louvin Brothers, and Johnny and Jack—but also black artists who were beginning to appear on the scene by the early 1950s. Like many white teenagers of the era, Buddy and Bob began twisting their radio dials to pull in the exotic sounds of blues and rhythm & blues. Buddy, in particular, was intrigued by the new sound. Tuned to clear channel radio stations from Nashville and Shreveport, Buddy listened intently to blues singers such as Muddy Waters and Howlin' Wolf, as well as rhythm & blues groups like the Drifters and Clovers.

When Lubbock radio station KDAV put out a call in late 1953 for local talent to audition for a new Sunday afternoon program patterned after the *Grand Ole Opry*, Buddy and Bob rushed over to the studio guitars in hand. One of the station's disc jockeys and co-owner, William "Hi-Pockets" Duncan, was impressed by the duo and suggested they would sound even better if they added a bass player. Shortly thereafter, Buddy and Bob returned with their friend Larry Welborn, and the group was given their own half-hour segment on the weekly radio show. "The Buddy and Bob Show" made them local celebrities, and Hi-Pockets got them numerous local bookings, playing dances, restaurants, laundromat openings, or any place else that was interested. Buddy, Bob, and Larry stuck mostly to country songs, but every once in a while they mixed in some rhythm & blues. Hoping to land a recording contract, the country group made a few demos in 1954, but nothing happened. Buddy and Bob had no way of knowing it as 1954 came to a close, but the two close friends and musical collaborators were about to hit a fork in their musical road to success.

Buddy Holly's world changed forever the moment he saw Elvis Presley perform in Lubbock, Texas, on Thursday, January 6, 1955. Holly witnessed the incredible performance as he stood backstage with Bob Montgomery. "Man, when I saw Elvis out there," said Buddy, "I started thinking different about music." Holly was awed by the entire scene—

Presley's wild cat clothes, his rockabilly sound, his dynamic performance style, the girls screaming, and the pandemonium throughout the hall. Buddy came away with a burning desire to follow Elvis's lead, telling his friends, "That's what I want to be!"[44]

From that point on, all Buddy Holly wanted to do was rock & roll. He began singing more R&B songs on the show. In recognition of their move toward Elvis's style of music, Buddy and Bob even printed up new business cards billing themselves as "Buddy and Bob" singers of "Western and Bop." J. I. Allison suggests that he and Buddy had actually been heading toward the new sound even before Presley arrived in Lubbock, but after Elvis's performance, there was no going back. "I think Buddy and I were [always] more interested in rock & roll than [Bob Montgomery and] the rest of the guys, and we started veering off in that direction," says Allison. "Then Elvis came to town and Buddy really got into rock & roll then."[45]

On October 14, 1955, Buddy and Bob were one of several opening acts at a Bill Haley and His Comets concert in Lubbock. A Nashville-based talent agent sitting in the audience was impressed enough to ask for some demos. J. I. Allison recalls what happened next: "We went and made some demos . . . at a studio in Wichita Falls, Texas . . . and Buddy and Bob did a couple of country duets and we did some Elvis-sounding records that just Buddy sang on—rockabilly—and we sent those to Nashville."[46] The talent agent then passed the songs on to music publisher Jim Denny, who in turn contacted Paul Cohen, the A&R man for Decca Records in Nashville.

Shortly thereafter, Decca contacted Holly. Unfortunately, there was a catch. Hoping to sign its own rockabilly version of Elvis Presley, Decca wanted Buddy as a solo artist. At first, Holly balked because he didn't want to betray Bob Montgomery. But Bob eventually convinced him that he had to give it a shot. According to Buddy's mother, "Bob said, 'You've got your chance—now go ahead!' And so Buddy did." The decision sent Buddy and Bob off in different directions. While Holly headed toward rock & roll, Montgomery stuck with country music. Bob never regretted his choice. Eventually, he became one of Nashville's most successful songwriters, music publishers, and record executives, scoring numerous hits with performers such as Jim Reeves, Patsy Cline, Mel Tillis, Eddie Arnold, Joe Diffie, and Collin Raye.[47]

Holly's first steps down the rock & roll path were tentative at best. Buddy's Decca sessions in 1956 were a disaster. He showed up in Nashville in late January 1956, with a backup band that included Lubbock friends Sonny Curtis on guitar and Don Guess on bass. But Decca producer Owen Bradley (who later produced Brenda Lee's numerous rock & roll hits) insisted that Holly had to use Nashville studio musicians instead. That was the first setback. Nothing jelled. Buddy wanted to rock & roll, while Bradley and his talented country pickers insisted on country stylings. The stalemate continued throughout two more recording sessions later in the year. Even though Bradley eventually allowed Buddy's Lubbock friends, including drummer J. I. Allison and bass player Don Guess, to play in the last two sessions, the results were still disappointing. "We went and recorded some in 1956," recalls Allison. "The records weren't very successful so Decca dropped Buddy."[48]

Despite the setback, Holly still had faith in the tracks he recorded for Decca, so he placed a long-distance phone call to A&R man Paul Cohen. The twenty-year-old was savvy enough to secretly tape the conversation just in case evidence was needed down the road. Buddy politely asked Cohen for a written release for five of the songs, which he wanted to market elsewhere. The Decca record man tried to stonewall him, saying the recordings belonged to the company and that Buddy could not rerecord them with anybody for five years. The young singer was not intimidated by the more experienced businessman. He calmly argued his case, to which Cohen replied in a patronizing tone that Holly could not redo the songs. He even had the nerve to tell the singer not to feel bad about it. "Well, I can hardly keep from it, Paul, because it seems like a heck of way to do a guy," responded an upset Holly. Cohen assured him that this was simply business and Decca had money tied up in the recordings. Who knows what might happen down the road, said Cohen—Decca might even decide to release the records. "So, you can't record them for another company," repeated Cohen, "but you can record anything else you want to." Holly refused to budge, insisting that he wanted to rerecord his songs in an effort to get them released on another label. The cold, calculating Cohen then tried a different approach. "Why don't you let me hear them [new masters] before you give them to anybody," he said, "and I'll tell you what to do." An incredulous Holly did not take the bait. "Well, I didn't much want to stay with Decca, because they didn't seem to want to push me," said Holly.

Clearly exasperated, Cohen repeated once again that Holly could not record the songs for five years, and he urged Buddy to call back if he recorded any new dubs. Holly avoided a direct reply, saying simply, "Well, talk to you later about it, then. Thank you a lot. Good-bye." They both hung up.[49]

Subsequently, Buddy Holly and J. I. Allison began reworking the songs, along with other new material. "We got to listening even more to Little Richard, Fats Domino, and Chuck Berry," recalls Allison. "We decided we'd be a group as opposed to just Buddy Holly, so we came up with the name "The Crickets" because of an old [R&B] group called the Spiders."[50]

Prior to 1957, Holly and Allison were the only two constants in a group that was always changing. "There really wasn't any steady group," says Allison. "It was just whatever came up and whoever was hanging around at the time and was available to play." Buddy and J. I. were eager to play with anyone willing to jump in. So the band's lineup often changed from one gig to the next. Sometimes, just Holly and Allison showed up. Sonny Curtis, who played with the Crickets both before and after Holly's death, suggests that necessity was the mother of Holly and Allison's musical invention. "Boy, that was some good stuff when Allison and Holly were just picking by themselves," he explains. "And that's how they got to picking together so good—they simply had to fill up every hole." Allison agrees, and adds with a smile, "Sure made the money go farther, too."[51]

After the Decca deal fizzled, Holly and Allison eventually wound up contacting Norman Petty, who owned a recording studio in nearby Clovis, New Mexico. Things happened fast after that. The Crickets wrote and recorded several songs, including "That'll Be the Day," which made it all the way to number 1 on the pop charts in 1957. For Buddy Holly, it was the beginning of a meteoric career that would end tragically in rock & roll martyrdom.

Holly was just one of many country singers who followed Elvis Presley down the rock & roll highway in the late 1950s. Some, like Carl Perkins, Gene Vincent, and Johnny Cash, would find immediate success; others—including Buddy Holly and the Crickets, Jerry Lee Lewis, the Everly Brothers, Eddie Cochran, Brenda Lee, Jack Scott, Conway Twitty, and Roy Orbison—would not make it big until later in the 1950s. Still others such as Thomas Wayne, Ronnie Hawkins, Clyde

Stacy, Dale Hawkins, and Wanda Jackson would never find sustained success, although they, too, would have their moment in the rock & roll spotlight.

By the end of 1956, rockabilly music had become mainstream rock & roll. The roots of rockabilly were planted deep in southern soil. Rockabilly was the product of a southern cultural melting pot that mixed together working class whites and blacks. It was the sound of the urban and rural South in post–World War II America. It reverberated with the emotionalism of Southern Baptists and Pentecostal singers, and gave voice to sharecroppers, working-class whites, and rural blacks. It was at once a tradition and an innovation, a musical, cultural, and racial hybrid that mixed gospel, blues, rhythm & blues, and country & western. The style demonstrates how early rock & roll blended country music and rhythm & blues with pop-oriented lyrics aimed at white teenagers. Rockabilly's transformation from an underground southern music into mainstream rock & roll both reflected and helped shape the era's emerging youth culture. The new sound spoke of teenage rebellion, as well as the conventional dreams and fears of young people.

The rockabilly singers who arrived on the pop music charts in 1956 found some success, but in the end they remained just the court for the "King of Rock & Roll." Elvis Presley would continue to be the main rockabilly draw throughout the rest of the decade and beyond.

CONCLUSION

Crazy Man, Crazy! The Birth of Rock & Roll and 1950s America

The world has changed a great deal since Bill Haley and His Comets recorded "Crazy Man, Crazy" in 1953. Not only is it a new century but in many ways it is also a different world with new technologies, new realities, new hopes, and new fears. America of the 1950s may be gone, but it is not forgotten. It lives on in many ways. Even Bill Haley, who died in 1981, did not fade away completely. Black-and-white images of Haley and his group performing "Crazy Man, Crazy" back in the early '50s can still be seen flickering in old film clips or on the Internet.

One vintage Haley video begins with a cacophony of drums. An electric guitar joins in as Haley sings the phrase "Crazy Man, Crazy" three times. Viewers—then and now—quickly realize this sound is different, very different. Haley and his group jubilantly push forward. Dressed in matching plaid tuxedos with black bowties, they bounce to the beat. Haley with his ever-present grin looks to the left, then to the right, recognizing each of the Comets at just the right moment when—like jazz players from earlier days—they take turns with solos. Haley drops to his knees almost in reverence as the saxophone player blows hot riffs and the bass player stands atop his instrument. Without missing a beat, the performers jump back into original formation and finish up strong. Listeners get caught up in the big beat, while Haley careens through the lyrics like a pinball bouncing from one slang term to another: *crazy, chick, rockin', wild*. All the while, he keeps driving home the main point: the new sound was really cool. Or, to quote the slang used in the song, "man, that music's gone, gone."[1]

The phrase "crazy, man, crazy" could just as easily be used to describe what many people thought about the numerous changes that were occurring in both popular music and American culture in the 1950s. Throughout the decade, Americans experienced rapid social, cultural, economic, and political change, struggling to keep up with a burgeoning cold war culture that permeated all levels of American life and thought. Popular music likewise underwent tremendous change when rock & roll exploded onto the scene. More often than not, the new music was in tune with the changing times.

THE RISE OF ROCK & ROLL

While fans and critics might argue about whether "Crazy Man, Crazy" was the first rock & roll record, one thing is certain: Haley's record was at the vanguard of a new musical style that emerged in the 1950s.

The coming of Elvis Presley in 1956 launched rock & roll to even greater heights. The innovative rocker reshaped the music's image and style. He influenced numerous performers and riveted public attention on the new sound, expanding its market if not guaranteeing rock & roll's survival. By the end of the decade, all the main forms of early rock & roll were evident. There was vibrant rockabilly, with Elvis leading the way and Carl Perkins, Gene Vincent, and others in tow. There was excellent rhythm & blues–based rock & roll sung by artists such as Chuck Berry, Fats Domino, and the Five Satins. And there was both original and derivative pop rock, featuring singers like Bill Haley and His Comets, Pat Boone, and the Diamonds, to name just a few. In addition, there were numerous offshoots, including instrumental rock, novelty rock, dance songs, and more. These various rock & roll styles would dominate pop music for most of the next two decades. Each blended various ingredients from traditional white pop, black rhythm & blues, and white country & western.

The rise of rock & roll was one of the most important cultural developments of the post–World War II era. Not only did it serve as a cultural binding force for the generation that came of age following

World War II, but it reflected—and perhaps helped shape—American life and thought of the 1950s.

ROCK & ROLL AND 1950S AMERICA

The emergence of the new music was linked to major changes of the post–World War II era. White America's discovery of black rhythm & blues was the result of the movement of large numbers of African Americans from the South to large urban areas in the North and West during and after World War II. When blacks migrated northward to jobs in New York City, Chicago, Cleveland, and other industrial cities, they brought along cultural baggage, including rhythm & blues. For the first time on a large scale, whites living outside the South could listen to black music in bars and record stores or on the radio. Before long, whites across the country were integrating black rhythms and beats into white pop and country & western, helping to give birth to rock & roll.

If the birth of rock & roll was linked to the emergence of blacks in American society, its growth was dependent upon another major demographic change—the coming of a new postwar youth culture. This new generation was raised on prosperity with more consumer goods and opportunities than their parents could have imagined when they were growing up during the Great Depression. The new teenage cohort would be reinforced by millions of baby boomers reaching puberty in the 1950s and '60s. The boom began after World War II and would continue until 1964, eventually producing 76.5 million babies or one-third of America's population.[2]

Like the young generation, rock & roll came of age after World War II. The new sound, with its distinctive beat and adolescent themes, was perfect for a new postwar youth culture that considered itself unique. Rock & roll became the boundary marker for the youth culture and its various subcultures. It contributed to teenagers' collective memory and group identity, allowing the new generation to clarify who they were by listening to the type of music that appealed to their particular subculture. Rock & roll taught adolescents how to dance, how to dress, how to date, how to use slang, and how to act as it communicated group attitudes about school, parents, and everyday life and thought.[3]

Rock & roll was intertwined with American prosperity after World War II. There was no better growth industry in 1950s America than rock & roll, which offered abundant opportunities for expectant capitalists, including owners of record companies, media moguls, or young singers hoping to strike it rich. The new music was a perfect fit for the era's consumer culture. Just as adults spent lavishly on a cornucopia of consumer goods, the market for rock & roll expanded rapidly as teenage consumers created their own culture of consumption based on a variety of rock & roll–related products, including records, record players, transistor radios, movies, radio shows, fan magazines, or fashions such as Elvis Presley jewelry or blue suede shoes.

Technological change powered the growth of rock & roll. Prior to World War II, the recording industry had been limited to elaborate and expensive studios in New York City, Chicago, or Los Angeles. But by the mid-1950s, the introduction of magnetic tape recorders enabled small, independent companies to record local rock & roll talent anywhere in the country, reinforcing the music's grassroots connection. Rock & roll thrived on other technological innovations. The rise of television and the resulting changes in radio programming beamed rock & roll into expanding markets throughout the country. New 45-rpm records with their wide hole in the middle gave the music a more distinct appearance and made it easier to transport and play on new portable record players. And transistor radios and radios in cars made the music portable, allowing it to be played while cruising the streets or parked at drive-ins or lovers' lanes.

ROCK & ROLL AND REBELLION

To a large extent, rock & roll reflects conflict and tensions in 1950s America. Critics linked the music to a variety of social ills, insisting that rock & roll would turn innocent youths into violent hoodlums, sexual perverts, or worse. The stage was set in 1955 when Bill Haley's "Rock Around the Clock" appeared in the opening sequence of *Blackboard Jungle*, a film about teenage gangs and hoodlums in an inner-city school. That connection was quickly etched into the public consciousness.[4]

Opponents of rock & roll soon piled on, claiming that the deviant music was undermining American values in every way imaginable. *Variety* ran a three-part series in 1955 criticizing obscene "leer-ics" of R& B and rock & roll songs. A two-part series that ran in the *New York Daily News* in early 1956 claimed rock & roll was turning youths into hoodlums and touching off riots across the country. The story pointed out that adults were finally fighting back, outraged by the "barrage of primitive jungle-beat rhythms, which when set to lyrics at all, frequently sound off with double meaning leer-ics few adults would care to hear."[5]

The use of the phrase "jungle-beat" by the *New York Daily News* was a thinly veiled racist attack on rock & roll. Others were more blatant. Fearing that rock & roll would blur the racial divide, paranoid critics denounced the music's black roots and black singers. The North Alabama White Citizens' Council insisted that not only was rock & roll "sexualistic" and "immoral," but it was also an NAACP plot to further integration and it dragged whites "down to the level of the Negro." "Help save the youth of America," pleaded a leaflet prepared by another racist group. "Don't let your children buy or listen to these Negro records. The screaming, idiotic words and savage music are undermining the morals of our white American youth." Similar comments could be heard from more mainstream sources, too. Congressman Emanuel Celler from New York stated bluntly that rock & roll "has its place . . . among the colored people."[6]

At times, it seemed as if the entire American establishment was lined up against rock & roll. The FBI began a file on Elvis. Cultural critics such as Dwight Macdonald and Vance Packard maintained that the teenage music was undermining traditional culture. A psychiatrist from Hartford, Connecticut, insisted that the teenage fad was "a communicable disease with music appealing to adolescent insecurity and driving teen-agers to do outlandish things." Another compared rock & roll to mass movements throughout history, cautioning that the music could lead toward fascism. *Time* magazine issued a similar warning, suggesting that teenagers' adulation of rock & roll stars was similar to "Hitler's mass meetings."[7]

Given the anti–rock & roll hysteria, radio and TV stations thought twice before playing certain singers or records. "The recently headlined controversies over the effect of rock and roll music on the morals of minors have prompted the broadcast industry—in particular the major networks—to keep an especially cautious ear open for material that might lead youngsters astray," reported a trade publication in 1956. "Songs which are profane, ridicule physical deformities, contribute to juvenile delinquency, are offensive to minorities, and more often, songs which are lascivious, are considered improper for broadcast."[8]

If Marshall McLuhan was right when he said "the medium is the message," then rock & roll's message for many listeners was rebellious, if not outright subversive. A *Time* magazine article in 1956 described the new sound and style as "an unrelenting, socking syncopation that sounds like a bull whip; a choleric saxophone honking mating calls; an electric guitar turned up so loud that its sound shatters and splits; a vocal group that shudders and exercises violently to the beat while roughly chanting either a near-nonsense phrase or a moronic lyric in hillbilly idiom."[9] Most teenagers understood that rock & roll was making a statement, albeit a very loud one. The statement was that things would never be the same.

Rock & roll was different from earlier pop. It sounded different with its big beat, raucous sound, and teen-oriented lyrics. Its performers—generally younger than traditional pop singers and frequently from minority, ethnic, and working class backgrounds—were different. And the performance style was different. Rock & rollers often danced around on stage, shaking their bodies in sexy ways or using instruments and microphones as suggestive props.

Rock & roll defiantly distanced itself from other types of music, as evidenced by Chuck Berry's 1956 hit "Roll Over Beethoven," which warned older styles of music to get out of the way. Rock & roll performers didn't look or act like traditional pop singers. They frequently wore outrageous clothes, sported wild hair styles, and spoke in teenage idioms. Elvis Presley is a perfect example. People took notice of his fashion sense and were either attracted or repelled by the young rocker's performance style, colloquial speech patterns, and propensity for black or wild, tailored "cat" clothes of bright pink, chartreuse, and purple.[10]

Rock & roll's very existence was a threat to 1950s notions of race. The new music was offering 1950s audiences visions of racial equality and harmony. In an era of segregation, rock & roll featured black artists such as Chuck Berry and Fats Domino, who wrote and recorded songs for the white audience, as well as white singers like Elvis Presley and

Pat Boone, who copied black styles. All these rock & rollers blended elements of white country & western, black rhythm & blues, and traditional white pop. The result was a musical hybrid that mixed sounds, styles, and people from different races (figure C.1).

Early rock & roll reflected—maybe even contributed to—the rise of integration in 1950s America. The Ramparts' "Death of Emmett Till" (1956), which memorialized a twelve-year-old black boy who was murdered for allegedly flirting with a white girl, was the most obvious attempt to plug into the era's rising civil rights movement. Not surprisingly, the record did well with black listeners but flopped on the national pop charts. Yet the very existence of rock & roll music—which was based in part on black R&B and featured numerous black artists—was proof that cultural integration had arrived. White rockabilly artist Carl Perkins saw the irony between segregation patterns in the South and the lack of racial distinctions in rock & roll. "When you walked up to an old . . . Wurlitzer jukebox, it [didn't say] 'Blue Suede Shoes,' Carl

Figure C.1. This photo of Little Richard and Bill Haley suggests the connection between rock & roll and integration in the 1950s. (Richard Aquila Collection)

Perkins, white; 'Blueberry Hill,' Fats Domino, black," explains Perkins. "No. There was no difference. Kids danced to Little Richard, Chuck Berry, Elvis."[11]

The connection between rock & roll and race did not go unnoticed. Segregationists and other critics became nearly apoplectic, condemning the music in print, smashing records in public, organizing protests, petitioning TV networks to ban rock & roll singers, and boycotting radio stations that played the music. "The obscenity and vulgarity of the rock 'n' roll music," warned Asa Carter of the Alabama White Citizens' Council in 1956, "is obviously a means by which the white man can be driven to the level of the nigger."[12]

Other observers applauded the impact the new music was having on race relations. An editorial in *Cashbox* praised rock & roll as "The Great UNIFYING FORCE," explaining that everyone in the music industry should be proud of the musical and cultural mixing taking place because of rock & roll. *DownBeat* reporter Ruth Cage was impressed by the integrated audiences that frequented rock & roll concerts: "For those who say that the music with a beat is doing terrible things to the nation's youth, it might be pointed out that this music is doing a job in the Deep South that even the U.S. Supreme Court hasn't been able to accomplish." Years later, civil rights leader Julian Bond offered a similar appraisal, suggesting that 1950s rock & roll "exposed white youth to black America for the first time." The experience "helped prepare them for the civil rights movement then yet to come."[13]

Race was not the only fault line for rock & roll. The music's sexuality created other fissures. Rock & roll's sexual power threatened 1950s sensibilities by allowing erotic dreams to penetrate previously forbidden racial, ethnic, or class borders. White middle- and upper-class teenage girls could fantasize about Elvis and other blue-collar rockabilly singers, as well as black rock & rollers like Bo Diddley and Frankie Lymon. Teenage boys had similar rock & roll fantasies, dreaming about sexy rock & roll girls like the uninhibited, blue-collar country rocker Wanda Jackson or the sensuous R&B singer LaVern Baker.

The music's sexuality was both explicit and implicit. Sometimes, it was the suggestive performance style of rock & rollers. Other times, it was the sensual sound of hot electric guitar licks, insistent beats, or throbbing sax solos. On other occasions, rock & roll dance steps, vocals, or lyrics aroused young listeners. Some hit records from the mid-1950s probably should have been labeled *for mature audiences only*. Teenagers got excited by Gene Vincent's orgasmic delivery and heavy breathing on "Be-Bop-a-Lula" (1956). Adolescent girls went into overdrive when they heard Elvis sing, "Baby Let's Play House" (1955). Even reverent audiences understood the true meaning behind the Platters' "My Prayer" (1956), which featured the lead singer asking for divine assistance so he "could linger" with his girl "at the end of the day." [14]

Many rock & roll artists oozed sex. Elvis was the most obvious. Wherever he went, whenever he performed, whatever he did sent females into a state of frenzy. When *Life* magazine asked him to explain "what is about him that makes all the ladies go limp," the King of Rock & Roll just smiled and replied, "I don't know, but I sure hope it doesn't stop." [15]

Rock & roll girls could be just as sexy. Like their counterparts in American society, girls in rock & roll songs sometimes were willing to go the extra mile if not all the way to please the boy of their dreams. A perfect example is Mickey and Sylvia's provocative "Love Is Strange" (1956). Like a good girl of the '50s, Sylvia starts out slowly, but she makes it clear that she might be willing to go further. The song's insistent rhythms and sensual beat become foreplay for an erotic exchange between the two singers, which culminates with Sylvia whispering erotically to her "sweet baby" that he's "the one." Mickey and Sylvia's voices then come together in the refrain, as electric guitars and drums explode in a musical climax. [16]

Rock & roll threatened the status quo in other ways. Rock & roll's working-class roots made it suspect. Elvis Presley's overnight leap from truck driver to top recording artist was not unusual in the world of rock & roll where many singers came from working-class backgrounds. For good or bad, singers and song lyrics were often seen as low class. Lew Chudd, the owner of Imperial Records, remembers sending an advance copy of Fats Domino's "Ain't That a Shame" (1955) to Cleveland deejay Bill Randle. "[Randle] liked it because it was ignorant," said Chudd. The erudite disc jockey, who taught part-time at a local university, was probably fascinated by the vernacular lyrics for the same reason that literary scholars praise Mark Twain's use of dialect in *Huckleberry Finn*. But the low-class music was too authentic for the tastes of many middle-class and upper-class listeners. When Pat Boone was asked to cover the song, the young singer initially tried to make the lyrics grammatically correct. "I tried to change it to 'Isn't That a Shame,'" says Boone. "I was just transferred to Columbia University in New York and I was majoring in English." In the end, Pat recorded the song as originally written, and both the Boone and Domino versions of "Ain't That a Shame" became major hits, much to the chagrin of gatekeepers of American culture. Dave Bartholomew, the co-writer and producer of "Ain't That a Shame," remembers sitting in a restaurant one night with Fats watching Steve Allen's *Tonight Show*. All of a sudden, Allen launched into a parody of the song. He adjusted his glasses and dramatically recited the lyrics to "Ain't That a Shame" just as a scholar would give a reading of a serious poem. The two songwriters cringed as viewers laughed nationwide. "Steve Allen made us feel like shit," Bartholomew later said. "He was making fun of us."[17] What Allen did to the two rock & rollers that night was no different from what upper- and middle-class people frequently did to perceived inferiors. Like sophisticated urbanites who looked down their noses at country bumpkins, Steve Allen and his middle- and upper-class audience shared laughs by condemning allegedly low-class rock & roll upstarts.

Allen's vicious attack suggests that rock & roll was a battleground across a generational divide. The new music gave as well as it got. For every attack by Steve Allen or some other adult, rock & roll took its own shots at the establishment or glorified the new youth culture. Popular songs celebrated the uniqueness of teenage culture, particularly young romance, teenage fashions, interests, and slang.[18] The more rock & roll became a cultural binding force for the emerging youth culture, the more it came under attack by the establishment. The music became a dividing line between the young and the old. But the division was not based solely on age. The music's attitude also had a lot to do with it. Many songs had lyrics that were innocent enough, but when rock & roll singers shouted them out, slurred the words, or sang them with a sneer, they took on new meaning. Sometimes, just the wild appearance and outrageous performance styles of rock & rollers such as Elvis Presley and Little Richard were enough to send critics into apoplexy.

One of rock & roll's pioneers insists that rock & roll's attitude is what set it apart from other musical styles. "You know, we used to think that you had to be young to sing rock & roll," explains Dion DiMucci, who found success in the 1950s as the lead singer of Dion and the Belmonts and later as a solo artist with hits such as "Runaround Sue" (1961) and

"Abraham, Martin, and John" (1968). "But, [rock & roll] is an attitude and it's an expression. . . . I think it's honest, it's simple, you have something to say, and you're going to say it. . . . There's always a real honest expression coming out. You can't suppress it."[19] That rock & roll attitude—the in-your-face way that rock & roll freely expressed itself about sex, race, and other topics—probably caused many people to view the music as a threat to the status quo in 1950s America.

Clearly, there were elements of rebellion in rock & roll, yet in many ways the new teenage music was no more rebellious than other segments of American culture. For example, race was taking center stage not just in rock & roll but throughout 1950s America.[20] The civil rights movement picked up momentum in the years following World War II, causing an avalanche of media coverage of *Brown vs. Board of Education*, Rosa Parks, the Montgomery bus boycott, and Martin Luther King Jr. Hollywood spotlighted black actors and subjects with films such as *Carmen Jones* (1954) and *The Defiant Ones* (1958). By the end of the decade, mainstream audiences were as familiar with black actors and actresses such as Sidney Poitier, Harry Belafonte, and Dorothy Dandridge as they were with African American rock & rollers like Chuck Berry and Fats Domino. Blacks also emerged as TV stars. In 1956, Nat "King" Cole became the first African American to host a variety show on network television; *Amos and Andy*—with an almost entirely black cast—emerged as one of TV's top sitcoms; and black performers such as Lena Horne, Sammy Davis Jr., and Eartha Kitt made regular TV appearances. African American authors made their mark with bestsellers such as Ralph Ellison's *Invisible Man* (1952) and James Baldwin's *Go Tell It on the Mountain* (1953), while black-operated magazines such as *Ebony* and *Jet* enjoyed major gains in readership. In sports, African Americans followed Jackie Robinson's lead, gaining recognition as some of the top athletes in the nation, including Willie Mays and Hank Aaron in baseball, Sugar Ray Robinson in boxing, and Bill Russell in basketball.

Just as rock & roll was not alone when it came to issues of race in 1950s America, the same can be said about matters involving sex. Rock & roll was not the only area of pop culture treating sex more openly. As the motion picture production code unraveled after World War II, the movie industry began pushing the limits of what could be depicted on the big screen with suggestive films such as *And God Created Woman*,

From Here to Eternity, and *Baby Doll.* Brigitte Bardot and Marilyn Monroe emerged as the era's top sex goddesses, joined by other buxom blonde bombshells such as Mamie Van Doren and Jayne Mansfield. The obvious talents of those actresses sparked the popularity of "falsies." By the end of the decade, Sears was offering twenty different varieties designed to help young ladies look more like big-screen sex goddesses.

Television—because it was beamed into living rooms across the nation—had to be more circumspect about sex. But the result was often just as titillating. Bob Cummings's popular sitcom, *Love That Bob,* related the escapades of a playboy fashion photographer whose charms were irresistible to all the super models. Another popular show, *Sheena of the Jungle,* provided a contrived setting and the means for its beautiful, blonde, six-foot-one-inch star, Irish McCalla, to parade around African jungles in skimpy leopard-skin costumes. Equally provocative were the two dancing girls featured in Old Gold cigarette commercials. They wore giant cigarette boxes that covered everything but their legs, guaranteeing viewers' attention would be riveted on the shapely legs dancing sensuously in black mesh stockings and white boots. Popular writing of the 1950s was even steamier with best-selling novels such as Vladimir Nabokov's *Lolita* and Grace Metalious's *Peyton Place,* or provocative new magazines such as Hugh Hefner's *Playboy.*

America of the 1950s was obsessed with sex. People could not stop talking about Professor Alfred Kinsey's analytical report published in 1953, *Sexual Behavior in the Human Female.* And the media found delight in sexy stories about the latest rages, such as bikini bathing suits, panty raids on college campuses, voluptuous pinups like Bettie Page, and suggestive advertising campaigns such as "I dreamed I [did whatever] in my Maidenform bra."

Rock & roll was not even the only form of popular culture that spotlighted teenagers or rebellious youth. Hollywood served up numerous feature films about defiant youth, including *The Wild One, Blackboard Jungle,* and *Rebel Without a Cause.* The publishing industry got in on the action with sensational books like *Jailbait Street* and *Rumble,* as well as confession magazines such as *True Story,* which offered first-person accounts with titles like "We Were Truant Teens" and "They Called Us High School Hoodlums."[21]

When all is said and done, rock & roll was no more rebellious or unruly than other areas of pop culture. The music clearly pushed the limits on sex, race, juvenile delinquency, and new fads, but it was not alone. So did other media, as well as American culture and society in general.

ROCK & ROLL AS CONSENSUS BEHAVIOR

While opponents of rock & roll sometimes had good reason to claim the music was rebellious, their histrionics actually say more about cold war America than they do about rock & roll. Fear was everywhere in the 1950s. People railed against anything different. They eyed foreigners with suspicion and were quick to judge as un-American anyone who criticized the U.S. government or the status quo, citing the Rosenbergs and Alger Hiss as evidence of internal subversion. Given the mood of the country, it is not surprising that the new, weird-sounding music was seen as a threat. In reality, though, rock & roll was not a sinister force determined to undermine the American way of life. Most teenagers did not view the music as a vehicle for rebellion. Rock & roll was simply their form of popular music. And, in many ways, the music was more a sign of consensus between the generations than conflict.

Rock & roll was born in the midst of the cold war. The same culture that produced "Rock Around the Clock," "Maybellene," and "Hound Dog" was also responsible for the Berlin Crisis, McCarthyism, House Un-American Activities Committee (HUAC), and the Korean War. Therefore, it should not be surprising that much of early rock & roll was informed by that ubiquitous cold war culture. The 1950s are generally viewed as a period of consensus and conformity in American history, an era marked by fears of communism and praise for traditional American values that supported God, country, and family. Early rock & roll was part of—not apart from—the era's cold war culture.

Numerous scholars have described in detail the various ways anti-communism permeated American life and thought in the years following World War II. They argue that a cold war culture emerged, influencing institutions involving government, religion, marriage, and the family, as well as everyday life and attitudes toward race, ethnicity, and gender.[22]

Rock & roll records demonstrate that teenagers were eager participants in the cold war culture. The music subscribed wholeheartedly to
the era's rising patriotism. Historian Stephen Whitfield suggests, "The
search to define and affirm a way of life, the need to express and
celebrate the meaning of Americanism, was the flip side of stigmatizing
Communism."[23] Rock & roll celebrated Americanism in various ways.
For one thing, the new sound was 99.9 percent pure American. Usually,
only American singers made the charts. Rock & roll was reserved for
American artists; foreign performers were viewed as mere imitators.
This mind-set reflected the patriotism of the day and the generally
accepted ethnocentric notion that foreign products were vastly inferior
to American ones. A rock & roll record by European artists was no
more welcome than consumer goods marked "Made in Japan."

Rock & roll displayed patriotism in other ways. Gene Vincent named
his rockabilly group, the Blue Caps, after the golf hat made popular by
President Eisenhower. An R&B group named the Treniers tapped into
young people's mainstream political attitudes in an election year with
their 1956 release, "Rock and Roll President." And Pat Boone's "I'll Be
Home" (1956) told the tale of a guy in uniform who promises to come
home to "serve" his girl just as he has his country.[24]

Rock & roll singers—like other good American boys of the 1950s—
exhibited traditional values. Most rock & roll idols were cut from the
same mold as earlier American heroes. The ultimate rock & roll hero
was basically just an updated version of Jack Armstrong, the All-
American Boy—a good-looking, talented, athletic, self-made, honest,
sensitive, polite, and humble white male. Any rock & roller who did not
fit that mold (i.e., racial and ethnic minorities, females, or anyone with a
character flaw) had a much harder time becoming a top-tier teenage
idol. Elvis Presley and Pat Boone were bookends on opposite ends of
the spectrum for rock & roll heroes, yet they were remarkably similar.
Boone came from a loving family, respected his parents, believed in
God, loved his country, was well groomed, didn't drink or smoke, and
was loved by girls because of his good looks, boyish charm, and singing
ability. Elvis, despite his rebellious image, really wasn't that much different. He, too, loved God, country, and family, was polite to elders and
women, dressed well (even though some adults were appalled by his
fashion tastes), and made it big because of God-given talent.

Given Presley's All-American Boy qualities, no wonder many adults supported him. Journalist Fred Sparks even came to Elvis's defense when critics claimed he was "a bad example for our young people." In a story syndicated across the country, Sparks refuted all the charges, pointing out that Elvis "is of the soil itself, like Will Rogers and Carl Sandburg." Presley and other rock & rollers would later demonstrate their patriotism by serving in the nation's armed forces. Before entering the army in 1958, Elvis assured his fans, "It is an honor and privilege to serve our country." Once in, Presley was just a typical G.I. "You can treat Presley like any other soldier. He never asked for one special preference," reported a sergeant. "He is a fine lad."[25]

Rock & roll endorsed cold war America in other ways. In the 1950s, American life and thought was dominated by what historian Godfrey Hodgson calls the "liberal consensus"—a centrist ideology that promoted the unquestioned supremacy of American democracy and capitalism. America's economic success story reverberated with cold war significance. In 1956, the Advertising Council coined the phrase "People's Capitalism" as the title for an exhibit designed to promote the American way of life. President Eisenhower praised the display when it was set up in Washington, D.C.'s Union Station. Subsequently, the exhibit toured the world through the auspices of the United States Information Agency, promoting America's economic success story to people throughout Europe, Africa, Asia, and Latin America. Its main message was summed up succinctly in a General Electric magazine advertisement that read: "Our American brand of capitalism is distinctive and unusually successful because it is 'people's capitalism': all the people share in its responsibilities and benefits."[26] The success of American capitalism seemed self-evident to 1950s Americans, who reveled in the availability of jobs, abundance of consumer goods, and myriad opportunities for leisure activities.

American capitalism and rock & roll went hand in hand. Singers, producers, and record label owners were all expectant capitalists. If Sam Phillips's famous statement—"If I could only find a white man who had the Negro sound and the Negro feel, I could make a billion dollars"—captures the hope of music producers and independent record owners hoping to make it big, then Elvis Presley's meteoric rise to fame, fortune, and glory gave hope to everyone who believed in Horatio Alger stories and the American Dream. Rock & roll was one of the hottest growth industries in 1950s America—a wide-open field where any rugged individualist with good ideas, talent, grit, and determination could make it big.

Rock & roll was people's capitalism at its best or worst, depending upon one's viewpoint. In true entrepreneurial fashion, the music business identified a new market and went after it. "By 1958, teen spending was an estimated $9.5 billion yearly, much of it in impulse purchases and almost all, for the first time, free from adult control," notes historian Tom Engelhardt. Rock & roll did its best to relieve young people of all those dollars. Rock & roll marketed not just hit records but also celebrities, fashions, products, and lifestyles. Teenagers eagerly scooped up anything related to rock & roll—magazines, transistor radios, record players, and assorted paraphernalia. For example, along with Elvis's best-selling records, there were popular items such as Elvis bubble gum cards, Elvis dolls, Elvis hats, Elvis shoes, Elvis lipstick, Elvis purses, Elvis jewelry, Elvis shirts, Elvis jeans, and Elvis books. *Look* estimated that by the end of 1956, teenagers were paying "nearly $20,000,000 a year to worship the young rock 'n' roller."[27]

Sometimes rock & roll reflected trends. Other times it caused them. In either case, the new music sold products. There were hits about blue suede shoes, black denim trousers, blue jeans, and other fashions, as well as songs about more durable products like cars. The entire rock & roll scene exemplifies the 1950s as an age of affluence, planned obsolescence, and conspicuous consumption. Some songs did not even try to be subtle. The title of Elvis Presley's "Money Honey" (1956) sums up what the singer believed to be the most important thing in life, while Little Richard's "Rip It Up" (1956) describes a guy who spent cash as fast as he got it. The latest hits served the same function for teenagers that brand new automobiles and other consumer goods did for adults. They met Americans' demand for newness and novelty, and they became visible symbols of personal progress and success. Sometimes, record companies could not keep pace with the tremendous demand for new product. Planned obsolescence was built into rock & roll. With the release of a performer's new record, the previous hit immediately became old and obsolete. The Top 40 record charts reinforced this trend. As many a disc jockey said, "The hits just keep on coming." And teenagers just kept on buying.[28]

The capitalist nature of rock & roll enabled teenagers to participate in the era's conformity as young people began identifying with particular singers, styles, and forms. The process was not new. Historian Daniel Boorstin notes that the rapid growth of American industry following the Civil War resulted in a new type of American community based on the consumption of manufactured goods. "The acts of acquiring and using had a new meaning," he writes. "Nearly all objects from the hats and suits and shoes men wore to the food they ate became symbols and instruments of novel communities. Now men were affiliated less by what they believed than by what they consumed."[29]

Rock & roll became the means to America's newest consumption community—that of the American teenager. Groups with names such as the Six Teens or Frankie Lymon and the Teenagers, along with hit records such as Boyd Bennett's "Seventeen" (1955), Sonny James's "Young Love" (1956), and the Chordettes' "Teen Age Goodnight" (1956) drove home the point that this was a unique generation with special needs, hopes, and dreams. Rock & roll acted as a cultural binding force, providing teenagers with their own music, fashions, slang, and styles. The Top 40 charts, a weekly listing of the most popular rock & roll hits, showed teenagers what songs their friends were listening to. Purchasing those records enabled young people to become part of the group. Nationwide, teenagers could cheer on the same performers and enjoy the same songs, the same dance steps, the same fashions, even the same speech patterns and behavior. As a style, rock & roll may have seemed alien to many adults, but as a process, the new music should have been all too familiar. Teenagers—like adults—were simply trying to conform, as "good" Americans of the 1950s were wont to do.

Rock & roll was in tune with other aspects of America's cold war culture. Throughout the 1950s, Americans promoted traditional values—or at least what they viewed as traditional values—in a variety of ways. Leading the charge was religion. The 1950s were boom times for organized religion. God could be found everywhere. There were billboards praising the Lord, drive-in churches in California, and *Time* and *Newsweek* covers about God and church. Sales of Bibles and other religious books soared. Hollywood cranked out blockbuster movies like *The Robe* and *The Ten Commandments*. Not to be outdone, Congress added "under God" to the Pledge of Allegiance, as well as "In God We Trust" to coins.

Many theories exist to explain the enormous popularity of organized religion during the 1950s. Historians Douglas T. Miller and Marion Nowak link the rise in religion to cold war anxieties. "There were two main reasons for the religiosity of fifties politics," they write. "First, it was simply good politics. Democrats as well as Republicans tried to appear godly. . . . The second and more significant reason for the close identification of religion with politics was the cold war." Miller and Nowak explain: "Communists were our mortal enemies and they were atheists. Religion, therefore, came to seem essential to the fight against Communism, and it is not surprising that the religiosity of the era became entwined with super patriotism."[30]

While adults were flocking to churches at a record-setting pace or watching the Reverend Billy Graham on TV, teenagers were worshiping in their own way by listening to numerous hits about God and heaven, including Gloria Mann's "Teenage Prayer" (1955) and the Platters' "My Prayer" (1956). There were also religious-influenced hits such as the Harptones' "A Sunday Kind of Love" (1953) and Pat Boone's "Friendly Persuasion" (1956), as well as myriad songs about angels and demons, including the Penguins' "Earth Angel" (1954), the Crew-Cuts' "Angels in the Sky" (1955), and Gene Vincent's "Race with the Devil" (1956).[31]

Rock & roll likewise endorsed mainstream attitudes toward marriage and the family. During the cold war, many Americans turned to the home for shelter from communism.[32] With marriage rates on the rise in cold war America, rock & roll did all it could to reinforce the importance of monogamy. Marriage was glorified on numerous hits, including the Willows' "Church Bells May Ring" (1956) and the Rover Boys' "From a School Ring to a Wedding Ring" (1956). Other hits such as Johnny Ace's "Pledging My Love" (1955), the Platters' "Only You" (1955), and Elvis Presley's "I Want You, I Need You, I Love You" (1956) focused on traditional notions of courtship and monogamous relationships.

Rock & roll never questioned cold war attitudes toward gender. Throughout the 1950s, women were idealized as wives, mothers, and girlfriends, as well as the righteous upholders of religion, morals, truth, and justice, and other aspects of the American way of life. The cold war model for female behavior was spelled out in Marynia Farnham and Ferdinand Lundberg's influential book *Modern Woman: The Lost Sex* (1947), which encouraged women to accept their natural roles by becoming wives and homemakers and by denying "masculine-aggressive" outside interests. Women were expected to be passive and defer to more active and competitive males. Other popular writing encouraged women to cheerfully accept 1950s domesticity. In 1956, *Reader's Digest* published an article called "You Don't Know How Lucky You Are to Be Married." That same year, a special Christmas issue of *Life* assured women: "Of all the accomplishments of the American woman, the one she brings off with the most spectacular success is having babies."[33]

Americans of the 1950s were convinced that if both men and women lived up to their potential and carried out their expected roles, the nation would benefit and the communist threat could be checked. If men were the leaders in the cold war against communism, women were the auxiliary support. In a 1955 commencement address at Smith College, a women's school, Senator Adlai Stevenson explained the role of women in cold war America. "I think there is much you can do about our crisis in the humble role of housewife. . . . You can do it in the living-room with a baby in your lap or in the kitchen with a can opener in your hand. If you're really clever, maybe you can even practice your saving arts on that unsuspecting man while he's watching television," explained the former and future presidential nominee. Stevenson noted that for centuries a battle has been raging between individualism and collectivism, and the current collision between American democracy and Soviet communism would be won not on the battlefield but in hearts and minds. "Women, especially educated women, have a unique opportunity to influence us, man and boy, and to play a direct part in the unfolding drama of our free society." As housewives and mothers, said Stevenson, women have "the primary task of making homes and whole human beings in whom the rational values of freedom, tolerance, charity and free inquiry can take root."[34]

Adlai Stevenson's commencement address to Smith College students summed up the common wisdom that a woman's job in 1950s America was to serve and provide support for her man and her family. "In keeping with the American tradition, it was up to women to achieve successful families," explains historian Elaine Tyler May. "If women fulfilled their domestic roles, as adapted to the atomic age, they would rear children who would avoid juvenile delinquency (and homosexuality), stay in school, and become future scientists and experts to defeat the Russians in the cold war."[35]

Early rock & roll enthusiastically supported prescribed gender roles in cold war America. The feminine mystique that was in full bloom in the 1950s contained several important elements: females existed to please males, become wives, have babies, keep house, be attractive, be nurturing, be subservient, provide comfort, be passive, and follow a man's lead in all matters. Rock & roll girls fit the bill perfectly. They were portrayed on rock & roll hits as objects, possessions, and playthings. Although rock & roll may have been revolutionary in some ways, it was outright conservative in its attitudes toward females. Put another way, rock & roll of the 1950s—despite its radical image—was every bit as sexist as the rest of American society and culture.[36]

Like the dominant culture, the new music objectified women. Songs such as the Penguins' "Earth Angel" (1954) placed women on pedestals. Other hits treated women as sex objects. Like many Americans of the 1950s, rock & rollers believed young women could be both sexy and marriage material. "In Victorian times, woman was either sexless saintly wife or sensual dirty whore," note historians Douglas T. Miller and Marion Nowak. "Fifties America maintained the premarital dichotomy of good girl versus bad girl. Yet it invested the wife with both ideals. Sexual repression was remodeled. A wife could enjoy sex as long as she obediently obeyed her man." Many rock & roll hits were blatant odes to women as sex objects. Gene Vincent's "Be-Bop-a-Lula" (1956) describes a sexy teenage girl in tight jeans who gets everybody's attention by the way she walks, dances, and treats her man. Other songs such as Little Richard's "Long Tall Sally" (1956) and Little Willie John's "Fever" (1956) likewise treated women as sex objects, pure and simple.[37]

Following the lead of mainstream America, rock & roll usually relegated women to secondary status as dependents or passive objects. It was up to the guys to ask girls out and to propose marriage. At dances and record hops, guys took the initiative to ask girls to dance and not vice versa, unless, of course, it was a "lady's choice" as popularized at school dances and later on TV's popular *American Bandstand*. Numerous songs reinforced the belief that teenage girls were dependent upon boys for their very existence. The Teen Queens' "Eddie My Love" (1956), for example, features a depressed if not suicidal girl pining for her absent boyfriend. Desperate and sick in bed, she pleads with Eddie to return soon because the very next day could be her last.[38]

While rock & roll treated females as passive subordinates or submissive playthings, the music's flip side idealized males as aggressive, dominant individuals. Teenage males ruled their world, just as adult males did the rest of society. Two Bo Diddley songs offer perfect examples. Bo's macho image came through loud and clear on "I'm a Man" (1955) and "Who Do You Love?" (1956). On the former, Bo recalls how even as a little boy he had "somethin' in his pocket" that kept people alive. Now that he's a man, spelled "M–A–N—Man," he invites all the pretty women to stand in line, promising they won't be able to resist the way he makes love. The lyrics on "Who Do You Love?" are even more provocative. Diddley's vocal almost drips with testosterone as he vividly describes his virility and ability to please women. He sets the stage with vivid tough-guy images. He boasts he can walk forty-seven miles on barbed wire; he uses a cobra for a necktie; and he has a house and chimney made of rattlesnake hides and human skulls. He then goes in for the kill: "Now come on take a walk with me, Arlene, and tell me, who do you love?"[39]

Rock & roll likewise shared the dominant culture's attitudes toward race, reflecting both continuity and change in 1950s America. A close look at rock & roll reveals continuing patterns of segregation, as well as negative stereotypes and racial attitudes that can be traced back to colonial America. The public response to the new music all too often mirrored the era's racism. Prejudiced whites frequently condemned the music as "African" or "jungle" music, fearing the allegedly lustful sound would lead to miscegenation. Black rock & rollers felt the sting of racial prejudice when they toured in the segregated South or when their songs were covered by white artists. Rock & roll often found it difficult to break free from traditional racial shackles. At times, even African American singers themselves perpetuated old racial images. For example, Chuck Berry's "Brown-Eyed Handsome Man" (1956), the Robins' "Smokey Joe's Café" (1955), and the Cadets' "Stranded in the Jungle" (1956) all made use of traditional stereotypes that portrayed blacks as sexy, violent, or comic figures.

But if rock & roll reflected traditional racial attitudes, it also anticipated the nation's move toward integration. Hit records like the Dominoes' "Sixty Minute Man" (1951) and the Chords' "Sh-Boom" (1954), along with the popularity of Chuck Berry, Fats Domino, the Platters, and other black rock & roll artists, suggest that African Americans were gaining ground in America years before the civil rights movement blossomed. Yet we usually do not read about the coming of black rock & rollers in history textbooks. Instead, historians focus on legal and political challenges to segregation, highlighting court cases, boycotts, protest marches, demonstrations, or landmark civil rights legislation.

Early rock & roll offers proof that the winds of change were already sweeping across America's racial landscape in the immediate years following World War II. By the early 1950s, whites were cheering on black artists and copying black rhythms and beats, suggesting that cultural integration was becoming a reality in the United States. Rock & roll offers a view from "the bottom up" of the racial tensions and progress in America of the 1950s. Musical evidence proves that cultural integration was occurring long before *Brown vs. Board of Education* or the Montgomery bus boycott.

Along with reflecting mainstream attitudes toward race, rock & roll exhibited the general anxieties usually associated with America's cold war culture. The 1950s were anxious years due to international crises, new lifestyles, and rapid social and economic change. Fears of atomic power and nuclear holocaust, for example, led to the building of communal and individual fallout shelters nationwide, as well as the development of "duck-and-cover drills" and air-raid drills to protect people against surprise attack. Americans' preoccupation with atomic power and external attack, according to many experts, might even help explain the proliferation of UFO sightings and Hollywood films such as "Creature from the Black Lagoon" (1954), "Earth versus the Flying Saucers" (1956), or other horror movies about monsters, mutants, and creatures from outer space. Rock & roll reflected similar preoccupations. Elvis Presley was billed on a club marquee as the "Atomic Power Singer." Bill Haley and His Comets alluded to atomic bombs on "Thirteen Women" (1954). The Cadets, on their 1956 hit "Stranded in the Jungle," described something heavy hitting them "like an atomic bomb." The Cuff-Links' "Guided Missiles (Aimed at My Heart)" (1956) placed atomic power and the threat of nuclear attack in the context of teenage romance. And Goodman and Buchanan's "Flying Saucer" (1956) poked fun at creatures from outer space.

ROCK & ROLL AS HISTORY

Rock & roll songs are literally records of the past. These vinyl tracks offer valuable clues about 1950s America from the bottom up. Like a vast oral history project, musical records enable us to tap into the collective memory of the era's youth. Rock & roll yields a wealth of information about everyday life and ordinary people; it offers fascinating glimpses of cold war politics, youth culture, religion, class, race, ethnicity, and gender; and it echoes the hopes, dreams, and fears of everyday Americans. In addition, rock & roll reveals the tensions and often contradictory forces at work in American society and culture: the affluence and anxiety, the conflict and consensus, the continuity and change.

Early rock & roll was anything but monolithic. There was no one message in the music. It was contested terrain where divergent forces coexisted and struggled to be heard. Rock & roll became a public arena where rivals battled for control. Producers and consumers vied for supremacy, while the establishment and proponents of social engineering sparred repeatedly with grassroots populists seeking change and participatory democracy. Similar contests occurred between the young and old or other adversaries divided along racial, ethnic, social, or economic lines. Without a doubt, cultural politics were being waged throughout the rock & roll world.

Rock & roll offers compelling evidence that America's cold war culture was much more broadly based than previously thought. The music reveals that, to an extent, some adolescents were rebelling against accepted norms and values. But, equally important, it shows that many— if not most—teenagers were not that different from their parents. Young people subscribed to the era's patriotism, traditional values, dislike of communism, and ubiquitous cold war culture. Much of 1950s rock & roll demonstrates that adults and teens shared similar beliefs, values, interests, and pastimes; it indicates that both adults and teenagers were concerned about the same sources of tensions and insecurities in American life. So although rock & roll may have contained elements of rebellion, it also reflected the era's consensus behavior and conservatism. This dichotomy suggests that youth culture has never been as monolithic or as radical as myth has it. The so-called generation gap would not open for another decade.

More than sixty years have passed since rock & roll first appeared on the national stage. In retrospect, it is clear that 1950s America created Elvis and the new music craze. Rock & roll went on to become one of the most important cultural developments of the post–World War II era. In tune with the times, the music reflected and shaped American life and thought. Rock & roll offered a virtual adolescent utopia that fulfilled the American Dream. It enabled youth to have it all: freedom, camaraderie, success, sex, and almost every imaginable pleasure available in the years after World War II. Yet it existed side-by-side with God, country, family, and other traditional values associated with the American way of life. Elvis Presley was living proof of the rock & roll promised land. By the end of the 1950s, teenagers could smile knowingly when they saw a new album of Presley's gold records (figure C.2). On the cover were multiple images of the "King of Rock & Roll" standing proud and defiant in a glitzy gold tuxedo. The album's title said it all: *50,000,000 Elvis Fans Can't Be Wrong*.

Figure C.2. Elvis Presley greatest hits album cover. (Richard Aquila Collection)

NOTES

INTRODUCTION

1. Good introductions to the history of the postwar years include William Chafe, *The Unfinished Journey: America since World War II* (New York: Oxford University Press, 1981); John Patrick Diggins, *The Proud Decades: America in War and Peace, 1941–1960* (New York: Norton, 1988); James T. Patterson, *Grand Expectations: The United States, 1945–1974* (New York: Oxford University Press, 1966).

2. Herb Abramson, "Rock 'n' Roll: Seen in Perspective," *Cashbox* (July 28, 1956): 78. Abramson is one of the individuals seen in figure 8.4.

3. Richard Aquila interview with Dion for NPR's *Rock & Roll America*, October 19, 1995; Mike Stoller quoted in Ed Ward, Geoffrey Stokes, and Ken Tucker, *Rock of Ages: The Rolling Stone History of Rock & Roll* (New York: Rolling Stone Press/Summit Books, 1986), 88.

4. For books dealing with youth culture, see William Graebner, *Coming of Age in Buffalo: Youth and Authority in the Postwar Era* (Philadelphia: Temple University Press, 1990); Jon Savage, *Teenage: The Creation of Youth Culture* (New York: Viking, 2007).

5. The Bruce Springsteen quote comes from the opening page of the Official Rock & Roll Hall of Fame and Museum website that appeared on www.rockhall.com on July 12, 2001.

I. MYSTERY TRAIN

1. Although much has been written about the birth of rock & roll, there is considerable disagreement about when and how the music first appeared. For examples, see Charlie Gillett, *The Sound of the City: The Rise of Rock and Roll* (New York: Dutton, 1970); Carl Belz, *The Story of Rock* (New York: Harper & Row, 1972); Jim Miller, ed., *The Rolling Stone Illustrated History of Rock & Roll* (New York: Random House/Rolling Stone, 1976); Simon Frith, *Sound Effects: Youth, Leisure, and the Politics of Rock 'n' Roll* (New York: Pantheon, 1981); Ed Ward, Geoffrey Stokes, and Ken Tucker, *Rock of Ages: The Rolling Stone History of Rock & Roll* (New York: Rolling Stone/Summit Books, 1986); Richard Aquila, *That Old Time Rock & Roll: A Chronicle of an Era, 1954–63* (New York: Macmillan/Schirmer Books, 1989); Joe Stuessy, *Rock & Roll: Its History and Stylistic Development* (Englewood Cliffs, N.J.: Prentice Hall, 1990); Philip H. Ennis, *The Seventh Stream: The Emergence of Rocknroll in American Popular Music* (Hanover, N.H.: Wesleyan University Press, 1992); David Szatmary, *A Time to Rock: A Social History of Rock 'n' Roll* (New York: Macmillan/Schirmer Books, 1996); Reebee Garofalo, *Rockin' Out: Popular Music in the USA* (Boston: Allyn and Bacon, 1997); James Miller, *Flowers in the Dustbin: The Rise of Rock and Roll, 1947–1977* (New York: Simon & Schuster, 1999); Glenn C. Altschuler, *All Shook Up: How Rock 'n' Roll Changed America* (New York: Oxford University Press, 2003); and Albin Zak III, *I Don't Sound Like Nobody: Remaking Music in 1950s America* (Ann Arbor: University of Michigan Press, 2013).

2. There were other jazz-influenced songs such as the Mills Brothers' "Rockin' Chair" (1932) and Chick Webb and Ella Fitzgerald's "Rock It for Me" (1938). The Boswell Sisters, a white pop group from New Orleans, made it all the way to number 7 on the pop charts in 1934 with "Rock and Roll," a song from the film *Transatlantic Merry-Go-Round*. It was probably the first popular song to use the entire phrase in its title. Information about hit records can be found in Joel Whitburn, *Pop Memories: The History of American Popular Music Compiled from America's Popular Music Charts, 1890–1954* (Menomonee Falls, Wis.: Record Research, 1986).

3. Information about early black performers who used the terms "rock" and "roll" can be found in Whitburn, *Pop Memories*; Joel Whitburn, *Top R&B Singles, 1942–1988: Compiled from* Billboard's *Rhythm & Blues Charts* (Menomonee Falls, Wis.: Record Research, 1988); and Jim Dawson and Steve Propes, *What Was the First Rock 'n' Roll Record?* (Boston: Faber and Faber, 1992). See also Nick Tosches, *Unsung Heroes of Rock and Roll* (New York: DaCapo Press, 1999) and Larry Birnbaum, *Before Elvis: The Prehistory of Rock 'n' Roll* (Lanham, Md.: Scarecrow Press, 2013).

4. Dawson and Propes, *What Was the First Rock 'n' Roll Record?*.

5. Jerry Wexler quoted in Robert Palmer, *Rock & Roll: An Unruly History* (New York: Harmony Books, 1995), 33.

6. Peter Grendysa, "Black Music: An Introduction," in Whitburn, *Top R& B Singles*, 9–11; Altschuyler, *All Shook Up*, 3–35; Ward, Stokes, and Tucker, *Rock of Ages*, chaps. 1–3.

7. Nicholas Lemann, *The Promised Land: The Great Black Migration and How It Changed America* (New York: Vintage, 1992); Szatmary, *A Time to Rock*, 3, 4.

8. Moore is quoted in Louis Cantor, *Wheelin' on Beale: How WDIA–Memphis Became the Nation's First All-Black Radio Station and Created the Sound That Changed America* (New York: Pharos Books, 1992), 72–73. Blues great Big Bill Broonzy has a similar explanation: "The blues won't die because spirituals won't die. Blues [is] a steal from spirituals. . . . Blues singers start out singing spirituals." Broonzy quoted in Szatmary, *A Time to Rock*, 3.

9. The following CD with liner notes is an excellent overview of Les Paul's career and music: *Les Paul Guitar Wizard and Mary Ford* (London: Proper Records, 2002); for details, see Robb Lawrence, *The Early Years of the Les Paul Legacy 1915–1963* (Milwaukee: Hal Leonard, 2008); Dave Hunter, *The Gibson Les Paul: The Illustrated Story of the Guitar That Changed Rock* (Minneapolis, Minn.: Voyageur Press, 2014)

10. Leo Fender's contributions are detailed in Forrest White, *Fender: The Inside Story* (Milwaukee: Backbeat, 1994).

11. Muddy Waters quoted in Szatmary, *A Time to Rock*, 6; Arnold Shaw, *The Rockin' 50s: The Decade That Transformed the Pop Music Scene* (New York: Bowles Book, 1970), 87–88. For additional information about the musical structure of blues and rhythm & blues, see Stuessy, *Rock & Roll*, 26–30.

12. Arnold Shaw, *The World of Soul: Black America's Contribution to the Pop Music Scene* (New York: Cowles Book, 1970), 95; John A. Jackson, *Big Beat Heat: Alan Freed and the Early Years of Rock & Roll* (New York: Schirmer Books, 1991), 4, 6. For additional information about R&B, see Arnold Shaw, *Honkers and Shouters: The Golden Years of Rhythm and Blues* (New York: Macmillan, 1978); Tosches, *Unsung Heroes of Rock and Roll*; Jerry Wexler and David Ritz, *Rhythm and the Blues: A Life in American Music* (New York: Knopf, 1993); Birnbaum, *Before Elvis*; and Zak, *I Don't Sound Like Nobody*.

13. The advertisement for "Rocket 88" can be found in Galen Gart, ed., *First Pressings: The History of Rhythm & Blues*, vol. 1: *1951* (Milford, N.H.: Big Nickel, 1991), 37.

14. Shaw, *The World of Soul*, 103–4; Steve Chapple and Reebee Garofalo, *Rock 'n' Roll Is Here to Pay: The History and Politics of the Music Industry* (Chicago: Nelson-Hall, 1977), 28–31.

15. Grendysa, "Black Music: An Introduction," 10–11.

16. Patrick R. Parsons, "The Business of Popular Music: A Short History," in *America's Musical Pulse: Popular Music in Twentieth-Century Society*, ed. Kenneth J. Bindas (Westport, Conn.: Greenwood Press, 1992), 139–40. For more on ASCAP and BMI, see Garofalo, *Rockin' Out*, 31–32, 36–37, 66–68, 86–87; Michael T. Bertrand, *Race, Rock, and Elvis* (Urbana: University of Illinois Press, 2000), 73–74; and Altschuyler, *All Shook Up*, 133–42.

17. Art Rupe quoted in Shaw, *The World of Soul*, 104; Sid Nathan quoted in Rick Kennedy and Randy McNutt, *Little Labels—Big Sound: Small Record Companies and the Rise of American Music* (Bloomington: Indiana University Press, 1999), 61.

18. Shaw, *The World of Soul*, 104; Chapple and Garofalo, *Rock 'n' Roll Is Here to Pay*, 29.

19. Chapple and Garofalo, *Rock 'n' Roll Is Here to Pay*, 20, 28–31; Ennis, *The Seventh Stream*, 176; see also liner notes to "Ram Records: Shreveport Stomp" (Ace Records, 1994). They explain how Mira Smith began the label in Shreveport, Louisiana, in 1955 with only a $250 investment in a single-track Crown tape machine and a Neumann U47 microphone. In similar fashion, Art Rupe established his rhythm & blues label, Specialty Records, with an investment of only $600. See also Kennedy and McNutt, *Little Labels—Big Sound*, xvi.

20. Chris Spindel quoted in Louis Cantor, *Wheelin' on Beale: How WDIA–Memphis Became the Nation's First All-Black Radio Station and Created the Sound That Changed America* (New York, 1992), 19.

21. Robert "Wolfman Jack" Smith, quoted in Ben Fong-Torres, *The Hits Just Keep on Coming: The History of Top 40 Radio* (San Francisco: Miller Freeman Books, 1998), 22.

22. George Klein, quoted in Cantor, *Wheelin' on Beale*, 53. See also Jonathan Kamin, "The White R&B Audience and the Music Industry, 1952–1956," *Popular Music and Society* 6 (1978): 150–68.

23. In the 1920s and '30s, both network radio and local stations frequently showcased local black announcers and performers. For examples, see Cantor, *Wheelin' on Beale*, 58, 156–57; Fong-Torres, *The Hits Just Keep on Coming*, 27–28; J. Fred MacDonald, *Don't Touch That Dial! Radio Programming in American Life, 1920–1960* (Chicago: Nelson-Hall, 1979), 329–31, 338–39; Mark Newman, *Entrepreneurs of Profit and Pride: From Black Appeal to Radio Soul* (New York: Praeger, 1988), 67.

24. "The Forgotten 15,000,000," *Sponsor* (October 10, 1949): 24–25; See also Cantor, *Wheelin' on Beale*, 20–22; MacDonald, *Don't Touch That Dial*, 395. The *Variety* magazine quote comes from Jackson, *Big Beat Heat*, 48–49. Other information about radio stations geared to black listeners can be found

in William Barlow, *Voice Over: The Making of Black Radio* (Philadelphia: Temple University Press, 1999); Kathy M. Newman, "The Forgotten Fifteen Million: Black Radio, Radicalism, and the Construction of the 'Negro Market,'" in *Communities of the Air: Radio Century, Radio Culture*, ed. Susan Merrill Squier (Durham, N.C.: Duke University Press, 2003), 109–33.

25. Hunter Hancock quoted in Garofalo, *Rockin' Out*, 88.

26. Cantor, *Wheelin' on Beale*, 164; "Hoss" Allen quoted in Palmer, *Rock & Roll*, 20.

27. For information about Phillips, see Louis Cantor, *Dewey and Elvis: The Life and Times of a Rock 'n' Roll Deejay* (Urbana: University of Illinois Press, 2005). A sample of Dewey Phillips may be found at http://memphismusichalloffame.com/inductee/deweyphillips/ (accessed July 23, 2014).

28. Miller, *Flowers in the Dustbin*, 34–39; Fong-Torres, *The Hits Just Keep on Coming*, 25–26; Gart, *First Pressings*, 1:64; Cantor, *Wheelin' on Beale*, 164–69.

29. Jackson, *Big Beat Heat*, 76–77; Galen Gart, ed., *The History of Rhythm & Blues*, vol. 4: *1954* (Milford, N.H.: Big Nickel, 1990), 100; Shaw, *The Rockin' 50s*, 108. The *New York Age Defender* quote can be found in James M. Salem, *The Late Great Johnny Ace and the Transition from R&B to Rock 'n' Roll* (Urbana: University of Illinois Press), 113–14.

30. Fong-Torres, *The Hits Just Keep on Coming*, 27.

31. The young Elvis Presley is a perfect example of a young white who frequently listened to R&B on the radio. And Elvis wasn't alone. Many whites were turning on to rhythm & blues in the same way. See Ahmet Ertegun interview in Shaw, *The Rockin' 50s*, 86; Miller, *Flowers in the Dustbin*, 38.

32. Good overviews of the civil rights movement include Robert Weisbrot, *Freedom Bound: A History of America's Civil Rights Movement* (New York: Norton, 1989) and Taylor Branch, *Parting the Waters: America in the King Years, 1954–1963* (New York: Simon & Schuster, 1988).

33. Garofalo, *Rockin' Out*, 89; Arnold Passman, *The Deejays* (New York: Macmillan, 1971), 185; Miller, *Flowers in the Dustbin*, 39.

34. The advertisement described can be found in Gart, *First Pressings*, 1:40. Additional advertisements for jukeboxes in 1951 are on pp. 50, 80.

35. Of course, not all storeowners welcomed the arrival of "race" music. John Vincent, who founded Ace Records, remembers the trouble he had back in the late 1940s trying to service jukeboxes in the segregated South. Vincent's comments can be found in Kennedy and McNutt, *Little Labels—Big Sound*, 127; The chance for big profits often cancelled out prejudices against rhythm & blues, however, leading to the integration of many jukeboxes nationwide. The jukebox industry soon became one of the nation's prime dealers in rhythm & blues records. When Memphis's WDIA switched to all-black music pro-

gramming in 1948, Don Kern recalls how difficult it was to locate R&B records: "The only place around was what you call a one-stop. That's where the juke-box operators come and they can buy everything they want [including rhythm & blues] at one stop." Don Kern quoted in Cantor, *Wheelin' on Beale*, 51.

36. The music industry quickly took notice. Playlists of popular radio and TV shows of the early 1950s such as *Your Hit Parade* and Peter Potter's *Jukebox Jury* were based in part on jukebox popularity. Record companies also monitored jukeboxes very closely to see what records were selling and what audiences wanted. See Chapple and Garofalo, *Rock 'n' Roll Is Here to Pay*, 6; Shaw, *The Rockin' 50s*, 69, 77; Garofalo, *Rockin' Out*, 60.

37. Gart, *First Pressings*, 1:45, 1:96.

38. Richard Aquila, interview with C. Warren Vander Hill (September 7, 2000); Bertrand, *Race, Rock, and Elvis*, 13; "Juke Box Sociology," *Ebony* (March 1954): 88.

39. Jackson, *Big Beat Heat*, 45; Bertrand, *Race, Rock, and Elvis*, 174; Gart, *First Pressings*, 1:35, 1:69, 1:101–2. For additional evidence of integrated night clubs, see Chapple and Garofalo, *Rock 'n' Roll Is Here to Pay*, 41. For a full treatment, see Preston Lauterbach, *The Chitlin Circuit and the Road to Rock 'n' Roll* (New York: W.W. Norton, 2011).

40. Gart, *First Pressings*, 1:69; Jackson, *Big Beat Heat*, 1–3. Bill Randle quoted in Jackson, *Big Beat Heat*, 7.

41. Jackson, *Big Beat Heat*, 46, 51–52; Alan Freed's brother, David, who attended the Moondog Coronation Ball in 1952, recalls that the audience "was almost all black." Photographs taken at Freed's concerts and dances staged in 1952 and 1953 depicted mostly black audiences. Freed acknowledged that his Cleveland dances "appealed most to colored people," which probably explains the "batches of poison-pen letters calling me a 'nigger-lover.'" All quotes come from Jackson, *Big Beat Heat*, 3, 34, 53.

42. Jackson, *Big Beat Heat*, 65, 34.

43. On another occasion, three hundred white females from Jackson, Mississippi, who belonged to a fan club for black singer Larry Darnell, traveled all the way to New Orleans to see him perform. These types of incidents did not go unnoticed in the black community. *Jet*—an African American magazine— reported in 1953 that "toppling racial barriers in the South, along with enticing salaries, are encouraging previously reluctant Negro performers to accept engagements below the Mason-Dixon Line." Bertrand, *Race, Rock, and Elvis*, 174–75; the original comments can be found in "Bull Moose Jackson," *Ebony* (January 1950): 27; "The Larry Darnell Story," *Our World* (June 1947): 32; "Florida's Color Bars Tumble as Jazz Invades Miami Beach," *Jet* (December 31, 1953): 60.

44. Chapple and Garofalo, *Rock 'n' Roll Is Here to Pay*, 56; Miller, *Flowers in the Dustbin*, 100; Garofalo, *Rockin' Out*, 89; Galen Gart, ed., *First Pressings: The History of Rhythm & Blues*, vol. 3: *1953* (Milford, N.H.: Big Nickel, 1990), 4.

45. Jerry Wexler interview in Shaw, *The Rockin' 50s*, 78–79; white R&B disc jockey William "Hoss" Allen has similar recollections of R&B music spreading to white audiences in the South. See Palmer, *Rock & Roll*, 19–20.

46. Sam Phillips quoted in Ren Grevatt, "It All Started with Elvis," *Saturday Evening Post* (September 1958): 92; Bertrand, *Race, Rock, and Elvis*, 67.

47. Aquila, interview with C. Warren Vander Hill. Whites often used the term "cat music" to refer to R&B. *Jet* magazine noted in 1954 that white teenagers were frequently buying and requesting R&B records, explaining that "when white teenagers in the South go into a record store and ask for a 'cat' record, they mean one featuring Negro musicians. Down there they call it 'cat music.'" Bertrand, *Race, Rock, and Elvis*, 66, 67; "New York Beat," *Jet* (August 12, 1954): 65. By 1954, that designation was so widespread that Atlantic Records chose it as the name for their subsidiary label, "Cat Records" (the Chords' "Sh-Boom"—touted by many experts as the first rock & roll record—was released on the Cat label in 1954).

48. Eric Lott, *Love and Theft: Blackface Minstrelsy and the American Working Class* (New York: Oxford University Press, 1993), 52; Bertrand, *Race, Rock, and Elvis*, 30. Bertrand also links the adoption of black rhythm & blues by white audiences to issues of race, class, and status. He applies Antonio Gramschi's theory of class conflict to the rise of rhythm & blues, as well as rock & roll. "Antonio Gramschi once wrote that it was not necessarily a music's 'historical origin' that should preoccupy scholars, instead, they should be concerned about why certain groups of people have embraced a cultural form not of their own creation that 'conceives the world and life in contrast with official society.' The more important aspect of cultural appropriation," adds Bertrand, "is to recognize that 'people adopt [these songs] because they conform to their [own] way of thinking and feeling.'" Bertrand argues that "rhythm and blues and rock 'n' roll became a shared vehicle of expression for various groups the mainstream had ignored, maligned, or rejected." Bertrand, *Race, Rock, and Elvis*, 195. The Gramschi quotes come from Antonio Gramschi, *Selections from Cultural Writings*, ed. David Forgacs and Geoffrey Nowell-Smith (Cambridge, Mass.: Harvard University Press, 1985), 195.

49. Norman Mailer, "The White Negro: Superficial Reflections on the Hipster," in Mailer, *Advertisements for Myself* (New York: G. P. Putnam's Sons, 1959), 337–75; Jack Kerouac, *On the Road*, 5th ed. (New York: Penguin Books, 1991), 180; Rufus Thomas quoted in Cantor, *Wheelin' on Beale*, 95.

50. The *Cashbox* quote is cited in Bertrand, *Race, Rock, and Elvis*, 67. The original can be found in an article entitled "American Music Becomes National Rather Than Regional," *Cashbox* (April 2, 1955): 76.

51. Stuessy, *Rock & Roll*, 26, 27.

52. Wynonie Harris, "Good Rockin' Tonight" (King Records, 1948).

2. GOOD ROCKIN' TONIGHT

1. "Good Rockin' Tonight." Words and music by Roy Brown, c. 1948. Wynonie Harris recorded his version for King Records in 1948. Elvis Presley's version was done on Sun Records in 1954.

2. Minstrel music, spirituals, blues, ragtime, and jazz are discussed in Michael Campbell, *And the Beat Goes On: An Introduction to Popular Music in America, 1840 to Today* (New York: Schirmer Books, 1996); Ian Whitcomb, *After the Ball: Pop Music from Rag to Rock* (New York: Penguin Press, 1972); Robert Toll, *Blacking Up: The Minstrel Show in Nineteenth-Century America* (New York: Oxford University Press, 1974); Reebee Garofalo, *Rockin' Out* (Boston: Allyn and Bacon, 1997), chaps. 1 and 2; and Burton W. Peretti, "Emerging from America's Underside: The Black Musician from Ragtime to Jazz," in *America's Musical Pulse*, ed. Kenneth Bindas (Westport, Conn.: Greenwood Press, 1992), 63–72. For information about black influences on Jimmie Rodgers and Hank Williams, see Nolan Porterfield, "The Day Hank Williams Died: Cultural Collisions in Country Music," in Bindas, *America's Musical Pulse*, 175–84; Nolan Porterfield, *Jimmie Rodgers: The Life and Times of America's Blue Yodeler* (Urbana: University of Illinois Press, 1979); Roger M. Williams, *Sing a Sad Song: The Life and Times of Hank Williams* (Urbana: University of Illinois Press, 1981). The information about Frankie Laine and Johnny Ray can be found in Arnold Shaw, *The Rockin' 50s: The Decade That Transformed the Pop Music Scene* (New York: Bowles Book, 1970), 48–49, 53.

3. Bill Haley interview in Shaw, *The Rockin' 50s*, 139; a good, brief summary of the importance of Bill Haley and His Comets can be found in James Miller, *Flowers in the Dustbin: The Rise of Rock and Roll, 1947–1977* (New York: Simon & Schuster, 1999), 87–94; the definitive biography of Haley is John Swenson, *Bill Haley: The Daddy of Rock and Roll* (New York: Stein and Day, 1982).

4. Bill Haley interview in Shaw, *The Rockin' 50s*, 140. See also Haley's comments in the liner notes included with *Rock the Joint: The Original Essex Recordings, 1951–1954*, a Bill Haley and His Comets CD (SchoolKids' Records, 1994).

5. Liner notes of the CD, Bill Haley and His Comets, *Rock the Joint*.

6. Liner notes of the CD, Bill Haley and His Comets, *Rock the Joint.*

7. Bill Haley interview in Charlie Gillett, *The Sound of the City: The Rise of Rock and Roll* (New York: Dutton, 1970), 30–31; Johnny Grande quoted in the liner notes, Bill Haley and His Comets' CD, *Rock the Joint.*

8. Bill Haley in Shaw, *The Rockin' 50s*, 141; Johnny Grande quote comes from the liner notes, Bill Haley and His Comets CD, *Rock the Joint*; the last Haley quote appears in David Szatmary, *A Time To Rock: A Social History of Rock 'n' Roll* (New York: Macmillan/Schirmer Books, 1996), 45.

9. The ten hits were the Crows' "Gee"; Bill Haley and His Comets' "Rock Around the Clock"; the Midnighters' "Work with Me, Annie"; the McGuire Sisters' cover of the Spaniels' "Goodnight, Sweetheart, Goodnight"; the Chords' "Sh'Boom"; the Crew-Cuts' cover of "Sh'Boom"; Joe Turner's "Shake, Rattle, and Roll"; Bill Haley and His Comets' cover of "Shake, Rattle, and Roll"; the Midnighters' "Annie Had a Baby"; and the Drifters' "Honey Love." Information about the *Billboard* report comes from Galen Gart, ed., *First Pressings: The History of Rhythm & Blues*, vol. 4: *1954* (Milford, N.H.: Big Nickel, 1990), 33–34. See also Shaw, *The Rockin' 50s*, 81.

10. Bob Hyde, "Track by Track Annotation," *The Doo Wop Box* (Santa Monica, Calif.: Rhino Records, 1993), 8, in liner notes booklet.

11. Richard Aquila interview with Robert Pruter for NPR's *Rock & Roll America*, 1999. See also Robert Pruter, *Chicago Soul* (Urbana: University of Illinois Press, 1991) and Robert Pruter, *Doowop: The Chicago Scene* (Urbana: University of Illinois Press, 1996).

12. Billy Vera, "What Is Doo Wop?" in liner notes booklet of *The Doo Wop Box*, 14.

13. Ed Ward, Geoffrey Stokes, and Ken Tucker, *Rock of Ages: The Rolling Stone History of Rock & Roll* (New York: Rolling Stone Press/Summit Books, 1986), 127, 167, 199.

14. Hyde, "Track by Track Annotation," 32; Richard Aquila, *That Old Time Rock & Roll: A Chronicle of an Era, 1954–63* (repr., Urbana: University of Illinois Press, 2000), 201–2.

15. The interview appeared on CNN in 1995; for details about how "Sh-Boom" and other early rock & roll songs dealt with the atomic bomb and other aspects of the cold war culture, see Richard Aquila, "Sh-Boom; or How Early Rock & Roll Taught Us to Stop Worrying and Love the Bomb," in *The Writing on the Cloud: American Culture Confronts the Atomic Bomb*, ed. Alison M. Scott and Christopher D. Geist (New York: University Press of America, 1997), 106–18.

16. Shaw, *The Rockin' 50s*, 73–75.

17. For examples, see Carl Belz, *The Story of Rock* (New York: Harper & Row, 1972), 25–30; Shaw, *The Rockin' 50s*, 77; Joel Whitburn, *Pop Memories:*

The History of American Popular Music Compiled from America's Popular Music Charts, 1890–1954 (Menomonee Falls, Wis.: Record Research, 1989), 102; Szatmary, *A Time to Rock*, 23.

18. "Shake, Rattle, and Roll," written by Charles E. Calhoun, performed by Joe Turner, 1954, and Bill Haley and His Comets, 1954.

19. Bill Haley quoted in Gillett, *The Sound of the City*, 21.

20. Alan Freed was not shy about tooting his own horn about alleged accomplishments. Not only did he claim that he was the one who coined the phrase "rock & roll," but he also claimed to be both "the father of rock & roll" and "the king of rock & roll." See Carl Belz, *The Story of Rock*, 51; liner notes to *Alan Freed Top 15* record album; Steve Chapple and Reebee Garofalo, *Rock 'n' Roll Is Here to Pay: The History and Politics of the Music Insutry* (Chicago: Nelson-Hall, 1977), 56; see also the photograph of a WINS advertisement that is included in the photo essays located after p. 112 in John A. Jackson, *Big Beat Heat: Alan Freed and the Early Years of Rock & Roll* (New York: Schirmer Books, 1991). The official Alan Freed website can be found at www.alanfreed.com. The information about Freed in most books is extremely unreliable. By far the most accurate account of Freed's rise and fall can be found in Jackson's pathbreaking study, *Big Beat Heat*.

21. See Shaw, *The Rockin' 50s*, chap. 12.

22. Ward, Stokes, and Tucker, *Rock of Ages*, 69–70; Gillett, *Sound of the City*, 13; Chapple and Garofalo, *Rock 'n' Roll Is Here to Pay*, 56.

23. Jackson, *Big Beat Heat*, 35–39; see also Miller, *Flowers in the Dustbin*, 57–61.

24. Shaw, *The Rockin' 50s*, 106; Freed's tour manager, Teddy Reig, is quoted in Robert Palmer, *Rock & Roll: An Unruly History* (New York: Harmony Books, 1995), 135. A sample of Alan Freed's on-air personality can be heard at www.alanfreed.com/wp/on-the-air-audio-2/audio-wins-1955/ (accessed July 23, 2014).

25. See Gillett, *Sound of the City*, 13; Chapple and Garofalo, *Rock 'n' Roll Is Here to Pay*, 56; Jim Miller, ed., *The Rolling Stone Illustrated History of Rock & Roll* (New York: Random House, 1980), 92.

26. Shaw, *The Rockin' 50s*, 105–6; Jackson, *Big Beat Heat*, 42.

27. The audio clip is an MP3 file of a Moondog show obtained from the Official Alan Freed Website, which was found at www.alanfreed.com.

28. Jackson, *Big Beat Heat*, 82–83.

29. The 1953 audio tape was found on the Official Alan Freed website (www.alanfreed.com). The photograph of the Record Rendezvous event can be found in Michael Ochs, *Rock Archives: A Photographic Journey through the First Two Decades of Rock & Roll* (Garden City, N.Y.: Doubleday, 1984), 38 (picture #4). Although the photograph is not dated, most likely it was taken in

1951 or early 1952, since the audience is still almost all African American. After Freed had been on the air for several months, his audiences became more integrated. A photograph of a poster for Freed's first major R&B concert in Cleveland can be found in Palmer, *Rock & Roll*, 128.

30. Jackson, *Big Beat Heat*, chap. 1. See also Gillett, *Sound of the City*, 13; Chapple and Garofalo, *Rock 'n' Roll Is Here to Pay*, 56–57; Philip H. Ennis, *The Seventh Stream: The Emergence of Rocknroll in American Popular Music* (Hanover, N.H.: Wesleyan University Press, 1992), 218; Palmer, *Rock & Roll*, 133.

31. Alan Freed quoted in Jackson, *Big Beat Heat*, 59.

32. Gart, *First Pressings*, 4:47, 4:57, 4:67; Ennis, *The Seventh Stream*, 218.

33. Jackson, *Big Beat Heat*, 66; Gart, *First Pressings*, 4:80; Palmer, *Rock & Roll*, 135; Ward, Stokes, and Tucker, *Rock of Ages*, 96; Chapple and Garofalo, *Rock 'n' Roll Is Here to Pay*, 56–57.

34. Information about Louis Hardin and the lawsuit can be found in Gart, *First Pressings*, 4:113, 4:125; Jackson, *Big Beat Heat*, 80–82; Miller, *Flowers in the Dustbin*, 83, 84; Fredric Dannen, *Hit Men: Power Brokers and Fast Money inside the Music Business* (New York: Vintage Books, 1991), 42; Ward, Stokes, and Tucker, *Rock of Ages*, 96.

35. Levy quoted in Dannen, *Hit Men*, 42.

36. The aircheck is quoted in Ben Fong-Torres, *The Hits Just Keep on Coming: The History of Top 40 Radio* (San Francisco: Miller Freeman Books, 1998), 32; See also Miller, *Flowers in the Dustbin*, 84–86; Jackson, *Big Beat Heat*, 86, 87; Gart, *First Pressings*, 4:128.

37. Jackson, *Big Beat Heat*, 85, 86.

3. ROCK AROUND THE CLOCK

1. Arnold Shaw, *The Rockin' 50s: The Decade That Transformed the Pop Music Scene* (New York: Hawthorn Books, 1974), 122, 138. See also Linda Martin and Kerry Segrave, *Anti-Rock: The Opposition to Rock 'n' Roll* (New York: DaCapo Press, 1993), 7.

2. Richard Aquila interview with Dave Bartholomew for NPR's *Rock & Roll America*, July 2, 1998; Ruth Brown quoted in Divine Laboratories Collective, comp., *The Little Black Leather Book of Rock 'n' Roll* (Vancouver, B.C.: Arsenal Pulp Press, 1994), 13; Richard Aquila interview with Bo Diddley for NPR's *Rock & Roll America*, January 21, 1998.

3. Galen Gart, ed., *First Pressings: The History of Rhythm & Blues*, vol. 4: *1954* (Milford, N.H.: Big Nickel, 1990), 33–35; James Miller, *Flowers in the Dustbin: The Rise of Rock and Roll, 1947–1977* (New York: Simon & Schuster,

1999), 86; John A. Jackson, *Big Beat Heat: Alan Freed and the Early Years of Rock & Roll* (New York: Schirmer Books, 1991), 60, 86, 34.

4. Gart, *First Pressings*, 4:104.

5. Jackson, *Big Beat Heat*, 87–88.

6. The Jumping George Oxford program is available on CD or cassette as part of the *Cruisin'* series issued by Increase Records. The CD is entitled *Cruisin' 1955: Jumping George Oxford, KSAN, San Francisco.*

7. Galen Gart, ed., *First Pressings: The History of Rhythm & Blues*, vol. 5: *1955* (Milford, N.H.: Big Nickel, 1990), 67, 123, 137.

8. For information about *The Wild One*, see Douglas Brode, *The Films of the Fifties* (New York: Citadel Press Book, 1992), 86–87; Judge Victor Wylega-la quoted in William Graebner, *Coming of Age in Buffalo: Youth and Authority in the Postwar Era* (Philadelphia: Temple University Press, 1990), 87. For additional information about concerns over juvenile delinquency, see Graeb-ner, *Coming of Age in Buffalo*, 15, 86–103; Douglas T. Miller and Marion Nowak, *The Fifties: The Way We Really Were* (Garden City, N.Y.: Doubleday, 1975), 280–87.

9. Information about *Rebel Without a Cause* can be found in Brode, *Films of the Fifties*, 163–66; the Nicholas Ray quote comes from Peter Guralnick, "Elvis Presley," in *The Rolling Stone Illustrated History of Rock & Roll*, ed. Jim Miller (New York: Random House/Rolling Stone, 1976), 19; see also Peter Guralnick, *Last Train to Memphis: The Rise of Elvis Presley* (Boston: Little, Brown, 1994), 323–24.

10. Information about how Bill Haley came to record "Rock Around the Clock" comes from several sources. Especially useful were Jim Dawson and Steve Propes, *What Was the First Rock 'N' Roll Record?* (Boston: Faber and Faber, 1992), 142–47; Miller, *Flowers in the Dustbin*, 87–94; and John Swenson, *Bill Haley: The Daddy of Rock and Roll* (New York, 1982). Jimmy Myers is quoted in Dawson and Propes, *What Was the First Rock 'N' Roll Record*, 146.

11. Robert Palmer, *Rock & Roll: An Unruly History* (New York: Harmony Books, 1995), 51; Shaw, *The Rockin' 50s*, 122.

12. Ed Ward, Geoffrey Stokes, and Ken Tucker, *Rock of Ages: The Rolling Stone History of Rock & Roll* (New York: Rolling Stone Press/Summit Books, 1986), 106–7; Martin and Segrave, *Anti-Rock*, 7–8; Marshall Crenshaw, *Hollywood Rock: A Guide to Rock 'n' Roll in the Movies* (New York: HarperPerenni-al, 1994), 41; Palmer, *Rock & Roll*, 51; Jackson, *Big Beat Heat*, 95; Miller, *Flowers in the Dustbin*, 88, 93.

13. Gart, *First Pressings*, 5:55.

14. Graebner, *Coming of Age in Buffalo*, 4, 5; *Buffalo Evening News*, July 5, 1955, p. 6.

15. Richard Aquila, *That Old Time Rock & Roll: A Chronicle of an Era, 1954–63* (New York: Shirmer Books, 1989), 177. Biographical information can be found on the official Boyd Bennett website: www.boydbennett.com.

16. Boyd Bennett, "Seventeen" (King Records, 1955).

17. Gart, *First Pressings*, 5:3, 5:5–7.

18. In 1955 and 1956, Pat Boone had hits with cover versions of the Charms' "Two Hearts," Fats Domino's "Ain't That a Shame," the El Dorados' "At My Front Door," the Five Keys' "Gee Whittakers," the Flamingos' "I'll Be Home," Little Richard's "Tutti Frutti" and "Long Tall Sally," Ivory Joe Hunter's "I Almost Lost My Mind," and Joe Turner's "Chains of Love." His only early hit that was not a cover record was "Friendly Persuasion (Thee I Love)," which he recorded for the Gary Cooper film *Friendly Persuasion*.

19. Richard Aquila interview with Pat Boone for NPR's *Rock & Roll America*, June 12, 1998.

20. Pat Boone quoted in the liner notes to the album, *Pat Boone's Greatest Hits: The Original Dot Recordings*, 1993.

21. Aquila, interview with Pat Boone.

22. Jackson, *Big Beat Heat*, 77, 79–80; Shaw, *The Rockin' 50s*, 127.

23. Gart, *First Pressings*, 5:27, 5:30.

24. Gart, *First Pressings*, 5:91.

25. Shaw, *The Rockin' 50s*, 120–21.

26. A good overview of the civil rights movement is Harvard Sitkoff, *The Struggle for Black Equality: 1954–1992* (New York: Hill and Wang, 1993).

27. Aquila, *That Old Time Rock & Roll*, 7; Shaw, *The Rockin' 50s*, 126.

28. Shaw, *The Rockin' 50s*, 126.

29. For examples of how 45s were gaining dominance in the music industry, see Gart, *First Pressings*, 4:91, 5:9; 6:45; Steve Chapple and Reebee Garofalo, *Rock 'n' Roll Is Here to Pay: The History and Politics of the Music Industry* (Chicago: Nelson-Hall, 1977), 241.

30. Aquila, interview with Pat Boone.

31. Jackson, *Big Beat Heat*, 80; Miller, *Flowers in the Dustbin*, 102.

32. Aquila, interview with Pat Boone; Shaw, *The Rockin' 50s*, 128.

33. Aquila interview with Pat Boone.

34. Aquila interview with Pat Boone.

35. Ward, Stokes, and Tucker, *Rock of Ages*, 100; Shaw, *The Rockin' 50s*, 128–29; Jackson, *Big Beat Heat*, 78.

36. Aquila, interview with Dave Bartholomew.

37. Johnny Otis quoted in Chapple and Garofalo, *Rock 'n' Roll Is Here to Pay*, 246.

38. Gart, *First Pressings*, 5:3, 6:116.

39. Jackson, *Big Beat Heat*, 80; Miller, *Flowers in the Dustbin*, 101.

40. Fred Parris quoted in Jackson, *American Bandstand*, 83.

41. Mercury advertisement in Gart, *First Pressings*, 5:34; the Blend Records' ad can be found in the same volume, p. 60. See also Jackson, *Big Beat Heat*, 88–89.

42. Rick Coleman, *Blue Monday: Fats Domino and the Lost Dawn of Rock 'n' Roll* (Cambridge, Mass.: DaCapo Press, 2006), 8, 10, 73.

43. Aquila, interview with Dave Bartholomew.

44. Bumps Blackwell quoted in Paul Friedlander, *Rock and Roll: A Social History* (Boulder, Colo.: Westview Press, 1996), 29; Aquila, interview with Dave Bartholomew.

45. Aquila, interview with Dave Bartholomew.

46. Guralnick, "Fats Domino," in Miller *The Rolling Stone Illustrated History of Rock & Roll*, 50–51; Coleman, *Blue Monday*, 17, 19, 22, 26, 28.

47. Aquila, interview with Dave Bartholomew.

48. Aquila, interview with Dave Bartholomew; see also Dawson and Propes, *What Was the First Rock 'n' Roll Record?*, 62–65.

49. Aquila, interview with Dave Bartholomew.

50. Aquila, interview with Dave Bartholomew.

51. Chuck Berry quoted in *History of Rock & Roll*, Episode 1: *Renegades* (PBS/BBC documentary, 1995).

52. Miller, *Flowers in the Dustbin*, 103–5; Patricia Romanowski and Holly George-Warren, eds., *The New Rolling Stone Encyclopedia of Rock & Roll* (New York: Fireside/Rolling Stone Press Book, 1995), 71; Joe Stuessy, *Rock & Roll: Its History and Stylistic Development* (Englewood Cliffs, N.J.: Prentice Hall, 1990), 61.

53. Chuck Berry, *Chuck Berry: The Autobiography* (New York: Fireside Book/Simon & Schuster, 1987), 89–91; see also Miller, *Flowers in the Dustbin*, 103–5; Friedlander, *Rock and Roll*, 33–34, 307.

54. Berry, *Chuck Berry: The Autobiography*, 98; Romanowski and George-Warren, *The New Rolling Stone Encyclopedia of Rock & Roll*, 71; Miller, *Flowers in the Dustbin*, 101; Friedlander, *Rock and Roll*, 34; Chapple and Garofalo, *Rock 'n' Roll Is Here to Pay*, 38.

55. Berry, *Chuck Berry: The Autobiography*, 100–101; for information about Chess Records, see Nadine Cohodas, *Spinning Blues into Gold: The Chess Brothers and the Legendary Chess Records* (New York: St. Martin's Press, 2000).

56. Berry, *Chuck Berry: The Autobiography*, 103; Bob Shannon and John Javna, *Behind the Hits: Inside Stories of Classic Pop and Rock and Roll* (New York: Warner Books, 1986), 222; Ward, Stokes, and Tucker, *Rock of Ages*, 101; Shaw, *The Rockin 50s*, 145; Miller, *Flowers in the Dustbin*, 105.

57. Gart, *First Pressings*, 5:87; Glenn C. Altschuler, *All Shook Up: How Rock 'n' Roll Changed America* (New York: Oxford University Press, 2003), 63.

58. Stuessy, *Rock & Roll*, 62; Charlie Gillett, *The Sound of the City: The Rise of Rock and Roll* (New York: Pantheon Books, 1983), 30; Coleman, *Blue Monday*, 108; Chapple and Garofalo, *Rock 'n' Roll Is Here to Pay*, 39; Gart, *First Pressings*, 5:104–5, 5:140.

59. Bob Hyde, "Track by Track Annotation," in liner notes booklet of *The Doo Wop Box* (Santa Monica, Calif.: Rhino Records, 1993), 36–37; Wayne Stierle, "Earth Angel and the Birth of Rock 'n' Roll" in liner notes booklet of *The Doo Wop Box*, 26.

4. I WAS THE ONE

1. Elvis Presley, "I Was the One." Music and lyrics by Schroeder, DeMetrius, Blair, and Pepper, 1956.

2. Peter Guralnick, *Last Train to Memphis: The Rise of Elvis Presley* (New York: Little, Brown, 1994), 188.

3. Sam Phillips may or may not have actually said that to Marion Keisker. It has been repeated on numerous occasions and is now commonly featured in books on rock history.

4. Most likely, this story of Elvis first entering Sun Studios to record a song for his mother began with a questionable news article that appeared in the *Memphis Press-Scimitar* on July 28, 1954. A reprint of the story can be found in *Elvis: Commemorative Edition* (Lincolnwood, Ill.: Publications International, 2002), 18. Ever since then, the story has been repeated in books, magazines, TV shows, and movies about Elvis. For examples of books, see David Szatmary, *A Time to Rock: A Social History of Rock 'n' Roll* (New York: Macmillan/Schirmer Books, 1996), 37; Ed Ward, Geoffrey Stokes, and Ken Tucker, *Rock of Ages: The Rolling Stone History of Rock & Roll* (New York: Rolling Stone Press/Summit Books, 1986), 77; Elizabeth McKeon and Linda Everett, *Elvis Speaks: Thoughts on Fame, Family, Music, and More in His Own Words* (Nashville: Cumberland House, 1997), 3. Magazines repeat the same story, for example, Anthony Thorton, ed., *Elvis: Uncut Legends, The Definitive Guide to Rock's Ultimate Icons* (2005): 27; "A Legend Is Born," *Forever Elvis: The 15th Memorial Anniversary Salute* (1992): 10; *Life, Collector's Edition* (February 10, 1995): 6.

5. Dixie Locke is quoted in Guralnick, *Last Train to Memphis*, 69.

6. Gladys Presley quoted in Jerry Hopkins, *Elvis: A Biography* (New York: Simon & Schuster, 1971), 26.

7. Nancy Anderson, "Elvis by His Father Vernon Presley," *Good House-keeping* (January 1978): 156; Guralnick, *Last Train to Memphis*, 15.

8. Gladys Presley quoted in Guralnick, *Last Train to Memphis*, 15.

9. The Elvis quote comes from McKeon and Everett, *Elvis Speaks*, 15; the neighbor was Mrs. Ruby Black, who was the mother of Bill Black, who played bass in Elvis's first band. She is quoted in Jerry Hopkins, *Elvis*, 40.

10. Red West, Sonny West, and Dave Hebler, *Elvis: What Happened?* (New York: Ballantine Books, 1977), 53.

11. Ernst Jorgensen, *Elvis Presley: A Life in Music; The Complete Recording Sessions* (New York: St. Martin's Press, 1998), 8.

12. McKeon and Everett, *Elvis Speaks*, 203.

13. Guralnick, *Last Train to Memphis*, 47, 48.

14. Guralnick, *Last Train to Memphis*, 20–21, 23, 48, 51, 53, 92; McKeon and Everett, *Elvis Speaks*, 27, 146; Jorgensen, *Elvis Presley*, 7, 8.

15. Jorgensen, *Elvis Presley*, 7–8; Guralnick, *Last Train to Memphis*, 17–19, 23, 25, 26, 40–41, 45–47; Hopkins, *Elvis*, 29, 31, 43.

16. Hopkins, *Elvis*, 25, 29, 43–44, 49; Marie Clayton, *Elvis Presley: Unseen Archives* (Bath: Parragon, 2003), 13; Guralnick, *Last Train to Memphis*, 16, 23, 34–35, 38, 40, 43, 46; McKeon and Everett, *Elvis Speaks*, 3, 5–6, 8–9, 11, 159, 191.

17. Sam Phillips's quotes can be found in James Miller, *Flowers in the Dustbin: The Rise of Rock and Roll, 1947–1977* (New York: Simon & Schuster, 1999), 73; and Guralnick, *Last Train to Memphis*, 43. Other indications of Elvis's insecurity can be found in Hopkins, *Elvis*, 25, 43–44; West, West, and Hebler, *Elvis*, 55; McKeon and Everett, *Elvis Speaks*, 34, 47, 183, 205, 236.

18. Red West quoted in Hopkins, *Elvis*, 41–42. See also Hopkins, *Elvis*, 49; Guralnick, *Last Train to Memphis*, 25–26, 28, 44, 50, 77, 93; West, West, and Hebler, *Elvis*, 16; Greil Marcus, *Mystery Train: Images of America in Rock 'n' Roll Music* (New York: Dutton, 1975), 155.

19. McKeon and Everett, *Elvis Speaks*, 21, 22.

20. Hopkins, *Elvis*, 27, 38, 41–42, 48, 52; Marcus, *Mystery Train*, 161; Guralnick, *Last Train to Memphis*, 20, 23, 25, 27, 38–39, 44–48, 50–51, 91, 111; *Elvis: Commemorative Edition*, 14, pictures on 22, 23; McKeon and Everett, *Elvis Speaks*, 16, 22, 89, 114, 121–22, 125, 138.

21. Marcus, *Mystery Train*, 154; Dixie Locke quoted in Guralnick, *Last Train to Memphis*, 68.

22. The Phillips quote can be found in Miller, *Flowers in the Dustbin*, 73; the Elvis quote appears in Jorgensen, *Elvis Presley*, 1.

23. West, West, and Hebler, *Elvis*, 55; McKeon and Everett, *Elvis Speaks*, 23.

24. McKeon and Everett, *Elvis Speaks*, 171.

25. Pictures of Sun Studios and the restaurant can be found in *Elvis: Commemorative Edition*, 19–20.

26. Rick Kennedy and Randy McNutt, *Little Labels—Big Sound: Small Record Companies and the Rise of American Music* (Indianapolis: Indiana University Press, 1999), 93.

27. Kennedy and McNutt, *Little Labels—Big Sound*, 90–92; Guralnick, *Last Train to Memphis*, 60–62.

28. Kennedy and McNutt, *Little Labels—Big Sound*, 91–92; Colin Escott, with Martin Hawkins, *Good Rockin' Tonight: Sun Records and the Birth of Rock 'n' Roll* (New York: St. Martin's Press, 1991); Louis Cantor, *Wheelin' on Beale: How WDIA–Memphis Became the Nation's First All-Black Radio Station and Created the Sound That Changed America* (New York: Pharos Books, 1992), 20–21.

29. Guralnick, *Last Train to Memphis*, 57–58.

30. McKeon and Everett, *Elvis Speaks*, 51.

31. Hopkins, *Elvis*, 54; Guralnick, *Last Train to Memphis*, 62–63.

32. Scotty Moore as told to James Dickerson in Scotty Moore, *That's Alright, Elvis: The Untold Story of Elvis's First Guitarist and Manager, Scotty Moore* (New York: Schirmer Trade Books, 2005), 45–47; Guralnick, *Last Train to Memphis*, 63–64; Hopkins, *Elvis*, 56.

33. Hopkins, *Elvis*, 57; Guralnick, *Last Train to Memphis*, 65.

34. Guralnick, *Last Train to Memphis*, 84–85.

35. Moore, *That's Alright, Elvis*, 58–59; Guralnick, *Last Train to Memphis*, 91–94; Jorgensen, *Elvis Presley*, 12–13.

36. For information about Elvis's first early recording session, see Jorgensen, *Elvis Presley*, 12–15; Moore, *That's Alright, Elvis*, 57–61; Guralnick, *Last Train to Memphis*, 95–97.

37. Moore, *That's Alright, Elvis*, 62–66.

38. Jorgensen, *Elvis Presley*, 12–15; Guralnick, *Last Train to Memphis*, 102–14.

39. Guralnick, *Last Train to Memphis*, 108.

40. The newspaper article and photograph can be found in *Elvis: Commemorative Edition*, 18.

41. Moore, *That's Alright, Elvis*, 71–73.

42. Elvis Presley quoted in Jerry Osborne, *Elvis: Word for Word* (New York: Gramercy Books, 1999), 53–54.

43. Hopkins, *Elvis*, 65; Guralnick, *Last Train to Memphis*, 111–15, 121.

44. Hopkins, *Elvis*, 65–66; Guralnick, *Last Train to Memphis*, 116–19.

45. Jorgensen, *Elvis Presley*, 16–19; Guralnick, *Last Train to Memphis*, 111–12; Gerald Nachman, *Raised on Radio* (Los Angeles: University of California Press, 1998), 157.

46. Jorgensen, *Elvis Presley*, 19–21.

47. Richard Aquila interview with J. I. Allison for NPR's *Rock & Roll America*, January 5, 1999.

48. Peter Guralnick, "Elvis Presley," in Jim Miller, ed., *The Rolling Stone Illustrated History of Rock & Roll* (New York: Rolling Stone Press/Random House, 1976), 30.

49. Jorgensen, *Elvis Presley*, 19–21.

50. Bob Neal quoted in Guralnick, "Elvis Presley," in *The Rolling Stone Illustrated History of Rock & Roll*, 36.

51. Ward, Stokes, and Tucker, *Rock of Ages*, 112, 117; Guralnick, "Elvis Presley," in *The Rolling Stone Illustrated History of Rock & Roll*, 36; Guralnick, *Last Train to Memphis*, 233; Kennedy and McNutt, *Little Labels—Big Sound*, 97.

52. West, West, and Hebler, *Elvis*, 57, 58; McKeon and Everett, *Elvis Speaks*, 216.

53. Bob Neal quoted in Hopkins, *Elvis*, 99.

54. Jorgensen, *Elvis Presley*, 26; Guralnick, *Last Train to Memphis*, 190; Hopkins, *Elvis*, 102.

55. Moore, *That's Alright, Elvis*, 108.

56. Ward, Stokes, and Tucker, *Rock of Ages*, 112; Hopkins, *Elvis*, 106.

57. Galen Gart, ed., *First Pressings: The History of Rhythm & Blues*, vol. 5: *1955* (Milford, N.H.: Big Nickel, 1990), 133.

5. MONEY HONEY

1. Elvis Presley's final performance on *Stage Show* occurred on March 24, 1956. A black-and-white video can be viewed online at www.youtube.com. Elvis's version of "Money Honey" is almost identical to the hit version by Clyde McPhatter and the Drifters (Atlantic Records, 1953), which was a number 1 hit on the R&B charts.

2. Colonel Tom Parker quoted in Luke Crampton and Dafydd Rees, *Rock & Roll: Year by Year* (London: DK Books, 2003), 42.

3. James Baughman, *The Republic of Mass Culture: Journalism, Filmmaking, and Broadcasting in America since 1941* (Baltimore: Johns Hopkins University Press, 1997), 41–42; Peter Guralnick, *Last Train to Memphis: The Rise of Elvis Presley* (New York: Little, Brown and Company, 1994), 230–31; Ed Ward, Geoffrey Stokes, and Ken Tucker, *Rock of Ages: The Rolling Stone History of Rock & Roll* (New York: Summit Books, 1986), 116.

4. The advertisement is reproduced in David P. Szatmary, *A Time to Rock: A Social History of Rock and Roll* (New York: Schirmer Books, 1996), 51;

Guralnick, *Last Train to Memphis*, 235–36; the *Memphis Press-Scimitar* article can be found in *Elvis: Commemorative Edition* (Lincolnwood, Ill.: Publications International, 2002), 37.

5. Ward, Stokes, and Tucker, *Rock of Ages*, 116; Ernst Jorgensen, *Elvis Presley: A Life in Music; The Complete Recording Sessions* (New York: St. Martin's Press, 1998), 41.

6. Jorgensen, *Elvis Presley*, 41.

7. Elvis, Scotty, and Bill are quoted in Guralnick, *Last Train to Memphis*, 271; D. J. Fontana is quoted in Scotty Moore, as told to James Dickerson, in *That's Alright, Elvis: The Untold Story of Elvis's First Guitarist and Manager, Scotty Moore* (New York: Schirmer Trade Books, 2005), 121–22.

8. The two reviews are reproduced in *Elvis: Commemorative Edition*, 42.

9. Moore, *That's Alright, Elvis*, 123.

10. Detailed information about Elvis Presley's TV performances and recording sessions can be found in Jorgensen, *Elvis Presley*. For information about Elvis's hit records, see Richard Aquila, *That Old Time Rock & Roll: A Chronicle of an Era, 1954–63* (New York: Shirmer Books, 1989), 299–301; Joel Whitburn, *Top Pop Singles, 1955–1990* (Menomonee Falls, Wisc.: Record Research, 1991), 457–62.

11. Pictures of Elvis singing on the Milton Berle show can be found in Marie Clayton, *Elvis Presley: Unseen Archives* (Bath: Parragon, 2003), 31–36.

12. *Elvis: Commemorative Edition*, 46; Clayton, *Elvis Presley*, 37; James Miller, *Flowers in the Dustbin: The Rise of Rock and Roll, 1947–1977* (New York: Simon & Schuster, 1999), 132–33; Guralnick, *Last Train to Memphis*, 284.

13. Clayton, *Elvis Presley*, 37; Steve Allen quoted in Guralnick, *Last Train to Memphis*, 287.

14. Detailed information about Elvis Presley's TV performances and recording sessions can be found in Jorgensen, *Elvis Presley*.

15. Guralnick, *Last Train to Memphis*, 296.

16. Szatmary, *A Time to Rock*, 56–58; Guralnick, *Last Train to Memphis*, 323–33; Jorgensen, *Elvis Presley*, 55–60; *Elvis: Commemorative Edition*, 137.

17. Jorgensen, *Elvis Presley*, 55–60; Guralnick, *Last Train to Memphis*, 329–30; Jerry Hopkins, *Elvis: A Biography* (New York: Simon & Schuster, 1971), 159–60; Clayton, *Elvis Presley*, 62.

18. Hopkins, *Elvis*, 144–49; *Elvis: Commemorative Edition*, 60–63.

19. *TV Guide* article is reprinted in *Elvis: Commemorative Edition*, 57; Moore, *That's Alright, Elvis*, 131–32.

20. Guralnick, *Last Train to Memphis*, 337–38; Jorgensen, *Elvis Presley*, 65.

21. Guralnick, *Last Train to Memphis*, 378–79; Jorgensen, *Elvis Presley*, 74.

22. Elizabeth McKeon and Linda Everett, *Elvis Speaks: Thoughts on Fame, Family, Music, and More in His Own Words* (Nashville: Cumberland House, 1997), 50.

23. *Elvis: Commemorative Edition*, 78–79.

24. Tom Engelhardt, *The End of Victory Culture: Cold War America and the Disillusioning of a Generation* (New York: Basic Books, 1995), 136.

25. Nat D. Williams quoted in Guralnick, *Last Train to Memphis*, 370.

26. Linda Martin and Kerry Segrave, *Anti-Rock: The Opposition to Rock 'n' Roll* (New York: DaCapo Press, 1993), 64–66.

27. Guralnick, *Last Train to Memphis*, 400–401; Jerry Osborne, *Elvis: Word for Word* (New York: Gramercy Books, 2000), 97–98, 113.

28. Martin and Segrave, *Anti-Rock*, 65; *Elvis: Commemorative Edition*, 87.

29. Elvis quotes can be found in Osborne, *Elvis*, 66, 95, 101.

30. Elvis quoted in James Gregory, ed., *The Elvis Presley Story* (New York: Hillman Books, 1957), 67.

31. Elvis quoted in Guralnick, *Last Train to Memphis*, 486; Elvis's comments about juvenile delinquency can be found in Osborne, *Elvis*, 101.

32. Elvis quoted in Gregory, *The Elvis Presley Story*, 69.

33. Fred Sparks's newspaper article is reprinted in *Elvis: Commemorative Edition*, 76.

34. Gregory, *The Elvis Presley Story*, 106.

35. *Tupelo Daily Journal* (September 27, 1956), quoted in Crampton and Rees, *Rock & Roll*, 47.

36. Elvis quoted in McKeon and Everett, *Elvis Speaks*, 192.

37. Sonny West quoted in Red West, Sonny West, and Dave Hebler, *Elvis: What Happened?* (New York: Ballantine Books, 1977), 20–21.

38. *[Elvis] On His 60th Birthday: Life: Collector's Edition* (February 10, 1995): 39, 87; Clayton, *Elvis Presley*, 50; *Ladies Home Journal* (July 2003): 106.

39. Sam Phillips's comments are from an article that appeared in the *Memphis Press-Scimitar*, February 5, 1955, quoted in *Elvis: Commemorative Edition*, 28; Leiber and Stoller quote comes from Ken Emerson, *Always Magic in the Air: The Bomp and Brilliance of the Brill Building Era* (New York: Viking, 2005), 8; Elvis quote can be found in McKeon and Everett, *Elvis Speaks*, 56.

40. Pictures can be found in *Elvis: Commemorative Edition*, 24,

41. West, West, and Hebler, *Elvis: What Happened?*, 17.

42. West, West, and Hebler, *Elvis: What Happened?*, 55–56; *Elvis: Commemorative Edition*, 35, 17.

43. The U.P.I. article is reprinted in *Elvis: Commemorative Edition*, 131.

44. Clayton, *Elvis Presley*; Elvis quoted in McKeon and Everett, *Elvis Speaks*, 151, 206.

45. Elvis quoted in McKeon and Everett, *Elvis Speaks*, 167.

46. Guralnick, *Last Train to Memphis*, 108, 91.

47. Sonny West quoted in *Elvis: What Happened?*, 128.

48. Bruce Springsteen's comments are from his keynote address at the South by Southwest Music Festival in Austin, Texas (March 28, 2012), www.rollingstone.com/music/news/exclusive-the-complete-text-of-bruce-springsteens-sxsw-keynote-address-20120328 (accessed July 23, 2014). The address may be viewed online at *Elvis Presley: The Official Site of the King of Rock 'n' Roll*, www.elvis.com/photos-video/videos.aspx?id=140 (accessed July 23, 2014).

49. McKeon and Everett, *Elvis Speaks*, 216.

50. Osborne, *Elvis*, 80, 70.

51. Osborne, *Elvis*, 8, 16–17, 42, 72, 76, 84, 100.

52. Buddy Holly quoted in Ellis Amburn, *Buddy Holly: A Biography* (New York: St. Martin's Press, 1995), 35.

53. Bruce Springsteen, keynote address.

54. Written by Jerry Leiber and Mike Stoller, the Coasters' "What Is the Secret of Your Success?" was released in 1957 on Atco Records.

6. THE GIRL CAN'T HELP IT!

1. Douglas Brode, *The Films of the Fifties* (New York: Citadel Press, 1992), 243.

2. Little Richard, "The Girl Can't Help It" (Specialty Records, 1956).

3. Poster can be found in Brode, *The Films of the Fifties*, 243.

4. Marshall Crenshaw, *Hollywood Rock: A Guide to Rock 'n' Roll in the Movies* (New York: HarperPerennial, 1994), 94–95.

5. Newspaper stories are reprinted in *Elvis: Commemorative Edition* (Lincolnwood, Ill.: Publications International, 2002), 41–42, 54.

6. Michael Barson and Steven Heller, *Teenage Confidential: An Illustrated History of the American Teen* (New York: Barnes & Noble, 1998), 67; see also *Elvis: Commemorative Edition*, 40, 42, 45–56; E. Condon, "What Is an Elvis Presley?" *Cosmopolitan* (December 1956): 54–61.

7. Letter to the editor quoted in *Elvis: Commemorative Edition*, 56.

8. Douglas T. Miller and Marion Nowak, *The Fifties: The Way We Really Were* (Garden City, N.Y.: Doubleday, 1975), 291; Galen Gart, ed., *First Pressings: The History of Rhythm & Blues*, vol. 6: *1956* (Milford, N.H.: Big Nickel, 1991), 4; the *Time* quotes appear in Peter Jennings and Todd Brewster, *The Century* (New York: Doubleday, 1998), 345, 343.

9. Barson and Heller, *Teenage Confidential*, 120–21; *Elvis: Commemorative Edition*, 55, 57, 75, 79.

10. Ben Fong-Torres, *The Hits Just Keep on Coming: The History of Top 40 Radio* (San Francisco: Miller Freeman Books, 1998), 16–17. For more on the rivalry between radio and television, see Jay Black and Jennings Bryant, *Introduction to Mass Communication* (Dubuque, Ia.: Wm C. Brown, 1992), 222–24; James L. Baughman, *The Republic of Mass Culture: Journalism, Filmmaking, and Broadcasting in America since 1941*, 2nd ed. (Baltimore: Johns Hopkins University Press, 1997), 42, 67–74.

11. The 1953 research study done by the Arthur Politz research firm is quoted in Fong-Torres, *The Hits Just Keep on Coming*, 17; Baughman, *The Republic of Mass Culture*, 67–68.

12. Fong-Torres, *The Hits Just Keep on Coming*, 18.

13. Sound clips from some of Lorenz's later shows are available at www.hounddoglorenz.com/shows.php (accessed July 23, 2014).

14. Richard Aquila, interview with Danny Neaverth for NPR's *Rock & Roll America*, June 10, 1998. A sampling of Danny Neaverth's on-air style can be found at www.youtube.com/watch?v=1ub7GBbkhM0 (accessed July 23, 2014).

15. William Graebner, *Coming of Age in Buffalo: Youth and Authority in the Postwar Era* (Philadelphia: Temple University Press, 1990), 32–34.

16. Fong-Torres, *The Hits Just Keep on Coming*, 29–30.

17. Anyone who would like to sample Top 40 radio can find excellent examples in the Cruisin' series, a collection of CDs issued by Increase Records/ Chess INCM. The series features individual CDs for each of the following disc jockeys who became legendary figures of Top 40 Radio: Jumpin' George Oxford, Robin Seymour, Joe Niagara, Jack Carney, Hunter Hancock, Dick Biondi, Arnie Ginsberg, Russ Knight, B. Mitchel Reed, Johnny Holliday, Robert W. Morgan, Pat O'Day, Dr. Don Rose, Johnny Dark, and Kris Eric Stevens.

18. Herman Land, "The Storz Bombshell," *Television* (May 1957): 3–4; Marc Fisher, *Something in the Air: Radio, Rock, and the Revolution That Shaped a Generation* (New York: Random House, 2007), 8–9; Fong-Torres, *The Hits Just Keep on Coming*, 37–39; Christopher H. Sterling and John M. Kittross, *Stay Tuned: A Concise History of American Broadcasting*, 2nd ed. (Belmont, Calif.: Wadsworth, 1990), 338–39.

19. Fisher, *Something in the Air*, 8–9; Dick Clark quoted in Fong-Torres, *The Hits Just Keep on Coming*, 40

20. Fisher, *Something in the Air*, 3–10; Sterling and Kittross, *Stay Tuned*, 338–39.

21. Sterling and Kittross, *Stay Tuned*, 338–39; Steve Chapple and Reebee Garofalo, *Rock 'n' Roll Is Here to Pay: The Music and Politics of the Music Industry* (Chicago: Nelson-Hall, 1977), 58–59.

22. Land, "The Storz Bombshell," 4; Fisher, *Something in the Air*, 15.

23. Fisher, *Something in the Air*, 15; Fong-Torres, *The Hits Keep on Coming*, 117–18; transcript of Scott Simon's NPR interview of Dick Biondi (September 21, 2013) www.npr.org/templates/story/story.php?storyId=224715929 (accessed July 24, 2014).

24. Fong-Torres, *The Hits Keep on Coming*, 117–18.

25. Readers can hear this segment, as well as more of the Dick Biondi show on WKBW on the following CD: *Cruisin' 1960: Dick Biondi* (Increase Records/Chess INCM, 2005). Biondi air checks are also available online at www.radiohof.org/dick_biondi.htm (accessed July 23, 2014).

26. Quotes can be found in Fisher, *Something in the Air*, 10.

27. The quote is from station owner David Segal and can be found in Fisher, *Something in the Air*, 21.

28. Fong-Torres, *The Hits Keep on Coming*, 57.

29. Richard Aquila, interview with Tom Shannon for NPR's *Rock & Roll America*, June 17, 1998.

30. Aquila, interview with Tom Shannon.

31. Aquila, interview with Tom Shannon.

32. Richard Aquila, interview with Casey Kasem for NPR's *Rock & Roll America*, November 25, 1996; the Sensations, "Please Mr. Disc Jockey" (Atco Records, 1956).

33. Fisher, *Something in the Air*, 25–26; *Time* (July 14, 1958).

34. Gart, *First Pressings*, 6:43; Karal Ann Marling, *As Seen on TV: The Visual Culture of Everyday Life in the 1950s* (Cambridge, Mass.: Harvard University Press, 1994), 179.

35. Tim Brooks and Earle Marsh, *The Complete Directory to Prime Time Television and Cable TV Shows, 1946–Present* (New York: Ballantine Books, 2003), 1342–43.

36. Fats Domino quoted in Rick Coleman, *Blue Monday: Fats Domino and the Lost Dawn of Rock 'n' Roll* (Cambridge, Mass.: DaCapo Press, 2006), 139.

37. Gart, *First Pressings*, 6:17–18.

38. Gart, *First Pressings*, 6:152.

7. THE ROCK AND ROLL WALTZ

1. Kay Starr, "Rock and Roll Waltz" (RCA, 1956).

2. The "Hilltoppers" who sang "Ka Ding Dong" were not the group that scored numerous hits under that name. When the real Hilltoppers were not available to record, Dot Records brought in some replacements for the session. See Carlton Jackson, *P.S. I Love You: The Story of the Singing Hilltoppers* (Lexington: University Press of Kentucky, 2007), 82.

3. Atlantic Records advertisement is reprinted in Galen Gart, ed., *First Pressings: The History of Rhythm & Blues*, vol. 6: *1956* (Milford, N.H.: Big Nickel, 1991), 138.

4. Gart, *First Pressings*, 6:153.

5. Gart, *First Pressings*, 6:87, 6:92, 6:103.

6. Buchanan and Goodman, "The Flying Saucer (Parts 1 & 2)" (Luniverse, 1956).

7. Stan Freberg, "Heartbreak Hotel" (Capitol, 1956).

8. Gart, *First Pressings*, 6:29; *Time* (July 23, 1956).

9. Bill Haley and His Comets, "Teenager's Mother (Are You Right?)" (Decca Records, 1956).

10. Bill Haley and His Comets, "Skinny Minnie" (Decca Records, 1958).

11. John Charles Peterson, *The True-Life Adventures of Captain Wa Wah—Fifty Years of Music, Meditation, and Politics* (Muncie, Ind.: Katydid, 2009), 17, 18, 16.

12. Crew-Cuts, "Angels in the Sky" (Mercury Records, 1956).

13. James Miller, *Flowers in the Dustbin: The Rise of Rock and Roll, 1947–1977* (New York: Simon & Schuster, 1999), 102; William O'Neill, *American High: The Years of Confidence, 1945–1960* (New York: Free Press, 1986), 268; Charlie Gillett, *The Sound of the City: The Rise of Rock and Roll* (New York: Pantheon, 1983), 25; Reebee Garofalo, *Rockin' Out: Popular Music in the USA* (Boston: Allyn and Bacon, 1997), 156.

14. Richard Aquila, interview with Pat Boone for NPR's *Rock & Roll America*, June 25, 1998.

15. Jerry Osborne, *Elvis: Word for Word* (New York: Gramercy Books, 1999), 111; Peter Guralnick, *Last Train to Memphis: The Rise of Elvis Presley* (New York: Little, Brown, 1994), 452, 177.

16. Aquila, interview with Pat Boone.

17. Aquila, interview with Pat Boone.

18. Aquila, interview with Pat Boone.

19. Aquila, interview with Pat Boone.

20. Aquila, interview with Pat Boone.

21. Aquila, interview with Pat Boone.

22. Aquila, interview with Pat Boone.

23. Aquila, interview with Pat Boone.

24. Aquila, interview with Pat Boone.

25. Aquila, interview with Pat Boone.

26. Audrey, "Dear Elvis (Pages 1&2)" (Plus Records, 1956).

8. LET THE GOOD TIMES ROLL

1. Shirley and Lee, "Let the Good Times Roll" (Aladdin Records, 1956).

2. Shirley and Lee, "Let the Good Times Roll"; Langdon Winner in Anthony DeCurtis and James Henke with Holly George-Warren, eds., *The Rolling Stone Illustrated History of Rock & Roll* (New York: Random House, 1992), 42.

3. Richard Aquila, interview with Dave Bartholomew for NPR's *Rock & Roll America*, July 2, 1998.

4. Galen Gart, ed., *First Pressings: The History of Rhythm & Blues*, vol. 6: *1956* (Milford, N.H.: Big Nickel, 1991), 13–14, 27.

5. Paul Robi quoted in Joe Smith, *Off the Record: An Oral History of Popular Music* (New York: Warner Books, 1988), 108.

6. Arnold Shaw, *The Rockin' 50s: The Decade That Transformed the Pop Music Scene* (New York: Hawthorn Books, 1974), 168.

7. Wayne Jancik, *The Billboard Book of One-Hit Wonders* (New York: Billboard Books, 1990), 26–28; Patricia Romanowski and Holly George-Warren, eds., *The New Rolling Stone Encyclopedia of Rock & Roll* (New York: Fireside/Rolling Stone Press Book, 1995), 661.

8. The Cadillacs, "Speedoo" (Josie Records, 1956).

9. The Five Satins, "In the Still of the Nite" (Ember, 1956).

10. Gart, *First Pressings*, 6:129.

11. For details about McPhatter's early Atlantic sessions, see Jerry Wexler interview in Shaw, *The Rockin' 50s*, 78. See also Jerry Wexler and David Ritz, *Rhythm and the Blues: A Life in American Music* (New York: Knopf, 1993).

12. Charlie Gillett, *The Sound of the City: The Rise of Rock and Roll* (New York: Dutton, 1970), 201.

13. Aquila, interview with Dave Bartholomew.

14. Aquila, interview with Dave Bartholomew.

15. Rick Coleman, *Blue Monday: Fats Domino and the Lost Dawn of Rock 'n' Roll* (Cambridge, Mass.: DaCapo Press, 2006), 83–84; Aquila, interview with Dave Bartholomew.

16. Aquila, interview with Dave Bartholomew; Coleman, *Blue Monday*, 56, 144; Jim Miller, ed., *The Rolling Stone Illustrated History of Rock & Roll* (New York: Random House/Rolling Stone, 1976), 51; Dave Bartholomew quoted in liner notes of Fats Domino's CD, *My Blue Heaven: The Best of Fats Domino* (Legendary Masters Series, EMI/Imperial Records, 1990).

17. Aquila, interview with Dave Bartholomew.

18. Aquila, interview with Dave Bartholomew.

19. Coleman, *Blue Monday*, xvi, xviii.

20. Fats Domino, "I'm in Love Again" (Imperial Records, 1956); Coleman, *Blue Monday*, 114.

21. Aquila, interview with Dave Bartholomew.

22. Aquila, interview with Dave Bartholomew.

23. Chuck Berry, "Roll Over Beethoven" (1956).

24. Galen Gart, ed., *First Pressings: The History of Rhythm & Blues*, vol. 5: *1955* (Milford, N.H.: Big Nickel, 1990), 104–5.

25. Coleman, *Blue Monday*, 149; Paul Friedlander, *Rock and Roll: A Social History* (Boulder, Colo.: Westview Press, 1996), 309; Ed Ward, Geoffrey Stokes, and Ken Tucker, *Rock of Ages: The Rolling Stone History of Rock & Roll* (New York: Rolling Stone Press/Summit Books, 1986), 107; Arnold Shaw, *The World of Soul: Black America's Contribution to the Pop Music Scene* (New York: Cowles Book, 1970), 149–50; Gillett, *Sound of the City*, 384; Chuck Berry, *Chuck Berry: The Autobiography* (New York: Fireside Book/Simon & Schuster, 1987), 91.

26. Shaw, *The World of Soul*, 149.

27. Joe Stuessy, *Rock & Roll: Its History and Stylistic Development* (Englewood Cliffs, N.J.: Prentice Hall, 1990), 61, 63.

28. Berry, *Chuck Berry: The Autobiography*, 93.

29. Keith Richards quoted in the film *Chuck Berry Hail! Hail! Rock 'n' Roll*, directed by Taylor Hackford (Delilah Films, 1987); Michael MacCambridge, "Review of *Chuck Berry Hail! Hail! Rock 'n' Roll*," in *Belles Lettres: A Literary Review* (Washington University in St. Louis) 7 (no. 2, January/May 2008): 8.

30. Gillett, *Sound of the City*, 81, 254; Berry, *Chuck Berry: The Autobiography*, 142–43.

31. Carl Belz, *The Story of Rock*, 2nd ed. (New York: Harper Colophon Books, 1972), 64; Berry, *Chuck Berry: The Autobiography*, 95, 139.

32. Coleman, *Blue Monday*, 197, 141, 140.

33. Berry, *Chuck Berry: The Autobiography*, 115, 139; Coleman, *Blue Monday*, 170.

34. Coleman, *Blue Monday*, 10.

35. Coleman, *Blue Monday*, 10; Glenn C. Altschuyler, *All Shook Up: How Rock 'n' Roll Changed America* (New York: Oxford University Press, 2003), 62, 64–65.

36. Berry, *Chuck Berry: The Autobiography*, 155–58, 150.

37. Coleman, *Blue Monday*, 169; Berry, *Chuck Berry: The Autobiography*, 136; Michael Bertrand, *Race, Rock, and Elvis* (Urbana: University of Illinois Press, 2000), 186, 41.

38. Conner quoted in David Szatmary, *A Time to Rock: A Social History of Rock 'n' Roll* (New York: Schirmer Books, 1996), 18–19. Information about Little Richard can be found in Szatmary's book, as well as Friedlander, *Rock*

and Roll, 36–40; Ward, Stokes, and Tucker, *Rock of Ages*, 103–4; James Miller, *Flowers in the Dustbin: The Rise of Rock and Roll, 1947–1977* (New York: Simon & Schuster, 1999), 108–13; and Langdon Winner, "Little Richard," in Miller, *The Rolling Stone Illustrated History of Rock & Roll*, 52–56.

39. Shaw, *The Rockin' 50s*, 161; Miller, *Flowers in the Dustbin*, 112.

40. Altschuler, *All Shook Up*, 58; Ward, Stokes, and Tucker, *Rock of Ages*, 104; see also Friedlander, *Rock and Roll*, 36–40; Miller, *Flowers in the Dustbin*, 108–13; and Winner, "Little Richard," 52–56.

41. Ward, Stokes, and Tucker, *Rock of Ages*, 104.

42. Little Richard, "Tutti Frutti" (Specialty Records, 1956).

43. Miller, *Flowers in the Dustbin*, 111.

44. Little Richard quoted in the TV documentary, *Rock & Roll*, episode 1: *Renegades* (PBS series produced by WGBH Public Television, Boston, 1995).

45. Gart, ed. *First Pressings*, 6:29.

46. Miller, *Flowers in the Dustbin*, 112.

47. There is disagreement over how and why Little Richard decided to give up rock & roll. See Winner, "Little Richard," 54. Little Richard is quoted in Shaw, *The Rockin' 50s*, 209–10.

48. Shaw, *The Rockin' 50s*, 161; Little Richard quoted in Shaw, *The Rockin' 50s*, 161.

49. Richard Aquila, interview with Bo Diddley for NPR's *Rock & Roll America*, January 21, 1998; see also Bo Diddley interview in Shaw, *The Rockin' 50s*, 133.

50. Aquila, interview with Bo Diddley.

51. Aquila, interview with Bo Diddley.

52. Aquila, interview with Bo Diddley.

53. Robert Palmer, "Rock Begins," in *The Rolling Stone Illustrated History of Rock & Roll*, ed. Anthony DeCurtis and James Henke (New York: Random House, 1980), 15.

54. Bo Diddley, "Hey Bo Diddley" (Chess Records, 1957).

55. Coleman, *Blue Monday*, 9.

56. Aquila, interview with Bo Diddley.

57. Bo Diddley's account can be found on his official website, www.bodiddley.com; see also Coleman, *Blue Monday*, 138.

58. Aquila, interview with Bo Diddley.

59. Aquila, interview with Bo Diddley.

60. Aquila, interview with Bo Diddley.

61. Aquila, interview with Bo Diddley.

62. Jerry Leiber and Mike Stoller, *Hound Dog: The Leiber and Stoller Autobiography* (New York: Simon & Schuster, 2009), 32–33. See also Robert Palm-

er, *Baby That Was Rock & Roll: The Legendary Leiber and Stoller* (New York: Harcourt Brace Jovanovich, 1978).

63. Leiber and Stoller, *Hound Dog*, 35; Jerry Leiber quoted in Ken Emerson, *Always Magic in the Air: The Bomp and Brilliance of the Brill Building Era* (New York: Viking Press, 2005), 6–7.

64. Leiber and Stoller, *Hound Dog*, 63–65; Jerry Leiber quoted in Emerson, *Always Magic in the Air*, 11–12.

65. Leiber and Stoller, *Hound Dog*, 57–76; Shaw, *The Rockin' 50s*, 134–35.

66. Leiber quoted in Emerson, *Always Magic in the Air*, 10.

67. Emerson, *Always Magic in the Air*, 11.

68. Quotes come from the TV documentary entitled *Rock & Roll: The Producer*, episode 2: *In the Groove*.

69. Charlie Thomas quoted in Emerson, *Always Magic in the Air*, 122–23.

9. DIXIE FRIED

1. Wayne Jancik, *One-Hit Wonders* (New York: Billboard Books, 1990), 14–16.

2. James Miller, *Flowers in the Dustbin: The Rise of Rock and Roll, 1947–1977* (New York: Simon & Schuster, 1999), 120–26.

3. Carl Perkins quoted in Miller, *Flowers in the Dustbin*, 122.

4. Miller, *Flowers in the Dustbin*, 123.

5. Carl Perkins, "Dixie Fried" (Sun Records, 1956).

6. Peter Guralnick, "Rockabilly," in Jim Miller, ed., *The Rolling Stone Illustrated History of Rock & Roll* (New York: Rolling Stone Press, 1976), 64; Craig Morrison, *Go Cat Go! Rockabilly Music and Its Makers* (Urbana: University of Illinois Press, 1996).

7. Jerry Naylor and Steve Halliday, *The Rockabilly Legends: They Called It Rockabilly Long before They Called It Rock and Roll* (Milwaukee: Hal Leonard, 2007), 26, 16.

8. Peter Guralnick, "Rockabilly," 64.

9. Naylor and Halliday, *The Rockabilly Legends*, 28; see also Paul Kingsbury and Alana Nash, *Will the Circle Be Unbroken: Country Music in America* (New York: DK, 2006), 353.

10. Charlie Feathers quoted in Rick Kennedy and Randy McNutt, *Little Labels—Big Sound: Small Record Companies and the Rise of American Music* (Bloomington: Indiana University Press, 1999), 96–97.

11. Both the Johnny Cash and Carl Perkins versions of the story appear in Bob Shannon and John Javna, *Behind the Hits: Inside Stories of Classic Pop and Rock and Roll* (New York: Warner Books, 1986), 218.

12. Carl Perkins quoted in Kennedy and McNutt, *Little Labels—Big Sound*, 98.

13. Miller, *Flowers in the Dustbin*, 125.

14. Peter Guralnick, *Last Train to Memphis: The Rise of Elvis Presley* (Boston: Little Brown, 1994), 236, 246, 259; Ernst Jorgensen, *Elvis Presley: A Life in Music; The Complete Recording Sessions* (New York: St. Martin's Press, 1998), 37, 39.

15. Kennedy and McNutt, *Little Labels—Big Sound*, 98, 100; Jorgensen, *Elvis Presley*, 40, 44; Patricia Romanowski and Holly George-Warren, *The New Rolling Stone Encyclopedia of Rock & Roll* (New York: Fireside/Rolling Stone Press Book, 1995), 759; Jancik, *The Billboard Book of One-Hit Wonders*, 15.

16. Carl Perkins quoted in Jancik, *The Billboard Book of One-Hit Wonders*, 15.

17. Guralnick, *Last Train to Memphis*, 179.

18. Romanowski and George-Warren, *The New Rolling Stone Encyclopedia of Rock & Roll*, 759; Jancik, *The Billboard Book of One-Hit Wonders*, 15; Guralnick, *Last Train to Memphis*, 103.

19. Charlie Daniels quoted in Naylor and Halliday, *The Rockabilly Legends*, 136.

20. Jancik, *The Billboard Book of One-Hit Wonders*, 16.

21. *The Complete Million Dollar Quartet: Elvis Presley, Carl Perkins, Jerry Lee Lewis, Johnny Cash* (Sun Records/RCA/Sony, 2006).

22. Kingsbury and Nash, *Will the Circle Be Broken*, 223.

23. Naylor and Halliday, *The Rockabilly Legends*, 153.

24. Naylor and Halliday, *The Rockabilly Legends*, 154–57.

25. Romanowski and George-Warren, *The New Rolling Stone Encyclopedia of Rock & Roll*, 158–59; Paul Kingsbury, *The Grand Ole Opry History of Country Music* (New York: Villard Books, 1995), 106; Kennedy and McNutt, *Little Labels—Big Sound*, 96.

26. Kingsbury, *The Grand Ole Opry History of Country Music*, 107; Naylor and Halliday, *The Rockabilly Legends*, 167.

27. Bob Dylan's recollection can be found at www.frankgrizzard.info/public_html/cash.html (accessed July 26, 2014)

28. Johnny Cash's acceptance speech into the Rock and Roll Hall of Fame can be found at www.rockhall.com/inductees/johnny-cash/transcript/johnny-cash-accepts-induction/ (accessed July 26, 2014).

29. Bob Dylan's comments about Johnny Cash are available at www.frankgrizzard.info/public_html/cash.html (accessed July 26, 2014).

30. Sam Phillips quoted in Kennedy and McNutt, *Little Labels—Big Sound*, 105.

31. Gene Vincent, "Be-Bop-a-Lula" (Capitol Records, 1956).

32. Naylor and Halliday, *The Rockabilly Legends*, 217–19.

33. Gene Vincent and His Blue Caps, "Be-Bop-a-Lula" (Capitol, 1956); the performance can be found in the 1956 film *The Girl Can't Help It*.

34. Guralnick, *Last Train to Memphis*, 282, 301; Naylor and Halliday, *The Rockabilly Legends*, 223, 219.

35. Kennedy and McNutt, *Little Labels—Big Sound*, 103.

36. Janis Martin, "Will You, Willyum" (RCA, 1956); for more information, see entry for Janis Martin in Wikipedia (http://en.wikipedia.org/wiki/Janis_Martin).

37. Galen Gart, ed., *First Pressings: The History of Rhythm & Blues*, vol. 6: *1956* (Milford, NH: Big Nickel Publications, 1991), 125.

38. Rick Kienzle, CD liner notes, *Vintage Collections: Wanda Jackson* (Capitol Nashville Records, 1996).

39. Rick Kienzle, CD liner notes.

40. Rick Kienzle, CD liner notes.

41. The Buddy Holly quote comes from a newspaper article that Holly wrote for a British newspaper while the Crickets were touring England in March 1958. The article is reprinted in John Beecher and Malcolm Jones, eds., *The Buddy Holly Story: A Pictorial Account of His Life and Music,*" booklet included in *The Complete Buddy Holly* box set (London· MCA/Coral Records Box Set, 1079).

42. Richard Aquila, interview with Jerry Ivan Allison for NPR's *Rock & Roll America*, January 5, 1999.

43. Peggy Sue Gerron quoted in Naylor and Halliday, *The Rockabilly Legends*, 62; Buddy Holly's essay is reprinted in John Goldrosen, *The Buddy Holly Story* (New York: Quick Fox Press, 1979), 32–33.

44. Buddy Holly quoted in Naylor and Halliday, *The Rockabilly Legends*, 63.

45. John Goldrosen, *The Buddy Holly Story*, 9–31; Aquila, interview with Jerry Ivan Allison.

46. Aquila, interview with Jerry Ivan Allison.

47. Mrs. Holley is quoted in Goldrosen, *The Buddy Holly Story*, 41.

48. Aquila, interview with Jerry Ivan Allison.

49. Phone call between Buddy Holly and Paul Cohen of Decca Records (February 28, 1957), available from YouTube.com.

50. Aquila, interview with Jerry Ivan Allison. For further information, see Malcolm Jones and John Beecher, liner notes, *The Complete Buddy Holly*.

51. Curtis and Allison quoted in Goldrosen, *The Buddy Holly Story*, 64–65.

CONCLUSION

1. Bill Haley and His Comets, "Crazy Man, Crazy" (Essex Records, 1953). Videos of Haley and his group performing the song are now available on www.youtube.com and various DVDs.

2. Information about the post–World War II youth culture may be found in Landon Y. Jones, *Great Expectations: America and the Baby Boom Generation* (New York: Ballantine Books, 1980) and Jon Savage, *Teenage: The Creation of Youth Culture* (New York: Viking, 2007).

3. For specific examples of hit records that promoted youth culture, see Richard Aquila, *That Old Time Rock & Roll: A Chronicle of An Era, 1954–63* (Urbana: University of Illinois Press, 2000), 63–105.

4. James Gilbert, *A Cycle of Outrage: America's Reaction to the Juvenile Delinquent in the 1950s* (New York: Oxford University Press, 1986), 184–85, 18; James T. Patterson, *Grand Expectations: The United States, 1945–1974* (New York: Oxford University Press, 1996), 373; Linda Martin and Kerry Segrave, *Anti-Rock: The Opposition to Rock 'n' Roll* (New York: DaCapo Press, 1993), 7, 25.

5. Charles L. Ponce De Leon, *Fortunate Son: The Life of Elvis Presley* (New York: Hill and Wang, 2006), 84–85; Martin and Segrave, *Anti-Rock*, 18–19, 23, 48, 52; Father Kelliher quoted in William Graebner, *Coming of Age in Buffalo: Youth and Authority in the Postwar Era* (Philadelphia: Temple University Press, 1990), 94.

6. Martin and Segrave, *Anti-Rock*, 13, 41–42. See also Michael T. Bertrand, *Race, Rock, and Elvis* (Urbana: University of Illinois Press, 2000), 101, 162, 188; Glenn C. Altschuler, *All Shook Up: How Rock 'N' Roll Changed America* (New York: Oxford University Press, 2003), 37–38; Congressman Celler quoted in LeRoy Ashby, *With Amusement for All: A History of American Popular Culture since 1930* (Lexington: University Press of Kentucky, 2006), 342.

7. Ashby, *With Amusement for All*, 343; Martin and Segrave, *Anti-Rock*, 46–47, 50–51; Douglas T. Miller and Marian Nowak, *The Fifties: The Way We Really Were* (New York: Doubleday, 1975), 313, n.21; Tom Englehardt, *The End of Victory Culture: Cold War America and the Disillusioning of a Generation* (New York: Basic Books, 1995), 140; Altschuler, *All Shook Up*, 6.

8. Galen Gart, ed., *First Pressings: The History of Rhythm & Blues*, vol. 6: *1956* (Milford, N.H.: Big Nickel, 1991), 47, 71.

9. Marshall McLuhan, *Understanding Media: The Extensions of Man* (New York: Signet Books, 1964), 23; Peter Jennings and Todd Brewster, *The Century* (New York: Doubleday, 1998), 345.

10. News clips can be found in *Elvis: Commemorative Edition* (Lincoln-wood, Ill.: Publications International, 2002), 41, 45, 52.

11. Carl Perkins interview in "Rock 'n' Roll Explodes," episode 1: *The History of Rock 'n' Roll* (DVD, 2004).

12. Rick Coleman, *Blue Monday: Fats Domino and the Lost Dawn of Rock 'n' Roll* (Cambridge, Mass.: DaCapo Press, 2006), 117, 113.

13. Ruth Cage, "Rhythm & Blues," *Down Beat* (October 5, 1955), 18; Coleman, *Blue Monday*, 107, 116, 226.

14. Elvis Presley, "Baby, Let's Play House" (Sun Records, 1955); Little Richard, "Long Tall Sally" (Specialty Records, 1956); Gene Vincent and His Blue Caps, "Be-Bop-a-Lula" (Capitol Records, 1956); The Platters, "My Prayer" (Mercury, 1956).

15. Clip from *Life* magazine, April 30, 1956, in *Elvis: Commemorative Edition*, 40.

16. Mickey and Sylvia, "Love Is Strange" (Groove Records, 1956).

17. Coleman, *Blue Monday*, 105, 106.

18. See Aquila, *That Old Time Rock & Roll*, 63–105.

19. Richard Aquila, interview with Dion DiMucci for NPR's *Rock & Roll America*, October 19, 1995.

20. For evidence of African American gains after World War II, see Harvard Sitkoff, *The Struggle for Black Equality: 1954–1992* (New York: Hill and Wang, 1993); Robert Weisbrot, *Freedom Bound: A History of America's Civil Rights Movement* (New York: Norton, 1989); Taylor Branch, *Parting the Waters: America in the King Years, 1954–1963* (New York: Simon & Schuster, 1988).

21. Michael Barson and Steven Heller, *Teenage Confidential: An Illustrated History of the American Teen* (New York: Barnes & Noble, 1998), 41–48.

22. Stephen J. Whitfield, *The Culture of the Cold War* (Baltimore: Johns Hopkins University Press, 1991); Elaine Tyler May, *Homeward Bound: American Families in the Cold War Era* (New York: Harper/Collins, 1988); Miller and Nowak, *The Fifties*; William L. O'Neill, *American High: The Years of Confidence, 1945–1960* (New York: Free Press, 1986).

23. Whitfield, *The Culture of the Cold War*, 53.

24. Pat Boone, "I'll Be Home" (Dot Records, 1956); the Tassels, "To a Soldier Boy" (Madison Records, 1959).

25. Jerry Osborne, ed., *Elvis: Word for Word* (New York: Gramercy Books, 2006), 116; *Elvis: Commemorative Edition*, 76–77, 121.

26. Godfrey Hodgson, *America in Our Time: From World War II to Nixon, What Happened and Why* (New York: Vintage/Random House, 1976), chap. 4; Miller and Nowak, *The Fifties*, chap. 4. The GE ad is quoted on pp. 11–12.

27. Engelhardt, *The End of Victory Culture*, 134; *Elvis: Commemorative Edition*, 60–63.

28. Aquila, *That Old Time Rock & Roll*, 27.

29. Daniel Boorstin, *The Americans: The Democratic Experience* (New York: Vintage/Random House, 1973), 89–90.

30. Miller and Nowak, *The Fifties*, 90–91.

31. For examples of rock & roll hits dealing with religion, see Aquila, *That Old Time Rock & Roll*, 106–8.

32. May, *Homeward Bound*, 3.

33. Miller and Nowak, *The Fifties*, 150–55.

34. Adlai Stevenson, "A Purpose for Modern Woman," commencement address, Smith College, 1955," excerpted in *Women's Home Companion* (September 1955).

35. May, *Homeward Bound*, 109.

36. Aquila, *That Old Time Rock & Roll*, 112–17.

37. Miller and Nowak, *The Fifties*, 157; for examples of songs that endorsed traditional gender attitudes, see Aquila, *That Old Time Rock & Roll*, 112–17.

38. The Teen Queens, "Eddie, My Love" (RPM 453, 1956).

39. A list of rock & roll songs that portray men in macho ways can be found in Aquila, *That Old Time Rock & Roll*, 117–18; the Bo Diddley songs can be found on Bo Diddley's album, *Bo Diddley* (Chess Records, 1958).

BIBLIOGRAPHY

BOOKS AND ARTICLES

Abramson, Herb. "Rock 'n' Roll: Seen in Perspective." *Cashbox* (July 28, 1956): 78.

Altschuyler, Glenn C. *All Shook Up: How Rock 'n' Roll Changed America.* New York: Oxford University Press, 2003.

Amburn, Ellis. *Buddy Holly: A Biography.* New York: St. Martin's Press, 1995.

"American Music Becomes National Rather Than Regional." *Cashbox* (April 2, 1955): 76.

Anderson, Nancy. "Elvis by His Father Vernon Presley," *Good Housekeeping* (January 1978).

Aquila, Richard. "Sh-Boom; or How Early Rock & Roll Taught Us to Stop Worrying and Love the Bomb." In *The Writing on the Cloud: American Culture Confronts the Atomic Bomb,* ed. Alison M. Scott and Christopher D. Geist, 106–18. New York: University Press of America, 1997.

Aquila, Richard. *That Old Time Rock & Roll: A Chronicle of an Era, 1954–63.* New York: Macmillan/Schirmer Books, 1989; reprint with new introduction, Urbana: University of Illinois Press, 2000.

Ashby, LeRoy. *With Amusement for All: A History of American Popular Culture since 1930.* Lexington: University Press of Kentucky, 2006.

Barlow, William. *Voice Over: The Making of Black Radio.* Philadelphia: Temple University Press, 1999.

Barson, Michael, and Steven Heller. *Teenage Confidential: An Illustrated History of the American Teen.* New York: Barnes & Noble, 1998.

Baughman, James. *The Republic of Mass Culture: Journalism, Filmmaking, and Broadcasting in America since 1941.* Baltimore: Johns Hopkins University Press, 1997.

Belz, Carl. *The Story of Rock.* New York: Harper & Row, 1972.

Berry, Chuck. *Chuck Berry: The Autobiography.* New York: Fireside Book/Simon & Schuster, 1987.

Bertrand, Michael T. *Race, Rock, and Elvis.* Urbana: University of Illinois Press, 2000.

Betrock, Alan. *Girl Groups: The Story of a Sound.* New York: Delilah Books, 1982.

Bindas, Kenneth, ed. *America's Musical Pulse: Popular Music in Twentieth-Century America.* Westport, Conn.: Greenwood Press, 1992.

Birnbaum, Larry. *Before Elvis: The Prehistory of Rock 'n' Roll.* Lanham, Md.: Scarecrow Press, 2013.

Black, Jay, and Jennings Bryant. *Introduction to Mass Communication.* Dubuque, Iowa: Wm C. Brown, 1992.

Boorstin, Daniel. *The Americans: The Democratic Experience.* New York: Vintage/Random House, 1973.

Brackett, David. *The Pop, Rock, and Soul Reader: Histories and Debates*. New York: Oxford University Press, 2005.

Branch, Taylor. *Parting the Waters: America in the King Years, 1954–1963*. New York: Simon & Schuster, 1988.

Brode, Douglas. *The Films of the Fifties*. New York: Citadel Press Book, 1992.

Brooks, Tim, and Earle Marsh. *The Complete Directory to Prime Time Television and Cable TV Shows, 1946–Present*. New York: Ballantine Books, 2003.

Buffalo Evening News, July 5, 1955, p. 6.

"Bull Moose Jackson." *Ebony* (January 1950).

Cage, Ruth. "Rhythm & Blues." *Down Beat* (October 5, 1955).

Campbell, Michael. *And the Beat Goes On: An Introduction to Popular Music in America, 1840 to Today*. New York: Schirmer Books, 1996.

Cantor, Louis. *Dewey and Elvis: The Life and Times of a Rock 'n' Roll Deejay*. Urbana: University of Illinois Press, 2005.

Cantor, Louis. *Wheelin' on Beale: How WDIA–Memphis Became the Nation's First All-Black Radio Station and Created the Sound That Changed America*. New York: Pharos Books, 1992.

Chafe, William. *The Paradox of Change: American Women in the 20th Century*. New York: Oxford University Press, 1991.

Chafe, William. *The Unfinished Journey: America since World War II*. New York: Oxford University Press, 1991).

Chapple, Steve, and Reebee Garofalo. *Rock 'n' Roll Is Here to Pay: The History and Politics of the Music Industry*. Chicago: Nelson-Hall, 1977.

Clayton, Marie. *Elvis Presley: Unseen Archives*. Bath: Parragon, 2003.

Cohen, Ronald D., and Rachel Clare Donaldson. *Roots of the Revival: American and British Folk Music in the 1950s*. Normal: University of Illinois Press, 2014.

Cohn, Nik. *Rock from the Beginning*. New York: Stein and Day, 1969.

Cohodas, Nadine. *Spinning Blues into Gold: The Chess Brothers and the Legendary Chess Records*. New York: St. Martin's Press, 2000.

Coleman, Rick. *Blue Monday: Fats Domino and the Lost Dawn of Rock 'n' Roll*. Cambridge, Mass.: DaCapo Press, 2006.

Condon, E. "What Is an Elvis Presley?" *Cosmopolitan* (December 1956): 54–61.

Cotten, Lee. *Shake, Rattle, & Roll: The Golden Age of American Rock 'n' Roll*. Ann Arbor, Mich.: Popular Culture Ink, 1989.

Crampton, Luke, and Dafydd Rees. *Rock & Roll: Year by Year*. London: DK, 2003.

Crenshaw, Marshall. *Hollywood Rock: A Guide to Rock 'n' Roll in the Movies*. New York: HarperPerennial, 1994.

Daniel, Pete. *Lost Revolutions: The South in the 1950s*. Chapel Hill: University of North Carolina Press, 2000.

Dannen, Fredric. *Hit Men: Power Brokers and Fast Money Inside the Music Business*. New York: Vintage Books, 1991.

Dawson, Jim, and Steve Propes, *What Was the First Rock 'n' Roll Record?* Boston: Faber and Faber, 1992.

DeCurtis, Anthony, and James Henke with Holly George-Warren, eds. *The Rolling Stone Illustrated History of Rock & Roll*. New York: Random House, 1992.

Denisoff, R. Serge, and William L. Schurk. *Tarnished Gold: The Record Industry Revisited*. New Brunswick, N.J.: Transaction Books, 1986.

Diggins, John Patrick. *The Proud Decades: America in War and Peace, 1941–1960*. New York: Norton, 1988.

Divine Laboratories Collective, comp. *The Little Black Leather Book of Rock 'n' Roll*. Vancouver, B.C.: Arsenal Pulp Press, 1994.

Douglas, Susan. *Where the Girls Are: Growing Up Female with the Mass Media*. New York: Random House, 1994.

Elvis: Commemorative Edition. Lincolnwood, IL: Publications International, 2002.

[Elvis] On His 60th Birthday: Life: Collector's Edition. February 10, 1995.

Emerson, Ken. *Always Magic in the Air: The Bomp and Brilliance of the Brill Building Era.* New York: Viking, 2005.

Engelhardt, Tom. *The End of Victory Culture: Cold War America and the Disillusioning of a Generation.* New York: Basic Books, 1995.

Ennis, Philip H. *The Seventh Stream: The Emergence of Rocknroll in American Popular Music.* Hanover, N.H.: Wesleyan University Press, 1992.

Escott, Colin, with Martin Hawkins. *Good Rockin' Tonight: Sun Records and the Birth of Rock 'n' Roll.* New York: St. Martin's Press, 1991.

Fisher, Marc. *Something in the Air: Radio, Rock, and the Revolution That Shaped a Generation.* New York: Random House, 2007.

"Florida's Color Bars Tumble as Jazz Invades Miami Beach." *Jet* (December 31, 1953): 60.

Fong-Torres, Ben. *The Hits Just Keep on Coming: The History of Top 40 Radio.* San Francisco: Miller Freeman Books, 1998.

"The Forgotten 15,000,000." *Sponsor* (October 10, 1949).

Friedlander, Paul. *Rock and Roll: A Social History.* Boulder, Colo.: Westview Press, 1996.

Frith, Simon. *Sound Effects: Youth, Leisure, and the Politics of Rock 'n' Roll.* New York: Pantheon, 1981.

Gans, Herbert. *The Levittowners: Ways of Life and Politics in a New Suburban Community.* New York: Columbia University Press, 1982.

Garofalo, Reebee. *Rockin' Out: Popular Music in the USA.* Boston: Allyn and Bacon, 1997.

Gart, Galen, ed. *First Pressings: The History of Rhythm & Blues*, vol. 1: *1951.* Milford, N.H.: Big Nickel, 1991.

Gart, Galen, ed. *First Pressings: The History of Rhythm & Blues*, vol. 3: *1953.* Milford, N.H.: Big Nickel, 1990.

Gart, Galen, ed. *First Pressings: The History of Rhythm & Blues*, vol. 4: *1954.* Milford, N.H.: Big Nickel, 1990.

Gart, Galen, ed. *First Pressings: The History of Rhythm & Blues*, vol. 5: *1955.* Milford, N.H.: Big Nickel, 1990.

Gart, Galen, ed. *First Pressings: The History of Rhythm & Blues*, vol. 6: *1956.* Milford, N.H.: Big Nickel, 1991.

Gilbert, James. *A Cycle of Outrage: America's Reaction to the Juvenile Delinquent in the 1950s.* New York: Oxford University Press, 1986.

Gillett, Charlie. *The Sound of the City: The Rise of Rock and Roll.* New York: Dutton, 1970.

Goldman, Eric. *The Crucial Decade.* New York: Vintage, 1960.

Goldrosen, John. *The Buddy Holly Story.* New York: Quick Fox Press, 1979.

Graebner, William. *Coming of Age in Buffalo: Youth and Authority in the Postwar Era.* Philadelphia: Temple University Press, 1990.

Gramschi, Antonio. *Selections from Cultural Writings*, ed. David Forgacs and Geoffrey Nowell-Smith. Cambridge, Mass.: Harvard University Press, 1985.

Gregory, James, ed. *The Elvis Presley Story.* New York: Hillman Books, 1957.

Grendysa, Peter. "Black Music: An Introduction." In *Top R&B Singles, 1942–1988*, ed. Joel Whitburn, 9–11. Menomonee Falls, Wisconsin: Record Research, 1988.

Grevatt, Ren. "It All Started with Elvis." *Saturday Evening Post* (September 1958): 92.

Guralnick, Peter. *Dream Boogie: The Triumph of Sam Cooke.* Boston: Little, Brown 2005.

Guralnick, Peter. "Elvis Presley." In *The Rolling Stone Illustrated History of Rock & Roll*, ed. Jim Miller. New York: Rolling Stone Press/Random House, 1976.

Guralnick, Peter. "Fats Domino." In *The Rolling Stone Illustrated History of Rock & Roll*, ed. Jim Miller. New York: Rolling Stone Press/Random House, 1976.

Guralnick, Peter. *Last Train to Memphis: The Rise of Elvis Presley.* Boston: Little, Brown, 1994.

Guralnick, Peter. "Rockabilly." In *The Rolling Stone Illustrated History of Rock & Roll*, ed. Jim Miller. New York: Rolling Stone Press, 1976.

Guralnick, Peter. *Sam Phillips: The Man Who Invented Rock 'n' Roll.* Boston: Little, Brown, 2015.

Halberstam, David. *The Fifties.* New York: Fawcett Columbine, 1993.

Hall, Mitchell K. *The Emergence of Rock and Roll: Music and the Rise of American Youth Culture*. New York: Routledge, 2014.

Helander, Brock. *The Rockin' 50s: The People Who Made the Music*. New York: Schirmer Books, 1998.

Hodgson, Godfrey. *America in Our Time: From World War II to Nixon; What Happened and Why*. New York: Vintage/Random House, 1976.

Hopkins, Jerry. *Elvis: A Biography*. New York: Simon & Schuster, 1971.

Hunter, Dave. *The Gibson Les Paul: The Illustrated Story of the Guitar That Changed Rock*. Minneapolis, Minn.: Voyageur Press, 2014.

Jackson, Carlton. *P.S. I Love You: The Story of the Singing Hilltoppers*. Lexington: University Press of Kentucky, 2007.

Jackson, John A. *American Bandstand: Dick Clark and the Making of a Rock 'n' Roll Empire*. New York: Oxford University Press, 1999.

Jackson, John A. *Big Beat Heat: Alan Freed and the Early Years of Rock & Roll*. New York: Schirmer Books, 1991.

Jackson, Keith. *Crabgrass Frontier: The Suburbanization of the United States*. New York: Oxford University Press, 1985.

Jancik, Wayne. *The Billboard Book of One-Hit Wonders*. New York: Billboard Books, 1990.

Jennings, Peter, and Todd Brewster. *The Century*. New York: Doubleday, 1998.

Jones, Landon Y. *Great Expectations: America and the Baby Boom Generation*. New York: Ballantine Books, 1980.

Jorgensen, Ernst. *Elvis Presley: A Life in Music; The Complete Recording Sessions*. New York: St. Martin's Press, 1998.

"Juke Box Sociology." *Ebony* (March 1954): 88.

Kamin, Jonathan. "The White R&B Audience and the Music Industry, 1952–1956." *Popular Music and Society* 6 (1978): 150–68.

Kennedy, Rick, and Randy McNutt. *Little Labels—Big Sound: Small Record Companies and the Rise of American Music*. Bloomington: Indiana University Press, 1999.

Kerouac, Jack. *On the Road*, 5th ed. New York: Penguin Books, 1991.

Kingsbury, Paul. *The Grand Ole Opry History of Country Music*. New York: Villard Books, 1995.

Kingsbury, Paul, and Alana Nash. *Will the Circle Be Unbroken: Country Music in America*. New York: DK, 2006.

Ladies Home Journal (July 2003).

Land, Herman. "The Storz Bombshell." *Television* (May 1957).

"The Larry Darnell Story." *Our World* (June 1947).

Lauterbach, Preston. *The Chitlin' Circuit and the Road to Rock 'n' Roll*. New York: W. W. Norton, 2011.

Lawrence, Robb. *The Early Years of the Les Paul Legacy, 1915–1963*. Milwaukee: Hal Leonard, 2008.

"A Legend Is Born." *Forever Elvis: The 15th Memorial Anniversary Salute* (1992).

Leiber, Jerry, and Mike Stoller. *Hound Dog: The Leiber and Stoller Autobiography*. New York: Simon & Schuster, 2009.

Lemann, Nicholas. *The Promised Land: The Great Black Migration and How It Changed America*. New York: Vintage, 1992.

Life (April 30, 1956).

Life, Collector's Edition (February 10, 1995).

Lott, Eric. *Love and Theft: Blackface Minstrelsy and the American Working Class*. New York: Oxford University Press, 1993.

MacCambridge, Michael. "Review of *Chuck Berry Hail! Hail! Rock 'n' Roll*." *Belles Lettres: A Literary Review* 7 (no. 2, January/May 2008): 8.

MacDonald, J. Fred. *Don't Touch That Dial! Radio Programming in American Life, 1920–1960*. Chicago: Nelson-Hall, 1979.

Mailer, Norman. *Advertisements for Myself*. New York: G.P. Putnam's Sons, 1959.

Malone, Bill. *Country Music U.S.A*. Austin: University of Texas Press, 1985.

Marcus, Greil. *Mystery Train: Images of America in Rock 'n' Roll Music*. New York: Dutton, 1975.

Marling, Karal Ann. *As Seen on TV: The Visual Culture of Everyday Life in the 1950s*. Cambridge, Mass.: Harvard University Press, 1994.

Martin, Linda, and Kerry Segrave. *Anti-Rock: The Opposition to Rock 'n' Roll*. New York: DaCapo Press, 1993.

May, Elaine Tyler. *Homeward Bound: American Families in the Cold War Era*. New York: Harper/Collins, 1988.

May, Lary, ed. *Recasting America: Culture and Politics in the Age of the Cold War*. Chicago: University of Chicago Press, 1989.

McKeon, Elizabeth, and Linda Everett. *Elvis Speaks: Thoughts on Fame, Family, Music, and More in His Own Words*. Nashville: Cumberland House, 1997.

McLuhan, Marshall. *Understanding Media: The Extensions of Man*. New York: Signet Books, 1964.

Memphis Press-Scimitar, July 28, 1954; February 5, 1955.

Merriam, A. P. *The Anthropology of Music*. Evanston, Ill.: Northwestern University Press, 1964.

Miller, Douglas T., and Marion Nowak. *The Fifties: The Way We Really Were*. Garden City, N.Y.: Doubleday, 1975.

Miller, James. *Flowers in the Dustbin: The Rise of Rock and Roll, 1947–1977*. New York: Simon & Schuster, 1999.

Miller, Jim, ed. *The Rolling Stone Illustrated History of Rock & Roll*. New York: Random House/Rolling Stone, 1976.

Moore, Scotty, as told to James Dickerson. *That's Alright, Elvis: The Untold Story of Elvis's First Guitarist and Manager, Scotty Moore*. New York: Schirmer Trade Books, 2005.

Morrison, Craig. *Go Cat Go! Rockabilly Music and Its Makers*. Urbana: University of Illinois Press, 1996.

Nachman, Gerald. *Raised on Radio*. Los Angeles: University of California Press, 1998.

Naylor, Jerry, and Steve Halliday. *The Rockabilly Legends: They Called It Rockabilly Long before They Called It Rock and Roll*. Milwaukee: Hal Leonard, 2007.

"New York Beat." *Jet* (August 12, 1954): 65.

Newman, Kathy M. "The Forgotten Fifteen Million: Black Radio, Radicalism, and the Construction of the 'Negro Market.'" In *Communities of the Air: Radio Century, Radio Culture*, ed. Susan Merrill Squier, 109–33. Durham, N.C.: Duke University Press, 2003.

Newman, Mark. *Entrepreneurs of Profit and Pride: From Black Appeal to Radio Soul*. New York: Praeger, 1988.

Oakley, Ronald J. *God's Country: America in the 50's*. Fort Lee, N.J.: Barricade Books, 1990.

Ochs, Michael. *Rock Archives: A Photographic Journey through the First Two Decades of Rock & Roll*. Garden City, N.Y.: Doubleday, 1984.

O'Neill, William L. *American High: The Years of Confidence, 1945–1960*. New York: Free Press, 1986.

Osborne, Jerry. *Elvis: Word for Word*. New York: Gramercy Books, 1999.

Palmer, Robert. *Baby That Was Rock & Roll: The Legendary Leiber and Stoller*. New York: Harcourt Brace Jovanovich, 1978.

Palmer, Robert. *Rock & Roll: An Unruly History*. New York: Harmony Books, 1995.

Palmer, Robert. "Rock Begins." In *The Rolling Stone Illustrated History of Rock & Roll*, ed. Anthony DeCurtis and James Henke. New York: Random House, 1980.

Parsons, Patrick R. "The Business of Popular Music: A Short History." In *America's Musical Pulse: Popular Music in Twentieth-Century Society*, ed. Kenneth J. Bindas, 139–40. Westport, Conn.: Greenwood Press, 1992.

Passman, Arnold. *The Deejays*. New York: Macmillan, 1971.

Patterson, James T. *Grand Expectations: The United States, 1945–1974*. New York: Oxford University Press, 1996.

Peretti, Burton W. "Emerging from America's Underside: The Black Musician from Ragtime to Jazz." In *America's Musical Pulse: Popular Music in Twentieth-Century Society*, ed. Kenneth J. Bindas, 63–72. Westport, Conn.: Greenwood Press, 1992.

Peterson, John Charles. *The True-Life Adventures of Captain Wa Wah (Fifty Years of Music, Meditation, and Politics)*. Muncie, IN: Katydid, 2009.

Peterson, Richard. "Why 1955? Explaining the Advent of Rock Music." *Popular Music* (January 1990): 97–116.

Ponce De Leon, Charles L. *Fortunate Son: The Life of Elvis Presley*. New York: Hill and Wang, 2006.

Porterfield, Nolan. "The Day Hank Williams Died: Cultural Collisions in Country Music." In *America's Musical Pulse: Popular Music in Twentieth-Century Society*, ed. Kenneth J. Bindas, 175–84. Westport, Conn.: Greenwood Press, 1992.

Porterfield, Nolan. *Jimmie Rodgers: The Life and Times of America's Blue Yodeler*. Urbana: University of Illinois Press, 1979.

Pruter, Robert. *Chicago Soul*. Urbana: University of Illinois Press, 1991.

Pruter, Robert. *Doowop: The Chicago Scene*. Urbana: University of Illinois Press, 1996.

Romanowski, Patricia, and Holly George-Warren, eds. *The New Rolling Stone Encyclopedia of Rock & Roll*. New York: Fireside/Rolling Stone Press Book, 1995.

Salem, James M. *The Late Great Johnny Ace and the Transition from R&B to Rock 'n' Roll*. Urbana: University of Illinois Press, 2001.

Savage, Jon. *Teenage: The Creation of Youth Culture*. New York: Viking, 2007.

Shannon, Bob, and John Javna. *Behind the Hits: Inside Stories of Classic Pop and Rock and Roll*. New York: Warner Books, 1986.

Shaw, Arnold. *Honkers and Shouters: The Golden Years of Rhythm and Blues*. New York: Macmillan, 1978.

Shaw, Arnold. *The Rockin' 50s: The Decade That Transformed the Pop Music Scene*. New York: Hawthorn Books, 1974.

Shaw, Arnold. *The World of Soul: Black America's Contribution to the Pop Music Scene*. New York: Cowles Book, 1970.

Sitkoff, Harvard. *The Struggle for Black Equality*. New York: Hill and Wang, 1993.

Smith, Joe. *Off the Record: An Oral History of Popular Music*. New York: Warner Books, 1988.

Sterling, Christopher H., and John M. Kittross. *Stay Tuned: A Concise History of American Broadcasting*, 2nd ed. Belmont, Calif.: Wadsworth, 1990.

Stevenson, Adlai. "A Purpose for Modern Woman." Commencement address, Smith College, 1955, excerpted in *Women's Home Companion* (September 1955).

Stuessy, Joe. *Rock & Roll: Its History and Stylistic Development*. Englewood Cliffs, N.J.: Prentice Hall, 1990.

Swenson, John. *Bill Haley: The Daddy of Rock and Roll*. New York: Stein & Day, 1983.

Szatmary, David. *Rockin' in Time*, 8th ed.. New York: Pearson, 2013.

Szatmary, David. *A Time to Rock: A Social History of Rock 'n' Roll*. New York: Macmillan/Schirmer Books, 1996.

Talevski, Nick, and Robert D. West. *The Origins and Early History of Rock & Roll*. Green, Ohio: Guardian Express Media, 2011.

Thorton, Anthony, ed. *Elvis: Uncut Legends, The Definitive Guide to Rock's Ultimate Icons*, 2005.

Time (July 14, 1958); (July 23, 1956).

Toll, Robert. *Blacking Up: The Minstrel Show in Nineteenth-Century America*. New York: Oxford University Press, 1974.

Tosches, Nick. *Unsung Heroes of Rock and Roll*. New York: Da Capo Press, 1999.

Tupelo Daily Journal, September 27, 1956.

Ward, Ed, Geoffrey Stokes, and Ken Tucker. *Rock of Ages: The Rolling Stone History of Rock & Roll*. New York: Rolling Stone Press/Summit Books, 1986.

Weisbrot, Robert. *Freedom Bound: A History of America's Civil Rights Movement*. New York: Norton, 1989.

West, Red, Sonny West, and Dave Hebler. *Elvis: What Happened?* New York: Ballantine Books, 1977.

Wexler, Jerry, and David Ritz. *Rhythm and the Blues: A Life in American Music*. New York: Knopf, 1993.

Whitburn, Joel. *Pop Memories: The History of American Popular Music Compiled from America's Popular Music Charts, 1890–1954*. Menomonee Falls, Wis.: Record Research, 1986.

Whitburn, Joel. *Top Country Singles, 1944–1988*. Menomonee Falls, Wis.: Record Research, 1989.

Whitburn, Joel. *Top Pop Singles, 1955–1990*. Menomonee Falls, Wis.: Record Research, 1991.

Whitburn, Joel. *Top R&B Singles, 1942–1988*. Menomonee Falls, Wis.: Record Research, 1988.

Whitcomb, Ian. *After the Ball: Pop Music From Rag To Rock*. New York: Penguin Press, 1972.

White, Forrest. *Fender: The Inside Story*. Milwaukee: Backbeat, 1994.

Whitfield, Stephen J. *The Culture of the Cold War*. Baltimore: Johns Hopkins University Press, 1991.

Williams, Roger M. *Sing a Sad Song: The Life and Times of Hank Williams*. Urbana: University of Illinois Press, 1981.

Winner, Langdon. "Little Richard." In *The Rolling Stone Illustrated History of Rock & Roll*, ed. Jim Miller. New York: Rolling Stone Press, 1976.

Zak, Albin J., III. *I Don't Sound Like Nobody: Remaking Music in 1950s America*. Ann Arbor: University of Michigan Press, 2013.

INTERVIEWS

Conducted by Richard Aquila for NPR's *Rock & Roll America*:

Jerry Ivan Allison (drummer and cofounder of Buddy Holly and the Crickets). January 5, 1999

Dave Bartholomew (record producer). July 2, 1998.

Pat Boone. June 12, 1998; June 25, 1998.

Bo Diddley. January 21, 1998.

Dion (solo artist and lead singer of Dion and the Belmonts). October 19, 1995.

Casey Kasem (disc jockey). November 25, 1996.

Danny Neaverth (disc jockey). June 10, 1998.

Robert Pruter (music historian). October 20, 1999.

Tom Shannon (disc jockey). June 17, 1998.

C. Warren Vander Hill (historian). September 7, 2000.

ADDITIONAL SOURCES

Alan Freed's on-air personality can be heard at www.alanfreed.com/wp/on-the-air-audio-2/audio-wins-1955/ (accessed July 23, 2014). Other clips of Freed radio programs are available on the official Alan Freed website at www.alanfreed.com.

Bo Diddley's official website can be found at www.bodiddley.com

Bob Dylan's comments about Johnny Cash, www.frankgrizzard.info/public_html/cash.html (accessed July 26, 2014).

Bob Hyde. "Track by Track Annotation." In liner notes booklet of *The Doo Wop Box* (Santa Monica, Calif.: Rhino Records, 1993).

Boyd Bennett official web site, www.boydbennett.com.

Bruce Springsteen, keynote address at the South by Southwest Music Festival in Austin, Texas (March 28, 2012), www.rollingstone.com/music/news/exclusive-the-complete-text-of-bruce-springsteens-sxsw-keynote-address-20120328 (accessed July 23, 2014).

Buddy Holly, phone call to Paul Cohen of Decca Records (February 28, 1957). Available from YouTube.com.

Carl Perkins interview, in *Rock 'n' Roll Explodes*, episode 1 of *The History of Rock 'n' Roll* (DVD, 2004).

Chuck Berry Hail! Hail! Rock 'n' Roll (Delilah Films, 1987).

Colin Escott, "CD liner notes," *Sun's Greatest Hits* (BMG Music, 1992).

The Complete Million Dollar Quartet: Elvis Presley, Carl Perkins, Jerry Lee Lewis, Johnny Cash (CD issued by Sun Records/RCA/Sony, 2006).

Cruisin' is a series of Top 40 radio CDs issued by Increase Records/Chess INCM. The series features individual CDs for each of the following disc jockeys who became legendary figures of Top 40 Radio: Jumpin' George Oxford, Robin Seymour, Joe Niagara, Jack Carney, Hunter Hancock, Dick Biondi, Arnie Ginsberg, Russ Knight, B. Mitchell Reed, Johnny Holliday, Robert W. Morgan, Pat O'Day, Dr. Don Rose, Johnny Dark, and Kris Eric Stevens.

Dewey Phillips radio sound checks, http://memphismusichalloffame.com/inductee/dewey-phillips/ (accessed July 23, 2014).

Dick Biondi interview, a transcript of Scott Simon's NPR interview of Dick Biondi on September 21, 2013: www.npr.org/templates/story/story.php?storyId=224715929 (accessed July 24, 2014).

Dick Biondi's radio show on WKBW–Buffalo is available on the following CD: *Cruisin' 1960: Dick Biondi* (Increase Records/Chess INCM, 2005). Biondi air checks are available online at http://www.radiohof.org/dick_biondi.htm (accessed July 23, 2014).

Disc jockey Danny Neaverth's on-air style can be found at www.youtube.com/watch?v=1ub7GBbkhM0 (accessed July 23, 2014).

Elvis Presley: The Official Site of the King of Rock 'n' Roll. www.elvis.com/photos-video/videos.aspx?id=140 (accessed July 23, 2014).

George "Hound Dog" Lorenz Sound clips are available at www.hounddoglorenz.com/shows.php (accessed July 23, 2014).

History of Rock & Roll. PBS/BBC Documentary. 1995.

Hyde, Bob. "Track by Track Annotation." In liner notes booklet, *The Doo Wop Box*, Santa Monica, Calif.: Rhino Records, 1993.

Interview with members of the Chords (CNN, 1995).

Johnny Cash's acceptance speech into the Rock and Roll Hall of Fame. www.rockhall.com/inductees/johnny-cash/transcript/johnny-cash-accepts-induction/ (accessed July 26, 2014).

Jones, Malcolm, and John Beecher. Liner notes, *The Complete Buddy Holly* (London: MCA/Coral Records Box Set, 1979).

Liner notes to *Alan Freed Top 15* record album.

Liner notes to Fats Domino's CD, *My Blue Heaven: The Best of Fats Domino* (Legendary Masters Series, EMI/Imperial Records, 1990).

Liner notes to the album, *Pat Boone's Greatest Hits: The Original Dot Recordings* (1993).

Liner notes to *Ram Records: Shreveport Stomp* (Ace Records, 1994).

Liner notes to *Rock the Joint: The Original Essex Recordings, 1951–1954*, Bill Haley and His Comets (CD issued on SchoolKids' Records in 1994).

Liner notes to *Vintage Collections: Wanda Jackson* (CD, Capitol Nashville Records, 1996).

Rock & Roll Hall of Fame and Museum Website. www.rockhall.com (accessed July 12, 2001).

Vera, Billy. "What Is Doo Wop?" In Liner Notes Booklet of *The Doo Wop Box* (Santa Monica, CA: Rhino Records, 1993).

Video of Elvis Presley's final performance on *Stage Show* on March 24, 1956, is available online at YouTube.com.

Wayne Stierle, "Earth Angel and the Birth of Rock 'n' Roll." In liner notes booklet of *The Doo Wop Box* (Santa Clara, Calif.: Rhino Records, 1993), 26.

INDEX

ABOUT THE AUTHOR

Richard Aquila is professor emeritus of history at Penn State University and a Distinguished Lecturer for the Organization of American History. Previously, he served as the director of the School of Humanities and Social Sciences at Penn State's Behrend College and taught at Ball State University and Metropolitan State University of Denver. He specializes in U.S. social and cultural history, especially recent America, popular culture, the American West, and American Indians. His publications include numerous articles and reviews, as well as five books: *The Sagebrush Trail: Western Movies and Twentieth-Century America* (2015); *Home Front Soldier: The Story of a G.I. and His Italian American Family during World War II* (1999); *Wanted Dead or Alive: The American West in Popular Culture* (1996); *That Old Time Rock and Roll: A Chronicle of An Era, 1954–63* (1989); and *The Iroquois Restoration: Iroquois Diplomacy on the Colonial Frontier* (1983). Aquila has also written, produced, and hosted numerous documentaries for NPR. His weekly public history series, *Rock & Roll America*, was syndicated on NPR and NPR Worldwide. The series, which was nominated for a Peabody Award, is archived in the Rock & Roll Hall of Fame and Museum.